# Lecture Notes in Comp

161

*Commenced Publication in 1973*
Founding and Former Series Editors:
Gerhard Goos, Juris Hartmanis, and Jan van Leeuwen

Richard Harper   Matthias Rauterberg
Marco Combetto (Eds.)

# Entertainment Computing – ICEC 2006

5th International Conference
Cambridge, UK, September 20-22, 2006
Proceedings

 Springer

Volume Editors

Richard Harper
Microsoft Research Cambridge
Socio-Digital Systems
7 J.J: Thomson Ave, Cambridge, CB3 OFB, UK
E-mail: harper@microsoft.com

Matthias Rauterberg
Technische Universiteit Eindhoven
Department of Industrial Design
Den Dolech 2, 5612 AZ Einhoven, The Netherlands
E-mail: g.w.m.rauterberg@tue.nl

Marco Combetto
Micorsoft Research
External Research Office
7 J.J. Thomson Ave, Cambridge, CB3 OFB, UK
E-mail: Marco.Combetto@microsoft.com

Library of Congress Control Number: 2006932580

CR Subject Classification (1998): H.5, H.4, H.3, I.2, I.3, I.7, J.5

LNCS Sublibrary: SL 3 – Information Systems and Application, incl. Internet/Web
and HCI

ISSN        0302-9743
ISBN-10     3-540-45259-1 Springer Berlin Heidelberg New York
ISBN-13     978-3-540-45259-1 Springer Berlin Heidelberg New York

Springer is a part of Springer Science+Business Media

springer.com

© IFIP International Federation for Information Processing 2006
Printed in Germany

Typesetting: Camera-ready by author, data conversion by Scientific Publishing Services, Chennai, India
Printed on acid-free paper      SPIN: 11872320      06/3142      5 4 3 2 1 0

# Foreword

Welcome to the proceedings of ICEC 2006

Firstly, we are pleased with the solid work of all the authors who contributed to ICEC 2006 by submitting their papers. ICEC 2006 attracted 47 full paper submissions, 48 short paper submissions in total 95 technical papers. Based on a thorough review and selection process by 85 international experts from academia and industry as members of the Program Committee, a high-quality program was compiled. The International Program Committee consisted of experts from all over the world: 2 from Austria, 1 from Canada, 3 from China, 3 from Finland, 3 from France, 11 from Germany, 2 from Greece, 2 from Ireland, 5 from Italy, 10 from Japan, 1 from Korea, 7 from Netherlands, 2 from Portugal, 1 from Singapore, 3 from Spain, 3 from Sweden, 1 from Switzerland, 15 from UK, and 14 from USA. The final decision was made by review and conference chairs based on at least three reviewers' feedback available online via the conference management tool. As a result, 17 full papers and 17 short papers were accepted as submitted or with minor revisions. For the remaining submissions, 28 were recommended to change according to the reviews and were submitted as posters. This proceedings volume presents 62 technical contributions which are from many different countries: Belgium, Canada, P.R. China, Denmark, Finland, France, Germany, Italy, Japan, Korea, The Netherlands, Portugal, Singapore, Spain, Sweden, Taiwan, the UK, and USA. The technical papers accepted (17 full papers, 17 short papers) are compiled and presented in this volume in the order they were presented at the conference. In particular they are allocated to one of the following presentation sessions: (1) Agents; (2) Cultural and Psychological Metrics; (3) Transforming Broadcast Experience; (4) Culture, Place, Play (5) Display Technology; (6) Authoring Tools 1; (7) Object Tracking; (8) Edutainment (9) Networked Games; (10) Authoring Tools 2. All poster papers are listed separately and presented in a specific section of this book.

July 2006

Richard Harper
Marco Combetto

# Preface

Entertainment has come to occupy an extremely important part of our life by refreshing us and activating our creativity and providing different media for expression. Recently, with the advances made in computing, sensors and networks, new types of entertainment have been emerging such as video games, edutainment, robots, and networked games. In the meanwhile various degrees of entertainment are valuable to improve teaching, learning and in general knowledge and information sharing. New form of entertainment are appearing and are investigated by different disciplines and different sciences. Regrettably, until recently, entertainment has not been among the major research areas within the field of information processing. Since there are huge industries and markets devoted to entertainment, this unbalance seems very uncomfortable and is the subject of large discussions.

The new forms of entertainment have the potential to change our lives, so it is necessary for people who work in this area to discuss various aspects of entertainment and to promote entertainment-related research.

With this basic motivation, the General Assembly of the International Federation of Information Processing (IFIP) approved in August 2002 the establishment of the Specialist Group on Entertainment Computing (SG16). The responsibility of SG16 is to monitor and promote research and development activities related to entertainment computing throughout the world. One of the major activities of SG16 is to organize and support the International Conference on Entertainment Computing (ICEC). The ICEC is expected to bring together researchers, developers, and practitioners working in the area of entertainment computing. The conference covers a broad range of entertainment computing topics, such as theoretical studies, social and cultural aspects, new hardware/software development, integrated systems, human interfaces and interactions, and applications.

Let's take a brief look at the history of ICEC. The annual conference started in 2002 as the International Workshop on Entertainment (IWEC 2002), which was held May 14–17, 2002 in Makuhari, Japan. The workshop attracted more than 100 participants, and 60 papers were published in the proceedings by Kluwer. Based on the success of IWEC 2002, SG16 upgraded the workshop to a conference and organized ICEC 2003. ICEC 2003 was held May 8–10, 2003 at the Entertainment Technology Center of Carnegie Mellon University, Pittsburgh, USA. ICEC 2003 was also successful, with more than 100 attendees and 20 highly select papers. All of the papers of ICEC 2003 were accepted by ACM for inclusion in their ACM online digital library. The following year, ICEC crossed the Atlantic Ocean to move to Europe, and ICEC 2004 was held September 1–3, 2004 at the Technical University of Eindhoven in The Netherlands.

The conference attracted more than 150 attendees, and 27 full papers were published by Springer in the *Lecture Notes in Computer Science* (LNCS) series.

In 2005, ICEC came back to Japan, and was held at Kwansei Gakuin University, Sanda. In this conference the Committee selected more than 50 papers, and these papers are published in this LNCS volume.

Finally, in 2006, ICEC was hosted for the first time in the UK, in Cambridge, hosted by Microsoft Research and the University of Cambridge.

For the success of ICEC 2006, we express our special thanks to all the people who worked so hard to organize the conference: the University of Cambridge for the support and to all people of Microsoft Research Cambridge that supported the organization from end to end in the Local Organization Committee.

We are also grateful for the contribution of all the paper reviewers as well as the sponsors and cooperating societies.

July 2006                                                                 Richard Harper
                                                                          Marco Combetto

# Committees

## Chair

Richard Harper            Microsoft Research, UK

## International Chair

Matthias Rauterberg          TU Eindhoven, Netherlands

## Steering Committee

| | |
|---|---|
| Marc Cavazza | University of Teesside, UK |
| Tak Kamae | Tokyo Women's Medical University, Japan |
| Lizhuang Ma | Shanghai Jiao Tong University, China |
| Don Marinelli | Carnegie Mellon University, USA |
| Stéphane Natkin | CNAM, France |
| Ryohei Nakatsu | Kwansei Gakuin University, Japan |
| Matthias Rauterberg | TU Eindhoven, The Netherlands |
| Peter Robinson | University of Cambridge, UK |
| Andy Sloane | University of Wolverhampton, UK |
| Bill Swartout | University of Southern California, USA |

## Program Committee

| | |
|---|---|
| Christian Bauckhage | Deutsche Telekom, Germany |
| Matteo Bittanti | IULM, Italy |
| Michael Buro | University of Alberta, Canada |
| Alexander Braendle | Microsoft Research, UK |
| Christos Bouras | University of Patras, Greece |
| Brad J. Bushman | University of Michigan, USA |
| Gerhard Buurman | HGKZ, Switzerland |
| Nuno Correia | University of Lisbon, Portugal |
| Luca Chittaro | University of Udine, Italy |
| Paolo Ciancarini | University of Bologna, Italy |
| Antonio Cisternino | University of Pisa, Italy |
| Adrian David Cheok | Nanyang Technological University, Singapore |
| Ralf Dörner | FH Wiesbaden, Germany |
| David England | LJM University, UK |
| Steven Furnell | University of Plymouth, UK |
| Sidney Fels | University of British Columbia, Canada |

| | |
|---|---|
| Catherine Garbay | CNRS, France |
| Antonio Camara | YDreams, Portugal |
| Gianluca DiCagno | BSoft, Italy |
| Susan Gold | Sierra Nevada College, USA |
| Roberto Grossi | University of Pisa, Italy |
| Michael Haller | Upper Austria University, Austria |
| H.J. van den Herik | University of Maastricht, The Netherlands |
| Goffredo Haus | University of Milan, Italy |
| Michael Herczeg | University of Luebeck, Austria |
| Ernst A. Heinz | UMIT, Austria |
| Hiroyuki Iida | JAIST, Japan |
| Wijnand IJsselsteijn | TU/e, The Netherlands |
| Javier Jaén | Polytechnic University of Valencia, Spain |
| Francisco Javier Marin | Universidad de Málaga, Spain |
| Oskar Juhlin | Interactive Institute, Sweden |
| Börje Karlsson | PUC-Rio, Brazil |
| Haruhiro Katayose | Kwansei Gakuin University, Japan |
| Markus Koch | C-LAB, Germany |
| Oliver Lemon | Edinburgh University, UK |
| James Lester | North Carolina State University, USA |
| Olli Leino | University of Lapland, Finland |
| Ville-Veikko Mattila | Nokia, Finland |
| Ian Marshall | Coventry University, UK |
| Hitoshi Matsubara | Future University-Hakodate, Japan |
| Frans Mäyrä | University of Tampere, Finland |
| Carsten Magerkurth | Fraunhofer IPSI, Germany |
| Anton Nijholt | University of Twente, The Netherlands |
| Yoshihiro Okada | Kyushu, Japan |
| Kees Overbeeke | TU/e, The Netherlands |
| Zhigeng Pan | Zhejiang University, China |
| Mark Perry | Brunel University, UK |
| Christian Reimann | C-Lab, Germany |
| Paolo Remagnino | Kingston University, UK |
| Theresa-Marie Rhyne | North Carolina State University, USA |
| Abdennour El Rhalibi | Liverpool JM University, UK |
| Mark Riedl | University of Southern California, USA |
| Marco Roccetti | University of Bologna, Italy |
| Marcos Rodrigues | Sheffield Hallam University, UK |
| Ben Salem | Kwansei Gakuin University, Japan |
| Leonie Schäfer | EU-DG ISM, Belgium |
| Nikitas Sgouros | University of Piraeus, Greece |
| Leonid Smalov | Coventry University, UK |
| Scott Stevens | CMU, USA |
| Norbert Streitz | Fraunhofer IPSI, Germany |
| João Manuel R. S. Tavares | Universidade do Porto, Portugal |
| Ruck Thawonmas | Ritsumeikan University, Japan |
| Masahiko Tsukamoto | Kobe Univerity, Japan |

Christian Thurau          University of Bielefeld, Germany
Clark Verbrugge          Sable McGill, Canada
Frans Vogelaar           KHM, Germany
Annika Waern             SICS, Sweden
Lars Wolf                TU Braunschweig, Germany
Pierre-Louis Xech        Microsoft Research, UK
Iyun Seng Yang           KAIST, Korea
Michael Young            NCS University, USA
Robert Zubek             Northwestern University, USA
Michael Zyda             ISI, USA

## Organization Chair

Marco Combetto           Microsoft Research, UK

## Organization Support

TEAM Event Management

## In Collaboration With

University of Cambridge

## Sponsors

Microsoft Research

## Cooperating Societies

Association for Computing Machinery
British HCI Group
Digital Games Research Association
   Fun & Games  2006

# IFIP SG16

SG16 (Specialist Group on Entertainment Computing) was established at the General Assembly of IFIP (International Federation on Information Processing) in 2001. A new Technical Committee (TC) on Entertainment Computing was proposed to IFIP (approval pending) in the following way:

**Aims:**
To encourage computer applications for entertainment and to enhance computer utilization in the home, the Technical Committee will pursue the following aims:

- To enhance algorithmic research on board and card games
- To promote a new type of entertainment using information technologies
- To encourage hardware technology research and development to facilitate implementing entertainment systems, and
- To encourage haptic and non-traditional human interface technologies for entertainment.

**Scopes:**
1. Algorithms and strategies for board and card games

- Algorithms for board and card games
- Strategy controls for board and card games
- Level setups for games and card games

2. Novel entertainment using ICT
- Network-based entertainment
- Mobile entertainment
- Location-based entertainment
- Mixed reality entertainment

3. Audio
- Music informatics for entertainment
- 3D audio for entertainment
- Sound effects for entertainment

4. Entertainment human interface technologies
- Haptic and non-traditional human interface technologies
- Mixed reality human interface technologies for entertainment

5. Entertainment robots
- ICT-based toys
- Pet robots
- Emotion models and rendering technologies for robots

6. Entertainment systems
   - Design of entertainment systems
   - Entertainment design toolkits
   - Authoring systems

7. Theoretical aspects of entertainment
   - Sociology, psychology and physiology for entertainment
   - Legal aspects of entertainment

8. Video game and animation technologies
   - Video game hardware and software technologies
   - Video game design toolkits
   - Motion capture and motion design
   - Interactive storytelling
   - Digital actors and emotion models

9. Interactive TV and movies
   - Multiple view synthesis
   - Free viewpoint TV
   - Authoring technologies

10. Edutainment
   - Entertainment technologies for children's education
   - Open environment entertainment robots for education

## SG16 Members (2006)

**Chair**
Ryohei Nakatsu - Kwansei Gakuin University, Japan
**Vice-Chair**
Matthias Rauterberg –TU Eindhoven, The Netherlands
**Secretary**
Ben Salem - Kwansei Gakuin University, Japan

**National Representatives**
   - Galia Angelova - Bulgarian Academy of Sciences, Bulgaria
   - Sidney Fels - University of British Columbia, Canada
   - Zhigeng Pan - Zhejiang University, China
   - Ville-Veikko Mattila - Nokia Research Center, Finland
   - Bruno Arnaldi - IRISA-INRIA, France
   - Richard Reilly - University College Dublin, Ireland
   - Paolo Ciancarini - University of Bologna, Italy
   - Barnabas Takacs - Hungarian Academy of Science, Hungary
   - Takehiko Kamae - National Institute of Informatics, Japan
   - Hyun S. Yang - KAIST, Korea

- Matthias Rauterberg – TU Eindhoven, The Netherlands
- Geir Egil Myhr - University of Tromsö, Norway
- Nueno Correira - New University of Lisbon, Portugal
- Adrian David Cheok - National University of Singapore, Singapore
- Pedro Gonzalez Calero - Complutense University of Madrid, Spain
- Natanicha Chorpothong - Assumption University, Thailand
- Marc Cavazza - University of Teesside, UK
- Donald Marinelli - Carnegie Mellon University, USA

**WG Chair persons**
- **WG16.1** Marc Cavazza - University of Teesside, UK
- **WG16.2** Hitoshi Matsubara - Future University-Hakodate, Japan
- **WG16.3** Matthias Rauterberg – TU Eindhoven, The Netherlands
- **WG16.4** Jaap van den Herik - University of Maastricht, The Netherlands
- **WG16.5** Andy Sloane - University of Wolverhampton, UK

# Working Groups (WG)

### WG16.1 Digital Storytelling
Storytelling is one of the core technologies of entertainment. Especially with the advancement of information and communication technologies (ICT), a new type of entertainment called video games has been developed, where interactive story development is the key that makes those games really entertaining. At the same time, however, there has not been much research on the difference between interactive storytelling and conventional storytelling. Also, as the development of interactive storytelling needs a lot of time and human power, it is crucial to develop technologies for automatic or semiautomatic story development. The objective of this working group is to study and discuss these issues.

### WG16.2 Entertainment Robot
Robots are becoming one of the most appealing forms of entertainment. New entertainment robots and/or pet robots are becoming popular. Also, from a theoretical point of view, compared with computer graphics-based characters/animations, robots constitute an interesting research object as they have a physical entity. Taking these aspects into consideration, it was decided at the SG16 annual meeting that a new working group on entertainment robots is to be established.

### WG16.3 Theoretical Basis of Entertainment
Although the entertainment industry is huge, providing goods such as video games, toys, movies, etc., little academic interest has been paid to such questions as what is the core of entertainment, what are the technologies that would create new forms of entertainment, and how can the core technologies of entertainment be applied to other areas such as education, learning, and so on. The main objective of this WG is to study these issues.

**WG16.4 Games and Entertainment Computing**
The scope of this work group includes, but is not limited to, the following applications, technologies, and activities.
Applications:
- Analytical games (e.g., chess, go, poker)
- Commercial games (e.g., action games, role-playing games, strategy games)
- Mobile games (e.g., mobile phones, PDAs)
- Interactive multimedia (e.g., virtual reality, simulations)

Technologies:
- Search Techniques
- Machine Learning
- Reasoning
- Agent Technology
- Human Computer Interaction

**WG16.5 Social and Ethical Issues in Entertainment Computing**
The social and ethical implications of entertainment computing include:
- Actual and potential human usefulness or harm of entertainment computing
- Social impact of these technologies
- Developments of the underlying infrastructure
- Rationale in innovation and design processes
- Dynamics of technology development
- Ethical development
- Cultural diversity and other cultural issues
- Education of the public about the social and ethical implications of Entertainment computing, and of computer professionals about the effects of their work.

WG 16.5 explicitly cares about the position of, and the potentials for, vulnerable groups such as children, the less-educated, disabled, elderly and unemployed people, cultural minorities, unaware users and others.

Anyone who is qualified and interested in active participation in one of the working groups is kindly invited to contact one of the WG chairs.

# Invited Speakers

## Nicole Lazzaro

Nicole Lazzaro is the leading expert on emotion and the fun of games. President of XEODesign, her 14 years of interactive research has defined the mechanisms of emotion that drive play. The result for her clients is that XEODesign has improved over 40 million player experiences, transforming them from boring time wasters to emotionally engaging games by reshaping the fun. To do this she has heightened the emotions that create more captivating play. More and more her clients ask her to explore new game mechanics to create new genres and reach new audiences.

Her research on "Why People Play Games: 4 Keys to More Emotion without Story" has expanded the game industry's emotional palette beyond the stereotypical range of anger, frustration, and fear. Working for clients including Sony, LeapFrog, Sega, Ubisoft, PlayFirst and EA, Nicole has improved the player experiences for all levels of gamers in a wide range of genres and platforms including 3D adventures, casual games, camera based play and smart pens. Prior to founding XEODesign in 1992 and co-founding San Francisco State University's Multimedia Studies Program, Nicole earned a degree in Psychology from Stanford University and worked in film. Free white papers on emotion and games: www.xeodesign.com.

## Margeret Wallace

Margaret Wallace is a Co-founder and CEO of Skunk Studios, a San Francisco-based game development group, known for creating high-quality original games for the mass market. Prior to the establishment of Skunk Studios, she produced and designed games and other interactive content for Shockwave.com and for Mattel's Hot Wheels brand. Margaret also collaborated on CDROM and online content while at Mindscape Entertainment (then encompassing SSIGames Online and RedOrb Games) and also at PF.Magic, creators of the pioneering "virtual life" series of "Petz" programs. Margaret is a Steering Committee member of the International Game Developers Association (IGDA) Online Games Group. She holds a B.S. with Distinction in Communication from Boston University and an MA from the University of Massachusetts/Amherst in Cultural Studies. Because her academic interests dealt largely with the intersection of popular culture and emerging technologies, Margaret was drawn into the world of games and its potential for engaging people on a worldwide scale.

## Steve Benford

Steve Benford is Professor of Collaborative Computing. His research concerns new technologies to support social interaction across computer networks. Recently, this has focussed on collaborative virtual environments (CVEs) and has addressed issues such as socially inspired spatial models of interaction, user embodiment, information visualization and mixed reality interfaces. His research group has developed the MASSIVE CVE system and has collaborated with social scientists and psychologists to evaluate social interaction within MASSIVE through field trials and public demonstrations. Since 1992 he has been a principal investigator on four EPSRC grants (Virtuosi, The Distributed Extensible Virtual Reality Laboratory, Large-Scale Multi-user Distributed Virtual Reality and Multimedia Networking for Inhabited Television); an ESPRIT III Basic Research grant (COMIC); two ESPRIT IV Long-Term Research grants (eRENA and KidStory); an ACTS grant (COVEN); two UK HEFCE grants and four direct industry-funded grants. He has also been a co-investigator on two UK ESRC and one UK MRC funded grants. Research income for these grants has exceeded £3 million pounds. Professor Benford is an editor of the CSCW journal and has served on the program committees of VRST 1998, SIGGROUP 1997, ECSCW 1993, ECSCW 1995 and ECSCW 1997. He presented his work at the Royal Society in 1995 and at the Royal Society of Edinburgh in 1996. He has published over 100 works including recent papers in ACM TOCHI, *The Computer Journal*, *Presence* and also at the ACM CHI, ACM CSCW, ACM VRST and IEEE ICDCS conferences.

## Robert Stone

Professor Bob Stone holds a Chair in Interactive Multimedia Systems at the University of Birmingham, UK, where he is Director of the Human Interface Technologies Team within the Department of Electronic, Electrical and Computer Engineering. He graduated from University College London in 1979 with a BSc in Psychology, and in 1981 with an MSc in Ergonomics (Human Factors), and currently holds the position of Visiting Professor of Virtual Reality (VR) within the Faculty of Medicine at Manchester University. As a result of his pioneering in-theatre human task analysis research, which led to the development of the world's first commercial VR keyhole surgery trainer (Procedicus MIST), now marketed by Mentice of Sweden, Bob holds the position of Director of Virtual Reality Studies for the North of England Wolfson Centre for Human-Centred Medical Technologies. In 1996, he became an Academician of the Russian International Higher Education Academy of Sciences (Moscow) and an Honorary Cossack in 2003. In 2000, Bob was accredited by General Klimuk, Director of Russia's Gagarin Space Centre as responsible for "introducing virtual reality into the cosmonaut space programme". Bob undertakes research into the human factors aspects of virtual/synthetic environments and serious gaming, with regular contributions to projects in the fields of defense part-task training, defense medicine and general surgery/health care.

## Thore Graepel

Thore Graepel is a researcher in the Machine Learning and Perception Group at Microsoft Research Cambridge. His current work is focused on the application of machine learning techniques to games. Previously, he was a postdoctoral researcher at the Department of Computer Science at Royal Holloway, University of London working on learning theory and machine learning algorithms with Prof. John Shawe-Taylor.

Before that, he worked with Nici Schraudolph and Prof. Petros Koumoutsakos as a postdoctoral researcher at the Institute of Computational Science (ICOS) which is part of the Department of Computer Science of the Swiss Federal Institute of Technology, Zürich (ETH). Topics of research were machine learning and large-scale nonlinear optimization. He received his doctorate (Dr. rer. nat) from the Department of Computer Science of the Technical University of Berlin, where he was first a member of the Neural Information Processing group of Prof. Klaus Obermayer and later joined the Statistics group of Prof. Ulrich Kockelkorn

# Table of Contents

## Session 4: Culture, Place, Play

## Session 5: Display Technology

# Session 6: Authoring Tools 1

# Session 7: Object Tracking

# Session 8: Edutainment

## Session 9: Network Games

## Session 10: Authoring Tools 2

## Posters

# Towards Bi-directional Dancing Interaction

Dennis Reidsma, Herwin van Welbergen, Ronald Poppe,
Pieter Bos, and Anton Nijholt

Human Media Interaction Group
University of Twente, Enschede, The Netherlands
{reidsma, welberge, poppe, anijholt}@ewi.utwente.nl
http://hmi.ewi.utwente.nl/

**Abstract.** Dancing is an entertaining form of taskless interaction. When interacting with a dancing Embodied Conversational Agent (ECA), the lack of a clear task presents the challenge of eliciting an interaction between user and ECA in a different way. In this paper we describe our Virtual Dancer, which is an ECA that invites a user to dance. In our system the user is monitored using global movement characteristics from a camera and a dance pad. The characteristics are used to select and adapt movements for the Virtual Dancer. This way, the user can dance together with the Virtual Dancer. Any interaction patterns and implicit relations between the dance behaviour of the human and the Virtual Dancer should be evoked intuitively without explicit appeal. The work described in this paper can be used as a platform for research into natural animation and user invitation behavior. We discuss future work on both topics.

## 1  Introduction

Embodied Conversational Agents are usually sent into the world with a task to perform. They are asked to provide information about theater performances, engage the user in a training activity, sell a mortgage or help a user to successfully complete a hotel reservation. Users are often interested in interacting with these ECAs since they have an interest in the task to be performed. Since the user's focus is on the task, any nonverbal behavior exhibited by the ECA that aims at engaging the user will have a relatively low impact.

Our Embodied Agent, the Virtual Dancer (Fig. 1) tries to invite and engage the user, with the sole purpose of having an interaction. Existing dance-related entertainment applications usually introduce a task. The user should hit targets, stamp in certain patterns on a dance pad or mimic sequences of specific poses, gaining high scores by doing it fast, precise, or to the beat. We drop even that incentive. The user is simply invited to dance together with the Virtual Dancer; any interaction patterns and implicit relations between the dance behaviour of the human and the Virtual Dancer should be evoked intuitively without explicit appeal.

Viewing dancing as a taskless interaction gives us the opportunity to investigate more subtle aspects of engaging and inviting behavior in isolation, without

R. Harper, M. Rauterberg, M. Combetto (Eds.): ICEC 2006, LNCS 4161, pp. 1–12, 2006.
© IFIP International Federation for Information Processing 2006

the distraction of a concrete task that must be performed. Letting go of the goal-directed task presents us with the challenge of eliciting an interaction between user and ECA in a different way. The user should first be seduced to enter into interaction. When the user is involved with the application, the system should establish progressively more complex interaction patterns with the user, without explicit 'game rules' or commands, yet in a way that is clear enough to be able to say when the interaction is 'successful' or not. Achieving that will be a significant contribution to the field of engaging and entertaining ECAs.

**Fig. 1.** Screenshot of the Virtual Dancer

The basic idea of our application is to monitor global movement characteristics of the user, and then use those characteristics to select and adapt movements for the Virtual Dancer. We describe the modules that we have built, including the animation system, the beat detection and the computer vision observation. We also describe the initial interaction models with which we try to achieve interesting interaction patterns. Furthermore, we present our short-term plans to extend these interaction models and evaluate their impact.

## 2   Related Work

Applications of dancing avatars exist in several variations. In some cases, the main reason for working with dance is the fact that dancing provides an interesting domain for animation technology. Perlin *et al.* and Mataric *et al.* focus on animation specification and execution [1, 2] within the dancing domain. Shiratori *et al.*, Nakazawa *et al.* and Kim *et al.* [3, 4, 5] research the dance as a whole. They describe the regeneration of new dance sequences from captured dances. Captured sequences are segmented into basic moves by analysis of the movement properties and, optionally, the accompanying music. Then they are assembled into sequences using motion graphs, aligning the new dance to the beat structure of the music. Chen *et al.* use the traditional Chinese Lion Dance as domain for their function based animation, focussing on the possibilities for style adaptation: exaggeration, timing and sharpness of movements [6].

While above work focusses on the dance itself, we take this research one step further and look at the interaction with a human dancer. Ren *et al.* describe a system where a human can control the animation of a virtual dancer [7]. Computer vision is used to process the input from three cameras. The fact that they use a domain with a limited collection of known dance forms (swing dancing) allows them to obtain a very detailed classification of dance moves performed by the human dancer. The classified dance moves are used to control the animation of a dancing couple. For the physical dancing robot Ms DanceR [8], a dance robot that can be led through the steps of a waltz, the interaction between human and artificial dancer focusses on the mutually applied forces between a dancing couple. Detection of applied forces is used to determine the appropriate movements for the robot.

Our Virtual Dancer is not *controlled* by a human, but actively participates in the interaction process in which both the human and the Virtual Dancer influence each other and let themselves be influenced in turn.

## 3   Architecture

The architecture of our system is shown in Fig. 2. In our setup, the Virtual Dancer is projected on a screen. A user is observed by a camera that is placed above the screen, monitoring the area in front of the screen. A dance pad is placed in front of the screen. Our setup further includes a sound system with speakers to play the music to which both the user and the Virtual Dancer can dance. The different components of the architecture are described in this section.

### 3.1   Beat Detection

Both tempo and beats are detected from the music using a real-time beat detector. From a comparison of detectors in [9] it was found that the feature extracting and periodicity detection algorithm of Klapuri [10] performs best. The first part of this algorithm is an improvement of the algorithm of Scheirer [11]. Both algorithms use a number of frequency bands to detect accentuation in the audio signal, and employ a bank of comb filter resonators to detect the beat. Klapuri improved the accentuation detection and comb filter banks. The biggest difference between the two is the way these comb filter banks are used to detect periodicity. Scheirer's algorithm uses filter banks that can be used to detect tempo and beat directly. The comb filter with the highest output is selected. Klapuri uses many more, and slightly different, filters which detect periodicity

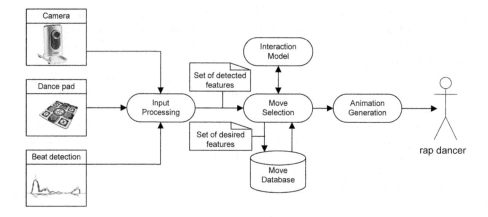

**Fig. 2.** Architecture of the Virtual Dancer system

in a broad range. A probabilistic model is used to detect the tactus, tatum and measure. For the Virtual Dancer we implemented Klapuri's algorithm.

### 3.2   Video Analysis

A single video camera is used to observe the user. Ideally, one would like to have complete knowledge about the movements of the user. This requires recovery of the pose of the user, usually described in terms of joint angles or limb locations. However, this is too demanding for our application for a number of reasons. Firstly, since only a single camera is used, no depth information is available. This makes it hard, if not impossible, to fully recover a complete pose. Secondly, there can be large variations in appearance and body dimensions between users. These can be estimated from the video, but this is hard since no pose information is present at first. An alternative is to add an initialization phase, in which these parameters can be estimated. However, such a phase prevents the more spontaneous use of our application that we aim for. Finally, when the movements of the user are known, our Dancer needs to extract certain characteristics and react to them. When poses are described in great detail, it is non-trivial how these can be used in the dancer's move selection phase (see also Section 3.5). Therefore, in our approach we use global movement features. These have a couple of advantages: they can be extracted more robustly, model variations between persons implicitly and can be used to determine selection criteria in the move selection phase. The set of characteristics $U$ that we extract from the video are summarized in Table 1. We distinguish between discrete values, that are either 0 or 1, and continuous values, that can have any value in the $[0 \ldots 1]$ interval.

As a first step, we extract the user's silhouette from the video image (Fig. 3(a)). This method requires a known background model, but it is computationally inexpensive. Moreover, silhouettes encode a great deal of information about the

**Table 1.** Summary of user characteristics, their types and input source

| Characteristic | Type | Source |
|---|---|---|
| BODY_HIGH | discrete | center of mass detector |
| BODY_LOW | discrete | center of mass detector |
| HORIZONTAL_ACTIVITY | continuous | center of mass detector |
| HAND_LEFT_TOP | discrete | radial activity detector |
| HAND_LEFT_SIDE | discrete | radial activity detector |
| HAND_RIGHT_TOP | discrete | radial activity detector |
| HAND_RIGHT_SIDE | discrete | radial activity detector |
| RADIAL_ACTIVITY | continuous | radial activity detector |
| FEET_MOVE_INTENSITY | continuous | dance pad |

user's pose. We employ two image processes to recover the movement characteristics. We describe these below.

**Center of Mass Detector.** The center of mass detector uses central moments to determine the 2D location of the silhouette's center of mass (CoM). Most changes in the silhouette due to pose changes will have only a small effect on the CoM. However, jumping or stretching the arms above the head will result in a higher CoM, whereas bending and squatting will lower the CoM considerably. Two thresholds are set on the vertical component of the CoM: a low threshold and a high threshold. If the CoM is below the low threshold, the BODY_LOW value is set. Similarly, if the CoM is above the high threshold, the BODY_HIGH value is set. The values of the thresholds are determined empirically. Furthermore, the average difference in successive values of the horizontal component is a measure for the HORIZONTAL_ACTIVITY value. This value is normalized with respect to the silhouette's width.

**Radial Activity Detector.** When the CoM is calculated, we can look at the distribution of silhouette pixels around the CoM. We are especially interested in the extremities of the silhouette, which could be the legs and arms. Therefore, we look at foreground pixels that lie in the ring centered around the CoM (Fig. 3(b)). The radius of the outer boundary equals the maximum distance between silhouette boundary and CoM. The radius of the inner boundary equals half the radius of the outer boundary. The ring is divided into 12 radial bins of equal size (see also Fig. 3(c)). A threshold on the percentage of active pixels within a bin is determined empirically. If the threshold within a bin is exceeded, the HAND_LEFT_SIDE, HAND_LEFT_TOP, HAND_RIGHT_TOP and HAND_RIGHT_SIDE values are set, for the corresponding bins. In addition, the RADIAL_ACTIVITY value is determined by the normalized average change in bin values between successive frames.

### 3.3   Dance Pad

To monitor feet movement we use a Dance Dance Revolution (DDR) pad. This pad contains eight 'buttons', that are pressed if a foot is placed on them. We do

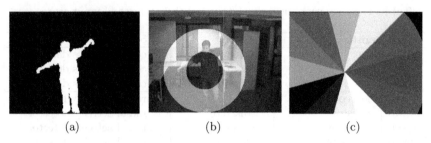

(a)                    (b)                    (c)

**Fig. 3.** (a) Extracted silhouette (b) Center of mass with ring (c) Radial activity bins

not force users to restrain their movement to the floor area covered by the pad. If the pad is used, we determine the FOOT_MOVE_INTENSITY characteristic by looking at the number of button presses that occurs in a given period of time.

### 3.4 Move Database

A human pose is described by setting the rotation values of the joints. Animations are defined as a number of keyframes that describing poses, and interpolation between them. The keyframes can be specified manually or obtained from motion capture. We can also use the location of end effectors to describe a pose. Using inverse kinematics (IK), we determine the rotation of joints involved in the animation. For example, we could describe the path of a hand and automatically calculate the rotation of the shoulder and elbow needed to place the hand on this path. Figure 4 visualizes the movement paths for the hands as defined in the 'car' move. Both hands move along a segment of an ellipse. Those paths are defined as a set of functions over time with adaptable movement parameters $(x(t,a), y(t,a)$ and $z(t,a))$. The parameter $t$ $(0 \leq t \leq 1)$ indicates the progress of the animation. The parameter $a$ can be seen as an amplitude parameter and is used to set the height of the hand's half-ellipse move. In a similar way, we defined formulae that describe joint rotation paths. We combine keyframe animation, rotation formulae for the joints and path descriptions for limbs and body center. Currently, we do not combine motion capture data with the other animation types.

For each move we stored key positions in time, that are aligned to the beats in the animation phase. Key points can have different weights, according to how important it is that they are aligned to a musical beat. For example, the time instance where a hand clap occurs is stored as a key position with high weight since we would like our Dancer to clap to the beat rather than between just anywhere.

### 3.5 Move Selection

The move selection is built to choose moves based on the current state of the Dancer and the characteristics of the dancing behaviour of the human (see Table 1). A mapping from this information to information stored about each

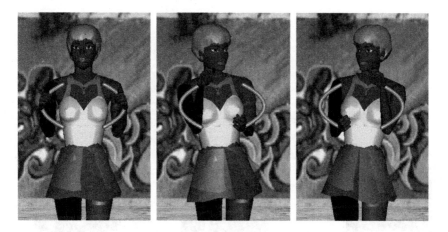

**Fig. 4.** Samples of the 'car' move, in which the hands are rotated in a driving movement. The path of the hands is shown by the white spheres.

move determines the selection of the next move of the Dancer. To support this mapping, each move $m$ in the database is annotated with its type (e.g. 'dancing' or 'bored') and the default duration. Furthermore, we manually set values for the each possible move characteristic $B^m \in M$. Currently, $M$ (the set of characteristics that a dance move can have) contains only a few components (HIGH_LOW, ACTIVITY, SYMMETRY, HAND_POSITION, REPEATING and DISPLACEMENT) but the set can be extended at any time.

To select a move, we first calculate the set of observed characteristics $O \in \wp(U)$ displayed by the human dancer. These characteristics are then mapped to a set of desired characteristics in the dance move ($D \in \wp(M)$) using mapping $G$:

$$G := U \longrightarrow M \tag{1}$$

By comparing the desired values $D_i$ with the value of the corresponding characteristic $B_i^m$ for each move $m$ in the database the most appropriate move is determined. The mapping $G$ is defined by the interaction model. A matching score $s_m$ is calculated for each move:

$$s_m = \sum_i (1 - |D_i - B_i^m|)w_i \tag{2}$$

$w_i$ is the weight of characteristic $i$. The weights are normalized to make sure they sum up to 1. The probability that a certain move $m$ is selected is proportional to its score $s_m$.

### 3.6   Animation Generation

**Dancing to the Beat.** One important feature in any dance animation is the alignment of the dance movements to the beat of the music. Our approach to this

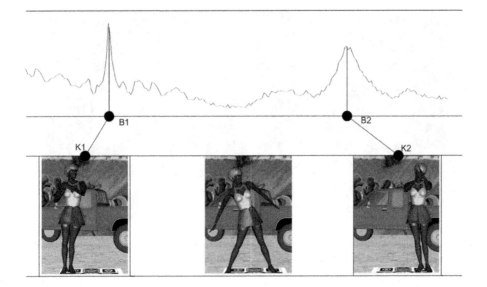

**Fig. 5.** Move alignment to the beat: beat $B_1$ is aligned to keyframe $K_1$; beat $B_2$ is aligned to keyframe $K_2$

is as follows. Whenever a new move is being planned, the beat detector module is queried for the current tempo and beat pattern of the music. This information is used to produce a vector of predictions of beats in the near future. The set of key points from the selected move and the beats from the beat prediction vector are time-aligned to each other using an algorithm inspired by the event-aligner from [12] (see Fig. 5). This algorithm takes into consideration the importance of the key points, the relative position of key points in the move, the beats in the vector and the strength of the beats.

**Interpolation.** To generate the transition from one dancing move to the next, we make use of a simple interpolation algorithm. The root position is linearly interpolated from the end position of the previous animation to the start position of the next animation. If there is no significant feet displacement, all joint rotations are interpolated. If significant feet displacement is needed to get from the previous animation to the next, the Dancer makes two intermediary steps. The movement of the feet and the vertical movement of the root are specified by the step formula described in [13].

### 3.7   Interaction Model

The interaction model is implemented as a state machine. Currently it has the states 'bored' 'invite' and 'dance'. During the 'bored' state, the Dancer exhibits bored behavior such as scratching her head or inspecting her fingernails. If the presence of a human is detected by the video analysis system, she tries to invite him or her to dance with her. This behavior is performed using nonverbal invitation gestures. Once the user steps on the dance pad, the dancing starts.

We implemented the dancing process as alternating phases of the ECA following and leading the user (or at least attempting to lead the user). 'Following' means dancing with movement properties that are similar to what the user shows. 'Leading' involves varying the movement properties considerably in one or more dimensions. The implicit intention is to get the the user to adapt in reaction. Based on the state of the Dancer, the mapping $G$ and the weights $w_i$ are adapted. This gives us a system which allows for all kinds of different dimensions of interactivity. The human and the Virtual Dancer will have a chance to influence the other. The can also observe the reactions to thatinfluence as well as the attempts at influencing by the other and can signal their reaction to that.

## 4   Results

The system described in this paper has been implemented and was exhibited on several smaller and larger occasions[1]. It has proved to be very robust. At the CHI Interactivity Chamber the program had been running non stop for two days in a row without needing any other intervention than occasionally making new snapshots of the changing background. The system currently runs on two 'average' laptops, one running the computer vision processes and the other running the real-time beat detection and all other processes for controlling and animating the Virtual Dancer, including the interaction algorithms.

During those demonstration events, many people interacted with the installation. Some of the interactions were recorded on video. The resulting recordings will be used to get a first idea of the interaction patterns to which people react as well as of the types of reactions. Then we will use this knowledge to improve the user observation modules and the interaction models to get closer to our aim of a system where interaction is not enforced but enticed.

## 5   Future Work

The work described in this paper can be used as a platform for research into natural animation, mutual dance interaction and user invitation behavior. This section describes our ongoing work on these topics.

### 5.1   Animation

Merging animations described by mathematical formulae with animations derived from motion capture by simply applying animating some joints with the one, and some with the other specification, results in unrealistically looking animations. The formula-based approach looks very mechanical, compared to the

---

[1] See Figure 1 for a screenshot and `http://hmi.ewi.utwente.nl/showcases/The Virtual Dancer/` for demos and movies.

movements obtained by motion capture, which contain a high level of detail. However, the formula-based animation gives us a high level of control on joint movements, which allows us to modify the path of movement and the amount of rotation of joints in real time. We have less control over motion captured movements. Currently, we can only align motion capture movement to the beat of the music and adapt its velocity profile. We would like to be able to modify not only the timing, but also the position of body parts in the animation.

The lack of control is a general problem in motion captured animation. There is much ongoing research in the domain of adaptation of motion capture data. A motion capture frame can be translated to IK data for certain body parts, so that the translation path of these parts can be adapted [14]. Motion capture data can be divided in small portions. Then, transitions between motions that show many similarities can be defined, which results in a motion graph [5, 15]. Suitable animations are created by selecting a path through the graph that satisfies the imposed animation constraints. Motion capture can also be used as 'texture' on generated or handmade keyframe animations [16], which improves the detail and naturalness of the animations. Different motion capture animations could be blended together to create new animations [17]. The movement style obtained from motion capture can be used to enhance animation generated by bio-mechanical models [18]. We plan to adapt our motion capture data to gain expressiveness of and control over our animations using such techniques as mentioned above.

## 5.2  Mutual Dance Interaction

Many issues still need to be resolved if we want to achieve the kind of interaction patterns that we are aiming for. Amongst others, the system should be able to detect when its attempts at leading are successful (see e.g. [19], where this is partially done for two dancing humans), the system should have a (natural) way to signal acknowledgement and approval to the user when the user reacts appropriately to the leading attempts of the system, the system should be able to detect situations when the user is attempting to lead, the interaction pattern should become progressively more complex when the first interaction is established and we should determine which dimensions in the dance moves are most suitable for variation. Such topics will shape some of our short-term future work on this project.

## 5.3  Invitation

In our ongoing work centered around the Virtual Dancer installation, one of the themes is the *invitation of users to join the dance*. Because there is no practical application associated to the installation, users will have no compelling reason to engage in interaction with it. At the moment, the Virtual Dancer initiates the interaction by making inviting gestures to the user. This is a kind of 'enforced' interaction: without warning or consent the user finds herself in the middle of an ongoing interaction. This is about as subtle as a television advertisement or an outbound sales agent who still needs to meet his quota. In real life, interaction often starts in a more subtle way. For example, as described in [20], people use all kinds of mechanisms to signal their willingness and intention to interact, even before the first explicit 'communication' is started. Peters describes a theoretical model for perceived attention and perceived intention to interact. Primarily gaze and body orientation, but also gestures and facial expression, are proposed as inputs for synthetic memory and belief networks, to model the level of attention directed at the agent by an other agent, virtual or human. The resulting attention profile, calculated over time, is used to determine whether this other agent is perceived as 'intending to interact'. Quote from [20]: "For example, peaks in an otherwise low magnitude curve are interpreted as social inattention or salutation behaviors without the intention to escalate the interaction. A profile that is of high magnitude and increasing is indicative of an agent that has more than a passing curiosity in an other and possibly an intention to interact. Entries regarding locomotion towards the self actively maintain the level of attention in cases where the profile would otherwise drop due to the eyes or head being oriented away."

We intend to use these ideas to experiment with behavior that entices people in an implicit way into interaction with the Dancer. Simulations and models for eye contact and attention of the type described above will be implemented using robust computer vision and the eye contact detection technology of [21].

## Acknowledgements

The authors would like to thank Moes Wagenaar and Saskia Meulman for performing the dance moves that are used in this work. Furthermore, we thank Hendri Hondorp, Joost Vromen and Rutger Rienks for their valuable comments and their contributions to the implementation of our system.

## References

1. Perlin, K.: Real time responsive animation with personality. IEEE Transactions on Visualization and Computer Graphics **1**(1) (1995) 5–15
2. Mataric, M., Zordan, V., Williamson, M.: Making complex articulated agents dance. Autonomous Agents and Multi-Agent Systems **2**(1) (1999) 23–43
3. Shiratori, T., Nakazawa, A., Ikeuchi, K.: Rhythmic motion analysis using motion capture and musical information. In: Proceedings of the IEEE International Conference on Multisensor Fusion and Integration for Intelligent Systems. (2003) 89–94
4. Nakazawa, A., Nakaoka, S., Kudoh, S., Ikeuchi, K.: Digital archive of human dance motions. In: Proceedings of the International Conference on Virtual Systems and Multimedia. (2002)
5. Kim, T., Park, S.I., Shin, S.Y.: Rhythmic-motion synthesis based on motion-beat analysis. ACM Transactions on Graphics **22**(3) (2003) 392–401
6. Chen, J., Li, T.: Rhythmic character animation: Interactive chinese lion dance. In: Proceedings of the International Conference on Computer Animation and Social Agents. (2005)

7. Ren, L., Shakhnarovich, G., Hodgins, J.K., Pfister, H., Viola, P.: Learning silhouette features for control of human motion. ACM Transcactions on Graphics **24**(4) (2005) 1303–1331
8. Kosuge, K., Hayashi, T., Hirata, Y., Tobiyama, R.: Dance partner robot –ms dancer–. In: Proceedings of the IEEE/RSJ International Conference on Intelligent Robots and Systems. (2003) 3459–3464
9. Gouyon, F., Klapuri, A., Dixon, S., Alonso, M., Tzanetakis, G., Uhle, C., Cano, P.: An experimental comparison of audio tempo induction algorithms. IEEE Transactions on Speech and Audio Processing (2006) In press.
10. Klapuri, A., Eronen, A., Astola, J.: Analysis of the meter of acoustic musical signals. IEEE transactions on Speech and Audio Processing **14**(1) (2006) 342–355
11. Scheirer, E.D.: Tempo and beat analysis of acoustic musical signals. Journal of the Acoustical Society of America **103**(1) (1998) 558–601
12. Kuper, J., Saggion, H., Cunningham, H., Declerck, T., de Jong, F., Reidsma, D., Wilks, Y., Wittenburg, P.: Intelligent multimedia indexing and retrieval through multi-source information extraction and merging. In: International Joint Conference of Artificial Intelligence, Acapulco, Mexico (February 2003) 409–414
13. Meredith, M., Maddock, S.: Using a half-jacobian for real-time inverse kinematics. In: Proceedings of the International Conference on Computer Games: Artificial Intelligence, Design and Education. (2004) 81–88
14. Meredith, M., Maddock, S.: Adapting motion capture using weighted real-time inverse kinematics. ACM Computers in Entertainment **3**(1) (2005) (This is a Web-based journal).
15. Kovar, L., Gleicher, M., Pighin, F.H.: Motion graphs. ACM Trans. Graph. **21**(3) (2002) 473–482
16. Pullen, K., Bregler, C.: Motion capture assisted animation: texturing and synthesis. In: Proceedings of the annual conference on Computer graphics and interactive techniques. (2002) 501–508
17. Safonova, A., Hodgins, J.K., Pollard, N.S.: Synthesizing physically realistic human motion in low-dimensional, behavior-specific spaces. ACM Trans. Graph. **23**(3) (2004) 514–521
18. Liu, K.C., Hertzmann, A., Popovic, Z.: Learning physics-based motion style with nonlinear inverse optimization. ACM Trans. Graph. **24**(3) (2005) 1071–1081
19. Boker, S., Rotondo, J. In: Symmetry building and symmetry breaking in synchronized movement. (2003) 163–171
20. Peters, C.: Direction of attention perception for conversation initiation in virtual environments. In: Proceedings of the Intelligent Virtual Agents, International Working Conference, Springer (2005) 215–228
21. Shell, J., Selker, T., Vertegaal, R.: Interacting with groups of computers. Special Issue on Attentive User Interfaces, Communications of ACM **46**(3) (March 2003) 40–46

# An Emotional Path Finding Mechanism for Augmented Reality Applications

José A. Mocholí[1], José M. Esteve[1], Javier Jaén[1], Raquel Acosta[1], and Pierre Louis Xech[2]

[1] Polytechnic University of Valencia
Camino de Vera s/n
46022 Valencia, Spain
{jesteve, fjaen, jmocholi, racosta}@dsic.upv.es
[2] Microsoft Research
7 J J Thomson Avenue
Cambridge CB3 0FB, UK
plxech@microsoft.com

**Abstract.** In this paper we present *eCoology*, an AR edutainment application for children in which emotional and social aspects are taking into consideration to improve flow or optimal experience. Particularly, we investigate the introduction of emotional agents that react and move within the AR environment according to their emotional state. We propose a model for emotional agents and a path finding mechanism with backtracking that allows exploration of different movement alternatives. In this way, virtual entities may exhibit a complex number of emotional movement behaviors within the augmented space.

## 1 Introduction

Studying is the major task for children, teenagers and college students across cultures, covering a significant percentage of time in their daily life [1]. Students have to deal with classmates and teachers following adult social rules of behavior and interaction, but these interactions are associated with low control of the situation and implicit motivation [2]. On the contrary, the most positive experiences are reported in activities such as sports, gaming, arts and hobbies, which merge fun with concentration and goal setting [3]. Particularly relevant in these activities has been the identification of *optimal experience* or *flow* [4] which is characterized by the perception of high environmental challenges, adequate personal skills, high levels of concentration, enjoyment and engagement, loss of self-consciousness, control of the situation, focused attention, positive feedback, clear ideas about the goals of the activity and intrinsic motivation [5]. Therefore, incorporating *flow* into learning environments [6] would encourage students to use their abilities and to find rewarding and engaging opportunities for action during work class and homework.

In this paper we report on an experience of using Augmented Reality (AR) gaming [7][8] as a key element in moving children away from apathy, lack of involvement in

R. Harper, M. Rauterberg, M. Combetto (Eds.): ICEC 2006, LNCS 4161, pp. 13–24, 2006.

school subjects and searching alternative dangerous sources of *flow*. AR gaming has very important features that make it ideal for optimal *flow* in learning activities. As pointed out in [9], AR games may require physical skills to the same extent as real world games; support spatial reasoning with arbitrarily complex game models and rules; contain social elements of collaboration, negotiation and relationship building; and can stimulate players emotionally across a full range of senses in a potentially vast number of mixed-reality scenarios and environments. Therefore, AR games can contribute positively to achieve all the components that constitute an optimal experience.

Particularly important, in our opinion, are the emotional and social aspects of Augmented Reality for flow building. It has been proven [10] that older and younger brains are linked by emotional systems not only in the processes of care but also in the quest for skill and understanding. Human companions support growth of intelligence and, in AR environments, artificial companions or agents may also collaborate as social entities in the processes of knowledge discovery and interpretation of the real world.

In this paper we present *eCoology*, an AR edutainment application for children in which emotional and social aspects are taking into consideration to improve *flow* or optimal experience. Particularly, we investigate the introduction of emotional agents that react and move within the AR environment according to their emotional state, and a path finding mechanism based on particle systems contributing to emotional movements of entities within the augmented space. Section 2 will introduce the main features of the *eCoology* system. Section 3 will present a model for emotional entities and a mechanism for emotional path finding. Section 4 will describe an algorithm for path resolution supporting emotional backtracking. Finally, section 5 will present our conclusions and future work.

## 2 The Ecoology Ecosystem

*eCoology* is an acronym for "An Electronic Cool Way of Learning about Ecology", and the main goal is to teach children (aged 8 to 12) about healthy everyday values such as having a balance diet, taking care of the environment, using renewable sources of energy, and behaving respectfully with others by means of an optimal flow experience based on games.

The proposed mechanism is an AR game application consisting of an ecosystem with plants, animals, energy sources and people. Children are proposed gaming activities such as, feeding animals with different types of food and, evaluating over time the health status of the animals under their responsibility. Animals that are only given unhealthy food eventually appear to be sick, and children have to find out the ultimate reasons of their illness. This problem solving task is mediated by social artificial agents and it will be presented later in this paper. The rationale behind this activity is to make children think about their own feeding behavior, and its consequences by analyzing a similar situation with virtual animals in an AR ecosystem (see Figure 1).

**Fig. 1.** *eCoology* augmented space

Living entities in *eCoology* behave emotionally to show happiness when healthy states are achieved, or to express different forms of aggressive behavior and unhappiness when animals detect situations related to past unhealthy states (emotional recall). This emotional behavior is not only expressed in terms of short duration reactions but even affect the movement of entities within the AR ecosystem. As a result, entities with emotional feelings about other entities, be they artificial or real, modify their movement trajectories accordingly to be near of good friends and go away from enemies or entities that could harm and entity's health.

Social learning is integrated within *eCoology* by making children aware of person-to-person and artificial agent-to-person relationships. Children have mechanisms to keep track of good and bad behaviors of other members in the ecosystem to help them to build partnership relationships with good friends, or try to fix a bad relationship if it is detected. Besides, trust building is supported by using negotiation spaces in which users interact to exchange items such as tools and needed food. The ultimate goal is, besides reinforcing responsibility values on children, to contribute to their personal growth by establishing personal relationships within the augmented reality space.

In terms of architectural design, *eCoology* is a multi-player AR game in which all users of the ecosystem perceive the same snapshot of the system in real time. *eCoology* leverages the power of P2P technology to easily maintain up-to-date all users. To develop the P2P network of *eCoology* we have used the PeerChannel [11] infrastructure present in the Windows Communication Foundation [12], which allowed us to create easily a multi-party communication network and to broadcast the simulation data to all client rendering engines.

## 3   Emotional Model

Emotional computing is a research area that is recently receiving a lot of attention [13] [14]. Although several definitions for "emotional behavior" can be found, all existing approaches refer to "human-like" agents when speaking about software systems that mimic human behavior biased by emotions.

Having entities in *eCoology* with emotional behavior is a key feature for children to perceive the augmented ecosystem as an attractive interactive environment for learning. Particularly interesting when dealing with immersive augmented reality experiences is the representation of emotional behavior that has an impact on entities movement. This interest arises from the need of user engagement: an augmented reality environment with virtual animals moving around according to some emotions improves users' immersion and engagement with the system.

In our first prototype we have defined a small set of emotional state ranges that influence movement of entities, namely, "fear-courage", "aggressiveness-calmness", "happiness-sadness", and "faithfulness-disloyalty". Each emotional range can be seen as a continuous variable with two extreme values. For instance, an entity may reach a very low level of fear-courage and "feel" fear when encountering another entity that behaves aggressively against it; or may "feel" aggressive (see Figure 2) if it is alone (no nearby entities of its kind) and surrounded by other types of entities. It may also reach the happiness-sadness emotional state and feel happy (see Figure 2) if it is side by side with its owner or with other entities of its kind. In terms of user interaction, the user can learn that some kind of food is not suitable for an entity if, after offering it, the entity does not obey further user commands. In the same way, if the entity likes the food, it could feel faithfulness and would follow the movements of the user. This emotional behavior affects the destination used in the path-finding of the entity.

**Fig. 2.** Depiction of a dog that "feels" aggressive and a happy chicken

To achieve this type of complex emotional behavior, we have designed an emotional model consisting of three subsystems (Figure 3):

− **Perception:** This is a basic component of any behavioral model for entities (be they emotional or not) that have to interact with their surrounding environment. It is responsible for extracting data from the environment (stimuli). This information may be obtained from an entity's field of vision, obstacles and objects, presence of other nearby entities (their emotional state), and also from what an entity can hear, such as the call from its owner.

- **Emotional Profile:** An important point to increase user engagement is to endow each entity with a different type of behavior, i.e., not just a differentiation among types of entities but also among individuals of the same type. This approach is a totally established trend in entertainment industry (games, movies, commercials [15]). This subsystem establishes the character of an entity in terms of what an entity will feel for a certain type of stimulus. Besides, it also contains an *emotional memory* to remember past interactions with other entities so that an entity may express emotional feelings with respect to them. Based on an entity's character and its emotional memory this subsystem generates a vector of emotional state ranges (as defined earlier) that are processed by the behavioral performer subsystem.

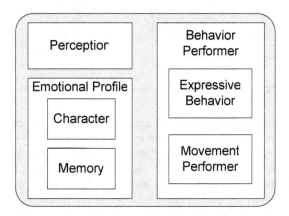

**Fig. 3.** Model of an emotional entity of *eCoology*

- **Behavioral performer:** This subsystem is responsible for expressing reactions and behaviors that relate to emotions generated by the emotional profile subsystem. These reactions include body expressions such as those depicted in Fig. 2 and movement behaviors. This subsystem takes a stimulus from the perception subsystem and the set of emotions associated to it from the emotional profile. Then, it makes the entity react either with a body expression and/or a movement in the augmented space towards a specific destination according to the emotion the stimulus produces. For example, if the stimulus is a person calling an animal and the animal feels a certain level of happiness and loyalty towards him, then it will select the person's current position as its next movement target. The details of how this process is done will be described next.

**Emotional Selection of a Destination**

Entities in *eCoology* perceive stimuli in many forms such as: detection of nearby entities, food being thrown at the ecosystem, and voice commands. These stimuli belong two categories: stimuli related to presence of objects or entities in the ecosystem such as "saw a cake next to you", "saw user A is at position (20,30)", or "saw dog C at position (2,3)"; and stimuli related to actions performed on an entity by another entity such as "user A is screaming at you", "user B is giving you a carrot", or

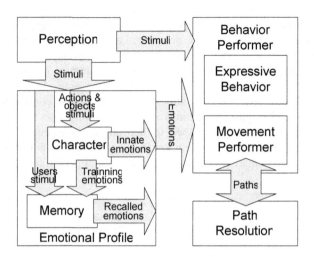

**Fig. 4.** Emotional selection of reactions and destinations

"dog C is barking at you". These stimuli are collected by the perception subsystem and passed to the Emotional profile and Behavioral Performer subsystems.

Actions and objects may produce "*innate emotions*" per se with different intensities. For instance, "barking at me causes I feel a certain level of aggressiveness", "Giving me love makes me feel happy and loyal", or "cakes make me feel happy". These emotions are part of the innate emotional profile of an entity and are generated by our character module within the emotional profile (Figure 4).

However, innate emotions caused by actions are particularly interesting because they are used as training sets for the memory component. This component uses emotions related to actions together with the entity that performed them to create "emotional memories". Emotional memories make an entity "remember" emotions that were caused as a result of actions performed by other entities in the past. Therefore, whenever an entity A perceives the presence of another entity B as a stimulus, the emotional profile of A uses its emotional memory to generate evoked emotions about B. To perform this process, the emotional memory component uses a machine learning mechanism based on clustering algorithms. Clustering deals with the construction of subsets (clusters) based on similarity mechanisms from input data sets. In our case, input data sets are innate emotions produced by the character module and a single cluster is obtained for each external entity that interacted in the past with a given entity. This way, whenever an entity A perceives another entity B, the centroid of the cluster representing B in the emotional memory of A is obtained and the emotional values contained in this centroid are generated as an emotional response. These emotional responses are called "recalled emotions".

Once an emotional response (innate or recalled) has been generated and passed to the behavioral performer, the latter can start its task. The first step is to select among the perceived stimulus the one the entity will react to. To do this, the behavioral performer analyzes the emotions associated to each stimulus to evaluate the one with the most intense set of emotions. Once this selection is done, the expressive behavior component uses the emotion with highest level of intensity to make the entity react visually (3D animation) according to the emotion. Besides, if the selected stimulus determines a movement towards or away from a given target in the augmented space then the movement performer component (Figure 4) communicates with a path resolution subsystem. This subsystem calculates all feasible routes (see next section) and returns them on demand to the movement performer which selects the best possible route based on the remaining stimuli and associated emotions. For instance, a certain route may be rejected if it passes close to the location of a stimulus that has produced a negative set of emotions. This way, entities exhibit emotional movements in the augmented space.

## 4   Ecoology Path Finding

Emotional behavior, as was described earlier, can be expressed in many forms including motion in a surrounding space. We describe in this section a path-finding service in charge of providing alternative paths to reach targets which the higher level behavioral system evaluates and, eventually, accepts or discards.

In the context of autonomous moving agents, the path-finding problem can be addressed as the problem of providing, given the current and final position, and a set of spatial constraints (usually a map), one or more possible ways of reaching our goal without violating any of the constraints.

There are several approaches which are commonly used to solve the path-finding problem but most path-finding algorithms work with graphs in the mathematical sense, a set of vertices with edges connecting them. In the most general case, a graph-based path finding algorithm will try to find a set of nodes to visit in order to be able to connect two requested nodes. Many of these algorithms try to find out the path of *minimum* cost, given a cost function to evaluate the alternative paths and a set of spatial constraints. However, despite graphs are widely used, and there exist very efficient algorithms to deal with them, they also have important implications that must be considered.

Probably the most important issue is the fact that graph-based algorithms work in a *discrete* version of the space, i.e. the map. This may not be a problem in some kind of tiled maps, where graphs fit effortlessly, but it is when the map is described as a continuous space as it occurs in *eCoology*.

Graph nodes are considered the positions of the space that can be reached and therefore, it quickly becomes obvious that an infinite amount of nodes would be necessary to cover the whole area of the map. Moreover, those moving entities could be flying entities as well, which would mean having three-dimensional maps with an exponential number of nodes. Since this is usually not feasible, the immediate consequence of having a finite amount of possible destinations is that moving entities are only able to reach *certain* places on the map, which is not acceptable in an interactive augmented reality application.

Think about a frequent situation in *eCoology* where an animal is wandering around the map. Then it is called by its owner, located in a random position on that map which the animal *can not reach* according to the underlying graph. The perceived experience would be that the animal disobeys his orders, or acts silly, coming closer and then stopping at some point before actually reaching him.

Extreme solutions like a massive graph covering the whole map do not seem the way to work around the problem due to computational costs, besides that reducing their density with variable-grain discretisation would result in an accuracy decrease. On the other hand, the user cannot be expected to move to a *reachable* position for the animal, in order to be able to call it. Trying to force users to behave this way would evidence the inner working of the application and, therefore, heavily penalize the immersive user's experience. Thus, an approach based only on graphs seems not to fit well enough the *eCoology* path-finding requirements, and will be enhanced in our context with a different technique: particle systems.

**Particle Systems**

A particle system can be seen as a small physics simulator where individual elements, the particles, are treated according to a set of real-physics laws [16]. Particles are defined with a set of physic properties (e.g. position, speed, acceleration, mass, etc.) and they are usually treated as punctual entities, they have no extents in space. Given a set of particles, usually generated by an *emitter*, a simulator is in charge of updating each particle life cycle, which is usually limited. Since the moment a particle is spawn, its properties are updated on discrete time spans according to the current active physic laws –i.e. the *rules* of the simulation.

In order to define a way for particles to interact with their environment, another kind of element is introduced in the simulation: deflectors. Deflectors are objects which the particles can collide with. They are characterized by their shape –a plane, sphere...- and properties like friction, which determine particles' reaction when colliding with them. The horizontal bar in Figure 5 is a plane deflector.

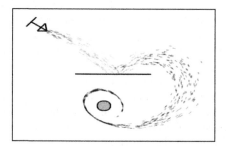

**Fig. 5.** A particle system

Using the elements defined so far, a simple navigating system can be implemented. Moving entities are modeled as particles, providing them with physical properties like their mass and, optionally, constants that constraint their maximum velocity and acceleration. The desired destination for a given entity is defined as an attractor, which will make its particle tend towards to it and eventually reach the destination. Finally the environment is modeled using deflectors which prevent the particles from going through the walls. See Figure 6.

One substantial benefit of this approach with respect to graphs is that particle simulation works in continuous space rather than discrete. This means an entity would

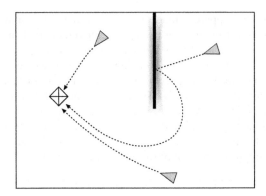

**Fig. 6.** Particle-based navigation

be able to move as smoothly as desired across the map. Moreover, since it is not restricted by a discrete space, it is possible for it to reach –almost- everywhere.

The continuous evaluation of the environment conditions –i.e. existing forces- makes paths able to _react_ to changing conditions, which a static generated path can not take into account. Reaction to changing emotional as well as physical space conditions is a fundamental requirement in *eCoology*.

**Path Finding in *eCoology***

When evaluating the requirements for the path-finding component in *eCoology* it was decided to take the best from both graph and particles, in order to create a powerful yet flexible system. This way, our hybrid approximation is based on a particle system but also reinforced with graph-based algorithms concepts.

In general terms, the characteristics of a scenario in *eCoology* are indoor spaces where the activities take place. Thus, scenarios are built up from sets of planar and spherical **deflectors** that define the walls or solid elements, and **attractors** which define points of interest a given entity may want to walk towards. Each particle also implements a repelling force for the rest of particles, preventing entities to "collapse" when forming groups.

However, these elements in isolation result in entities colliding and bouncing against the walls, making them appear as non natural elements in the augmented space. To solve this problem several refinements are introduced. Firstly, entities are given properties commonly used in *vehicle physics* [17] such as mass, acceleration, and velocity, which results in a smooth and more pleasant movement. Secondly, besides having normal colliding functions, deflectors play two more important roles in *eCoology*. On the one hand, they are considered as **repelling elements,** forcing particles not only to avoid colliding with them, but also to try to dodge them as long as the remaining forces allow it. Note this *smoothes* the performed trajectories and, even more important, it makes entities not looking blind when trying to "touch" the walls before dodging them.

On the other hand, deflectors are also **occluding elements**, i.e., entities cannot see through them. This is to simulate a natural behavior, the sight sense. In our path-finding system, a particle is not –directly- attracted, or repelled, by an object if it cannot be seen. So this apparent hinder in the normal functioning of the particle system actually has its justification for the sake of movement realism.

However, at the end, it is always desired for an entity to be able to reach its attractor whenever the map allows it. To achieve this goal we cover the map with a simple graph, making sure the important areas have a node in them. We call these nodes *buoys*, and they are not actually used to solve the path but helping the particle system to do so. Each buoy links those other buoys that are *visible* from its position, those that are not hidden by any occluding element. Then, when a particle looks for its attractor, it may make use of the underlying net of buoys to find it, in case it is not directly visible. A simplified version of the algorithm is given next:

```
Given a destination D for an entity
While D not reached do
    If have an assigned attractor which is visible then
        Update physics simulation
    else
        Check D's visibility against occluders
        If  D is directly visible then
            Assign an attractor located at D
        Else
            Obtain a suitable buoy which leads us to D
        End if
    End if
end while
```

**List 1.** Pseudo code of path solving process

A practical example of this process is shown in Figure 7. The upper figure shows two particles sharing the same attractor. The one on the left has direct visibility, so it can perform the simulation and accelerate towards its destination. However, the remaining particle has two deflectors hindering its way. It will then make use of the buoys, symbolized as "b" in the figure, to solve the way to go, and sequentially locate its attractor on each of them. Moreover, note its trajectory will be smoothed due to the vehicle physics –accelerations and decelerations-, and the repulsion of the deflectors, preventing from sudden changes in direction.

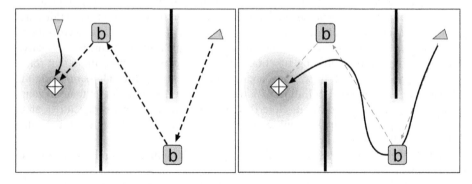

**Fig. 7.** Path solving

Obtaining a suitable buoy, as it is pointed out in our algorithm, is a slightly more complex process, which involves both "low" level information –the map- and the higher level behavioral processes. Think about a destination for an entity that can be reached from several alternative ways. Our algorithm would not obtain a single buoy, but rather a **set** of possible alternatives. Each one of those alternative paths is then presented to the controlling emotional behavioral layer, requesting a validation or rejection for it, as it was described in the previous section. If a proposal is rejected, then a backtracking process is performed, obtaining another possible alternative until an emotionally valid path is found. If the algorithm runs out of possible paths, the behavioral system is notified, so it can perform the proper actions. This backtracking method produces paths that exhibit both individual and collective group emotional behaviors [18]. For instance, in case of a group of frightened entities having a common threat, a collective defensive movement can be easily included in the system by assigning the same attractor to all the entities forming a group and dynamically positioning it in the geometrical center of the group. This makes our path finding mechanism a flexible tool for implementing multiple emotional movement schemes within the augmented space.

## 5  Conclusions

We have presented in this paper *eCoology*, an AR edutainment application with emotional components to enhance the learning process. Particularly interesting are our model of emotional entities that calculate their paths in the augmented space according to emotional states encouraging children to analyze and solve existing problems in the ecosystem. The proposed model is generic enough to implement a whole range of emotional movements in the augmented space in a non procedural way. Our future work includes the study of more complex emotional interaction mechanisms based on voice analysis that help users to interact with entities in the ecosystem in a natural way. The final goal is to evaluate how social and emotional concepts may help to reach *flow* not only in learning environments but also in any other AR application.

## Acknowledgments

Our thanks to the Microsoft Research Labs in Cambridge for supporting us, under grant "Create, Play and Learn" [19].

## References

[1] Brown, B., Larson, R.W. and Saraswathi, T.S.: The worlds' youth: adolescence in eight regions of the world. Cambridge University Press. 2002.
[2] Delle Fave, A., Bassi, M., Massimini, F.: Quality of experience and daily social context of Italian adolescents. In A.L. Comunian, U.P. Gielen eds. It's all about relationships. 2002.

[3] Verma, S. and Larsson, R.W.: Examining Adolescent Leisure Time Across Cultures: Developmental Opportunities and Risks. New Directions in Child and Adolescent Development Series. 2003.

[4] Csikszentmihalyi, M. and Csikszentmihalyi, I.: Optimal Experience. Psychological Studies of Flow in Consciousness. Cambridge University Press. 1988.

[5] Deci, E.L. and Ryan, R. M.: Intrinsic Motivation and Self-Determination in Human Behaviour. Plenum Press. 1985.

[6] Wakkary, R., Hatala, M., Lovell, R. and Droumeva, M.: An ambient intelligence platform for physical play. ACM Multimedia 2005.

[7] Thomas, B., Piekarski, W., Hepworth, D., Gunther, B. and Demczuk, V.: A Wearable Computer System with Augmented Reality to Support Terrestrial Navigation. Second International Symposium on Wearable Computers (ISWC'98) page 168.

[8] Billinghurst, M. and Hirokazu, K.: Collaborative Augmented Reality. Communication of the ACM Vol.45, No.7, 64-70. 2002.

[9] Nilsen, T., Linton, S. and Looser, J.: Motivations for Augmented Reality Gaming. New Zealand Game Developers Conference. 2004.

[10] Schore, A.N.: Affect Regulation and the Origin of the Self: The Neurobiology of Emotional Development. Erlbaum. 2004.

[11] A Preview of Microsoft Windows Vista Developer Opportunities. http://msdn. microsoft. com/library/en-us/dnlong/html/vistatopten.asp. Last visited on March 13th, 2006.

[12] Windows Communication Foundation (WCF). *http://msdn.microsoft.com/webservices/ indigo/ default.aspx*. Last visited on March 13th, 2006.

[13] Research on Emotions and Human-Machine Interaction. Bibliography section of *http://emotion-research.net*. Last visited on June 8th, 2006.

[14] Cavazza, M., Lugrin, J. L., Hartley, S., Le Renard, M., Nandi, A., Jacobson, J. and Crooks, S.: Intelligent virtual environments for virtual reality art. Computers & Graphics, Volume 29, Issue 6, 1 December 2005, Pages 852-861.

[15] Massive Software. *http://www.massivesoftware.com*. Last visited on March 9th, 2006.

[16] Building and advanced particle system. *http://www.gamasutra.com/features/20000623/ van derburg_01.htm*. Last visited on March 9th, 2006.

[17] Eberly, D.H.: Game Physics. Morgan Kaufmann, 2003.

[18] Reynolds, C. W.: Steering Behaviors For Autonomous Characters. Sony Computer Entertainment America. Game Developers Conference, 1999.

[19] MSR External Research Office. Create Play and Learn: Innovative Technologies with Social and Cultural Value. 2004.

# Interacting with a Virtual Conductor

Pieter Bos, Dennis Reidsma, Zsófia Ruttkay, and Anton Nijholt

HMI, Dept. of CS, University of Twente,
PO Box 217, 7500AE Enschede, The Netherlands
anijholt@ewi.utwente.nl
http://hmi.ewi.utwente.nl/

**Abstract.** This paper presents a virtual embodied agent that can conduct musicians in a live performance. The virtual conductor conducts music specified by a MIDI file and uses input from a microphone to react to the tempo of the musicians. The current implementation of the virtual conductor can interact with musicians, leading and following them while they are playing music. Different time signatures and dynamic markings in music are supported.

## 1 Introduction

Recordings of orchestral music are said to be the interpretation of the conductor in front of the ensemble. A human conductor uses words, gestures, gaze, head movements and facial expressions to make musicians play together in the right tempo, phrasing, style and dynamics, according to his interpretation of the music. She also interacts with musicians: The musicians react to the gestures of the conductor, and the conductor in turn reacts to the music played by the musicians. So far, no other known virtual conductor can conduct musicians interactively.

In this paper an implementation of a Virtual Conductor is presented that is capable of conducting musicians in a live performance. The audio analysis of the music played by the (human) musicians and the animation of the virtual conductor are discussed, as well as the algorithms that are used to establish the two-directional interaction between conductor and musicians in patterns of leading and following. Furthermore a short outline of planned evaluations is given.

## 2 Related Work

Wang *et al.* describe a virtual conductor that synthesizes conducting gestures using kernel based hidden Markov models [1]. The system is trained by capturing data from a real conductor, extracting the beat from her movements. It can then conduct similar music in the same meter and tempo with style variations. The resulting conductor, however, is not interactive in the sense described in the introduction. It contains no beat tracking or tempo following modules (the beats in music have to be marked by a human) and there is no model for the interaction between conductor and musicians. Also no evaluation of this virtual conductor has been given. Ruttkay *et al.* synthesized conductor movements to demonstrate the capabilities of a high-level language to

R. Harper, M. Rauterberg, M. Combetto (Eds.): ICEC 2006, LNCS 4161, pp. 25–30, 2006.
© IFIP International Federation for Information Processing 2006

describe gestures [2]. This system does not react to music, although it has the possibility to adjust the conducting movements dynamically.

Many systems have been made that try to follow a human conductor. They use, for example, a special baton [3], a jacket equipped with sensors [4] or webcams [5] to track conducting movements. Strategies to recognize gestures vary from detecting simple up and down movements [3] through a more elaborate system that can detect detailed conducting movements [4] to one that allows extra system-specific movements to control music [5]. Most systems are built to control the playback of music (MIDI or audio file) that is altered in response to conducting slower or faster, conducting a subgroup of instruments or conducting with bigger or smaller gestures.

Automatic accompaniment systems were first presented in 1984, most notably by Dannenberg [6] and Vercoe [7]. These systems followed MIDI instruments and adapted an accompaniment to match what was played. More recently, Raphael [8] has researched a self-learning system which follows real instruments and can provide accompaniments that would not be playable by human performers. The main difference with the virtual conductor is that such systems follow musicians instead of attempting to explicitly lead them.

For an overview of related work in tracking tempo and beat, another important requirement for a virtual conductor, the reader is referred to the qualitative and the quantitative reviews of tempo trackers presented in [9] and [10], respectively.

## 3   Functions and Architecture of the Virtual Conductor

A virtual conductor capable of leading, and reacting to, a live performance has to be able to perform several tasks in real time. The conductor should possess knowledge of the music to be conducted, should be able to translate this knowledge to gestures and to produce these gestures. The conductor should extract features from music and react to them, based on information of the knowledge of the score. The reactions should be tailored to elicit the desired response from the musicians.

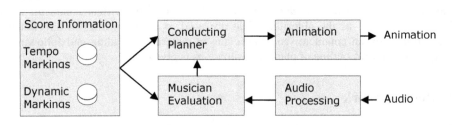

**Fig. 1.** Architecture overview of the Virtual Conductor

Figure 1 shows a schematic overview of the architecture of our implementation of the Virtual Conductor. The audio from the human musicians is first processed by the Audio Processor, to detect volume and tempo. Then the Musician Evaluation compares the music with the original score (currently stored in MIDI) to determine the conducting style (lead, follow, dynamic indications, required corrective feedback to musicians, etc). The Conducting Planner generates the appropriate conducting movements based on the score and the Musician Evaluation. These are then animated. Each of these elements is discussed in more detail in the following sections.

## 3.1 Beat and Tempo Tracking

To enable the virtual conductor to detect the tempo of music from an audio signal, a beat detector has been implemented. The beat detector is based on the beat detectors of Scheirer [11] and Klapuri [12]. A schematic overview of the beat detector is presented in Figure 2. The first stage of the beat detector consists of an accentuation detector in several frequency bands. Then a bank of comb filter resonators is used to detect periodicity in these 'accent bands', as Klapuri calls them. As a last step, the correct tempo is extracted from this signal.

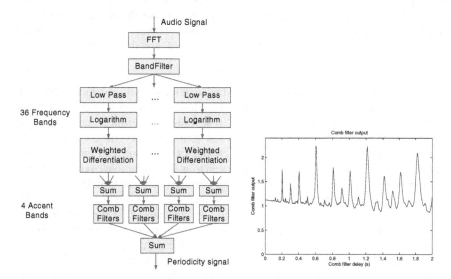

**Fig. 2.** Schematic overview of the Beat detector          **Fig. 3.** Periodicity signal

To detect periodicity in these accent bands, a bank of comb filters is applied. Each filter has its own delay: delays of up to 2 seconds are used, with 11.5 ms steps. The output from one of these filters is a measure of the periodicity of the music at that delay. The periodicity signal, with a clear pattern of peaks, for a fragment of music with a strong beat is shown in Figure 3. The tempo of this music fragment is around 98 bpm, which corresponds to the largest peak shown. We define a peak as a local maximum in the graph that is above 70% of the outputs of all the comb filters. The peaks will form a pattern with an equal interval, which is detected. Peaks outside that pattern are ignored. In the case of the virtual conductor an estimate of the played tempo is already known, so the peak closest to the conducted tempo is selected as the current detected tempo. Accuracy is measured as the difference between the maximum and minimum of the comb filter outputs, multiplied by the number of peaks detected in the pattern.

A considerable latency is introduced by the sound card, audio processing and movement planning. It turned out that in the current setup the latency was not high enough to unduly disturb the musicians. However, we also wrote a calibration method where someone taps along with the virtual conductor to determine the average latency. This latency could be used as an offset to decrease its impact on the interaction.

## 3.2  Interacting with the Tempo of Musicians

If an ensemble is playing too slow or too fast, a (human) conductor should lead them back to the correct tempo. She can choose to lead strictly or more leniently, but completely ignoring the musicians' tempo and conducting like a metronome set at the right tempo will not work. A conductor must incorporate some sense of the actual tempo at which the musicians play in her conducting, or else she will lose control. A naïve strategy for a Virtual Conductor could be to use the conducting tempo $t_c$ defined in formula 1 as a weighted average of the correct tempo $t_o$ and the detected tempo $t_d$.

$$t_c = (1-\lambda)\, t_o + \lambda\ t_d \qquad (1)$$

If the musicians play too slowly, the virtual conductor will conduct *a little bit* faster than they are playing. When the musicians follow him, he will conduct faster yet, till the correct tempo is reached again. The ratio $\lambda$ determines how strict the conductor is. However, informal tests showed that this way of correcting feels restrictive at high values of $\lambda$ and that the conductor does not lead enough at low values of $\lambda$. Our solution to this problem has been to make $\lambda$ adaptive over time. When the tempo of the musicians deviates from the correct one, $\lambda$ is initialised to a low value $\lambda_L$. Then over the period of $n$ beats, $\lambda$ is increased to a higher value $\lambda_H$. This ensures that the conductor can effectively lead the musicians: first the system makes sure that musicians and conductor are in a synchronized tempo, and then the tempo is *gradually* corrected till the musicians are playing at the right tempo again. Different settings of the parameters result in a conductor which leads and follows differently. Experiments will have to show what values are acceptable for the different parameters in which situations. Care has to be taken that the conductor stays in control, yet does not annoy the musicians with too strict a tempo.

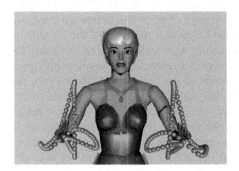

**Fig. 4.** A screenshot of the virtual conductor application, with the path of the 4-beat pattern

### 3.3  Conducting Gestures

Based on extensive discussions with a human conductor, basic conducting gestures (1-, 2-, 3- and 4-beat patterns) have been defined using inverse kinematics and hermite splines, with adjustable amplitude to allow for conducting with larger or smaller gestures. The appropriately modified conducting gestures are animated with the animation framework developed in our group, in the chosen conducting tempo $t_c$.

## 4  Evaluation

A pre-test has been done with four human musicians. They could play music reliably with the virtual conductor after a few attempts. Improvements to the conductor are being made based on this pre-test. An evaluation plan consisting of several experiments has been designed. The evaluations will be performed on the current version of the virtual conductor with small groups of real musicians. A few short pieces of music will be conducted in several variations: slow, fast, changing tempo, variations in leading parameters, etcetera, based on dynamic markings (defined in the internal score representation) that are not always available to the musicians. The reactions of the musicians and the characteristics of their performance in different situations will be analysed and used to extend and improve our Virtual Conductor system.

## 5  Conclusions and Future Work

A Virtual Conductor that incorporates expert knowledge from a professional conductor has been designed and implemented. To our knowledge, it is the first virtual conductor that can conduct different meters and tempos as well as tempo variations and at the same time is also able to *interact* with the human musicians that it conducts. Currently it is able to lead musicians through tempo changes and to correct musicians if they play too slowly or too fast. The current version will be evaluated soon and extended further in the coming months.

Future additions to the conductor will partially depend on the results of the evaluation. One expected extension is a score following algorithm, to be used instead of the current, less accurate, beat detector. A good score following algorithm may be able to detect rhythmic mistakes and wrong notes, giving more opportunities for feedback from the conductor. Such an algorithm should be adapted to or designed specifically for the purpose of the conductor: unlike with usual applications of score following, an estimation of the location in the music is already known from the conducting plan.

The gesture repertoire of the conductor will be extended to allow the conductor to indicate more cues, to respond better to volume and tempo changes and to make the conductor appear more lifelike. In a longer term, this would include getting the attention of musicians, conducting more clearly when the musicians do not play a stable tempo and indicating legato and staccato. Indicating cues and gestures to specific musicians rather than to a group of musicians would be an important addition. This would need a much more detailed (individual) audio analysis as well as a good implementation of models of eye contact: no trivial challenge.

## Acknowledgements

Thanks go to the "human conductor" Daphne Wassink, for her comments and valuable input on the virtual conductor, and the musicians who participated in the first evaluation tests.

## References

1. Wang, T., Zheng, N., Li, Y., Xu, Y. and Shum, H. Learning kernel-based HMMs for dynamic sequence synthesis. Veloso, M. and Kambhampati, S. (eds), Graphical Models 65:206-221, 2003
2. Ruttkay, Zs., Huang, A. and Eliëns, A. The Conductor: Gestures for embodied agents with logic programming, in Proc. of the 2nd Hungarian Computer Graphics Conference, Budapest, pp. 9-16, 2003
3. Borchers, J., Lee, E., Samminger, W. and Mühlhäuser, M. Personal orchestra: a real-time audio/video system for interactive conducting, Multimedia Systems , 9:458-465, 2004
4. Marrin Nakra, T. Inside the Conductor's Jacket: Analysis, Interpretation and Musical Synthesis of Expressive Gesture. Ph.D. Thesis, Media Laboratory. Cambridge, MA, Mass. Inst. of Technology, 2000
5. Murphy, D., Andersen, T.H. and Jensen, K. Conducting Audio Files via Computer Vision, in GW03, pp. 529-540, 2003
6. Dannenberg, R. and Mukaino, H. New Techniques for Enhanced Quality of Computer Accompaniment, in Proc. of the International Computer Music Conference, Computer Music Association, pp. 243-249, 1988
7. Vercoe, B. The synthetic performer in the context of live musical performance, Proc. Of the International Computer Music Association, p. 185, 1984
8. Raphael C. Musical Accompaniment Systems, Chance Magazine 17:4, pp. 17-22, 2004
9. Gouyon, F. and Dixon, S. A Review of Automatic Rhythm Description Systems, Computer music journal, 29:34-54, 2005
10. Gouyon, F., Klapuri, A., Dixon, S., Alonso, M., Tzanetakis, G., Uhle, C. and Cano, P. An Experimental Comparison of Audio Tempo Induction Algorithms, IEEE Transactions on Speech and Audio Processing, 2006
11. Scheirer, E.D. Tempo and beat analysis of acoustic musical signals, Journal of the Acoustical Society of America, 103:558-601, 1998
12. Klapuri, A., Eronen, A. and Astola, J. Analysis of the meter of acoustic musical signals, IEEE transactions on Speech and Audio Processing, 2006

# Animal Controlled Computer Games: Playing Pac-Man Against Real Crickets

Wim van Eck and Maarten H. Lamers

Media Technology MSc Program, Leiden University, The Netherlands
wimeck@hotmail.com

**Abstract.** We explore the possibilities of replacing behaviour-generating code in computer games by real-time behaviour of live animals, and the question of whether one can play computer games against animals. To experience the differences for a human between playing against an animal or against computer code, we experimented with a variant of Pac-Man where the behaviour of virtual game characters is derived from that of live crickets in a real maze. Initial results are described in this paper.

## 1 Introduction

When I was young I loved to play games with my cat. Throwing a ball across the room which it would chase, letting a ball of wool bungle above its head which it would try to grab, or putting food in a difficult place for it to reach, seeing if it could manage to get it. You never knew how the cat would react or what it would do. It could play the game along, get aggressive, find new ways to solve its problem, or simply loose interest.

These days I play games against a computer. These games take you to different worlds and tell unbelievable stories. But what they fail to do, is to surprise me, like my cat would. Computer games are pre-programmed, and will not do anything except what their programmers programmed them to do. If the programmer did not think of it, it can not happen. Donkey Kong (Nintendo, 1981) will never get tired of throwing heavy barrels at you, or strain a muscle, or get hungry and just eat the princess. After playing a computer game for some time, you know what you can expect from it.

But is it possible to take the unpredictability of an animal, and merge this behaviour with a computer game, by this replacing parts of the computer code by animal behaviour? Can you play a computer game against an animal? What will be the differences? In this study, we will explore these questions and their possibilities.

## 2 Playing Computer Games Against Animals

While searching for relevant projects and research on the question if you can play computer games against animals, no direct comparison was found. However, there is an art project made by Dan Young called "Lumberjacked"[1], which enables you to play a computer game against a tree. With the aid of sensors, movement of the leafs of the tree are translated into movement within the game.

R. Harper, M. Rauterberg, M. Combetto (Eds.): ICEC 2006, LNCS 4161, pp. 31 – 36, 2006.
© IFIP International Federation for Information Processing 2006

We could not find direct examples of playing computer games against animals. But when we look at the three keywords of this question, namely computer, games and animals, we can make interesting combinations. The combination computer-games needs no further research; it is a standard term. Lets have a look at the other ones.

## 2.1 Animals and Games

It is quite common for humans and animals to play games together. This can be voluntary and enjoyable for the animal, like a dog fetching a stick. But it can also be forced upon the animal, like bullfighting. From the bulls viewpoint this is not play.

Animals do not need humans to stimulate them to play games. Many animals show natural play behaviour. It is not easy to tell if an animal is playing or not, because animal play may imitate adult behaviour so closely it is difficult to make a distinction between them. However, there are clear examples of animal play[2,3]. A common example has young lions wrestling, trying to overpower each other.

## 2.2 Animals and Computer Games

It is possible to learn animals to play computer games. After learning Rhesus monkeys to manipulate a joystick and perform computerized game-like tasks[4], animals such as pigs and rats[5] followed. Computer games can act as a platform for comparative research, permitting direct comparison of performance by humans and for example primates, with identical software and hardware under equal conditions.

Not only can animals learn to play computer games, some even enjoy playing them. Research with Rhesus monkeys found that they actually prefer game-like computer tasks above their normal toys, and replace boredom related behaviour[6]. It is not clear what precisely makes the game-like tasks enjoyable to the monkeys.

## 2.3 Merging Computers and Animals

With the AIBO, Sony introduced an "entertainment robot" in the shape of a dog (1999). It tries to simulate the behaviours of an animal pet, but eliminates the responsibilities and problems of a real pet. It does recognize its boss, likes to play and develops its own "personality". The purpose of AIBO is actually opposite to the goal of our study. It uses computer code trying to simulate a real animal, while we want to use real animals to perform a task which is usually done by computer code.

Instead of making a robotic representation of an animal, it is also possible to keep the representation digital. In 1996 the Tamagotchi was released by Bandai; a handheld digital pet, which you have to play with and feed through button operations.

Another approach is to let an animal control a computer. Artist Ken Rinaldo's "Augmented Fish Reality"[7] is an installation of 5 robotic fish-bowl sculptures with Siamese fighting fish inside of them. By swimming to an edge of the bowl, the fish moves the sculpture in the corresponding direction. This lets the fish get within a centimetre of each other, allowing the normally aggressive fish to interact without killing each other and explore their environment beyond the limits of the fish-bowls.

Garnet Hertz created "The Cockroach Controlled Mobile Robot"[8]. It consists of a giant hissing Madagascan cockroach, which controls the movements of a three-wheeled robot. The cockroach is placed above a pingpong ball, which it spins with its feet, like a trackball device. When the robot detects an object ahead, one of many small lights which encircle the front of the cockroach starts to flash. As the cockroach tries to scuffle away from the light, the robot moves away from the obstacle.

The "Augmented Fish Reality" project puts the fish in direct control of the robot, it moves in the direction the fish is facing. Hertz's project has a slightly different approach: it is hard to say if the cockroach is controlling the robot, or if the robot is controlling the cockroach. The robot is moved by the movement of the animal, but the sensor-driven lights influence the direction the animal is moving in.

The previous two projects already get close to creating a cyborg, an organism which is a mixture of organic and mechanical parts. At the Duke University Medical Center, researchers even went a step further in accomplishing this. Here they taught a Rhesus monkey to consciously control the movement of a robot arm in real-time, using only direct signals from its brain and visual feedback on a video screen[9].

The opposite can also be found, namely an electrical device controlling an animal[10]. Isao Shimoyama, head of the bio-robot research team at Tokyo University, developed a way of controlling a cockroach with a remote control.

## 3 Using Animal Intelligence in Pac-Man

Our goal is to see if it is possible to replace behaviour-generating computer code by animal behaviour. We will not focus on making it a "pleasing" (as implied when playing a game) experience for the animal. We want to concentrate on the differences in playing against an animal or against computer code. To test this, we replaced the "artificial intelligence" part of a computer game by "animal intelligence".

The computer game we used for our experiment is "Pac-Man" (Namco, 1980). This is a well-known game, which gives us the advantage that people already have expectations of how the game should play. Also, if we designed our own game there is a risk that the game itself is judged, rather than the replacing of computer code by animal behaviour. In "Pac-Man" you control a character trapped in a maze full of small dots. If you eat all the dots, the level is finished. Four ghosts wander in the maze, you lose one life when they touch you. There are four power-up items, which when eaten scare the ghosts, giving Pac-Man the temporary ability to eat them.

Instead of computer code, we want to have animals controlling the ghosts. To enable this we built a real maze for the animals to walk around in, measuring 20x20x1,8 cm. Its proportions and layout match the maze of the computer game. The position of the animals in the maze is detected using colour-tracking, and linked to the ghosts in the game, which let the real animals directly control the virtual ghosts.

Our "Pac-Man" game is not an exact copy of the original game. The maze is smaller, so you are more likely to encounter the ghosts. When a ghost gets eaten it is not temporarily locked in the middle of the maze. Instead it changes in a blinking pair of eyes, indicating that it was eaten. Furthermore there are no bonus-fruits.

### 3.1 Crickets

While choosing which animal to use we made some practical decisions. The animal could not be too large. The larger the animal, the larger the maze would need to be.

This costs more money, takes more time to build and requires more space. This time and effort would be better spent testing and doing research. Furthermore, the animal should not be too hard to find. Decease of an animal should not give problems finding a replacement. It should also be fairly active. Lack of movement will result in lack of resistance for the player in the game. We were not especially looking for an intelligent animal, since it is not our goal to learn an animal how to play a game. The field cricket (*Gryllus campestris*) complies very well with these requirements and therefore became our test subject. It measures 18-27mm and has a dark brown or black colour.

In their natural environment crickets prefer to sit together during daytime. The strongest ones sit in the middle, being more protected against predators. Since crickets are cold-blooded they get more active with high temperatures, around 33° Celsius is preferred. When hungry, crickets search for food, otherwise the males will try to lure and impress females by singing loudly.

### 3.2 Game Play

The natural behaviour of crickets is very apparent when they are controlling the ghosts. Just after being placed in the maze, they are very active, probably because they are agitated. After inspecting the maze individually they are likely to find a place to group together. This had a strong effect on our game-play. While being agitated, their speed is so fast that it is hard to avoid them, but when they group together they stop moving, which makes it possible for Pac-Man to eat most of the dots in the maze unhindered. However, this also makes it impossible to eat the dots on the place where they sit, preventing the player from finishing the level. Only by eating a power-up one is able to eat the ghosts, and therefore also the remaining dots. While grouping together gives the crickets protection in nature, in our virtual game it results in the opposite, making it easy to eat all the ghosts in one go.

In contrast to the fixed speed of the original Pac-Man ghosts, the movement of the crickets is very unpredictable, sometimes making short stops, and continuing with a different speed. Their speed also depends on the temperature inside of the maze, since they are cold-blooded. We could change the speed of the crickets by altering the temperature, this way having different difficulty levels.

## 4   Feedback to the Animal

Up till now we had one-way interaction: the game play depends on the movement of the animals. But if we want a bit more intelligent game play, the animals should react to the actions within the game also. It is possible to attract or repel an animal with stimuli such as sound, vibration, temperature, pheromones, light, electricity and smell.

Most of these stimuli are not suitable for our game. Once pheromones or a smell are released in the maze, they will be very difficult to control or remove. Heat takes time to increase or decrease, making it a slow stimulus. Using electricity on an animal is rather cruel, and would quite likely result in complaints of animal abuse. Vibration, sound and light can be activated and deactivated very quickly. It is difficult for crickets however to pinpoint a sound in the maze. A possibility is to darken the part of the maze where Pac-Man is located. The crickets are attracted to this dark place, but they must be able to directly see it to know it is there, which is difficult in a maze. Otherwise they will just sit still in the light, hoping not to be noticed by predators.

In nature, vibration of the ground warns crickets for an approaching predator. We chose to use this behaviour to stimulate the crickets in the game. We divided the floor of the maze into six parts, each with a motor attached underneath that vibrates when switched on. When the crickets should chase Pac-Man, we switch on the motors furthest away from his location in the maze, so the crickets will flee in his direction. When Pac-Man eats a power-up, the crickets are supposed to run away from him, so we then vibrate the part of the floor that contains Pac-Man's position.

### 4.1  Game Play

When we started to play our modified game, the crickets reacted as we expected: they walked away from the vibrations. But surprisingly the crickets quickly got used to the vibrations, they habituated. After a couple of minutes they hardly reacted to them anymore, they seemed to have learned that the vibrations do not pose a threat. Only after making the vibrations much stronger they reacted on them for a longer time. After about half an hour they started ignoring the vibrations again recurrently.

When the crickets react to the vibrations, there is an apparent interaction between the player and the crickets. The ghosts really start to chase or avoid you, depending on the state of the game. Differences again are that the ghosts do not move with a constant speed, but frequently stop and continue with different speeds, and sometimes stop moving at all. When they should avoid Pac-Man, they occasionally run in the wrong direction, walking straight into him. The crickets also manage to go to places where they are not supposed to be. They sit on the walls of the maze, or manage to crawl in-between the top of the walls and the glass covering plate, effectively avoiding Pac-Man.

## 5  Discussion

With this project we succeeded to play a computer game against animals. It was very tempting to forget our main goal, namely to see what the *differences* are when replacing parts of a computer code by animal behaviour. For example, the crickets easily habituated to the vibrations of the floor. Our first reaction was to increase the strength of the vibration, so they would continue to run away from it. But the fact that the crickets seem to learn that the vibrations are not a threat to them, and that they can safely ignore them, is much more interesting. It is actually a sign that we have some intelligence in our system.

During our tests something else happened which was very intriguing. One of the crickets stopped moving at all, and on closer inspection we discovered it was shedding its skin. The cricket's new skin was very light, and therefore it did not get detected by our colour tracking anymore. We now had a cricket which could freely walk around in our maze, not getting detected by our system, which was still tracking its old skin. After about half an hour the cricket's skin turned dark enough to also be noticed by the colour tracking, resulting in five ghosts being put in the game. At this moment our game really surprised us, you could say the crickets generated an extra piece of code to the game. This kind of unexpected behaviour was exactly what we were hoping to encounter during this research.

For future research it would be interesting to track the animals in a more natural environment. The wooden maze we now use does not provide much stimulation for the animals. A possibility could be to track ants in an ant farm. This way they will not only react on stimuli the player gives them, but they will also have their own natural activities. Or, by using reward schemes, the animal behaviour could be adapted to yield more interesting game play situations.

# References

1. Dan Young, Lumberjacked, online resource: www.newdigitalart.co.uk/lumberjacked, 2005
2. Marc Bekoff, John A. Byers, Animal Play: Evolutionary, Comparative and Ecological Perspectives, Cambridge University Press, Cambridge, 1998
3. Robert Fagen, Animal Play Behavior, Oxford University Press, Oxford, 1981
4. Duane M. Rumbaugh, W. Kirk Richardson, David A. Washburn, "Rhesus Monkeys (Macaca mulatta), Video Tasks, and Implications for Stimulus-Response Spatial Contiguity", Journal of Comparative Psychology, Vol 103(1), 1989, pages 32-39
5. David A. Washburn, Michael J. Rulon, Jonathan P. Gulledge, "A new breed of computer users: Rats control a cursor via joystick manipulation", Behavior Research Methods Instruments and Computers, Vol 36, 2004, pages 173-179
6. David A. Washburn, "The games psychologists play (and the data they provide)", Behavior Research Methods Instruments and Computers, Vol 35, 2003, pages 185-193
7. Ken Rinaldo, Augmented Fish Reality, Presented at the Ars Electronica Festival, September 2004, Linz, Austria
8. Garnet Hertz, Control and Communication in the Animal and the Machine (Master's Thesis), University of California Irvine, 2004
9. Jose M. Camena, Mikhail A. Lebedev, Roy E. Crist, et al, "Learning to control a brain-machine interface for reaching and grasping by primates", PLoS Biology, Vol 1, 2003, pages 193-208
10. Isao Shimoyama, Raphael Holzer, "Bio-robotic Systems Based on Insect Fixed Behavior by Artificial Stimulation", International Symposium on Robotics Research (Hayama, Japan), 1997

# Leaving a Message with the PaPeRo Robot: The Effect of Interaction Experience with Real or Virtual PaPeRo on Impression Evaluation

Takanori Komatsu, Tomoki Iwaoka, and Misako Nambu

School of Systems Information Sciences, Future University-Hakodate,
116-2 Kamedanakano, Hakodate 041-8655, Hokkaido, Japan
{komatsu, m1202148, m-nambu}@fun.ac.jp
http://www.fun.ac.jp/~komatsu

**Abstract.** This paper describes a simple psychological experiment to investigate the effects of two aspects of user interactions with message taking artifacts. The first is the effect of the artifacts' physical appearance, and the other is prior interaction experience. We examined the effect of these two factors on the ability of users to feel comfortable and natural when interacting with the artifacts. Experimental results revealed that prior interaction experience was a much more important factor than the artifacts' appearance in determining whether participants could leave verbal messages smoothly.

## 1 Introduction

Recently various researchers have been working on achieving intimate relationships between humans and artifacts (e.g., partner robots, life-like agents or game characters) in various research fields, such as human-computer interaction (HCI) and Entertainment Computing (EC). In these situations, if users are uncomfortable interacting with an artifact and feel the interactions are unnatural they definitely cannot achieve an intimate relationship with it. Therefore, one can say that in the studies mentioned above have a common issue, and that is how to make users feel comfortable during these interactions, and to make them feel such interactions are natural.

In a related study, Harada [2] conducted a psychological experiment to investigate whether participants feel comfortable and natural when leaving verbal messages using the following three artifacts: window-based software appearing on a computer display, a character agent appearing on a computer display, and a child care robot (PaPeRo robot developed by NEC corporation, left in Fig. 1 [3]). In this experiment, participants were asked to leave verbal message about a memo by using those artifacts as if they were leaving messages on an answering machine. Harada's results revealed that participants felt comfortable when they passed messages to the robot and felt the interaction was natural, but they did not feel this way toward the software and the agent. Harada then concluded that an artifacts' appearance whether it had physical existence would be an important cue for making users feel comfortable with the artifacts and making them feel that the interaction was natural.

However, before participants used this robot to leave messages, they had verbal conversations with it, as it was equipped with systems for highly accurate speech

R. Harper, M. Rauterberg, M. Combetto (Eds.): ICEC 2006, LNCS 4161, pp. 37–42, 2006.
© IFIP International Federation for Information Processing 2006

recognition and fluent speech expression. Actually, Harada intended that this verbal conversation was an orientation phase for participants to learn and understand the functions and behaviors of this robot. However, they did not experience any interactions or conversations with the window-based software or the agent before leaving messages with these artifacts. Therefore, the question was still open as to whether an artifact's physical appearance is the more important cue that causes users to feel comfortable and natural using it, or whether prior interaction and/or conversation experience with the artifacts is more important.

The purpose of this paper is to investigate the effects of these two aspects of artifacts on users' interactions with them: the artifact's appearance whether it has physical existence, and prior experience interacting with artifacts. We examined the effect of these two factors on whether users feel comfortable and natural in these interactions. Specifically, we conducted a simple psychological experiment in which participants leave verbal messages with the PaPeRo robot or with a PaPeRo's character animation created with computer graphics on a PC screen (PaPeRo CG) in two different situations. In one instance, they experience verbal conversations with the PaPeRo before leaving messages, and in the other they do not. The results of this study will contribute to creating effective interactive artifacts, such as partner robots or video game characters, that can induce natural user behaviors, and it will contribute to finding the trigger that induces intimate interactions between users and artifacts.

## 2 Experiment

### 2.1 Participants

The participants were 40 Japanese university students (36 men and 4 women; 18-22 years old). They did not have any previous experience interacting with PaPeRo or of observing its behaviors. These 40 participants were randomly assigned into the four groups, and participants in each group were asked to leave verbal messages by using the following objects under the following conditions:

- **Group 1:** PaPeRo robot with having interaction experience prior to leaving messages.
- **Group 2:** PaPeRo robot without advance interaction experience.
- **Group 3:** PaPeRo CG with advance interaction experience.
- **Group 4:** PaPeRo CG without advance interaction experience.

### 2.2 Objects Used for Leaving Verbal Messages

Participants used two objective artifacts to leave messages. There were the PaPeRo robot (left in Fig. 1), and PaPeRo animation depicted by computer graphics as PaPeRo CG (center in Figure 1).

The PaPeRo robot is 385 mm tall, 248 mm wide, and 245 mm thick. The PaPeRo CG appeared on a 17-inch display so that its actual size was about 200 mm x 150 mm x 150 mm. Participants in Groups 1 and 2 were asked to leave messages with the PaPeRo robot, while participants in Groups 3 and 4 did so with the PaPeRo CG. Both the PaPeRo robot and PaPeRo CG were activated by the same robot controller and sound recognition and expression system. Therefore, both can express the same behaviors and the same speech sounds, so there are no apparent differences in their functions. In other words, the differences between these two are just whether PaPeRo exists in the physical world or the virtual world."

**Fig. 1.** PaPeRo robot (left), PaPeRo CG (center) and character agent (right)

## 2.3  Interaction Experiences

Participants in Group 1 and 3 were assigned to leave messages after having prior interaction experience, while participants in groups 2 and 4 were to do so without experiencing interactions before leaving messages. These two conditions were designed as the follows:

- (Group 1 and 3) Those participants who had interaction experience in advance were passed a memo that listed 10 simple words that PaPeRo could recognize, and respond to with comical actions, e.g., if participants selected the word hello and addressed PaPeRo, the robot responded by saying "bonjour!" and dancing. Before leaving messages, these participants were asked to use five words from this list. The total time of this interaction was within two minutes at maximum.
- (Group 2 and 4) The other participants did not have any advance interaction with PaPeRo robot or PaPeRo CG.

## 2.4  Procedure

The experimental procedure was the nearly same as in Harada's study mentioned above in the introduction of this report.

1. All 40 participants were asked to leave verbal messages with the character agent appearing on a computer display as a preliminary session (right in Fig. 1). Specifically, participants were passed a message memo, e.g., "To Mr. Suzuki. English Exam. 4 PM. Lecture Hall B." and asked to leave a verbal message about this memo with this agent as if leaving a message on an answering machine.
2. Afterward, participants were asked to answer questions about this character agent; the questions are Part 1 of the questionnaire that is presented in Fig. 2.
3. The participants were then asked to leave messages with the PaPeRo robot or PaPeRo CG according to the corresponding conditions described

above as the main session. In this session, the participants were passed a message memo different from that used in the preliminary session.

4.  Afterward, all participants were asked to answer questions about PaPeRo that are in Parts 1 and 2 of the questionnaire. In addition, the participants in Groups 1 and 3 who had prior interaction experience before leaving messages were asked to also fill in Part 3 of the questionnaire.

The three kinds of questionnaires mentioned above and shown in Fig. 2 were designed as a six-point likert scale (the lower the points, the poorer the assessment: zero was the worst assessment, and five points was the best).

| Part 1. About the object used for leaving message | Part 2. About your impression of PaPeRo | Part 3. About interaction experiences |
|---|---|---|
| Q1. Could you successfully leave messages? | Q7. Did you think PaPeRo was cute? | Q11. Could PaPeRo and you communicate smoothly? |
| Q2. Did you feel that the object was staring at you? | Q8. Did you think PaPeRo was sociable? | Q12. Did you enjoy the conversation with PaPeRo? |
| Q3. Did you feel embarrassed when you left messages? | Q9. Did you feel establish rapports with PaPeRo? | Q13. Did you want to experience these kinds of conversations? |
| Q4. Did you enjoy leaving messages with this object? | Q10. Did you think PaPeRo was reliable? | |
| Q5. Could you leave messages without being at a loss for words? | | |
| Q6. Did you want to use this way of leaving message again? | | |

**Fig. 2.** Questionnaire used in this experiment

## 2.5 Results

**Questionnaire Part 1: About the object used for leaving messages.** Each of the six questions in Part 1 was analyzed with a 2 (physical appearance: robot or CG) x 2 (interactions: with or without prior experience) x 2 (sessions: preliminary or main) mixed ANOVA. The results of the ANOVA revealed that there were significant differences in the answers to Q4, Q5, and Q6.

For Q4, *"Did you enjoy leaving messages with this object?"* a significant tendency in the second-order interaction ($F(1, 36) = 3.75$, $p < .075$ (+)) was revealed, and a significant difference in the main effects of a session factor ($F(1,36)=66.15$, $p < .01$(**)) was found. In sum, we can say that the participants enjoyed leaving message with the PaPeRo regardless of the two kinds of physical appearance.

For Q5, *"Could leave messages without being at a loss for words?"* significant differences in main effects were found for session factor ($F(1,36)= 7.62$, $p < .01$(**)). In sum, we can say that the participants could leave messages with the PaPeRo without being at a loss for words regardless of the two types of physical appearance.

For Q6, *"Did you want to use this way of leaving messages again?"* we found significant tendency in the interaction between prior interaction experience and session factors ($F(1,36)=3.88$, $p < .075$(+)), and a significant difference in the interaction between physical appearance and session factors ($F(1,36)=5.41$, $p < .05$(*)). In sum, we can say that participants who experienced prior interactions and conversations with the PaPeRo robot wanted to use it again as a way of leaving messages (Fig. 3).

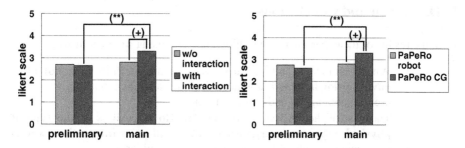

**Fig. 3.** Relationship between prior interaction experience and session factors (left) and that between physical appearance and session factors (right) for Q6

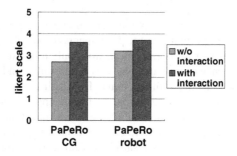

**Fig. 4.** Relationship between physical appearance and interaction experiment factors for Q8

**Part 2: About your impression of PaPeRo.** Each of the four questions in Part 2 was analyzed with a 2 (physical appearance: robot or CG) x 2 (interactions: with prior experience or without) ANOVA. The results of the ANOVA determined that there were significant differences answers to Q7, Q8, and Q9.

For Q7, *"Did you think PaPeRo was cute?"* a significant difference in the interaction between two factors ($F(1,36)=4.64$, $p<.01(**)$) was found. Therefore, we can say that particularly the participants who had prior interaction experiences thought that the PaPeRo robot was cute.

For Q8, *"Did you think PaPeRo was sociable?"* a significant tendency was found in the main effects of interaction experience factors ($F(1,36)=3.90$, $p<.075(+)$). Then, we can say that the participants who had prior interaction experiences thought that the PaPeRo was sociable regardless of the two types of physical appearance (Fig. 4).

For Q9, *"Did you feel establish rapport with PaPeRo?"* we found a significant tendency in the main effects of the interaction experience factor ($F(1,36)=8.73$, $p<.01(**)$). Thus, we can say that the participants who had prior interaction experiences felt rapport with the PaPeRo regardless of the two types of physical appearance.

**Part 3: About the interaction experiences.** The each of three questions in Part 3 answered by participants in Group 1 and 3 was analyzed by a 2 (interactions: with or without prior experience) ANOVA. This ANOVA result determined that there was no significant difference was found.

## 3 Discussion and Conclusions

From the results of the experiments, the following phenomena were confirmed.

- When participants left verbal messages with the **PaPeRo robot after having prior interaction experience**, they answered that they wanted to use the robot again, and that it was cute.
- They established rapport with the **PaPeRo regardless of the type of physical appearance presented if they had prior interaction experience**, and they felt that it was sociable and familiar.
- There were no significant differences in Part 3 of the questionnaire for Groups 1 and Group 3, both of whom had prior interaction experiences with the PePeRo, regardless of the type of physical appearance.

To summarize this result, we can say that prior interaction experience with the artifacts was a much more important cue for participants to be able to leave verbal messages smoothly. In other words, a prior interaction (only a few minutes) made participants feel that interaction with the artifacts was comfortable and natural. This result could contribute to advancement of HCI and EC applications, such as immersive video game characters or interactive virtual assistants appearing on a computer display or a PDA. Moreover, this result should have some impact on research in HCI and EC in that most researchers have previously believed that interactive artifacts must have physical existence and exist in the same physical world as humans [1].

However, this result also confirmed an advantage in the artifacts' having physical existence in that participants' impressions about them; that is, physical existence of artifacts might affect the emotional aspects of interactions, such as "I want to use this robot again (Q6)," or "this robot is cute (Q7)." Moreover, Q4 and Q5 revealed that the PaPeRo regardless of the type of physical appearance received a higher evaluation compared to the character agent appearing on a computer display. This means that the design of artifacts might also have some effects on whether users feel comfortable and natural when using them.

Therefore, to develop the artifacts required that induce natural user behaviors, two requirements are providing interaction experience for users, and designing an appropriate appearance for artifacts according to their use.

## References

1. Breazeal, C.: Towards sociable robots. Robotics and Autonomous Systems, 42 (3-4), (2003) 167-175.
2. Harada, T. E.: Effects of agency and social contexts faced to verbal interface system. In Proceedings of the 19th Japanese Cognitive Science Society Annual Meeting (In Japanese), (2002) pp. 14-15.
3. NEC PaPeRo personal Robot (2001): http://www.incx.nec.co.jp/robot/.

# Passive Interactivity, an Answer to Interactive Emotion

Nelson Zagalo, Ana Torres, and Vasco Branco

Department of Communication and Art, University of Aveiro,
3810-193 Aveiro, Portugal
{ntz, atorres, vab}@ca.ua.pt

**Abstract.** Sadness is a negative emotion, which aims at a deactivated physiological and behavioural state [21] and so this is easy to develop in film experiencing, where the viewer is passively watching and feeling. Interactive storytelling supposes active physiological behaviours and this raises the problematic -
how to create sad deactivated moments during interactive sequences. In this paper we intend to develop and present different ways to approach this problematic and methodologies to implement interactive sad moments in virtual environments, as videogames. These moments will be defined as situations of affective attachment supported by virtual body touching, visually represented by virtual gently stroking body parts (shoulders, hands, hair), bear hugs, soft kissing
and lying against each other cuddling.

**Keywords:** emotion, videogames, film, interactivity.

## 1 Introduction

It has been recently verified that the interactive storytelling finds a barrier regarding
the elicitation of sadness. We have come to this conclusion thanks to some results
given on a study supported by INSCAPE[1] Project [26]. None of the videogames used
on the referred study could elicit the Sadness cluster (as we can see on figure 1). On
the other hand the other clusters proposed by Russell's theory [21] were elicited by at
least one videogame.

The videogames industry has been trying to supplant this emotional difficulty. To
achieve this objective they were using filmic language, which consists on interactive
suspension moments (e.g. Max Payne [30]). These processes are designated as
"cutscenes", FMVs (Full Motion Videos) or simply film clips. It is important to re-
mark that this kind of video games' moments brings about a very low level of interest,
as we found in our study [26]. Therefore it seems that there is a clear connection between the interest in the object and the interaction possibility. This may be explained
through the users' expectations about the playing games activity (they usually expect
real interactive moments).

It is known that the range of game players is very restricted. For instance, the majority of them are medium age men as the Microsoft's Corporate vice-president J.
Allard, at E3 2005, pointed out - "the 18 to 34 year old male is the backbone of the
industry" [18]. As result we hypothesise that these restrictions on the target public are

---

[1] INSCAPE Integrated Project (EU RTD contract IST-2004-004150): www.inscapers.com

correlated with the emotional limitation referred. A reason to believe in this hypothesis is that the emotional limitation restricts the contents that can make the games more appealing to a specific public. As far as this hypothesis is concerned we can make reference to Fillingim's study as well, which demonstrated that gender exerts effect on experimental pain, with women exhibiting lower pain thresholds and tolerance [8]. These emotional differences between men and women supports the hypothesis that different emotional stimulus can be a focus for a different target public.

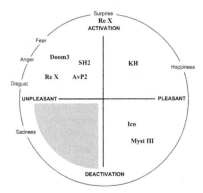

**Fig. 1.** Emotional Videogames Circumplex [26]

As result this study has the intention to give a possible way to solve this emotional difficulty. To get this purpose we will present a new concept of interactivity which we have designated as *passive interactivity*. This concept has foundation on a recent analysis of the sadness ways present in entertainment films [25]. The foundation is linked to the cognitive psychology [9] and neuropsychology [7] as well.

## 2  Interactive Emotion

Izard and Ackerman [14] argued that "induced emotion guides perception, increases the selectivity of attention, helps determine the content of working memory, in sum, it motivate, organize and sustain particular sets of behaviours". Thus emotion is a central cognitive and motor mechanism. As result it is clear that emotion is important in the interaction with video games, and this is the central phenomenon in this study.

The emotional basis of the fictional artefacts derives from the Interest [24]. Interest "motivates exploration and learning, and guarantees the person's engagement in the environment" [14]. We hypothesise that the origin of the Interest is on the emotional diversity of the artefact. We believe that it is not possible to get the player's engagement in a storytelling environment which presents a persistent tension, calm or euphoria. Instead of it, it is necessary an emotional alternation. This is the difficulty faced on the videogames in comparison to the cinema, which gets a wider emotional alternation.

The videogames industry has tried to find solutions to this problem of interactive sadness for a long time. In 1982 the Electronic Arts (EA)[2] in order to launch itself in the videogame industry initiated an advertising campaign which was based on the following announcement: "Can a Computer Make you Cry?". To Murray [19] this procedure led this institution to the interception between videogames and the storytelling old forms.

**Fig. 2.** Planetfall (1983)

**Fig. 3.** Final Fantasy VII (1997)

In 1983 the Infocom, more precisely Meretzky, became EA's rival with the game which has been recognised as the first being able to induce cry. Meretzky declared it later on an interview[3]. "Planetfall was an Infocom text adventure in which you spent a fair amount of time in the company of a rather smart-alecky robot named Floyd. Eventually, however, Floyd gave up his life for you, and there was no way to avoid it. It was a sad moment" [1]. Although this artefact is an interactive fiction, i.e. it consists on a text in which the only interaction is writing more text and which doesn't involve any visual form (see fig. 2). We know that the difference between literary fiction and cinematography fiction lies in the kind of the story presentation (the literary fiction lies in the "tell" while the cinematography lies in the "show"). If we attend to this difference we can easily understand the great difference present between an interactive text object and an object contained in a virtual narrative environment.

1997 was the year when the second key moment happened in the history of videogames interactive emotion. Final Fantasy VII has one of the well-known videogame sequences – the "Aeries death". It is the sequence when Aeries (who follows the player almost all the time of the game) is murdered by the evil of the story (Sphiroth). If we search for "Aeris Death" on Google we find hundreds of crying descriptions. However the problem of this moment is once more the interaction. The RPG[4] games are recognised for their narrative capacities and for their low interaction level as well. A wide number of RPG games consist on reading messages or watching films with a little level of interaction on some battles and limited displacement. So, the Aeris death is a big cinematography moment which contains Cloud carrying the death loved inside a sparkling blue lagoon with a sad music (see fig. 3).

---

[2] Eletronic Arts (EA) is the biggest company of the world on videogames production. It produced videogames as Sims, Harry Potter, Lord of the Rings, and the majority of sport games.

[3] "There was a little touch of a budding rivalry there, and I just wanted to head them off at the pass." [20].

[4] RPG – Role Playing Game. "is a type of game which players assume the roles of characters and collaboratively create narratives." (wikipedia.org, 2006).

In 2004, Steven Spielberg affirmed "I think the real indicator will be when somebody confesses that they cried at level 17" [4]. Finally in 2005 the EA contracted Steven Spielberg and announced through its sub-president (Neil Young): "We're trying to answer the question: Can a computer game make you cry? [..] Partnering with Steven, we're going to get closer to answering it, and maybe we'll answer it together." [23]. As we can realise through these statements this question is still very current (after 25 years) because the answers given are very unsatisfactory.

## 3   The Inactivity Paradox

The interactivity is generally an actions' cyclic process between men and machine. To Cameron [5] interactivity "means the ability to intervene in a meaningful way within the representation itself, not to read it differently". This presumes always the existence of an active user which involves a cognitive activity and also a motor activity because it is necessary that the interactive cycle continues and consequently the interaction has the expressivity needed at the representation level of the artefact. The interactivity lies in a user's action over the object in order to make this significant. Therefore the user's action is the energy point that produces the interactive art.

Art is always naturally dependent on the person who experiences it to make it happen. However the interactive art needs more action by the user than the traditional narratives. On the traditional art it is needed that the person who is experiencing does a cognitive activity about the representation. On the interactive arts it is needed that the user interacts with the representation to make it happen.

Concerning the Sadness emotion on its physiological component, if we attend to the circumplex model of Russell [21] we observe that this is characterised by motor inactivity. It is positioned on low left cluster which represents a physiological reaction of negative valence with a low or null activity (see fig.1).

We are confronted with a clear paradox because we need an active user to make the artefact work and on the other hand the sadness emotion needs an inactive user to be elicited.

Everyone knows that there is a big distinction between games and films in what concerns the motor action. This difference can explain the Gross [11] study's results. It is easier to develop states of sadness on films than on games because the spectator is on a passive mode of visualisation. We believe that we have found one of the possible causes of the problem linked to the answer of EA from 25 years old ago - "Can a computer make you Cry?"

Attending to what we have presented above and also to the fact that the activity on sadness cluster doesn't need to be null, we hypothesise that the interactive environments need to develop interaction structures which demand a low level of user action in order to stabilise his/her physiological state to be able to answer to an elicitation of sadness.

## 4   Design of Sadness Actions

It was necessary to analyse the genres and actions used on narrative cinema in order to find answers which promote solutions to the problem of inactivity paradox. As result we proceeded with a formalist study [25] of films' sequences tested by Gross and Levenson [11]. The highlights of this study are especially related to the influence of characters on spectator's emotions, originated by processes such as empathy, mental simulation, emotional contagious and memory resonance [25]. And regarding the narrative events we have realised the constant rupture of attachment relations [2] previously created by the narrative.

Accordingly to these results it is easy to understand our purpose to elicit sadness emotion on videogames which consist on three distinct phases: 1) The attachment – in which it is necessary to develop an attachment relation between the user and the artefact character 2) The rupture – in which it is created a situation that leads to a rupture of the attachment developed 3) Passivity – the creation of passivity in order to maintain sadness at least during a short period of time.

## 4.1 Attachment

The attachment is "the propensity of human being to make strong affectional bonds to particular others" [2, p.39]. This linkage established is constituted by a system of self-regulated "attachment behaviours" as cry behaviour. The intensity of individual emotion is amplified and generated through phases of "the formation, the maintenance, the disruption and the renewal of attachment relationships" [2, p.40]. As result the emotion is very dependent on the attachment systems.

Relating to attachment creation with fictional artefacts, if we take in consideration our film study already mentioned the characters would be the most important elements on the process of attachment relation creation. It is acknowledged that our empathy capacity depends on the presence of "other" similar to us. The "mirror neurons" concept [10] certainly justifies this last idea because it substantiates that we reproduce innately the behaviours of the other person. The empathy is apparently based on our neurological characteristic in order to experience the outlook of another being within oneself [29] – not through an identification process, but trough recognition and understanding of the states of mind of others which are followed by an emotional answer state [27].

The ability to develop attachment behaviour through the process of empathy requires firstly the development or presentation of a situation of attachment between narrative characters. To get this attachment it is necessary to present an attachment relation that should be familiar to the user in order to foment the empathy between user and artefact. The most used relation on films is the parent-child and this is maybe the most efficient on fictional sadness elicitation too (e.g. in "The Champ" when the father dies [3]). However there are other ways to develop adult sadness on films and they are very used (e.g. romantic/love relationships or deep friendship relations).

## 4.2 Rupture

A relation's rupture moment is a clear stimulus of the biological answer of sadness specially if it is irreversible [9]. It isn't correct to see Sadness as an avoidant or unnecessary emotion. Sadness has to be seen as a normal and healthy reaction to a bad thing [2]. It is natural that the user doesn't consciously look for a negative emotion because it denotes that something bad related to the artefact has happened. However people who usually look for fiction frequently recognise the motivation to feel Sadness. This emotion enables us at least to learn how to react in a certain real situation through the fictional environment.

For that it will be necessary to proceed to the rupture of this attachment after its creation and maintenance. It is the empathy assimilation of the rupture that can elicit the sadness emotion. However the user ability to feel this emotion depends on the success of the first phase – the attachment creation. Because the capacity to feel sadness after an attachment rupture depends on the deepness level of the immersion achieved which develop the interest for the characters.

Regarding the events usually used to elicit sadness on films, there are a set of them which we can mention but the death event is the most used on the cinema and certainly the one which has the strongest impact event that can elicit sadness. Bowlby defends this point of view [2, p.7], on arguing that the "loss of a loved person is one of the most intensely painful experiences any human being can suffer". Other researchers as Spitz [22] have supported empirically his ideas. A very relevant characteristic on the intensity of reaction to the rupture is the irreversibility. Death is the null extreme point of the reversibility continuum; consequently the sadness reaction is the most durable and intense too.

### 4.3  Passive Interactivity

After the creation of the sadness situation it will be necessary to create a situation adjusted to the user's sadness physiological state. Thus it is necessary to create a situation which enables a user's passive behaviour (related to the inertia state usually felt).

We want to develop this phase with the creation of interactive ways after the rupture moment of sadness creation. By now we have come to know how to develop the attachment and provoke the rupture of it but we haven't found out yet how to proceed after that. We don't know how the user should interact once he/she is in a sadness state composed by inactivity, without motivation to interact actively.

In order to achieve our purpose we will firstly dedicate to understand the relation of user, artefact and narrative. We know that the "mental simulation" [6] and the "mirror neurons" can help us realise the idea of "somatic displacement" defined by Holopainen and Meyers [13] as the "ability of a person to project the mental model of his or her own identity into another physical form, which represents the player in an alternate environment" [13]. This concept is on virtual reality basis and is behind what enables us to perform tasks inside virtual environments using a virtual hand as a visual connection to our own real hand [16].

If we follow this concept we can distinguish the character of the virtual narrative environment and the user who controls it and see it as a self projection inside the virtual universe. As result it is easy to understand the impact of a virtual touch on a user. It isn't a real touch but a visual communicational component (see Fig.4), however important on the communication of the necessary passive comfort during a sadness moment.

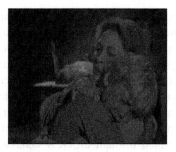

**Fig. 4.** Film, moment of body touching [3]          **Fig. 5.** Game, one virtual touch [31]

This situation should be more perceptible in environments experienced in third person, i.e. in which the user controls a character inside a world that he can see and manipulate simultaneously (in Fig. 5, ICO is a third-person game, in which, the player is controlling a boy, through whom he can hold the girl's hand). On the other side in the first person environment (see Fig.6) the user can only see the others NPC[5] and not the main character (Gordon Freeman), having nothing more than the hand to project himself inside the virtual world. Subsequently the somatic displacement should be more efficient in the third person environment because it is possible to project a full body with behaviours/movements into the body of the character (see fig. 5).

**Fig. 6.** Game, first person shooter [32]          **Fig. 7.** Film, first-person [28]

This third person environment, can also be seen as deeper on the empathy process because it consents the user a double way of elicit emotion. This way the user can feel emotions on experiencing the emotions of the character within oneself and experiencing emotions for the character and the world. While in the first person environment the user only feels for the world, that he experiences as a character himself and so having no empathetic character/object to feel for. In Fig.7, we can see one of the rarest movies [28] that made use of a first-person view during the entire movie, being scenes with mirrors the only sequences where viewers could see the hero/character, as in the figure. It was, completely unsuccessful, mainly because of the impossibility to establish empathy with the hero, because of the lack of an image of a body and all his communicative cues, a body-person to whom the viewer could build attachment.

---

[5] NPC non-player characters: "a character in the game story that is not controlled by the player, but by the game engine or AI" *in http://www.igda.org/writing/WritersGlossary.htm*

If we understand the process of the relation man-machine this way we can apply the necessary activity actions to the moments after the rupture, i.e. it is necessary to look for actions which create comfort and lower activity actions (which involve lower displacement). These actions can involve attempt actions of reattachment of attachment relations or of the creation of new attachment relations which can be initiated by the virtual touch between the characters. Therefore body virtual touching is a way of sensitive comfort that the character can look for and consequently which the user can feel by somatic simulation. Moreover it can help the user with the continuity of the sadness moment. The body touching can be defined through different behaviours, which express affection on body language (e.g. to do give pats in the shoulders or hands, to slip the hands on the hair or body, to hug, to kiss, to seat or to lie down leaned). The importance of body touching has been well highlighted since Harlow's study [12], in which he concluded that the comfort of body touching is determinant for the attachment creation. The fact that attachment propitiates sensations of security is already known and therefore the existence of body touching at this phase is crucial. The knowledge of the importance of body touching is supported by ethologic studies about "appeasement behaviours" as well. From this point of view the important social mechanism of "Human appeasement involves affiliative behaviours such as smiles and physical contact" [15, p.361].

## 5   Conclusions

As far as the emotions are concerned, the words are less important than non verbal language. The body expressivity and the relation that we may have with it in a virtual world are very important regarding the creation of a wide range of emotions by those who experience the interactive virtual fiction.

Despite our solution proposal, the creation of the interactive sadness emotion is a design process which will keep on suffering from different problems.

Because our purposes are especially related to the moment after the sadness elicitation hence it will be necessary to develop the precedent phases in a better way. The two first phases are very important to achieve the elicit sadness because it is on these phases that a strong attachment and consequently a profound immersion will be set up, which will subsequently predict the rupture impact.

We can as well suggest that the methodology suggested to the last phase related to passive interactivity can be also applied to the first one to promote the user attachment.

## Acknowledgments

This research is performed in the frame of the INSCAPE Integrated Project (EU RTD contract IST-2004-004150), which is funded by the European Commission under the sixth Framework Programme. More information on the project is available at www.inscapers.com

# References

1. Adams, E. (1999). How To Be Weird. Gamasutra.com.
2. Bowlby, J. (1969). Attachment and Loss Vol. 3. Loss: Sadness and depression. New York, Basic.
3. The Champ, (1979), Franco Zeffirelli, MGM
4. Breznican, A. (2004). Spielberg, Zemeckis say video games, films could merge.USA Today.
5. Cameron, A. (1995). "Dissimulations - illusions of interactivity." Millennium Film Journal No. 28, Spring.
6. Currie, G. (1995). Image and mind: film, philosophy and cognitive science. Cambridge, Cambridge University Press.
7. Damasio, A. R. (1994). Descartes' error: emotion, reason, and the human brain. New York, G.P. Putnam.
8. Fillingim RB, Maixner W. Gender differences in the responses to noxious stimuli. Pain Forum.1995;4:209-221.
9. Frijda, N. H. (1986). The emotions. Cambridge, Cambridge University Press.
10. Gallese, V. and A. Goldman (1998). "Mirror neurons and the simulation theory of mind-reading." Trends in Cognitive Sciences 2(12).
11. Gross, J. J. and R. W. Levenson (1995). "Emotion elicitation using films." Cognition and Emotion(9): 87-108.
12. Harlow, H. F. & Harlow, M. K. (1969) Effects of various mother-infant relationships on rhesus monkey behaviors. In B. M. Foss (Ed.) "Determinants of infant behavior" (Vol.4). London: Methuen.
13. Holopainen, J. and S. Meyers (2001). Neuropsychology and Game Design. Consciousness Reframed III, http://www.stephan.com/NeuroBio.html.
14. Izard, C. E. and B. P. Ackerman (2000). Motivational, organizational and regulatory functions of discrete emotions. Handbook of Emotion. M. Lewis and M. Haviland-Jones. New York, Guilford Press.
15. Keltner, D., Young, R.C. & Buswell, B. N. (1997), Appeasement in Human Emotion, Social Practice, and Personality, Aggressive Behavior 23: 359-374.
16. Krueger, M. W. (1991). Artificial reality II. Reading, Addison-Wesley.
17. Lang, P. J., M. M. Bradley, et al. (1998). "Emotion, Motivation and Anxiety: Brain Mechanisms and Psychophysiology." Biological Psychiatry 44: 1248-1263.
18. Microsoft (2005), Robbie Bach, J Allard, Peter Moore: Electronic Entertainment Expo (E3) 2005, transcripts, http://www.microsoft.com/presspass/exec/rbach/05-16-05E3.mspx
19. Murray, J. (2005). Did it make you cry? Creating Dramatic Agency in Immersive Environments. Virtual Storytelling 2005, Strasbourg, Lecture Notes in Computer Science, Springer Ed.
20. Rouse, R. (2001). "Games on the Verge of a Nervous Breakdown: Emotional Content in Computer Games." Computer Graphics Volume 35, Number 1.
21. Russell, J., Lemay, G., (2000). Emotion Concepts. Handbook of Emotion. M. H.-J. Lewis, M. New York, Guilford Press.
22. Spitz R: Hospitalism: An inquiry into the genesis of psychiatric conditions in early childhood. In: Psychoanalytic Study of the Child. Vol 1. New York, NY: International Universities Press; 1945: 53-74.
23. Tamaki, J. (2005). EA, Spielberg Team Up to Make Video Games. Los Angeles Times.
24. Tan, E. S. (1996). Emotion and the structure of narrative film: film as an emotion machine. Hillsdale, NJ, L. Erlbaum Associates.

25. Zagalo, N., Barker, A., Branco, V., (2005). Princípios de uma Poética da Tristeza do Cinema. 4º Congresso da Associação Portuguesa de Ciências da Comunicação - SOPCOM, Universidade de Aveiro, Portugal.
26. Zagalo, N., Torres, A. & Branco, V. (2005). Emotional Spectrum developed by Virtual Storytelling. Virtual Storytelling 2005, Strasbourg, Lecture Notes in Computer Science, Springer Ed.
27. Zillmann, D. (1994). "Mechanisms of emotional involvement with drama." Poetics (23): 33-51.
28. Lady in the Lake, (1947), Robert Montgomery, MGM
29. Gallese, Vittorio (2001), The 'Shared Manifold' Hypothesis - From Mirror Neurons To Empathy, Journal of Consciousness Studies, 8, No. 5–7, 2001, pp. 33–50
30. Max Payne, (2001), Sam Lake, Rockstar Games
31. Ico, (2001), Fumito Ueda, Sony Computer Entertainment Inc.
32. Half-Life 2, (2004), Gabe Newell, Valve Software

# Entertainment on Mobile Internet Services: From the Korean Consumer Perspectives

Seongil Lee[1] and Joo Eun Cho[2]

[1] Sungkyunkwan University, Department of Systems Management Engineering
300 Chunchun-Dong, Jangan-Gu, Suwon, Korea
silee@skku.edu
[2] Kyungpook National University, Department of Sociology
1370 Sankyuk-Dong, Daegu, Korea
june@mail.knu.ac.kr

**Abstract.** Elaborating on the rapid evolution of mobile internet services in Korea, this paper investigated young consumers' preferences and attitudes towards mobile entertainment services through person-to-person questionnaires. We tried to find out "how" mobile entertainment services differ from other mobile services from the consumer perspectives: expectation and satisfaction. After careful investigation of what the consumers actually said, it could be said that the speed of services was never met to consumer expectation in mobile entertainment services, while they never really cared about contents aspects of mobile internet services.

## 1 Introduction

It has been reported that South Korea is one of the leading countries in the world in number of people owning a mobile phones with 64% of the total population (KMIC, 2001). According to the NIDA(National Internet Development Agency of Korea, 2003, 2004, 2005), the subscribers of mobile internet services through major mobile telecommunication service carriers has dramatically increased over the past 4 years, reaching from approximately 32% in 2002 to 42.8% in 2005 of the entire mobile telecommunication service subscribers. The figure is approximately 39% of the total population of Korea.

Among the internet contents provided by the mobile telecommunication service carriers, ring tone and melody download service has consistently been the consumer favorite, while the services for mp3 music file download instantly became the second most popular services since its introduction to the market in 2004. Download of games and multimedia files has been also consistently requested (see Table 1). All these heavily requested contents and services can be viewed as entertainment services since they do not particularly convey information on certain purpose nor provide functions for daily transactions such as banking and purchasing. That means entertainment became the single most important revenue stream source for mobile internet contents providers and telecommunication service carriers. Therefore, while the market is expected to expand enormously, the factors that contribute to consumers' expectation on current mobile entertainment services as well as to their satisfaction or

R. Harper, M. Rauterberg, M. Combetto (Eds.): ICEC 2006, LNCS 4161, pp. 53–58, 2006.
© IFIP International Federation for Information Processing 2006

lack of satisfaction would be important for the providers and carriers to keep generating consistent revenue streams. Consumer behavior research, particularly on consumer perception on service quality is critical for identifying consumer preferences, attitudes and predispositions towards innovative mobile services.

**Table 1.** Trends of mobile internet services and usage for Korean customers (%)

| Mobile Internet Services | 2003 | 2004 | 2005 |
|---|---|---|---|
| Ring tone download | 32.8 | 82.9 | 96.8 |
| Multimedia file download * | 6.1 (0.0) | 56.5 (46.0) | 87.5 (45.4) |
| Game | 18.0 | 55.0 | 37.1 |
| Information search | 12.6 | 15.6 | 19.9 |
| Mobile banking | -- | 4.5 | 8.4 |
| GPS location service | -- | 3.1 | 7.6 |
| **Total No. of Respondents** | **3,276** | **3,103** | **3,063** |

When a service needs to be evaluated, it is the consumers' experience what ultimately counts. The consumers are not concerned about how a service is provided, but only the resulting quality they receive. The notion is well reflected in ETSI's (1990) definition of quality of service(QoS) in the context of digital networks as "... the collective effect of service performances, which determine the degree of satisfaction of a user of the service". Choi et al. (2003) revealed that service repurchase intention among Korean mobile internet users was significantly related to experienced value and satisfaction. This may particularly be true for entertainment services through mobile internet, with ever increasing consumers and service applications in this technology-driven business. For mobile service providers, balancing customer satisfactions and expectations is an important issue to maintain customers' royalty.

This paper investigates customers' perception towards mobile internet services in Korea through in-depth questionnaire surveys. We tried to identify the attributes of mobile internet services where the customers have the greatest or the least expectations and satisfaction in the services provided. Though we did not engage in a quantitative measurement of specific mobile network parameters related to the user perception, the study generally provides guidelines for the mobile entertainment services to meet the expectation with growing network performance demands of consumers in Korea. We tried to explain the relationship between the intangible user experiences of satisfaction and expectation and rather tangible attributes of mobile internet services. We also examined how the mobile entertainment services in Korea met to the challenge from the customers' expectation compared to the other mobile services.

## 2 Research Methodology

Data was collected from young consumers living in Metropolitan Seoul area, using questionnaires on current wireless internet services through mobile telecommunication service carriers. A total of 370 consumers (215 males and 155 females) whose age ranges from 14 to 40 years old (with the average age of 23.2 years) participated in the study over the span of 2 weeks. About 67% of the participants were high school and college students, considered in general to be the major mobile consumer groups. The data was collected by a person-to-person questionnaire which asks participants their satisfaction and expectation levels using a 7-point scale subjective rating method.

The mobile services examined were grouped in four categories: 1) personalization services, with such services as ring tone, background figure, or avatar figure download to decorate and customize consumer's mobile phones, 2) entertainment services, with such services as game or multimedia file (ex. mp3 music and mpeg files) download, 3) communication services, with SMS, MMS, and instant messengers to send and receive messages of different types, and 4) information provision, with such services as stock quotes, news and weather telecasting, and traffic information. Participants were advised with constituent services for each category prior to questionnaire responding.

Two aspects of mobile services were examined: system and contents. In each aspect, five different attributes of the mobile services in that aspect were examined through questionnaires. These attributes examined for each aspect of mobile services are important since they have been used for market research by mobile telecommunication service carrier companies in Korea, for monitoring and evaluating the behaviors and attitudes of the consumers (NIDA, 2005).

(1) System Aspect
- Reliability and Stability of System (reliability)
- Download Speeds (speed)
- Degree of Privacy in Services (privacy)
- Usability of System (usability)
- Screen Aesthetics (aesthetics)

(2) Contents Aspect
- Validity of Contents (validity)
- Accordance with Users' Intent (accordance)
- Contents Update Rate (update)
- Volume of Contents (volume)
- Variety of Contents (variety)

For each aspect, the questionnaire first asks users subjective satisfaction ratings in terms of the five attributes that influence the perceived quality of mobile internet services: How would you rate your satisfaction with your current mobile internet services in terms of the above attributes on the scale of 7 (with 1 being the lowest and 7 being the highest)? The questionnaire then asks users subjective expectation ratings with the same scale: How would you rate your expectation with your current mobile internet services in terms of the five attributes, based upon the current mobile telecommunication technology status in Korea on the scale of 7 (with the same manner)?

The questionnaire was carefully designed to ask consumers on the satisfaction first and on the expectation later since it could influence respondents' perceived satisfaction by evaluating in comparative manners.

# 3   Results and Analysis

## 3.1   System Aspect

*Satisfaction.* Korean consumers' overall satisfaction with the current mobile internet services was not great, scoring at around 4.4 out of 7 points. ANOVA shows a strongly significant difference between services ($\underline{F}$= 5.10, $\underline{p}$= 0.002). A Tukey Post-Hoc test shows that consumers were more satisfied with entertainment services and communication services than with other services. No significant attribute could be found that affects the user satisfaction in system aspect. However, consumers seemed not happy with download speeds for the personalization and entertainment services, while satisfaction levels for all the other interactions between services and attributes remained very similar. These two services consist mostly of downloading multimedia files: ring tones, background graphics, and avatar figures for the personalization service, and movie and music files, and game contents for the entertainment service. Consumers were not satisfied with the speed in these download services, since downloading multimedia files with bigger size with the current speed raised the costs.

*Expectation.* Overall consumer expectation with the current mobile internet services was generally higher, with average scores at around 5.6 out of 7 points. Consumers had significantly greater expectations with multimedia entertainment services and communication services ($\underline{F}$= 4.25, $\underline{p}$= 0.005) than with personalization and information services. The effects on attributes($\underline{F}$= 13.15, $\underline{p}$= 0.001) and service * attributes interaction were also found to be mildly significant ($\underline{F}$= 1.68, $\underline{p}$= 0.082). It was shown that consumers did not expect much on screen aesthetics compared to the other service attributes (Fig. 1). This was particularly apparent with the personalization, communication, and information services, while consumers expect rather higher aesthetics in entertainment services.

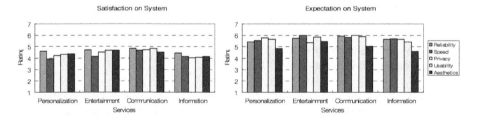

**Fig. 1.** Consumer satisfaction and expectation ratings on the system aspect of the current mobile internet services

## 3.2   Contents Aspect

*Satisfaction.* Overall user satisfaction with the current mobile internet services in contents aspect was similar to that in system aspect, scoring at 4.4 out of 7 points. No services or attributes was found to be significantly different from the others in consumer ratings.

*Expectation.* Overall user expectation with the current mobile internet services was slightly lower than that in system aspect, scoring at around 5.4 out of 7 points. Just like satisfaction, no services or attributes was found to be significantly different from the others in consumer ratings.

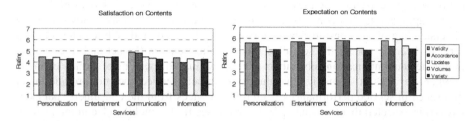

**Fig. 2.** Consumer satisfaction and expectation ratings on the contents aspect of the current mobile internet services

# 4 Conclusion

Based on the research carried out in this study with the current mobile services in Korea, which are regarded one of the leading mobile industries in the world, two conclusions can be drawn. First, the young consumers seemed not satisfied with the service speed, particularly for the services aiming for personalization and entertainment. Second, the young consumers seemed to be more sensitive to system aspect, such as speed, than to contents aspect, such as volumes and update rate, of mobile internet services.

Since the two categories of services in personalization and entertainment showed similar patterns in consumer attitudes, we can derive certain characteristics that are common to both services. Consumers enjoy self-engagement in those services: personalization in which users spend much time decorating and customizing to their delight and also to express their identity and preferences, and entertainment in which users engage in for their pleasure. Those two service categories differ from communication and information services since the services were designed to amuse consumers more than to provide simple telephony for communication or information. And it was speed that the consumers concerned the most in these services.

The personalization services can also be viewed as a sort of entertainment service since the activities the users engage in while personalizing their mobile phones, such as setting ring tones and background graphics, are intended to amuse the users themselves. From this perspective, it can be said that the whole mobile internet services are directed more and more towards entertainment, and consumers expect more and more speed to enjoy the services. While the consumers expected good screen aesthetics for the entertainment services, it seems, in general, unnecessary for the mobile telecommunication service carriers to invest lots of resources into the design for aesthetics, as it was shown that the users did not have great expectations in screen aesthetics for the other services.

Personalization services have continuously been an important revenue source for mobile service providers from the early days, while the entertainment services became the killer applications with the inclusion of the required functions and devices in the mobile phones recently, as such entertainment services became available for the mobile users as music, music videos, games, and now TV broadcasting.

The rapid evolution of mobile entertainment services in music, video, and games on mostly 2.5G or 3G phones provide new revenue streams for mobile telecommunication service carriers. For these carriers and content providers(CPs) to efficiently market applications and contents through mobile networks, extensive knowledge and understanding of the consumer behaviors and needs is required. While entertainment services become one of the so-called killer applications on the net and most young mobile telecommunication subscribers become willing to spend more money in entertainment services, it seems like that the entertainment service does not provide much difference in service performances from other services from the consumers' perspectives. It is expected that this study provide guidance for the mobile telecommunication service industries to build strategies to make their customers feel satisfied and happy in entertainment-dominant services, thus preventing to lose royalties in their services and maintaining customer retention (Karvonen and Warsta, 2004; Balaji, Landers, Kates, and Moritz, 2005).

# References

1. Balaji, T.S., Landers, B., Kates, J., and Moritz, B.: A Carrier's Perspective on Creating a Mobile Multimedia Service. Communications of the ACM. 48(7) (2005) 49–53
2. Choi, S.M., Lee, E.K., and Park, M.C.: An empirical study on the determinants of repurchase intention in Korean mobile internet services. Paper presented at the International Telecommunications Society, Asia-Australian Regional Conference, Perth, Australia (2003)
3. ETSI: Network Aspects (NA); general aspects of quality of service and network performance in digital networks, including ISDN (ETSI ETR 003 ed. 1) (1990)
4. Karvonen, J., and Juhani, W.: Mobile Multimedia Services Development – Value Chain Perspective. Proceedings of the 3rd International Conference on Mobile and Ubiquitous Multimedia MUM'04. (2004) 171-178
5. KMIC: Korean Ministry of Information and Communication, December (2001)
6. NIDA: 2005 Survey on the Wireless Internet Use. National Internet Development Agency of Korea, December (2005)
7. NIDA: 2004 Survey on the Wireless Internet Use. National Internet Development Agency of Korea, December (2004)
8. NIDA: 2003 Survey on the Wireless Internet Use. National Internet Development Agency of Korea, August (2003)

# Experimental Approach for Human Perception Based Image Quality Assessment

Jin-Seo Kim, Maeng-Sub Cho, and Bon-Ki Koo

CG Research Team, Digital Content Research Division,
Electronics and Telecommunications Research Institute,
161 Gajeong-dong, Yuseong-gu, Daejeon, 305-350, Republic of Korea
{kjseo, choms, bkkoo}@etri.re.kr
http://dcon.etri.re.kr

**Abstract.** The term 'image quality' is a subject notion so it is difficult to quantify. However, it can be reasonably quantified by using statistical and psychophysical approaches. Furthermore, it is also possible to model the human perception of image quality. In this paper, large scale psychophysical experiments including pair comparison and categorical judgment were carried out to judge the perception of image quality of photographic images. The evaluation of both image difference and absolute quality was also carried out. Test images were generated by rendering the eight selected original images according to the change of lightness, chroma, contrast, sharpness and noise attributes. Total number of 288 images were used as test images. The experimental results were used to calculate z-scores and colour difference threshold to verify the optimum level for each transform function. User preferred image content can be provided to entertainment, education, etc. when using the result of the study.

**Keywords:** Image quality, CIELAB, Psychophysical experiment.

## 1 Introduction

Image quality is an ideal concept and, therefore it can be determined by many different attributes such as colour, resolution, sharpness and noise. A number of metrics have been published that could be used to predict image quality including CIECAM02 [1], iCAM [2], MTFA, SNR and MSE. However, none of these metrics can easily predict certain perceptual attributes of human vision such as the naturalness of the image [3]. CIE TC8-02 is studying the calculation of colour difference using spatial characteristics.

The aim of this study is to derive a colour-appearance model which can predict both the spatial and subjective attributes of image quality (sharpness, noise, naturalness, etc.) so that many of image content based applications can provide the best quality image content to their users. To determine image-quality attributes psychophysical experiments have been conducted and the performance of current colour-difference formulae was evaluated. Six attributes were evaluated in this study (lightness, chroma, contrast, noise, sharpness and compression) using CIELAB and S-CIELAB to calculate thresholds. CIELAB is one of the CIE standard colour spaces in which the

R. Harper, M. Rauterberg, M. Combetto (Eds.): ICEC 2006, LNCS 4161, pp. 59–68, 2006.

Euclidean distance between two points in the CIELAB space is considered as colour difference. S-CIELAB is the updated version of CIELAB so that the spatial attributes can be considered when calculating the colour difference of two images, original and spatially corrupted image.

## 2   Experimental Method

Psychophysical experiments were conducted in order to collect the individual preference data of some test images for the development of image-quality modelling algorithm. A BARCO Reference Calibrator 121 was used in a darkened room as a reference display device for the experiments. Some device characteristics such as spatial and temporal uniformity and the channel additivity were tested and found to be satisfactory for conducting a psychophysical experiment. The GOG model was used to characterise the display used in the experiment [4].

Two types of psychophysical experiments were carried out; pair comparison and categorical judgment. Pair comparison was conducted for the evaluation of appearance difference between pairs of sample images. Categorical judgment which uses single image was also conducted for the evaluation of naturalness of individual test images.

Eight different test images were chosen to represent photo-realistic images (e.g. fruit, foliage, flower, plant) and artificial objects (e.g. balloon, bicycle, clothes). Fig. 1 shows the test images used in the experiment.

Six image-quality attributes (lightness, chroma, contrast, noise, sharpness, and compression) were chosen in this study and, six different levels of transform for each attribute were applied to prepare test images. Total numbers of 36 rendered images were generated as a result. The colour transform functions used in the experiments are summarised in Table 1.

(a) Musician      (b) Fruit      (c) Metal wares      (d) Balloons

(e) Bicycle      (f) Happy girl      (g) Mirror image      (d) Chair

**Fig. 1.** Test images

**Table 1.** Image quality transformation functions

| Parameter | Lightness | Chroma |
|---|---|---|
| Formula | $L^*_{out} = kL^*_{in}$ | $C^*_{out} = kC^*_{in}$ |
|  | $k$: scaling factor | $K$: scaling factor |
| Abb. | L | C |

| Parameter | Contrast | Noise |
|---|---|---|
| Formula | $L^*_{out} = L^*_{mid} + L^*_{in} \times k$, where, $L^*_{in} \geq L^*_{mid}$ | Gaussian |
|  | $= L^*_{mid} - L^*_{in} \times k$, where, $L^*_{in} < L^*_{mid}$ | random |
|  | $C^*_{out} = C^*_{mid} + C^*_{in} \times k$ , where, $C^*_{in} \geq C^*_{mid}$ | noise |
|  | $= C^*_{mid} - C^*_{in} \times k$ , where, $C^*_{in} < C^*_{mid}$ | |
|  | $k$: scaling factor | |
|  | $L^*_{mid}$: average lightness of the image | |
|  | $C^*_{mid}$: average chroma of the image | |
| Abb. | CLC | N |

| Parameter | Sharpness | Compression |
|---|---|---|
| Formula | 3×3 mask | Adobe photoshop's jpeg compression function |
| Abb. | SB | CO |

Fig. 2. Six different lightness transformed images.

Example of transformed images for lightness rendering is shown in Fig. 2

Total number of 288 rendered images (8 images × 6 parameters × 6 levels) plus eight original images were prepared as test images. Overall, 18 observers participated in the pair-comparison experiment and 11 observers participated in the categorical-judgment experiment. All observers were tested and found to have normal colour vision. For the pair-comparison experiment, the original and one of the transformed images were displayed on a CRT, and observers were asked the questions listed in Table 2. A total number of 2,304 observations (8 images × 6 parameters × 6 levels × 4 questions × 2 repeats) were obtained for each observer. For the categorical-judgment experiment, a single image (either the original or one of the transformed ones) was

**Table 2.** Questions used in the experiments

| Experiment | Pair comparison | Categorical judgment |
|---|---|---|
| Questions | 1. Do they look the same? (overall)<br>2. Do they look the same in colour?<br>3. Do they look the same in sharpness?<br>4. Do they look the same in texture? | 1. How real is this image? (overall)<br>2. How real is the colour of this image?<br>3. How real is the texture of this image? |

displayed on a CRT in a random order, and observers were asked to assign a number from a scale 1-9 for equally stepped categories according to the questions listed in Table 2.

The experiments were divided into four sessions so that the observation time for any one session did not exceed 45 minutes in order to avoid fatigue. In total, 63,648 observations (41,472 for pair comparison and 22,176 for categorical judgment) were accumulated over one month.

The software tool was developed to carry out psychophysical experiments. It consisted of three parts; user information input, pair comparison experiments, and categorical judgment experiments. First, each observer should complete the user information part before starting the experiment. Then one of the two psychophysical experiments was carried out according to the pre-designed schedule. In Fig. 3, actual images for the experiments using the software were shown.

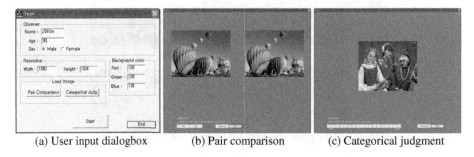

(a) User input dialogbox    (b) Pair comparison    (c) Categorical judgment

**Fig. 3.** Software tool for the experiment

## 3  Data Analysis

Two types of experiments were carried out and the results of the data analysis are summarised below.

For the categorical-judgment experiment, z-scores were calculated to evaluate the image quality of different levels of colour-transformed images. Fig. 4 shows the z-score results for categorical judgment of the 'balloons' image. Fig. 4(a) is the z-score results of lightness- and chroma-transformed images to the question 1; How real is the image? Fig. 4(b) is the chroma-transformed results for all three questions. Fig. 4(c) is the lightness transformed results for the same three questions. It can be seen from Fig. 4 that the results for lightness and chroma show a similar characteristics, i.e. the highest image quality occurs in the middle of lightness or chroma levels (that is, for images close to the original). This suggests that photographed images with small colour transformations applied tend to match best with the memory colour, so that they might have the highest image quality scores.

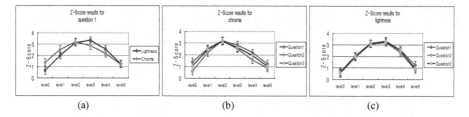

(a)                                    (b)                                    (c)

**Fig. 4.** Z-score results for balloons test images – Categorical judgment

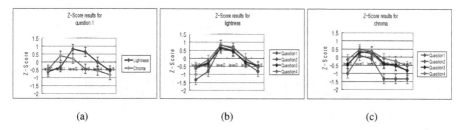

(a)                                    (b)                                    (c)

**Fig. 5.** Z-score results for balloons test images – Pair comparison

Z-score analysis was done for pair comparison experiment. Fig. 5 shows the results. In Fig. 4, the highest score for chroma rendering is level 2 which is slightly less chromatic than the original whereas the highest scores for other rendering attributes except for noise and compression rendering are level 3 which is slightly emphasized in each rendering attribute. In all of the 7 test images except fruit image, similar results were obtained. In fruit image, level 3 has the highest scores in chroma rendering. On the contrary, highest scores are distributed in level 2 and level 3 randomly in pair comparison showed in Fig. 5 except chroma rendering which has the highest score in level 2, and this is the same result as categorical judgment. In all of the 7 test images except fruit image, similar results were obtained. This means human perception of image quality is image dependent when the reference image is shown simultaneously with the test image. From these z-score analysis, it can be assumed that, observers recognise images as optimum quality when the image attributes exhibit slightly more than the original in case of determining the image quality with single test image except for the chroma attribute which observers recognise high image quality when the attribute exhibits slightly less than the original. However, when the original images are shown with the rendered images, this phenomenon disappears and the rendered images with attributes in either slightly more or less than the original images are selected as the highest image quality. The reason can be thought from the experimental results for pair comparison showed in Fig. 5 that observers pay more attention to discriminating the textural difference rather than colour and other attributes when both original and test images are displayed simultaneously. Also texture of the image has higher correlation with the overall image quality than other attributes. Details are explained in next data analysis. Besides, in case of fruit image, people recognise high image quality when test images have little more chromatic attribute than the original. That means people have memory colours about fruits which have

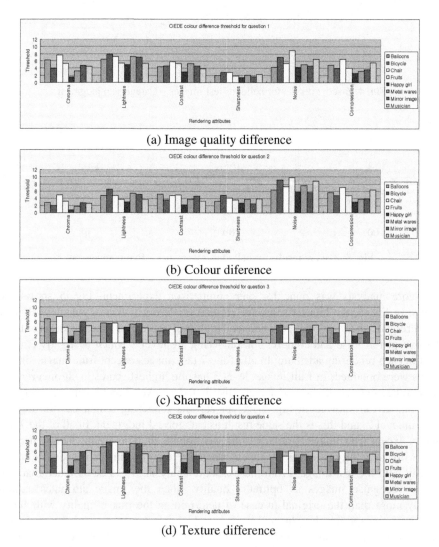

(a) Image quality difference

(b) Colour diference

(c) Sharpness difference

(d) Texture difference

**Fig. 6.** Colour difference thresholds for each question - CIELAB

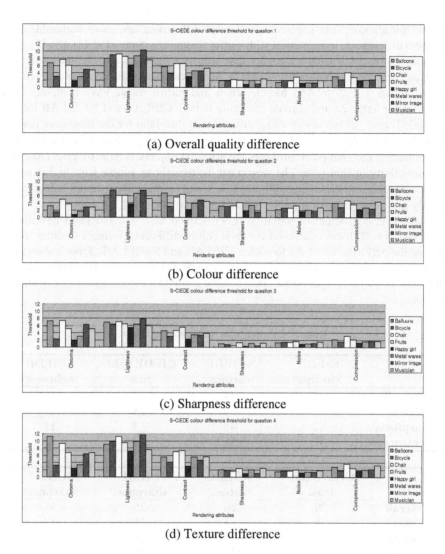

(a) Overall quality difference

(b) Colour difference

(c) Sharpness difference

(d) Texture difference

**Fig. 7.** Colour difference thresholds for each question – S-CIELAB

more chromatic than the original. In noise and compression rendering, level 0 has the smallest attribute change, so the plots are different from other attributes.

For pair-comparison experiment, colour-difference thresholds for each rendering attribute were calculated based upon CIELAB and S-CIELAB colour differences and Fig. 6, and Fig. 7 respectively. In Fig. 7, it was found that the 'Mirror' image had the highest threshold for most of the questions and the 'Happy girl' image had the lowest threshold for all questions. This means that people are less sensitive to the colour change in the 'mirror' image which includes natural objects such as tree, green foliage, blue sky, etc., while people are more sensitive to the 'happy girl' image which includes skin tones. In addition, the lightness has in general higher threshold values than the chroma thresholds. This implies that chroma differences are more noticeable than lightness differences, in agreement with earlier findings by Sano *et al.* [5], [6], [7]

Furthermore, S-CIELAB has higher thresholds for lightness and chroma rendering, whereas CIELAB has higher thresholds for sharpness, noise and compression rendering as shown in Fig. 6. And bicycle, chair and mirror image have relatively high threshold for lightness and chroma rendering in both CIELAB and S-CIELAB formulae while happy girl has lowest or relatively lower threshold for the remaining rendering in both CIELAB and S-CIELAB. This means that people have low sensitivity in discriminating the change of attributes the artificial objects such as bicycle, chair and high sensitivity in skin tone. The reason can be thought as people have higher sensitivity in recognising the change of human skin, and people have memory colours with slightly more chromatic of the objects than the real objects. [8], [9], [10]

Finally, the coefficient of variation (CV) defined as CV = (standard deviation / mean value) × 100 was calculated for each colour-difference formula in order to determine the performance of the formulae, CIELAB and S-CIELAB. Table 3 shows the results of CV calculation between CIEDE and SCIEDE for six different rendering functions. For a perfect agreement between the formula and visual results, CV should be zero.

**Table 3.** CV results for difference questions

|  | CIEDE chroma | SCIEDE chroma | CIEDE light-ness | SCIEDE lightness |
|---|---|---|---|---|
| **Overall** | 41 | 44 | 17 | 15 |
| **Colour** | 48 | 50 | 25 | 21 |
| **Sharptness** | 42 | 45 | 13 | 11 |
| **Texture** | 47 | 50 | 19 | 17 |

|  | CIEDE con-trast | SCIEDE contrast | CIEDE sharpness | SCIEDE sharpness |
|---|---|---|---|---|
| **Overall** | 20 | 26 | 25 | 31 |
| **Colour** | 26 | 34 | 21 | 32 |
| **Sharpness** | 21 | 27 | 29 | 45 |
| **Texture** | 23 | 26 | 21 | 32 |

|  | CIEDE noise | SCIEDE noise | CIEDE com-pression | SCIEDE compression |
|---|---|---|---|---|
| **Overall** | 29 | 32 | 30 | 30 |
| **Colour** | 21 | 24 | 28 | 28 |
| **Sharpness** | 17 | 21 | 31 | 30 |
| **Texture** | 15 | 17 | 30 | 29 |

It can be seen from Table 3 that the two formulae tested gave very similar result, although the CIELAB formula had a slightly better performance in predicting colour difference whereas the S-CIELAB formula was slightly better at predicting lightness and compression changes. The reason is that S-CIELAB uses spatial filtering that can predict spatial attributes such as compression, so its performance is better than CIELAB which only deals with colorimetric attributes of the pixel values. It was expected that most formulae would give similar performance because the transformed images used in the experiment had systematic spatial variations. The results also imply that all images had more or less the similar lightness threshold but large variations in other thresholds. In other words, people are less sensitive to lightness change than other attribute changes such as chroma, contrast, and sharpness changes.

## 4  Conclusion

An experiment was carried out to evaluate the image quality of colour-transformed images to test the performance of the CIELAB and S-CIELAB colour-difference formulae. Eight selected images were used and six colour-transform functions were generated. Each function had 6 distinct levels for rendering the images. Z-scores and colour difference thresholds were calculated from the original and 288 rendered images. The results reported here only include the data analysis of two colour-transform functions, lightness and chroma. The conclusions are summarised below and subsequent data analysis will be carried out for the remaining functions and reported elsewhere.

1) The results for the categorical judgment were similar for all the three questions asked.
2) People prefer a slightly lighter and higher chroma image to a darker and lower chroma one.
3) All images had similar lightness thresholds but large variations in chroma thresholds.
4) The performances of CIELAB and S-CIELAB were similar, but lightness and chroma attributes for each formula have different CV results.

Based on this study, future study will cover the development of image quality prediction model and apply it to the digital image applications such as computer game, digital cinema, digital broadcasting so as to provide the user preferred image content. Also more image quality factors which may affect the image quality of moving images such as temporal frequency will be considered as an advanced research in the future.

## References

1. Moroney N., Fairchild M.D., Hunt R.W.G., Li C., Luo M.R., Newman T.: The CIECAM02 Colour Appearance Model, Proceedings of the tenth Colour Imaging Conference. IS&T/SID, Scottsdale, Arizona, (2002) 23-27.
2. Fairchild M.D, Johnson G.: Meet iCAM: A next-generation colour appearance model, Proceedings of the tenth Colour Imaging Conference, IS&T/SID, Scottsdale, Arizona, (2002) 33-38.

3. Yendrikhovskij S.: Towards perceptually optimal colour reproduction of natural scenes, Colour Imaging Vision and Technology (Wiley, 1999), Chapter 18.
4. Berns S.: Methods for characterizing CRT displays, Displays vol. 6, no.4, (1996) 173-182
5. Sano C., Song T., Luo M.R.: Colour Differences for Complex Images, Proceedings of the eleventh Colour Imaging Conference, IS&T/SID, Scottsdale, Arizona, (2003) 121-125.
6. Uroz J., Luo M.R., Morovic J.: Perception of colour difference between printed images, Colour Science: Exploiting digital media, John Wiley & Sons Ltd., (2002) 49-73
7. Song T., Luo M.R.: Testing colour difference formulae on complex images using a CRT monitor, IS&T SID $8^{th}$ Colour Imaging Conference, (2000) 44-48
8. Coren S., Ward L.M., Enns J.T.: Sensation and perception, Six edition, Wiley, pp. 114-115 (2004)
9. Wichmann, F. A., Sharpe, L. T., Gegenfurtner, K. R.; Contributions of colour to recognition memory for natural scenes. Journal of Experimental Psychology: Learning, Memory & Cognition, 28, (2002) 509-520
10. Newhall, S. M., Burnham, R. W., Clark, J. R.: Comparison of successive with simultaneous colour matching. Journal of the Optical Society of America, 47, (1957) 43-56 (1957)

# Interaction and Participation in Radio Plays: A Novel Approach to an Old Medium

André Melzer, Michael Herczeg, and Oliver Jeskulke

University of Luebeck, Institute for Multimedia and Interactive Systems
Ratzeburger Allee 160, D-23538 Luebeck, Germany
{Melzer, herczeg, jeskulke}@imis.uni-luebeck.de

**Abstract.** Radio plays have recently regained both popular interest and commercial success. Yet, listeners are not provided with either feedback channels or the ability to actively participate in this medium. The TAPE-Player concept described in the present paper extends the radio play medium by adding interactivity as well as participation to the production process. The user takes the roles of both actor and director, which includes verbal interpretation, recording, and editing the dialogues for the selected role(s) as the play's script evolves. The creative freedom is supported by TAPE-Player's underlying hypermedia architecture: audio clips are managed separately and combined dynamically to produce a personalised radio play. The applicability of the concept was corroborated in an empirical study. Specifically, the users welcomed the interaction via TAPE-Player's easy-to-use interface, the creative freedom, and the substantial influence they had in producing radio plays in a personalised entertainment medium.

## 1 Introduction

The concept of radio plays dates back to the early 1920s. Its popularity, as an entertainment medium, is inextricably connected to the triumphant success of the radio medium. The term *radio drama* reflects the pronounced historical tendency to involve literary writers in the making of radio plays. Hence, narrative radio plays may be defined *"...as the acoustical art form that emerged from the development of the radio medium and in which stories are told or presented by means of electro-acoustically recorded and distributed sound material."* [7, p. 46].

Over the last years, radio plays regained popularity and commercial success. This success is surprising, for it contrasts much of the theories and findings of current human-computer interaction literature. While radio plays are confined to a single (i.e., acoustic) modality, current trends in entertainment media try to address multiple sensory channels to provide the user with multimodal experiences. Secondly, "traditional" radio plays do not provide interactivity: the recipient listens without having any adequate form of feedback channel. Thirdly, the listening audience is excluded from the production process. Each feature of a radio play (e.g., script, dialogues, music, and sound effects) is already tightly embedded in the final product that is sold commercially or broadcast.

R. Harper, M. Rauterberg, M. Combetto (Eds.): ICEC 2006, LNCS 4161, pp. 69–80, 2006.
© IFIP International Federation for Information Processing 2006

In the present paper, we argue that radio plays still bear great potential as an entertainment medium. In particular, we believe that some of the medium's apparent shortcomings are in fact its major strengths. These strengths refer to triggering the processes of role-taking, imagination, and immersion. We believe that to tap its full potentials, radio plays —like other well-established media— benefit from careful adaptation to changes in technology [4, 5, 11].

Following the analysis of theoretical concepts that are related to the topic of this paper, we will describe the TAPE-Player[1] concept that seeks to advance radio plays by enabling users to interact with and participate in the medium. We will then introduce the hypertext architecture as the basis of the concept. The detailed description of the implementation will be followed by a description of the evaluation and an analysis of the results. Finally, we will conclude this study with an outlook on future developments of the interactive and participative TAPE-Player concept.

## 2   Imagination and Immersion

Due to their historical background in radio-broadcasting, radio plays are confined to a single (i.e., acoustic) modality and, thus, address only the auditory sensory system of the recipients. Current trends in entertainment multimedia, however, provide the audience with a broad range of multimodal experiences by addressing multiple sensory channels (e.g., vision, haptics) [e.g., 19]. The employment of advanced multimodal elements is most prominent in computer and video games: spatial sound, 3D-animation, and haptic feedback, are thought to create the best possible realistic experience [e.g., 22]. However, rendering photorealistic impressions should not be equated *a priori* with joyful experiences. Rather, the high level of intended realism may also backfire on the medium causing a sense of general distrust to the visually displayed information. In particular, it may establish some form of cognitive set that the displayed picture is "not real", which may then induce confirmatory visual search. Any noticed leaks or glitches will be perceived as particularly disturbing [23]. This notion has already been acknowledged by the game industry. Hence, Satoru Iwata, Nintendo's CEO, stated at the Game Developers Conference 2005 that „*making games look more photorealistic is not the only means of improving the game experience*"[8]. As a consequence, games begin to incorporate more and more narrative content, thus blurring the boundaries between games and stories [e.g., 12].

Likewise, the confinement to a single human receptor system may not at all be disadvantageous for joyfully experiencing the medium. Rather, listening to radio plays challenges the recipient because it requires active participation and creative imagination. This is achieved by the medium's innate necessity for the listener to process cognitively the complexity of the incoming audio data stream. While listening, different acoustic signs (e.g., sound of different voices) have to be actively related to specific narrative functions (e.g., to indicate subjectivity). Radio plays thus follow the broadened approach to narration of media studies [7], which has been applied particularly to film, but also to digital media [13]. In radio plays, the recipient's imaginative processing integrates the different auditory perceptions into a

---

[1] The term TAPE-Player was chosen as a mark of respect to the historic standard carrier medium of radio plays.

coherent and meaningful whole. The resulting perception of the radio play represents the listener's inferred narrative meaning [7], which is based on knowledge, expectations, and preferences and is experienced as highly entertaining.

Imagination is closely related to the concept of immersion, which denotes the various degrees of mental involvement due to the user's focused attention [21]. When computer gamers are totally immersed, they report being cut off from reality and detachment to such an extent that the game is all that mattered [3]. In terms of radio plays, total involvement or the sense of "being there" was most prominent in the audience's reaction to Orson Welles' famous *War of the Worlds* in 1938. The quality of his work and the tendency at that time to believe anything presented on the radio in a realistic way [12] led to the tremendous success, though admittedly, with unexpected effects: Welles' basically far-fetched idea of Martians landing in New Jersey caused literal panic in the streets. Of course, media illiteracy (here: taking the media content for real) is not an indispensable prerequisite to feeling immersed and enjoying entertainment media. Even if people know that they are witnessing staged creations or that they are consuming fiction (e.g., in movies or books), they may nevertheless experience a high level of involvement and immersion [12]. When listening to radio plays, immersion will benefit to the extent people engage in what S. T. Coleridge called *"willing suspension of disbelief"*.

In sum, though radio plays are confined to a single (i.e., acoustic) modality, they challenge the recipients' active participation and creative imagination. The continuous and complex data stream of acoustical features has to be actively integrated to infer narrative meaning. The inherent immersive effect based on narrative storytelling in radio plays is an important source for joyful experiences. In the next section, we will argue that radio plays bear yet another potential: the different roles and voices that offer different character perspectives to the story. Multiple points-of-view serve as a further source for experiencing the story as novel, challenging, and entertaining.

## 3   Interaction and Multiple Points-of-View

People have a general interest in entertainment that provides immediate experiences of personal relevance and individual meaningfulness [e.g., 20]. This interest has its origin in the natural and intrinsic ambition of people to broaden their knowledge and to enhance their abilities [24]. However, this motivation is not solely confined to the individual level. Rather, actively gathering information is also functional behaviour in social interaction. Exploring other peoples' points-of-view reduces the likelihood of misinterpreting behaviour because it grants access to their way of thinking and feeling [6]. Perspective taking through interaction thus fosters essential human skills on a cognitive and emotional individual level, as well as on a socio-cultural level [4]. This is also reflected in theories that suggest storytelling may have originated from a human need to explain and understand their surrounding physical world [cf. 9]. Likewise, the intrinsic motivation to perspective taking is also an important aspect of performing as an active and expressive form of role taking in dramatics.

In human-computer research, however, the term *interaction* is commonly used in a sense to denote the degrees of freedom in controlling form and content of computer-mediated communication. Interaction includes both system input and system output (i.e., system feedback) as a result of user actions. Interaction has emerged as a core variable for the user's mental model or understanding of the system's functions [16]. In addition, the degree of interactivity provided by a system or medium was shown to be crucial for rich and meaningful experiences [20].

Various computer-mediated forms of entertainment have been presented that support perspective taking based on user interaction, while still providing immersive and joyful experiences [9]. Current extensions of experience design have been proposed on this issue [20]. In addition, various forms of interactive or participatory narrative concepts have been conceived to attract and maintain the attention of users, enabling them to switch between different perspectives or roles [13].

More specifically, Mazalek and colleagues [9, 10] suggested computer-mediated storytelling systems based on interactive multiple points-of-view narrative. The authors reasoned that interactive narratives offer the potential to tell more complex and personally meaningful stories than those delivered to a mass audience. By viewing different character perspectives to a given event, different insights may be revealed [9]. Tangible interfaces (i.e., computer-mediated physical objects) served as different points-of-view and provided an atmosphere for immersion in the story.

In accordance with the notion of multiple points-of-view narrative, Melzer et al. [11] proposed a DVD-based hyperfilm called *Deine Wahrheit/Your Truth* that enabled viewers to switch between different character perspectives and, thus, to gain insight into different subjective realities or perceptions. Perspective taking resulted in a comprehensive and coherent interactive, yet entertaining, story experience.

Cassell and Ryokai [4] introduced *StoryMat,* a tangible interface for children that supported perspective taking by recording and recalling children's narrating voices and the movements they make with stuffed toys on a story-evoking quilt. In contrast to the visually dominated DVD hyperfilm [11], the narrating voices in *StoryMat* primarily addressed children's hearing sense. In addition, a moving shadow of the toy was projected that accompanied the narrating voices.

As has already been mentioned, traditional forms of entertainment media, like radio plays or novels, are exclusively confined to non-interactive processes. This lack of interactivity may also have contributed to the little importance of radio plays in entertainment media research. Instead, the predominant focus of media research is on computer and video games and their high degrees of interactivity and participation in the stream of ongoing events [22].

There are only few attempts to bring interactivity into the radio play genre, one being Nick Fisher's *The Wheel of Fortune* for the BBC, which was aired in September 2001. *Wheel of Fortune* is a collection of three plays simultaneously broadcast on three different channels. Each of the three plays focused on the story of a different character. By switching between the channels at fixed key points, listeners actively created their own plays [5]. *Wheel of Fortune* thus resembles *Deine Wahrheit/Your Truth* [11] except for the different (i.e., auditory) sensory channel.

In conclusion, interaction is an important factor both for the user's mental model of the system functions and as a source for personal experiences. Interacting via multiple character viewpoints has proven fruitful in different entertainment media. Multiple points-of-view support perspective taking, which represents an important individual and socio-cultural human skill. This point is still missing in the radio play genre: the user/listener is actually *receiving*, not participating actively and creatively in the sense of speaking or interpreting dialogues like an actor, for example. To our knowledge, this attempt has not as yet been made; this medium is still lacking adequate forms of computer-mediated active user participation. In the next section, we will introduce TAPE-Player, a novel concept that was designed to address this particular issue.

# 4  The Concept of the Interactive Radio Play Environment

Based on the analysis in the previous sections we designed TAPE-Player, a computer-mediated interactive concept, which aims at supporting active and creative participation in radio plays. At the same time, TAPE-Player should perpetuate the entertaining and immersing effects that occur while listening to the medium. Due to the medium's origin as *radio drama*, user participation in our radio play concept was designed to match expressive performing in dramatics as closely as possible. This refers to the creative verbal interpretation of dialogues specified in a visually displayed script. Hence, after having selected a certain character or role, the user should play a significant part in the recording process without limitation to their creative freedom (e.g., time allotted for speaking the dialogue). The final play should thus become the result of creative idiosyncratic work, thereby reflecting the user's own personality. In addition, other functions, which usually require additional software tools (e.g., audio editing), should also be integrated in a single application.

As will be discussed in the next section, the TAPE-Player concept requires a flexible underlying architecture to manage separately stored tracks (e.g., voice recordings). This architecture supports the dynamic and seamless combination of information into a single and unique data file, the final radio play. Following the description of the form of interaction, we will present the modular structure of TAPE-Player as well as the application's actual use.

## 4.1  The Hypermedia Structure

Despite the tendency towards verbally dominated storytelling, a multiplicity of acoustical features (e.g., voice, music, sound effects, fading in/out, cutting, mixing) usually play an important role in radio drama production [7]. In traditional radio plays, these features form an interconnected system stored in a single continuous data stream. Interactive radio plays, however, inevitably require flexibility in terms of handling separate and interchangeable information or data files. In the TAPE-Player concept this refers to selecting and replacing speakers for different characters or roles. This issue has been addressed by hyperaudio [2], a concept that denotes an audio-based hypermedia system. Hypermedia systems like the *WorldWideWeb* allow authors to create hyperlinks between pieces of content (i.e., hypernodes or frames), thereby forming a non-linear graph structure or web that users may actively navigate [25]. According to their actions at each hypernode, single components will be combined at run time.

For the film medium, Naimark [14] presented the hyperfilms *Aspen Moviemap* and *3D Moviemap*. A related approach was suggested by Melzer et al. [11]. Viewers of their DVD-hyperfilm *Deine Wahrheit/Your Truth* were asked to select one of the different characters' points-of-view. The story then moved forward in a linear fashion from one chapter to the next. At each chapter, however, viewers either switched between different narrative perspectives or stayed with the current point-of-view.

The non-linear hypermedia structure was adopted for the TAPE-Player concept. Selecting and replacing individual speakers required a specific audio clip structure. Particularly, the system should not impose any restrictions on voice recordings for the selected character/role (i.e., time allotted for speaking a given dialogue, pronunciation, or accentuation). The system should also be able to insert seamlessly recordings into the story to result in a coherent, but entirely new radio play. Since it is common that more than one character will be speaking at the same time, it is impossible to reconstruct the play on the basis of simple relations between frames.

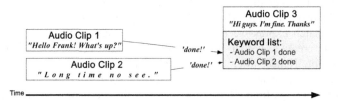

**Fig. 1.** Audio Clip 3 (*right*) may start because the keywords occurred

Rather, multiple relations need to be logically interconnected, as was suggested in the interval script concept [18]. Hence, the abstract audio clips in TAPE-Player were linked by keywords similar to token and transitions in a Petri net. Only when keywords occur, the preconditions of an audio clip for play-back are met (figure 1).

### 4.2 Combining Interaction and Immersion

Interactive entertainment media have to acknowledge the inherent conflict that exists between interaction and immersion [9]. Users, who are immersed in a story, are, for example, less inclined to interrupt the experience through complex interaction. Hence, any form of obstruction of immersion induced by the interface has to be minimized.

For the TAPE-Player concept, we speculated that, once the voice recording process starts, users will mainly direct their focal attention to the dialogues that are visually displayed. To avoid disruptive attention shifts, any form of necessary interaction should therefore be indicated and occur within the displayed script. Hence, indispensable events that require user actions are included as stage directions and indicated by embedded hyperlinks within the script. These hyperlinks follow Web design conventions (i.e., blue underlined letters) and are therefore likely to be coupled with the triggering of events in users' memory (i.e., established part of their mental model). Thus, they do not require unnecessary mental resources. Hyperlinks in TAPE-Player denote, for example, events like starting/stopping of additional sounds, or sending keywords to other roles. Simply moving the mouse across hyperlinks triggers the corresponding sound clip, thereby further reducing the mental effort associated with the interaction. In addition, this "mouse-over effect" helps to avoid clicking noises. More importantly, however, it supports natural interaction in form of a hand-like gesture that reduces the unwanted visibility of the computer interface [15].

Hence, during voice recording, users are totally free to interpret creatively their selected role by changing or adding words or noises (e.g., whistling, wheezing).

In conclusion, the TAPE-Player interface is designed to warrant an immersive experience by supporting the focalisation of attention to the evolving story, rather than to the handling of the interface: TAPE-Player lets the user interpret creatively her selected role with all the freedom of an actor [cf. 17]. Yet, whatever the user does will affect the radio play as a result of her work, thereby reflecting her own personality.

### 4.3  Using the TAPE-Player Application

The TAPE-Player uses audio files in the wave file format. Any other information (e.g., story content, user actions) is stored in XML. TAPE-Player was implemented in JAVA using the Java Media Framework (JMF).

In the application architecture (figure 2), the system input and output are provided via microphone, headphones, and TAPE-Player's graphical user interface (GUI). A dedicated module serves as a production manager and coordinates both processing of incoming signals and regulation of workflow. The knowledge and communication module synchronises the radio play. It directs the communication between different modules and stores keywords into a repository. Any part of the software that may send keywords also receives information of incoming keywords. Finally, a mixing module provides the export of the radio play into a single wave file.

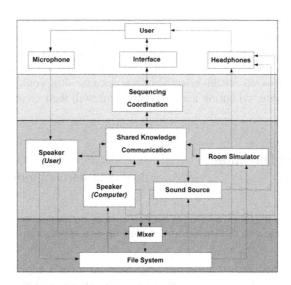

**Fig. 2.** The architecture of the TAPE-Player application

Pressing the record button causes TAPE-Player to run the radio play (figure 3). Stored sound clips play according to the course of the script. To guide the user visually, any current dialogue is highlighted in a grey-shaded frame in the application's GUI. Once a dialogue for the selected role(s) starts, the frame colour changes to red. This indicates that the user may now start interpreting and recording their dialogue.

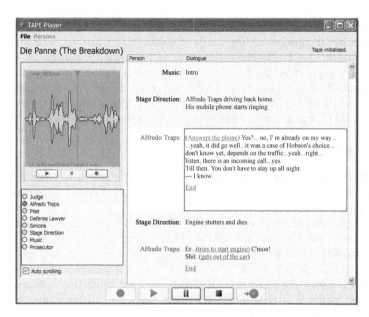

**Fig. 3.** Main control window in TAPE-Player with audio editor (*top left*) and script (*right*)

For stage directions, and if the cast is incomplete such that some roles are missing their audio sound files, a karaoke-like function will automatically and progressively colour the text red (figure 4). This visualisation (i.e., the visual anchor) provides the user with additional orientation in the course of the script. Please note that the karaoke function is not displayed for the selected role(s) because this would force the user to keep up with the letter colouring and, thus, interfere with their creative interpretation of the dialogues.

> **Stage Direction:** Alfredo Traps driving back home.
> His mobile phone starts ringing.

**Fig. 4.** Karaoke-like progressive letter colouring for stage directions and to compensate for absent speakers (Please note that letters turn red in the original application)

Sound effects specified in the script (e.g., starting a car's engine, closing doors) will be unobtrusively initiated by the user (see previous section) and played instantly during the recording process. Following the script's run-through, TAPE-Player automatically adds atmospheric background sound clips according to the script (e.g., reverberation). Users may then edit their audio recordings or listen to the resulting radio play by pressing the play button. Alternatively, pressing the export button will cause TAPE-Player to save the entire play as a single wave file that can be played with any other audio applications. Hence, TAPE-Player does not only support the joyful experience of acoustic play acting in the recording process, but also provides the rewarding experience of listening to a personalised version of the radio play, which may be shared with others.

# 5 Evaluation

TAPE-Player was empirically tested as an online tutorial that comprised 12 HTML pages. A total of 16 students and scientific researchers participated (11 male, 5 female). Their mean age was 25.6 ranging from 18-40 years ($SD$=5.18).

Participants were initially requested to download and install the required components. This included the JAVA and JMF environment, the TAPE-Player application, and the first ten minutes of a pre-produced version of F. Dürrenmatts 1961 radio play *Die Panne/The Breakdown* (German version only)[2]. For comparability reasons, participants selected the role of Alfredo Traps, one of the main characters. After the main menu and hyperlink functions had been introduced, participants were given an interactive example and practised the triggering of events (e.g., start/stop recording). They were particularly encouraged to bring their own individual interpretation into the voice recording of the dialogues for the selected character. Then, the audio editing functions were introduced and used with an interactive example. After participants had exported the final wave file, they listened to their radio play version. A novel thirty-one item questionnaire concluded the tutorial. The questionnaire determined demographics, the participants' interest in different forms of media, and the actual media use (e.g., radio plays, film). In addition, participants rated the quality of the tutorial and the complexity of the task. Similarly, they assessed the tangibility and the usability of the application, the interaction possibilities, and the overall TAPE-Player concept. Finally, participants gave future prospects to upcoming developments of the interactive radio play concept.

## 5.1 Results and Discussion

The following section presents the main results based on the questionnaire ratings. For each item, participants' ratings were recorded on a four-point scale, ranging from 1 (positive, e.g., *"I fully agree"*) to 4 (negative, e.g., *"I don't agree at all"*). The following details represent mean scores ($M$) and standard deviations ($SD$). Pearson's correlation coefficient ($r$) was used to denote correlations between items. For the statistical analysis, alpha was set at .05. An asterisk (*) indicates a significant result.

Mean ratings showed that participants thoroughly liked the TAPE-Player concept ($M$=1.06, $SD$=0.25). The concept also satisfied participants' expectations concerning the medium's performance ($M$=1.44, $SD$=0.51) and the overall usability of the system ($M$=1.50, $SD$=0.52). Participants reported that they were well aware of what to do in the course of the script ($M$=1.31, $SD$=0.48). Handling the interface ($M$=1.38, $SD$=0.50) and triggering the events by moving the mouse across hyperlinks ($M$=1.56, $SD$=0.63) was rated "easy". Specifically, controllability of the TAPE-Player interface was "rather good" to "very good" ($M$=1.38, $SD$=0.50).

---

[2] The use of *Die Panne* was kindly permitted by the publisher Diogenes Verlag, Zurich, Switzerland.

In line with our hypotheses, participants strongly appreciated both their creative freedom in interpreting the selected role ($M=1.25$, $SD=0.45$), and their influence on the entire radio play ($M=1.63$, $SD=0.50$). Moreover, a majority of the participants (.69) reported that they had felt like having been part of a vivid story. Their sense of immersion substantially benefited from being allowed to using their own voices to "interact" with the system, which strongly supported their own creativity ($r=.55*$).

Although the overall use of radio plays did not influence their ratings of the TAPE-Player concept ($r=-.02$), participants' prognosis concerning the further success of the concept was mediated by their overall interest in the radio play medium ($M=2.06$, $SD=0.93$). This is illustrated by the critical estimation of the applicability of the concept for visual media, like video and film ($M=2.31$, $SD=1.14$): though participants reported liking movies ($M=1.69$, $SD=0.60$), fans of radio plays were less interested in this medium ($r=-.56*$). However, it was the fans of radio plays that reported looking very much forward to more plays for the TAPE-Player ($r=.65*$). Similarly, they had a positive attitude towards social interaction and engagement in future communities ($r=.71*$) and also wished to use the TAPE-Player concept on the Internet ($r=.59*$).

To sum up, the evaluation data from the pilot study substantiated TAPE-Player as a successful interactive and participative concept. Though most participants came from the target group of radio play users, which might have positively biased their ratings, we conclude from the data that TAPE-Player satisfied even the high expectations in this group. The concept meets the requirements for the system functions. In addition, the interface also required only standard levels of computer literacy. Most importantly, participants thoroughly liked both the basic concept and the experience of creative freedom. The interactive and participative radio play concept was considered a promising supplement to traditional forms of the radio play medium.

# 6   Concluding Remarks

The TAPE-Player concept addresses the basic human motivation to exploring actively others' points-of-view. Perspective taking is provided by enabling the user to select a character or role, which may then be creatively verbally interpreted. In the voice recording process, the user may, in a sense, *become* the selected person. In addition, TAPE-Player lowers the organisational threshold for active participation in some form of dramatics: users become actors in the privacy of their home. Yet, they are a fully integrated part of the final radio play.

We believe that using TAPE-Player is not only entertaining, but also highly rewarding. On both cognitive and emotional levels, the outcome (i.e., the final radio play) may lead to experiencing *self-efficacy*, a term coined by Bandura [1], which denotes the individual belief that one has the capabilities to execute the courses of actions required to manage future situations. In current media research, self-efficacy is primarily associated with the rewarding effects of gaming [22]. This behaviour-influencing effect of productive creativity is not present in traditional radio plays that are confined to processes of imagination. TAPE-Player, however, directly supports the intrinsic motivation of people to broaden their knowledge and to enhance their abilities [24] by means of creative expression. We are currently developing a complementary authoring tool, *TAPE-Maker,* which will even further extend user participation such that writing scripts and composing interactive radio plays will be supported.

How can current state-of-the-art technology address the universal interest in stories and entertainment that provide experiences of personal relevance and individual meaningfulness? It has been suggested that the best and newest technology may well resemble the oldest forms of culture [4]. Likewise, Nick Fisher, writer of the interactive radio play *The Wheel of Fortune,* argued that *"… there can be a creative tension where interactivity and traditional narrative and character blend together"* [5]. In the present paper, we have presented a concept that follows this notion by offering creative participation in a popular entertainment medium. Based on its flexible hypermedia structure, TAPE-Player actively supports perspective and role-taking and triggers processes of imagination and immersion. Most importantly, then, the underlying technology supports the oldest-of-all human cultural behaviour, telling stories.

# References

1. Bandura, A.: Self-efficacy. In Ramachaudran, V.S. (Ed.): Encyclopedia of Human Behavior 4. Academic Press, New York (1994) 71-81
2. Barbará, D., Naqvi, S.A.: The AudioWeb. Proc. of CIKM 97, New York, ACM Press (1997) 97-104
3. Brown, E., Cairns, P.: A Grounded Investigation of Game Immersion. Proc. of CHI 2004, ACM Press, New York (2004) 1297-1300
4. Cassell, J., Ryokai, K.: Making Space for Voice: Technologies to Support Children's Fantasy and Storytelling. Personal and Ubiquitous Computing 5 (2001) 169-190
5. Eastgate Systems, Inc.: God, Random Access, or Roulette? Interview with Nick Fisher. http://www.eastgate.com/HypertextNow/archives/Fisher.html accessed 03/27/2006
6. Flavell, J.H., Botkin; P.T., Fry, C.L., Wright, J.W., Jarvis, P.E.: The development of role-taking and communication skills in children. New York, Wiley (1968)
7. Huwiller, E.: Storytelling by Sound: a Theoretical Frame for Radio Drama Analysis. The Radio Journal: Int. Stud. Broadcast Audio Media 3 (2005) 45-59
8. Iwata, S.: Speech held at the Game Developers Conference 2005. http://www.kotaku.com/gaming/text/2005_gdc_Iwata_Keynote.pdf accessed 03/23/2006
9. Mazalek, A.: Tangible Interfaces for Interactive Point-of-View Narratives. Unpublished MS Thesis, MIT Media Lab (2001)
10. Mazalek, A., Davenport, G., Ishii, H.: Tangible Viewpoints: A Physical Approach to Multimedia Stories. Proc. of Multimedia 2002, ACM Press, New York (2002) 153-160
11. Melzer, A., Hasse, S., Jeskulke, O., Schön, I., Herczeg, M.: The Interactive and Multi-protagonist Film: A Hypermovie on DVD. Proc. of ICEC 2004, Springer Verlag, Berlin Heidelberg New York (2004) 193-203
12. Miller, J.: Storytelling evolves on the web: case study: EXOCOG and the future of storytelling. Interactions, 12 (2005) 30-47
13. Murray, J.H.: Hamlet on the Holodeck: The Future of Narrative in Cyberspace. Free Press, New York (1997)
14. Naimark, M.: A 3D Moviemap and a 3D Panorama. Proc. of SPIE 1997 (1997)
15. Norman, D.A.: The Invisible Computer. MIT Press, Cambridge, MA (1999)
16. Norman, D.A., Draper, S.: User Centered System Design: New Perspectives on Human-Computer Interaction. Lawrence Erlbaum Associates, Hillsdale, NJ (1986)

17. Perlin, K., Goldberg, A.: Improv: A System for Scripting Interactive Actors in Virtual Worlds. Proc. of SIGGRAPH 96, ACM Press, New York (1996) 205-216
18. Pinhanez, C.S., Mase, K., Bobick, A.F.: Interval Scripts: a Design Paradigm for Story-Based Interactive Systems. Proc. of CHI 1997, ACM Press, New York (1997) 287-294
19. Ryoichi, W., Yuichi, I., Masatsugu, A., Yoshifumi, K., Fumio, K., Hideo, K.: The Soul of ActiveCube: Implementing a Flexible, Multimodal, Three-dimensional Spatial Tangible Interface. Comp. in Entertainment 2 (2004) 1-13
20. Shedroff, N.: Information Interaction Design: A Unified Field Theory of Design. In Jacobsen, R. (Ed.): Information Design. MIT Press, Cambridge (1999) 267-292
21. Sherman, W., Craig, A.: Understanding Virtual Reality. Interface, Application, and Design. Morgan Kaufmann Publishers, San Francisco (2002)
22. Vorderer, P., Hartmann, T., Klimmt, C.: Explaining the Enjoyment of Playing Video Games: the Role of Competition. Proc. of ICEC 2003, ACM Press, New York (2003) 1-9
23. Wages, R., Grünvogel, S., Grützmacher, B.: How Realistic is Realism? Considerations on the Aesthetics of Computer Games. Proc. of ICEC 2004, Springer Verlag, Berlin Heidelberg New York (2004) 216-225
24. White, R.W.: Motivation Reconsidered: The Concept of Competence. Psych. Rev., 66, (1959) 297-333
25. Woodhead, N.: Hypertext and Hypermedia: Theory and Applications. Addison-Wesley Longman, Boston, MA (1991)

# Real-Time Monitoring System for TV Commercials Using Video Features

Sung Hwan Lee, Won Young Yoo, and Young-Suk Yoon

Electronics and Telecommunications Research Institute (ETRI),
161 Gajeong-dong, Yuseong-gu, Deajeon, 305-350, Korea
{lovin, zero2, ys.yoon}@etri.re.kr

**Abstract.** For companies, TV commercial is a very important way to introduce and advertise their products. It is expensive to put an advertisement on TV. So these companies generally charge other companies to monitor that their TV commercials are broadcasted properly as contracted. Currently, these monitorings have been done manually. The monitoring company records all the TV programs and their air-times while they are being broadcasted. Then the agent checks the starting-times and the ending-times of TV commercials. Video retrieval and matching techniques can be used to monitor TV commercials automatically. By extracting visual features that can identify commercials, we can measure similarities and identify a target video from thousands of videos. To process all the TV programs of 24 hours a day, feature extraction and matching process must be done in real-time. In this paper, we designed the visual feature DB for real-time processing and implemented real-time TV commercial monitoring system. To construct the DB, we extracted scene change information, block-based dominant colors and edge pattern histograms of TV commercial clips.

## 1 Introduction

Many companies introduce their products on TV. It is very expensive to put a commercial on TV. So these companies generally charge other companies to verify that their TV commercials are actually broadcasted as contracted. Currently, monitoring-jobs are done by manually. All the TV programs are recorded with their air-time. Then the agent checks the start time and the length of the commercial. There are several tens of TV channels to monitor. It's a hard work to be done manually. However, using video identification techniques, we can automate the monitoring job. Most video identifications are done by feature extracting and matching it. There are many visual features that can be extracted from a video. The more features make it more accurate but requires more time. To make it useful, all the processes must be done in real-time.

In content based video retrieval and identification, the video sequence is often segmented into shots and the video content is described based on those shot content descriptors [1, 2, 3]. This shot based content representation is suitable for indexing and retrieval. After shot boundaries are located, the content of frames within the shot can be modeled and efficiently matched against those in the database. Key frame color

R. Harper, M. Rauterberg, M. Combetto (Eds.): ICEC 2006, LNCS 4161, pp. 81–89, 2006.
© IFIP International Federation for Information Processing 2006

histogram is a widely used color content descriptor for shot. One or more frames are selected to represent the shot, and the selection criterion can be based on color or motion [1, 4]. However, when noise is added or frame rate changes, different frames may be chosen as key frames, which will lead to variation of this color descriptor. To reduce this variation, robust color histogram descriptors are proposed [5]. In this descriptor, the color histogram is computed from all the frames within the shot. The simple way is averaging color histograms of all the frames, and it works well with most cases. Although this color histogram descriptor is robust to rotation, scaling, translation and outlier frames, it is not robust to color distortion that lasts in a group of frames. For example, brightness and contrast of the whole video are significantly modified in a way that the visual quality does not change much. Since this type of content modification can be conveniently implemented in many video editing tools, content attackers can take advantage of this means to produce pirated copies which can avoid detection of video identification methods based on color. Therefore robustness to such type of color distortions should be really considered in content based video copy detection. To avoid the color distortion difficulty, local edge descriptor is proposed as key frame feature [6], but this feature is sensitive key frame shift. In key frame representation one shot maps to a point in a feature space, while other approaches represent the shot content by feature trajectory. In [7, 8, 9] the color feature of each frame is quantized into symbols, and the shot is represented by a compact symbol sequence. Because the sequence length can be variable under different frame rates, shot matching often employs symbol edit operations or dynamic programming which can be very complex when the number of frames is large. The quantization process can tolerate some range of color variation, but if the feature vectors of group of frames shift across the quantization boundaries, this string representation will totally change to another one whose similarity with the original one can change dramatically based on symbol sequence matching. We used the scene change information and the block-based dominant color [10] and the edge pattern histogram of a scene as visual feature.

## 2   System Components

Our system consists of three major components – feature extractor, feature DB and matching module in Fig. 1. The 'feature extractor' extracts video features such as scene change information, block-based dominant color and edge pattern histogram. All the extracted features are stored in the 'feature DB'. The 'matching module' retrieves the feature DB and performs similarity measure.

We build the DB using about 250 TV commercials. Each commercial has a length of about 10 seconds. The DB is constructed with known commercials initially. While our system monitors the captured TV programs, a new commercial can be found. If an unidentified video clip that is located among two commercials and the length is shorter than 30 seconds, we consider it as a commercial. In most case, the commercials are located in series and the length is shorter than 30 seconds. The features of a new commercial are extracted and added to the feature DB.

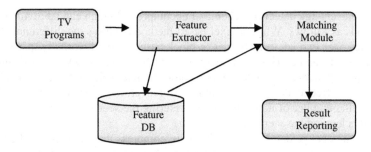

**Fig. 1.** System components

Our system works as follows. We build feature DB from already known TV commercials. At that time, feature extractor is used. Then, TV capture module captures all the TV programs and store the captured video clip. Feature extractor gets features from the captured clip and the matching module retrieves features from the feature DB. In matching module, each similarity functions of the features are used to find most similar commercial.

## 3 Feature Extraction

Comparing frames between two videos is a very simple and ignorant manner to find out whether they are absolutely the same or not. Although a video is semantically equal to another, the video can be slightly different from another because of all kinds of noise. Therefore, we should consider visual features to detect video data owing to both identifying the semantically same video and rising sharply a processing time in those schemes. There are many visual features that can be used to identify a video data. However, we cannot utilize a lot of features to detect exactly a video data owing to a waste of processing time. So, we chose three visual features such as scene change, edge, and dominant color.

Our approach progresses as follows. First, the scene change detection method reduces video clip into several key frames and produces scene length information. Next, the edge information for key frames obtains the shape of video data. Concurrently, we employ block-based dominant color in order to identify commercials with different caption because TV commercials have captions of broadcast company in many cases. Most captions are located in the corner of the video screen. So we applied block-based dominant color to identify video data with different caption despite the same video sequences. The proposed system works very well through simple and fast visual features.

### 3.1 Scene Length

Scene change is defined as a switch from a frame to a consecutive frame. Thus, scene change detection schemes are used to divide a video data into its elementary scenes. We can classify scene change detection methods in two groups such as compress or uncompress domain.

First, scene change detection scheme in uncompress domain can be divided by several methods as follows. While a pixel based method analyses the difference between pixel values over two adjacent frames, a block based method works by partitioning a frame into blocks and carrying out analysis on each of those blocks. Histogram representation uses that histogram has either colors or intensities grouped into bins and represented the frequencies of those values. Moreover, the edge change ratio involves calculating the number of new edge pixels entering the scene change and the number of old pixels leaving the scene change.

Next, scene change detection algorithms in compress domain can use the types of frames, DCT coefficients, and motion vectors. And an unsupervised clustering algorithm defines shot detection as a clustering problem where are clustered into 2 classes, a shot boundary class and non-shot boundary class.

**Scene Change Detection Scheme.** In a general pixel based method, the difference value at every pixel position within a frame is added and the result normalized, giving a difference which can be compared against a threshold to determine where this is a boundary frame. Eq. (1) defines $\Delta I_{x,y}(t)$ as the absolute value of pixel difference with $\Delta t$ frame distance

$$\Delta I_{x,y}(t) = \left| I_{x,y}(t + \Delta t) - I_{x,y}(t) \right| \tag{1}$$

where $I_{x,y}(t)$ denotes intensity value of pixel located at $(x,y)$ when time $t$. If we set $\Delta t = 1$, we could get the absolute value of consecutive frame difference.

We obtain the absolute sum of the inter-frame difference $Sum_{|FD|}(t)$ using Eq. (1). This is a simplest way of evaluating an image difference.

$$Sum_{|FD|}(t) = \sum_x \sum_y \left| \Delta I_{x,y}(t) \right| \tag{2}$$

Unfortunately, it is difficult to distinguish between a large change in a small area and a small change in a large area when we use the sum of frame difference value. So, we tend to be unable to detect cuts when a small part of a frame undergoes a large, rapid change.

To improve detection performance, we proposed $Rate_{|FD|}(t)$ meaning the number of pixels into the number of absolute values of inter-frame difference larger than a given threshold. Eq (3) denotes $Rate_{|FD|}(t)$,

$$Rate_{|FD|}(t) = \frac{n(\{\Delta I_{x,y}(t) \mid 2^{b-4} < \Delta I_{x,y}(t)\})}{x_{max} \times y_{max}} \tag{3}$$

where, the function $n$ represents the number of set, $b$ is defined as the used number of bits to represent the intensity of pixels. If we use 8 bits on the intensity channel, $2^{b-4}$ should be 16 in which $2^{b-4}$ is the empirical threshold. We can easily detect scene changes due to non-linear relationship between the proposed $Rate_{|FD|}(t)$ and $Sum_{|FD|}(t)$.

Furthermore, we designed a scene change detection filter so as to detect scene change in spite of frame rate conversion, slow motion, abrupt flash. The proposed method feeds $Rate_{|FD|}(t)$ the scene change detection filter composed of local maximum filter and minimum filter. Eq. (4) and Eq. (5) represent filters computing maximum and minimum value within the local range, respectively.

$$MAX_{range}(t) = \max(Rate_{|FD|}(t+i)) \quad (-\frac{range}{2} \leq i \leq \frac{range}{2} - 1) \quad (4)$$

$$MIN_{range}(t) = \min(Rate_{|FD|}(t+j)) \quad (-\frac{range}{2} + 1 \leq i \leq \frac{range}{2}) \quad (5)$$

And then, we define the scene change detection filter as Eq. (6) using Eq. (4) and Eq. (5)

$$SCDF(t) = MIN_4(MAX_4(t)) - MAX_2(MIN_2(MIN_4(MAX_4(t)))) \quad (6)$$

Figure 2 shows a simple process of proposed scene change detection filter. Fig. 2 (a) is a simple example in order to simulate those processes. The proposed scheme obtains the output of scene change detecting filter. It is getting on to zero but has value lager than 0.2 when a frame is scene change in general.

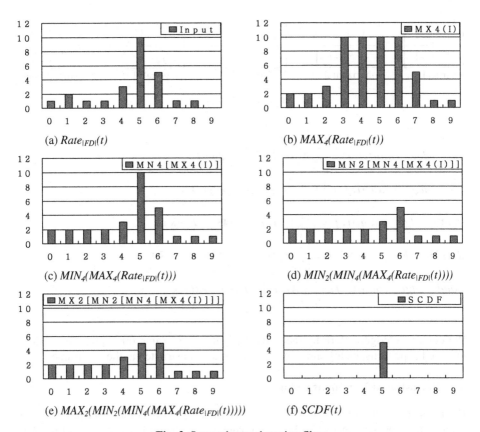

(a) $Rate_{|FD|}(t)$

(b) $MAX_4(Rate_{|FD|}(t))$

(c) $MIN_4(MAX_4(Rate_{|FD|}(t)))$

(d) $MIN_2(MIN_4(MAX_4(Rate_{|FD|}(t))))$

(e) $MAX_2(MIN_2(MIN_4(MAX_4(Rate_{|FD|}(t)))))$

(f) $SCDF(t)$

**Fig. 2.** Scene change detecting filter

**Property of Scene Change.** As we mentioned before, we make a good use of a detected scene change as a visual feature. The found scene changes offer largely two facts. First, the scene change represents key frame at a scene. Thus, we do not need to consider other frames to process in real-time at the scene. Next, the scene length computed from detected scene changes obtains a specific character of video data. Furthermore, we can overcome the synchronization problem detecting where the start position of stored video set is in quarry video.

## 3.2 Histogram for Edge Pattern

Edges can be used as a shape descriptor of an object in video data. There are many methods using edge to identify an object. However, we need only simple feature with edge characteristics to process a video identification system in real-time. Consequently, we used a histogram of main directions for the edges to describe the object. We classified the directions of edges with six patterns such as vertical edge, horizontal edge, diagonal_45 edge, diagonal_135 edge, no directional edge, and no edge. A frame occurred by the scene change is divided into small blocks and then we can compute the histogram of edge pattern for blocks with Eq. (7). Finally, we obtain edge directions using edge filters from Fig. 3.

| 1 | -1 |
|---|---|
| 1 | -1 |

a)vertical

| 1 | 1 |
|---|---|
| -1 | -1 |

b)horizontal

| $\sqrt{2}$ | 0 |
|---|---|
| 0 | $-\sqrt{2}$ |

c)diagonal_45

| 0 | $\sqrt{2}$ |
|---|---|
| $-\sqrt{2}$ | 0 |

d)diagonal_135

| 2 | -2 |
|---|---|
| -2 | 2 |

e)no directional

**Fig. 3.** Edge filters

$$ver\_edge\_count(i,j) = \left| \sum_{k=0}^{3} A_k(i,j) * ver\_edge(k) \right|$$

$$hor\_edge\_count(i,j) = \left| \sum_{k=0}^{3} A_k(i,j) * hor\_edge(k) \right|$$

$$dia45\_edge\_count(i,j) = \left| \sum_{k=0}^{3} A_k(i,j) * dia45\_edge(k) \right| \tag{7}$$

$$dia135\_edge\_count(i,j) = \left| \sum_{k=0}^{3} A_k(i,j) * dia135\_edge(k) \right|$$

$$nond\_edge\_count(i,j) = \left| \sum_{k=0}^{3} A_k(i,j) * nond\_edge(k) \right|$$

We determine edge pattern by the maximum number of same direction. After calculating edge patterns, histogram of edge patterns are constructed at the key frame.

## 3.3 Block-Based Dominant Color

Dominant color is defined in MPEG-7 standard [10]. This color descriptor is most suitable for representing local (object or image region) features where a small number of colors are enough to characterize the color information in the region of interest. Whole images are also applicable, for example, flag images or color trademark images.

Color quantization is used to extract a small number of representing colors in each region/image. The percentage of each quantized color in the region is calculated correspondingly. A spatial coherency on the entire descriptor is also defined, and is used in similarity retrieval.

```
1) Assign  each  color  to  its  cluster  using  Euclidean
   distance
2) Calculate cluster centroid.
3) Calculate  the  total  distortion  and  split  colorBins
   to  increase  CurrentBinNum  until  CurrentBinNum  =  Fi-
   nalBinNum.
4) Merge colorBins using a clustering method.
5) Repeat to 1) until process all pixels of a block.
```

TV commercials are captured with the captions of the broadcast company. It is required to identify a commercial with different logos. Figure 4 shows the logo area of TV commercials. Most logos are located at the corners of video screen. The logo-blocks are removed while we extract dominant color.

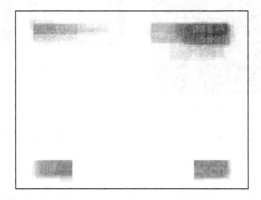

**Fig. 4.** Caption locations of captured TV commercials

## 4   Matching Method

The captured TV programs are processed by the feature extractor to produce features. The extracted features are passed to the matching module. Matching module retrieves candidates using scene length information using Eq. (8).

$$C_i = ID(V_j) \, if \, \sum \left|(SL_{q,k} - SL_{d,k})\right| < T$$

$$where \, ID(V) \, is \, ID \, of \, a \, video \, V, \tag{8}$$

$$SL_{q,k} \, is \, k\text{-}th \, shot \, length \, of \, query,$$

$$SL_{d,k} \, is \, k\text{-}th \, shot \, length \, of \, database$$

Using threshold $T$, we generate the candidates which have similar shot length. The final similarity function is Eq. (9).

$$S(C_i) = w1 * \sum |DC(C_i) - DC(q)| + w2 * \sum |EH(C_i) - EH(q)|$$

(9)

*where w1, w2 is weight constant*

We combined the summation of the differences of the shot length with weight value $w1$ and the summation of the differences of the dominant colors with $w2$.

## 5   Experimental Results

Figure 5 shows the implementation of our system. Fig. 5 (a) is main application that can manage the feature DB, identify captured video and add a new clip to the DB. Fig. 5 (b) is a result window that can compare the query video and the result.

Figure 6 shows feature DB management tool. With this tool, we can search, add, update and remove feature DB records.

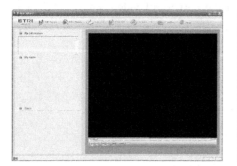

a) Main application                              b) Result window

**Fig. 5.** Implementation result

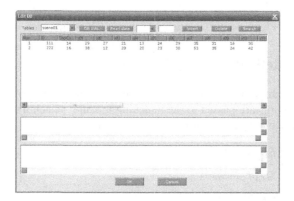

**Fig. 6.** Feature DB management tool

We used a computer with performance of P-4 3.0GHz CPU and 1GB memory. We constructed feature DB with recent 260 commercials in common database management system (DBMS). In order to check the performance of proposed system, we fed our TV commercial monitoring system into 364 minutes query video composed of 91 query video clips of 4 minutes length. Table 1 shows the experimental result. Our system requires about a half of playing time in order to identify video data. It's fast enough to process in real time. The matching rate is approximately 90%.

**Table 1.** Query result

| Length of Query video | Success | False Positive | False Negative | Processing Time |
|---|---|---|---|---|
| 364 minutes | 87.51% | 9.27% | 3.22% | 175 minutes |

## 6  Conclusion

TV commercials are effective and expensive way to introduce a product. Currently, TV commercials are monitored to verify the contract manually. We designed and implemented the TV commercial monitoring system. We employed shot detection method, histogram of edge patterns, and block-based dominant color to identify a video. By combining three features, our system can identify 90% commercials in real-time. Our system can be improved with other features. So we are still in progress to develop features that can be processed in real-time.

## References

1. Y. Rui, T. S. Huang, and S. Mehrotra, Exploring video structure beyond the shots, Proc. of IEEE Conf. on Multimedia Computing and Systems, June 1998.
2. H. J. Zhang, J.Wu, D. Zhong, and S.W. Somaliar, An integrated system for content-based video retrieval and browsing, Pattern Recognition 30 (1997), no. 4, 643–658.
3. J.M. Snchez, X. Binefa, and J. Vitri, Shot partitioning based recognition of tv commercials, Multimedia Tools and Applications 18 (2002), 233–247.
4. W. Wolf, Key frame selection by motion analysis, Proc. ICASSP, vol. II, 1996, pp. 1228–1231.
5. A.Mfit Ferman, A.MuratTekalp, and Rajiv Mehrotra, Robust color histogram descriptors for video segment retrieval and identification, IEEE Trans. on Image Processing 11 (2002), no. 5, 497–508.
6. Arun Hampapur and Ruud Bolle, Comparison of distance measures for video copy detection, International Conference on Multimedia and Expo, 2001.
7. D. A. Adjeroh and I. King M.C. Lee, A distance measure for video sequence, Computer Vision and Image Understanding 75 (1999), no. 1/2, 25–45.
8. Liping Chen and Tat-Seng Chua, A match and tiling approach to content-based image retrieval, IEEE Intl Conference on Multimedia and Expo (Tokyo, Japan), August 2001, pp. 417–420.
9. Xianfeng Yang, Qi Tian, and Sheng Gao, Video clip representation and recognition using composite shot models, ICICS-PCM, 2003.
10. MPEG-7, ISO/IEC TR 15938-8:2002, Information technology -- Multimedia content description interface -- Part 8: Extraction and use of MPEG-7 descriptions

# Interactive Dramaturgy by Generating Acousmêtre in a Virtual Environment

Wendy Ann Mansilla

ISNM - International School of New Media at the University of Luebeck
Willy-Brandt Allee 31c
23554 Luebeck, Germany
w.mansilla@isnm.de

**Abstract.** Acousmêtre, or the use of offscreen sounds and visual media to stimulate the imagination of the viewers was explored by Fritz Lang or Alfred Hitchcock in cinema. However, it's full potential is still waiting to be explored in interactive virtual environments. Based on the initial investigation, the inclusion of acousmêtre in a virtual environment effectively elicits suspense and increases the viewer's engagement. This paper further presents an approach on generating acousmêtre in a virtual storytelling application.

**Keywords:** Interactive Dramaturgy, Acousmêtre, Virtual Storytelling Environments, Experimentation.

## 1 Introduction

Interactive dramaturgy presents new forms of narration that move beyond the rules and conventions of narration and work to stimulate the sensations of the receiver. Interactive dramaturgy aims at creating binding effects in the listener and viewer [4]. To capture dramaturgy is often hard in virtual environments; oftentimes creating realistic visual setting is not enough. Current digital storytelling literature has given considerable attention to the importance of realism from the core of the visual medium (the eye and reason) but very little on the potentials of a medium's absence to reality. It is this very absence that gives a medium its illusion of depth. In cinema, the unique fusion of sound and images that creates an effect in the user is most effective when acousmêtre is employed.

Acousmêtre is a character hidden behind a curtain; the mysterious man talking on the phone; an offscreen sound that either speaks over the image or augments the sound naturally expected from the image. Visually, it is the silent character whose imaginary voice[1] is waiting to be heard. In other words, relative to what is shown on the screen, temporary or not, it is the offscreen character whose source is invisible [2]. Acousmatic sounds are also referred to as active offscreen sounds that engage the

---

[1] The discussions on cinema according to Chion [2] rarely use the term voice but instead use the word "soundtrack" which he sees as a deceptive notion. He argues that the aural elements in film do not exist as autonomous units. Instead they are received and analysed by the viewers relative to what is shown onscreen.

R. Harper, M. Rauterberg, M. Combetto (Eds.): ICEC 2006, LNCS 4161, pp. 90–95, 2006.
© IFIP International Federation for Information Processing 2006

spectator's anticipation to see the real source of the sound. In the movie *Psycho* by Alfred Hitchcock, the inability to see the image of the mother that can always be heard onscreen entirely builds up the curiosity of the viewer. On the other side, those that do not inspire the spectator to look for the source such as sounds that create an atmosphere (ambient sounds) are considered passive offscreen sounds [3].

Since antiquity, man has been in continuous search for ways to represent invisible forms, gods and fantasy. To express natural forms that cannot be explained, man created ways to represent obscurity. Through art and aesthetics ancient man was able to implicitly relate his life and touch the emotion of another. Dramaturgy is not new. What is new is the increasing demand to experience and interact with a fictional drama in real-time. The concept of acousmêtre is a powerful instrument in cinema that hasn't been fully realised in the interactive virtual entertainment arena to date. Perhaps this low popularity can be attributed to the hesitation on how an offscreen phenomenon can stimulate the creativity, aesthetics and real-life tension in virtual environments.

## 2 Suspense and Acousmêtre

According to Zillman [11], suspense and enjoyment are the essential emotional elements for viewers to judge the story as well formed. Brewer and Lichtenstein [1] supported this position, noting that suspense significantly contributes to the enjoyment of a narrative. Suspense is experienced when one fears a negative outcome, hopes for a positive outcome, and is uncertain about which outcome is going to happen [10]. According to Chion [3], sound controls human attention, unifies images, which would otherwise appear to be unrelated, and creates a sense of anticipation about what will follow in the story. In psychology, emotional responses to sound or music were found to have measurable effects on the autonomic nervous system and causes physiological changes in listeners, which are consistent with the emotions they report [7]. Thus, sounds can evoke emotional states. In addition, several studies also support the cognitivist position that uncertainty is one of the essential elements to achieve suspense [7, 10].

Murphy and Pitt [9] found that the inclusion of sound in a virtual environment conveys a sense of immersion. They noted that the use of spatial sound can affect the perception of an environment, the context of communication and meaning of the message. Theoretical and research literature suggests that acousmatic sounds integrated in the narrative add suspense and increase viewer's engagement in the virtual storytelling environment. These arguments led to the development of an application scenario called "Virtual Acousmatic Storytelling Environment" (VASE).

## 3 Audio-Visual Design

VASE simulates a doctor-patient conflict scenario. By evoking suspense it aims to represent the real-life drama and dilemma in the medical world using a virtual interactive environment [8]. VASE follows the three-act structure, composed of exposition (Act I), confrontation (Act II), and resolution (Act III). It also uses three typical forms of acousmêtre: "acousmatic mechanisms in motion"[2], "voiceless", and "bodi-less". The three acts are subdivided into seven scenes (3 scenes for Act I, 3 for Act II and 1 for Act III) each being associated with one instance of acousmêtre. Scenes are explored through interaction points (e.g. navigational command options) or deci-sion choices (in the form of multiple text descriptions of the next possible scenario). The decision made by the participant triggers the visual presentation (visual setting and virtual character reactions). Decision choices are hierarchical; each choice corre-sponds to some predefined visual presentations and branches to another set of decision choices. There are up to three possible choices shown after each scene com-pletes. Each possible scenario leads the viewer to a new scene, each of which has variations in the introductory presentation and unfolds to the same plot and next set of choices.

The first act provides exposition, an introduction to the environment and the main plot. There are three occurrences of acousmêtre that result in acousmatic mechanisms in motion in this act. They may appear in any order depending on the scene chosen by the user. All of these relate to the unresolved anxieties of the protagonist. Act I uses acousmatic voices that have no real-life relationship to the core of the image such as a hand holding an emerging syringe associated with the sound of an ambulance siren slowly getting closer to almost appear touching the camera from offscreen.

Act II shows the protagonist confronting obstacles. To heighten conflict and emo-tion in the story, there are two forms of acousmatic voices in this act. The acousmatic character of an injured boy and his mute character meet in two extremes. One extreme is the bodiless voice played by the acousmatic voice of the crying child accompanied by other offscreen sounds that fill the child's world. Another extreme is the child's voiceless body. It is the body without a voice in cinema that preserves the mystery of the character and serves as a conscience, a doubt, or a lack [2]. Finally, Act III, the resolution, reveals the acousmatic characters in the previous scenes. The offscreen sounds in this act consist only of flashback voices.

VASE uses five sounds: (1) access sounds, (2) ambient sounds, (3) visualised sounds, (4) offscreen sounds, and (5) silence. Once the user triggers an interaction point in the environment, the access sounds follow. Access sounds are representations of the virtual objects explored by the user. When the participant enters a new scene, the system plays ambient sounds that provide an atmosphere (e.g. people talking or distant noises) followed by visualised sounds (e.g. dialogues of the virtual character), if any. Acousmatic voices follow. An acousmatic voice in VASE is a combination of other aural elements – active offscreen sounds followed by *silence* or vice-versa. Silence refers to the transition of sounds to ambient silence (removal of other sounds except ambient); or to intimate and subtle sounds naturally associated with calmness (e.g. clocks in the nearby room, drops of water); or absolute silence. In VASE, silence plays in between two or more acousmatic voices or when the user moves back to the previous scene.

---

[2] Chion [2] used the term "acousmatic mechanisms in motion" to refer to the use of acousmatic voices that have relationships with each other. It is similar to Hitchcock's movie *Psycho* where parallel situations of offscreen discussions between the character (Norman) and his mother were shown.

# 4  Evaluation

An experiment was conducted in the current study consisting of 26 subjects (using an equal number of male and female subjects for each experiment) aged between 20 and 40 years from 8 nationalities, half of them being laymen and familiar with film and sound principles. The first and second experiments involve a continuous response measurement and self-report. A group of 10 subjects participated in an interactive application called AVP [6] having the same discourse transcripts as VASE's Act II (see Fig. 1b) but using only occasional background sounds. Another group consisting of 10 subjects participated with VASE. The third experiment involves a non-continuous response measurement consisting of 10 subjects (4 of which participated in AVP). Subjects were presented with series of offscreen sound samples together with a visual presentation (VASE as a series of movie excerpts).

The first and second experiments were administered in a laboratory room equipped with a computer terminal with electrodermal response (EDR) measurement software and device. Another computer terminal provided the subject with an AVP or VASE application. The experimenter recorded and monitored the interaction of the subject with the application. This data is used to track interactions such as the time when the participant enters a new scene or location. To verify the measured EDR, after the interaction, the subjects fill-out a questionnaire containing a descriptive summary of each major scene. Subjects were asked to rate (from 0-5) the feelings of hope and fear and perception of uncertainty for each scene. The experimenter also confirmed the subject's feeling of uncertainty through an interview based on Ortony, Clore, and Collins' (OOC)[3] appraisal of prospective event. Other questions include the subject's empathy for the character and understanding of the meaning of the scenes.

The third experiment was composed of 12 sound samples (consisting of either acousmatic voices, ambient sounds or visualised sounds). The materials are presented in the same linear sequence to each participant, with pauses for each sample, and are presented according to their possible appearance in VASE. Each sound sample classified as acousmatic voices may contain up to 4 offscreen sounds plus silence (combined to form a single meaning). The subjects were asked to scale their feelings of hope and fear and perception of uncertainty after each sample using the same rating scale method used in experiments 1 & 2.

A previous study by Hubert & de Jong-Meyer [5] suggests that suspense-evoking material results in greater changes in bodily sensations and increasing EDR. On the other side, materials that induce an amused state are marked by very few changes in bodily sensations, and a rapid decrease in EDR. These results are consistent in VASE, thus suggesting that the existence of acousmêtre adds suspense to an interactive narrative system. The EDR measured in AVP has lower and more clustered values of EDR compared to the data gathered with VASE (Fig 1a). The results correlate to the emotions reported by the viewers, suggesting that increasing EDR is consistent with the

---

[3] In the OOC emotion model [10], suspense is composed of fear, hope (emotivist response) and uncertainty (cognitivist response). Fear is classified as displeasure about the prospect of an undesirable event; hope as pleasure about the prospect of a desirable event. In addition, they also stated that, fear and hope as prospect emotions depend on the desirability and the likelihood that the prospective outcome will occur.

reported emotion of fear, hope and anticipation of an event. The results of experiment 3 also suggest that an increase in occurrence of offscreen sounds results in higher response (experiment 3) and this correlates to measured EDR (experiment 1). Data shows an increasing EDR response (Act I scene 2) on scenes with most offscreen sounds compared to Act II scene 1 when acousmêtre is reduced (Fig. 1c).

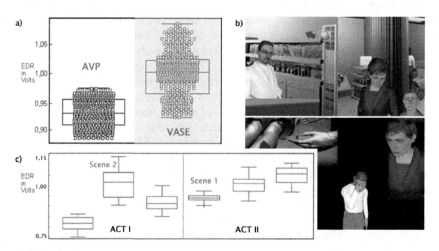

**Fig. 1.** VASE application scenario and experimental results plot (**a**) A dot plot comparison between the average mean EDR distributions of AVP and VASE in Act II. There is a significant difference between the standard deviations (SD) at 95,0% confidence level  The ratio of the variances: 0,28 to 0,45 at P-value 0,0001 (SD of AVP: 0,023 and SD of VASE: 0,039). (**b**) Snapshot of Act II (top) and Act III (bottom) in VASE. (**c**) A box-and-whiskers plot comparison between the mean EDR distributions decomposed into 6 segments for Act I and Act II.

## 5   Conclusions and Future Work

This paper has presented the potentials of using acousmêtre in an interactive virtual environment. The results obtained through the preliminary investigation of VASE suggest that suspense sensations occur when the viewer is presented with the right succession and combination of audio and visual stimulants that follow the principles of acousmêtre. The results also suggest that an increase in occurrence of offscreen sounds produces a correlated emotional effect to the participant.

Future work includes verifying the variables (e.g. length, succession, or delay of offscreen sounds in relation to the image) influencing the impact of acousmêtre to the viewer's state using more data samples. Although the participants in VASE came from different cultural backgrounds, no significant variations on the results were seen. A higher sample will also be helpful to verify if acousmêtre is independent of individual.

The process of generating acousmêtre in VASE is also presented in this paper. It attempts to combine visual scenes shown to the user and sounds played by tracking the level of interactivity of the user. The use of acousmêtre at the most relevant points in the story has the potential to greatly augment the user's engagement in the story and to create much more powerful feelings of suspense and emotion.

# References

1. Brewer, W.F., & Lichtenstein, E. H.: Event schemas, story schemas, and story grammars. In Long J. & Baddeley A., ed.: Attention and Performance IX. Hillsdale, NJ: Lawrence Erlbaum Associates (1981) 363-379
2. Chion, M.: La Voix au Cinéma. Paris: Cahiers du Cinéma (1982)
3. Chion M.: Audio-Vision: Sound on Screen. New York: Columbia University Press (1994)
4. Hagebölling H.: Aspects of Interactive Dramaturgies: Thematic Frame and Author's Contribution. In Hagebölling H., ed.: Interactive Dramaturgies. New Approaches in Multimedia Content and Design. Berlin; New York: Springer Verlag (2004) 1-5
5. Hubert W. & de Jong-Meyer R.: Autonomic, Neuroendocrine, and Subjective Responses to Emotion-inducing Film Stimuli, International Journal of Psychophysiology; 11(2) (1991) 131-40
6. Jung, B., et al.: The Affective Virtual Patient: An E-learning Tool for Social Interaction Training within The Medical Field. Proceedings of TESI - Training Education & Education International Conference. Nexus (2005).
7. Krumhansl, C.L.: An Exploratory Study of Musical Emotions and Psychophysiology.Canadian Journal of Experimental Psychology, 51(4) (1997) 336-352
8. Mansilla, W. A. & Jung B.: Emotion and Acousmêtre for Suspense in an Interactive Virtual Storytelling Environment. Proceedings of The Third Annual International Conference in Computer Game Design and Technology (2005) 151-156
9. Murphy D. & Pitt I.: Spatial Sound Enhancing Virtual Story Telling. In Virtual Storytelling: Using Virtual Reality Technologies for Storytelling. Berlin: Springer Verlag (2001) 20–29
10. Ortony, A. Clore, G.L. & Collins A.: The Cognitive Structure of Emotions. Cambridge: Cambridge University Press (1988)
11. Zillmann, D.: Anatomy of Suspense. In Tannebaum P. H., ed.: The Entertainment Functions of Television. Hillsdal. NJ: Lawrence Erlbaum (1980) 133-163

# Exposure to Violent Video Games and Desensitization to Violence in Children and Adolescents

Jeanne B. Funk

Department of Psychology, MS 948, University of Toledo, 2801 West Bancroft, Toledo, OH, USA
Jeanne.funk@utoledo.edu

**Abstract.** Entertainment computing is central to the leisure activities of many Americans, with a remarkable array of choices now available to the average person. Video and computer games, in particular violent games, are especially popular, even with relatively young children. With this popularity, concern has been raised about possible unintended consequences of participation in interactive violence. Desensitization to violence has been cited as one possible undesirable outcome of video game violence, but there is little evidence for this relationship. This paper presents a conceptual model and supporting data to begin the examination of possible relationships between exposure to violent video games and desensitization. Examining correlates of desensitization including empathy and attitudes towards violence, surveys of children and adolescents have identified a relationship between greater exposure to violent video games, lower empathy, and stronger proviolence attitudes. Additional research is needed to substantiate and to understand the causal implications of these results.

**Keywords:** Video Games, Violence, Desensitization, Children, Adolescents.

## 1 Introduction

Entertainment computing is central to the leisure activities of many Americans, with a remarkable array of choices now available to the average person. Violent video and computer games (referred to collectively as video games) are especially popular, even with relatively young children. [1] In a recent survey of 69 first through third graders, 53% of the children's favorite games had violent content, as rated by the children themselves. [2] In another recent survey of 213 middle school students, 99% of boys and 84% of girls reported that their preferred video games included violent content. [3] Given this popularity, concern has been raised about possible unintended consequences of repeated participation in interactive violence. [4 ,5] Desensitization to violence has been cited as one possible undesirable outcome. [4] This paper presents a conceptual model and supporting data to begin the examination of possible relationships between exposure to violent video games and desensitization to violence.

R. Harper, M. Rauterberg, M. Combetto (Eds.): ICEC 2006, LNCS 4161, pp. 96 – 102, 2006.
© IFIP International Federation for Information Processing 2006

## 2  Desensitization to Violence Defined

Desensitization to violence can be defined as an unconscious process that results in the reduction or eradication of cognitive and emotional, and as a result behavioral, responses to a violent stimulus. [6, 7, 8] Desensitization occurs when the individual is exposed to a previously disturbing stimulus under conditions that mitigate the disturbance.[9] The behavioral outcome of desensitization may be failure to intervene to stop violent actions or the voluntary commission of a violent act.

In normally developed individuals, moral reasoning processes will automatically be triggered prior to committing an aggressive or violent act. This allows for the assessment of the justification for, and possible outcomes of the potential action. However, if an individual becomes desensitized to violence, then the moral reasoning processes that could inhibit aggression may be bypassed. [7] As a real life example, it has been reported that the United States army has used violent video games to desensitize soldiers during combat training.[10] It is interesting that the American army disseminates its own video game, America's Army, to potential recruits. This game, available free of charge to anyone who claims to be 13 or older, allows the player to experience all aspects of military training and combat, including advanced activities such as participating in "sniper school." The Army hopes that this exposure to military life will encourage potential recruits to enlist. America's Army is also being used for training within government agencies, including the Secret Service. [11] It is unclear whether desensitization is an intended goal.

## 3  The Process of Desensitization to Violence

Desensitization to violence is an outcome of changes in several domains of psychological functioning. In the domain of active learning, violent video games expose the player to a powerful cycle of demonstration, reinforcement, and practice. In theory, this is the ideal way to transmit both messages and behaviors that will be easily learned and readily implemented. As a result of repetitive demonstration, reinforcement and practice, specific behavioral scripts may be developed. A script is a set of behavioral guidelines that tells a person what to expect in a particular situation, what the sequence of events will be, and what the response should be [12] The purpose of scripts is to make all the information and decisions that a person deals with on a continuous basis more manageable. People have scripts for a variety of different common activities. For example, most adults have driving scripts: get in, shut the door, put on the seat belt, turn on the ignition. These actions all take place without the individual making conscious choices. Once a script has been developed, decisions are made based on the existing script. A person tends to focus on information that is consistent with the script, and overlook or distort information that is not consistent. That is one reason that it takes a while to get used to driving a new car: a person needs to become aware of their driving script so it can be revised. This may not be easy or straightforward. For example, every car has a different way of activating the windshield wipers, and the driving script must be revised to accommodate these differences.

It is important to recognize that behavioral scripts do not function in isolation. [13] With repetition, networks of related scripts are formed. Memories and experiences with similar meanings, and those that are often activated together develop the strongest associations. The entire network of scripts can then be activated by a variety of different stimuli. If activation occurs frequently over time, then certain scripts or script networks may become easily and chronically accessible, easily triggered, and resistant to change. Repeated exposure to violent video games may lead to the development of scripts in which aggression and violence are normative behavior, indicating desensitization to violence. The desensitized individual whose behavioral scripts are primarily aggressive may not be capable of inhibiting an aggressive response once these scripts are automatically activated. For example, an innocent nudge in a crowded school hallway may trigger scripts for aggression, and aggressive behavior may result. It is worth noting that related research demonstrates that aggressive scripts are especially resistant to change. [14]

Exposure to violent video games will not desensitize every child or adolescent. A relative risk model is useful in understanding this caveat. [6] With few risk factors for desensitization, and some protective factors such as optimal parenting and safe neighborhoods, exposure to violent video games may have no obvious negative effects on a particular child. With additional risk factors such as poor parenting and poverty, the negative effects may be subtle, such as having lower empathy for victims, or more positive attitudes about the use of violence, reflecting the onset of desensitization to violence. As risk factors accumulate, desensitization may become pervasive, allowing the individual to exhibit increasingly severe forms of active aggression. Exposure to violent video games is just one possible risk factor for desensitization to violence. [15]

## 4 Desensitization and Moral Evaluation

Desensitization is a complex concept that has not been easily operationalized. Measuring correlates of desensitization to violence facilitates quantification. Empathy and attitudes towards violence are two of the critical measurable components of moral evaluation that reflect desensitization to violence.

### 4.1 Empathy

Empathy can be defined as the capacity to understand and to some extent experience the feelings of another. [3, 15] The experience of empathy results from the activation and interaction of perceptual, cognitive, and emotional processes.[3] Although based on inborn potential, the development of mature empathy requires opportunities to view empathic models, to interact with others, and to experience feedback about one's behavioral choices. Hoffman [16] emphasizes the role of inductive discipline in the development of empathy. Inductive discipline requires children to imagine how they would feel in a victim's situation, and encourages the development of moral scripts based on empathy. Theoretically, in a conflict situation, empathic scripts will automatically be triggered and guide behavioral choice. There is considerable experimental evidence that empathy inhibits aggressive behavior, with lower empathy being a factor in increased aggression. [17,18,19] In one study, exposure to community violence combined with low empathy predicted aggressive behavior in adolescents. [20]

Success playing violent games requires the repeated choice of violent actions that are presented as routine fun, concealing realistic consequences. Victims are typically dehumanized, a strategy that has been successful in minimizing empathy in real-life situations. Young players of violent video games are, therefore, in a situation that could interfere with the development of mature empathy, contributing to desensitization to violence.

## 4.2 Attitudes Towards Violence

Attitudes result from complex and selective evaluation processes, based on an individual's experience with, associated cognitions about, and affective reactions to a situation or object.[21] Attitudes may be formed out of awareness, as in advertising, or with purpose and conscious effort, as in the case of jury deliberations. [22] Established attitudes, like scripts, may interfere with accurate judgments in new situations, and can exert a direct impact on behavior. The development of attitudes towards violence is influenced by many factors including exposure to family and community violence, as well as exposure to violence in the media. For example, surveys of over 4,000 first through sixth grade children living in urban neighborhoods identified a relationship between exposure to community violence and attitudes and beliefs supporting aggression, as well as increases in aggressive behavior.[23] In another study, 473 inner-city middle school students were surveyed to determine their exposure to community violence and their level of distress and aggression.[24] Higher exposure to community violence was related to more aggression in girls. These researchers suggested that children with chronic violence exposure demonstrate desensitization to violence because they have developed the attitude that violence is normal. As previously noted, violent video games also promote the development of the attitude that violence is normal.

## 5  Violent Video Games and Desensitization

Several surveys have investigated possible relationships between exposure to violent video games, empathy, and attitudes towards violence. In one study of 307 Japanese fourth through sixth graders, there was a negative relationship between simple frequency of video game use and questionnaire-measured empathy. [25] In a survey of 229 15 to 19 year olds, those whose favorite game was violent had lower empathy scores on the "fantasy empathy" subscale of the Interpersonal Reactivity Index. [26] Fifty-two sixth graders were surveyed to examine relationships between a preference for violent video games, attitudes towards violence, and empathy.[27] Children listed up to three favorite games and categorized the games using previously established categories and definitions [see Table 1]. [28] It was anticipated that a stronger preference for violent games would be associated with lower empathy and stronger proviolence attitudes. Relationships were in the expected direction, though only marginally statistically significant. Perhaps more important, children with both a high preference for violent games and high time commitment to playing demonstrated the lowest empathy. Using a similar survey approach with 150 fourth and fifth graders, greater long-term exposure to violent video games was associated with lower empathy and stronger proviolence attitudes.[7] In another study, no difference was found in immediate empathic or aggressive responding after 66 five to twelve year old children played a violent or nonviolent video game. However, again using the established

**Table 1.** Revised video game categories with descriptions

| Category | Description |
| --- | --- |
| General Entertainment | Story or game with no fighting or destruction |
| Educational | Learning new information or figuring out new ways to use information |
| Fantasy Violence | Cartoon character must fight or destroy things and avoid being killed or destroyed while trying to reach a goal, rescue someone, or escape from something |
| Human Violence | Human character must fight or destroy things and avoid being killed or destroyed while trying to reach a goal, rescue someone, or escape from something |
| Nonviolent Sports | Sports without fighting or destruction |
| Sports Violence | Sports without fighting or destruction |

From "Video game controversies," by J. B. Funk and D. D. Buchman, Pediatric Annals, 24 (1995) p. 93. Copyright 1995 by SLACK, Inc. Adapted with permission.

category system, a long-term preference for violent video games was associated with lower empathy.[29]   Similar results were found in research using a comparable experimental paradigm with 69 first and second graders. [2] Results of this small body of research are consistent with the hypothesis that greater long-term exposure to violent video games may encourage lower empathy and stronger proviolence attitudes in some children and adolescents.

## 6   Behavioral Evidence for Media-Based Desensitization to Violence

At present, behavioral evidence for media-based desensitization to violence is limited to a handful of studies that includes only one study of violent video game exposure. In a classic media violence study, those children who first viewed a film with aggression took significantly longer to seek adult assistance when faced with an altercation between younger children than children who did not see the film.[30]  Using a similar paradigm, other researchers demonstrated that playing a violent video game slowed adults' response time to help a presumed violence victim, relative to those individuals who played a nonviolent game.[31] A long-term preference for playing violent video games was also associated with being less helpful to the presumed victim.

## 7   Summary and Implications

This paper begins the development of a conceptual model, and presents data that suggest that exposure to violent video games could contribute to desensitization to violence. Examining correlates of desensitization, relationships have been demonstrated between greater long-term exposure to violent video games, lower empathy, and stronger proviolence attitudes. There is also limited evidence of immediate desensitization after playing a violent video game. Desensitization concerns are strengthened by preliminary imaging research, whose full consideration is beyond the scope of the current presentation. Using fMRI technology, event-related changes in brain functioning have been found during video game play, specifically deactivation of the prefrontal cortex.[32] The prefrontal cortex is the gatekeeper for impulse control, planning, evaluation of the potential consequences of one's actions, as well as mature empathy. [4] Much more research is needed to substantiate and understand the implications of fMRI findings, and this seems especially important given that direct game-brain interfaces are now available (see http://www. smartbraingames.com).

It is critical that future research address the long-term relationships between exposure to violent video games, and desensitization as reflected in lower empathy and stronger proviolence attitudes to determine the causal direction of relationships identified thus far . Exposure to violent video games is only one potential route to desensitization to violence. If proven, however, this route is both optional and avoidable.

# References

1. Funk, J. B.: Video Games. Adolesc. Med. Clin. North Amer., 16 (2005) 395-411
2. Funk, J. B., Buchman, D., Chan, M., Brouwer, J. Younger Children's Exposure to Violent Media, Empathy, and Violence Attitudes.   Presented at the annual meeting of the American Psychological Association, Washington, DC, August, 2005
3. Funk, J. B., Fox, C. M., Chan, M., & Brouwer, J.:  The Development of the Children's Empathic Attitudes Questionnaire Using Classical and Rasch Techniques.  Manuscript in review
4. Funk, J. B. Children's Exposure to Violent Video Games and Desensitization to Violence. Child Adolesc. Psychiatry Clin. North Amer. 14 (2005) 387-40
5. Anderson C.A., Berkowitz L., Donnerstein E., Huesmann L.R., Johnson J.D., Linz D., et al.: The Influence of Media Violence on Youth. Psychol. Sci. in the Pub. Int. 4 (2003) 1-30
6. Funk, J. B., Hagan, J., Schimming, J., Bullock, W. A., Buchman, D. D., & Myers, M.: Aggression and Psychopathology in Adolescents with a Preference for Violent Electronic Games. Agg. Beh. 28 (2002) 134-144
7. Funk, J. B., Bechtoldt-Baldacci, H., Pasold, T., Baumgardner, J.:  Violence Exposure in Real-Life, Video Games, Television, Movies, and the Internet: Is There desensitization? J. Adolesc. 27 (2004) 23-39
8. Rule B.K., Ferguson. T.J.:  The Effects of Media Violence on Attitudes, Emotions, and Cognitions. J. Soc. Issues 42 (1986) 29-50
9. Funk, J.B.:  Video Violence. Amer. Acad. Pediatr. News, (1995) 16, 21
10. Grossman, D.: On Killing. Little, Brown, Boston (1995)
11. Snider, M.: Spies Will Learn Craft Via Games. USA Today, (2005, July 16) 5D
12. Funk,  J. B. Script Development.  In Arnett, J. J. (ed.): Encyclopedia of Children, Adolescents, and the Media. Sage, Thousand Oaks, California (in press)
13. Huesmann, L. R.: The Role of Social Information Processing and Cognitive Schema in the Acquisition and Maintenance of Habitual Aggressive Behavior. In Geen, R., Donnerstein, E. (eds.): Human Aggression: Theories, Research and Implications for Policy. Academic Press, New York, (1998) 73-109

14. Guerra, N. G., Nucci, L., Huesmann, L. R.: Moral Cognition and Childhood Aggression. In Huesmann, L. R. (ed.), Aggressive Behavior: Current Perspectives, Plenum, New York (1994) 153-186

15. Funk J. B.: Violent video games: Who's at risk? In: Ravitch D., Viteritti J, (eds.): Kid Stuff: Marketing Violence and Vulgarity in the Popular Culture. Johns Hopkins, Baltimore (2003) 168-192

16. Hoffman, M. L.: Varieties of Empathy-Based Guilt. In: Bybee J, (ed.): Guilt and Children. Academic Press, San Diego (1998) 91-112

17. Gallup, G. G., Platek, S.M.: Cognitive Empathy Presupposes Self-awareness: Evidence from Phylogeny, Ontogeny, Neuropsychology, and Mental Illness. Behav Brain Sci 25 (2002) 36-3

18. Vreek, G.J., van der Mark, I.L.: Empathy, an Integrated Model. New Ideas in Psychol 21 (2003) 177-207

19. Sams, D.P., Truscott, S.D. Empathy, Exposure to Community Violence, and Use of Violence Among Urban, At-Risk Adolescents. Child Youth Care 33 (2004) 33-50

20. Funk, J.B., Buchman, D.: Playing Violent Video and Computer Games and Adolescent Self-Perception. J. Comm. 46 (1996) 19-32

21. Fazio, R.H., Olson, M.A.: Attitudes: Foundations, Functions, and Consequences. In Hogg, M. A., Cooper, J. (eds.): The Sage Handbook of Social Psychology. Sage, London (2003) 139-160

22. Olson, M.A., Fazio, R.H.: Implicit Attitude Formation Through Classical Conditioning. Psychol Sci 12 2001 413-417

23. Guerra, N.G., Huesman, L.R., Spindler, A..: Community Violence Exposure, Social Cognition, and Aggression Among Urban Elementary School Children. Child Dev 74 (2003) 1561-1576

24. Farrell, A. D., Bruce, S. E.: Impact of Exposure to Community Violence on Violent Behavior and Emotional Distress among Urban Adolescents. J Clin Child Psychol 26 (1997) 2-14

25. Sakamoto, A.: Video Game Use and the Development of Sociocognitive Abilities in Children: Three Surveys of Elementary School Children. J App Soc Psychol 24 (1994) 21-42

26. Barnett, M.A., Vitaglione, G.D., Harper, K.K.G., Quackenbush, S.W, Steadman, L.A., Valdez, B.S.: Late adolescents' experiences with and attitudes towards videogames. J App Soc Psychol 27 (1997) 1316-1334

27. Funk, J.B., Buchman, D.D., Schimming, J.L., Hagan, J.D.: Attitudes Towards Violence, Empathy, and Violent Electronic Games. Presented at the annual meeting of the American Psychological Association, San Francisco, CA, August, 1998

28. Funk, J.B., Buchman, D.: Video Game Controversies. Pediatr Ann 24 (1995) 91-94

29. Funk, J.B., Buchman, D.D., Jenks, J., Bechtoldt, H.: Playing Violent Video Games, Desensitization, and Moral Evaluation in Children. J App Dev Psychol 24 (2003) 413-436

30. Drabman, R.S., Thomas, M.H.: Does Media Violence Increase Children's Tolerance of Real-Life Aggression? Dev Psychol 10 (1974) 418-421

31. Carnagey, N.L., Bushman, B.J., Anderson, C.: Video Game Violence Desensitizes Players to Real World Violence. Manuscript in review

32. Suzuki, K,, Tanaka, M., Matsuda, G.: The Effects of Playing Video Games on Brain Activity. Presented at the 34th Annual Conference of the International Simulation and Gaming Association, Tokyo, Japan, August, 2003

# Kansei Mediated Entertainment

Ben Salem[1,*] , Matthias Rauterberg[2], and Ryohei Nakatsu[1]

[1] School of Science and Technology, Kwansei Gakuin University, Sanda, Japan
mail@bsalem.info
[2] Department of Industrial Design, Eindhoven University of Technology, Eindhoven,
The Netherlands

**Abstract.** We present an extension of Kansei mediated communication in the field of entertainment. We propose to do so by implementing Cultural Computing concept and enriching it with Kansei Mediated Interaction. We present some inspiration for our approach in terms of culture and then discuss them. We relate our work to the Western and to the Eastern world. Thus we use cultural examples from England, France, Japan and China. Finally, we propose as a new direction for HCI, cultural computing with its related paradigm we call Kansei Mediated Interaction. Finally we propose Kansei Mediated Entertainment as a direction merging of Kansei and entertainment.

**Keywords:** cultural computing, Kansei mediation, unconscious, entertainment.

## 1 Introduction

From a historical perspective, Human-Computer Interaction (HCI) has evolved over more than five decades. Although the history of HCI is rich and complex, within the scope of this paper we will summarise some of the key milestones (see Fig. 1). The history of HCI stretches back to the 60s. Originally it was about Man-Machine Interaction and the emergence of the Personal Computing (PC) paradigm. In the 80s, HCI was investigating media rich computing with the paradigm of computer mediated interaction. Interactive multimedia was the focus of attention. More recently, at the turn of the century, HCI was about social computing and its associated paradigm: community mediated interaction (see also Rauterberg, 2004). The HCI research field investigated applications such as Computer Supported Cooperative Work (CSCW), and the Internet (on line communities). Nowadays, with mobile, portable and ubiquitous technology, HCI is looking at more personalised and intimate interaction (Nakatsu et al., 2005).

Several paradigms have emerged in recent years for the future directions of HCI: ubiquitous, nomadic, mixed-reality computing, and so on. In general all these new directions have some common properties. These are: (1) the disappearing computer; (2) from conscious to unconscious interaction (Rauterberg, 2006); and (3) the building of communities. A computer is not more the centre of interest or the focus of attention of the user. It is the running applications and the benefits and affects these have on the user that matter. The benefits and effects on the user are not limited to the

---

* Corresponding author.

R. Harper, M. Rauterberg, M. Combetto (Eds.): ICEC 2006, LNCS 4161, pp. 103–116, 2006.

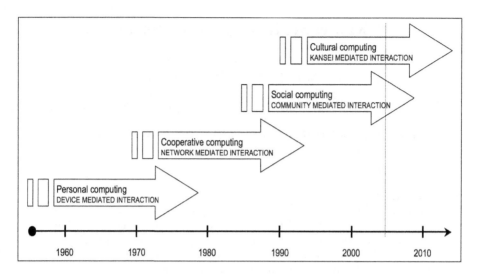

**Fig. 1.** From Personal to Cultural Computing

domain of the application but have been extended to include all aspects of interest to the user. In this perspective, cultural computing has emerged as an interesting direction. A direction we are interested to investigate.

## 1.1  Cultural Computing

Culture is the integration of human behaviour that includes attitudes, norms, values, beliefs, actions, communications and groups (ethnic, religious, social, etc.). These are exchanged between members of the same culture in an implicit way and with members of different culture in an explicit way (see Fig. 2).

Tosa et al (2005) think of *Cultural Computing* as a method for cultural translation that uses scientific methods to represent the essential aspects of culture (see also CCP, 2004). Including cultural concepts that heretofore have not been the focus of computing, such as mental images of Eastern thought and Buddhism, and the Sansui paintings, poetry and kimono that evoke these images, they projected the style of communication developed by Zen schools over hundreds of years into a world for the user to explore – an exotic Eastern Sansui world: the ZENetic computer. Through encounters with Zen Koans and haiku poetry, the user is constantly and sharply forced to confirm the whereabouts of his or her self-consciousness. Salem and Rauterberg (2005a) discuss the relationship of cultural computing and entertainment. What would be an equivalent system for Cultural Computing in the West? Nakatsu et al (2006) try to give a future direction in form of 'Kansei Mediation' to transform societies towards Enlightenment. In one astonishing, short period – the ninth century BCE – the peoples of four distinct regions of the civilized world created the religious and philosophical traditions that have continued to nourish humanity into the present day: Confucianism and Daoism in China; Hinduism and Buddhism in India; monotheism in middle east; and philosophical rationalism in Greece. 'Monotheism' and 'philosophical rationalism' is the religious and cultural foundation of the occident. Kant (1784) gave

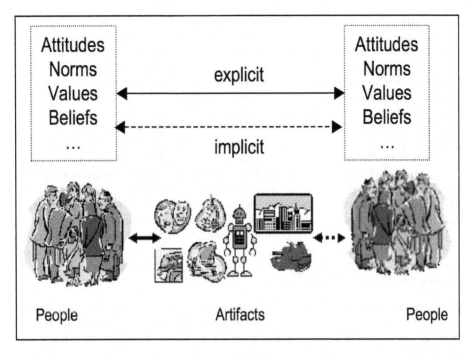

**Fig. 2.** Culture is determined partly by explicit (straight lines) and mainly by implicit communication (broken lines) about attitudes, norms, values, beliefs, etc. Different cultures are characterized by their social behaviour pattern and produced artefacts.

a first answer to the question, "What is Enlightenment?" He indicated that the 'way out' that characterizes Enlightenment in the West is a process that releases us from the status of 'immaturity'; and by 'immaturity,' he meant a certain state of our will that makes us accept someone else's authority to lead us in areas where the use of reason is called for. Enlightenment is defined by a modification of the pre-existing relation linking will, authority, and the use of reason.

**Commedia Virtuale:** Ben Salem (2005) has investigated face, hand and body expressions to be applied to avatars of a virtual environment to improve their communication capabilities and enrich and facilitate their perception by users of a virtual environment. He has based his work on inspiration from the world of theatre. In this perspective Commedia dell'Arte and Noh theatre have been the focus of his attention. He explored key features of Commedia dell'Arte namely improvisation, exaggerated gestures and expressive postures, and investigated how their adoption in the design of avatars are useful for Collaborative Virtual Environments. With the same objectives we looked at another theatre style, the Noh theatre. He investigated the variety of masks and the choreography. The outcome was a visual language for avatars made up of postures, gestures and appearances. He has concluded this investigation with the production of an experimental theatre play involving real and virtual actors and performing a classical plot from Commedia dell'Arte.

**Pet Robots:** There has been several investigations of various robotic systems for personal interaction: turning robots into pets and subjects of empathy. Developing a robot to nurture social and interpersonal skills to its user can be seen as a new dimension. The Tamagochi, Furby, micro-pets are examples that could be used as inspiration (Salem and Rauterberg, 2005b). The key issues they addressed were: (1) Rendering of emotion through postures and movements (Bartneck and Reichenbach, 2005), (2) effective human perception of the emotions expressed by the robot, (3) clear rules of engagement and social rules used by the human and the robot, (4) as natural as possible interaction between the user and the robot, and (5) real-time performance by the robot. Several modalities are available: body postures, body movements, simplified hand gestures, head movements, and the production of non-speech sounds. Social obligations and dialogue etiquette between the robot and his user will determine to a certain extent the experience the user will have of the robot. How the robot to be perceived is another major challenge. In our opinion to ensure a high level of empathy and the perception of real-like companionship, the robot should not be perceived as a tool, a pet or a cartoon creature but it should rather be perceived like an artificial being in between a pet and a human. This vision will be used as guideline for the robot(s) in ALICE (see next sections).

**The Sensorama Simulator:** A system to stimulate the senses of the user with the aim of simulating an actual experience realistically (see Fig. 3). Various applications were proposed for this system. It was designed to be an arcade game, a training and educational tool. Essentially it is a system that let the user experience a ride on a motorbike in the most realistic way (remembering the system was developed in the 1960s). Rightfully, Sensorama is considered as the pre-cursor of many interaction developments such as multi-media and Virtual Reality. Although not explicitly described as such, we consider the Sensorama as the precursor of cultural computing. It implemented a range of media with the intent of simulating a realistic experience. To do so it included medias such as smells, wind, noises that are associated in the Western World with a bike ride in a town (Heiling, 1962).

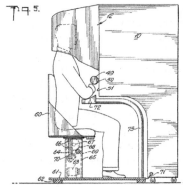

3.1. Picture of the system          3.2. Drawing from the patent application

**Fig. 3.** The Sensorama Simulator

Implementing similar systems for a range of applications rather than for the rendering of a single experience would be quite challenging. We advocate a different direction. One that relies on culture rather than experience.

## 1.2  Implementing Cultural Computing

Cultural computing (CC) is more than integrating a culture into the interaction. It is about allowing the user to experience an interaction that is closely related to the core aspects of his/her culture. In a way that let him/her engage with the interface using the values and attributes of his/her own culture. As such it is important to understand one's cultural values and how to render them during the interaction. As there are many cultures that we could investigate, there is a need to select a subset of cultures. In this paper we will focus on two representative sub-cultures, one from the Western world prevailing in England, and one from the Eastern World prevailing in Japan.

To understand both cultures in a way that would fit the objectives of our interests, we have sought illustrative examples of both. Thus, we have investigated illustrative stories that are well known, accessible, classical in their respective cultures and relevant from the point of view of cultural computing. We also looked for stories that would be helpful in the understanding of the essential aspects of both Western and Eastern cultures.

The origin of Western culture stories can be traced back to Greek mythology. An example of Greek mythology is the Illiad and the Odyssey written by Homer in the 8th Century BC. Illiad tells the story of the siege of the city of Illium during the Trojan War. The Odyssey describes the heroic journey back home from the Trojan war of Odysseus king of Ithaca. As for the Eastern Culture of Japan, the original works are the two mythological books Kojiki and Nihonshoki., completed in 712 and 720 respectively. Kojiki describes various myths and legends of Japan. It starts at the beginning of the world and ends at the reign of Empress Suiko. Nihonshoki is a compilation of the chronicles of Japan. Kojiki emphasise the mythical while Nihonshoki is more factual.

The historical mythologies could have been used, but within the context of our work they are rather complex in content, narrative and plot. We have selected less predominant stories but relevant none the less. These are for the Eastern culture: the story of The Ox herding attributed to a Ch'an master (circa 1200s), and the Journey to the West (1590). For the Western culture we have selected Alice in Wonderland by Lewis Carroll (1865), and Le Petit Prince by Antoine de Saint Exupery (1943). These stories help understand the underlying cultural value or question it. For the Eastern culture, the value dealt with is enlightenment, while it is orderly rational reason for the Western culture. In the next section we present an overview of these stories.

## 1.3  Eastern Culture: Story of the 'Ox Herding' (Enlightenment)

This short story has ten steps:

[1] **Seeking the ox:** Starting the journey, while being unaware that a dualist approach cannot lead to the understanding of the true nature of mind. There should not be a mind/body separation.

**[2] Seeing the ox tracks:** Although the ox is still not seen, the tracks confirm its existence, and lead to way to it. Through self discipline and training, it is possible to rediscover one's true self.

**[3] Seeing the Ox:** The path to enlightenment has been seen. It is about finding one's true self, through trial and errors (see Fig. 4.1).

**[4] Catching the Ox**: Although the ox has been seen, the difficulty now is to catch it (see Fig. 4.2).

**[5] Herding the Ox:** Kencho is finally obtained after a long period of disciplinary training. However, the Kencho attained is only a stepping stone towards Satori (see Fig. 4.3).

**[6] Coming Home on the Ox's Back:** The efforts paid off. The ox and the herder move together effortlessly. This shows the state in which one completely finds one's true self, that is, the state in which one obtains Satori (see Fig. 4.4).

**[7] Ox is forgotten:** The ox and the herder become one. Dualism has been overcome and the herder has no worldly attachments any more.

**[8] Both Ox and self forgotten:** The separation of reality from the mind is gone. Enlightenment is experienced and the mind has escaped.

**[9] Returning to the source:** Back to square one. The world carries on as always.

**[10] Returning to help others:** The enlightened has renounced all to selflessly help others (see Fig. 4.5).

| 4.1. Step 3 | 4.2. Step 4 | 4.3. Step 5 | 4.4. Step 6 | 4.5. Step 10 |

**Fig. 4.** Various representations of the Ox Herding Steps

The ten Ox Herding Pictures (Fig. 4) are an imagery of an illusion to be negated before a seeker can experience enlightenment. In these pictures, the ox symbolise the mind, while the herder the seeker. The illusion being that reality is separate from the mind (Budhanet, 2006). These metaphorical steps help one achieve Kencho and then Satori. Kencho is the initial awakening experience, while Satori is the more lasting experience of enlightenment. Both are however transitional compared with the Nirvana.

### 1.4 Eastern Culture: Story of 'Journey to the West' and 'Dragon Ball'

The Journey to the West is a Classical Chinese novel written circa 1590s.The story is a mythology describing the pilgrimage of a monk from China to India seeking religious texts called Sutras, and deals with *ideals*, *redemption* and *atonement*.

A modern version of this novel is the popular Dragon Ball Japanese Manga. It is loosely based the traditional Chinese tale. Dragon Ball is about the life and adventures of Son Goku, a monkey-tailed character, from his childhood all the way to being a grandfather. During his life he fights many battles and in the way becomes the strongest martial artist in the universe. The Dragon Balls are one component of the universe. They are magical spheres to summon a dragon and are scattered across the world.

5.1. Journey to the West    5.2. Son Goku (main)    5.3. Yamcha    5.4. Oolong

**Fig. 5.** Characters from 'Journey to the West' (5.1) and 'Dragon Ball' (5.2 – 5.4)

## 1.5   Western Culture: Story of 'Alice in Wonderland'

Alice adventures happen in a world of paradox, the absurd and the improbable (Wikipedia, 2006). The key aspects of Alice in Wonderland can be resumed in the following points: (1) a non linear non constant time flow; (2) a distortion of space and people; (3) a counter-intuitive, common sense defying heuristics. Alice's adventures are illustrative of English culture. Indeed English and Western culture in general are based on Monotheist religions (Judaism, Christianity, and Islam) which are concerned with certainty and absolutism: in the sense of absolute truth and certainty. Western culture is also based on Cartesian logic, analytical reasoning and a linear and constant flow of time.

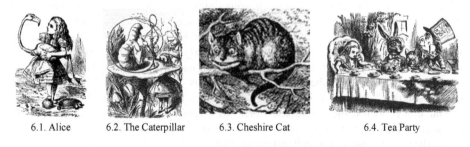

6.1. Alice    6.2. The Caterpillar    6.3. Cheshire Cat    6.4. Tea Party

**Fig. 6.** Characters from Alice Adventures in Wonderland

Alice in Wonderland can be used to give interesting examples of many of the basic concepts of adolescent psychology. Alice's experiences can be seen as symbolic depictions of important aspects of adolescent development, such as initiation, identity formation, and physical, cognitive, moral, and social development (Lough, 1983).

Alice's adventures are deconstructive[1] in nature and as such are directly challenging the strongly held belief of a linear, single track and sequential reality.

### 1.6 Western Culture: Story of 'Le Petit Prince'

This story is mainly about *wisdom* and *maturity*. A young child (the 'prince') lives in a small asteroid where there are two volcanoes and a rose (see Fig. 7). One day the prince leaves to visit the rest of the universe. He visits several asteroids where he meets adults who are all caricature in their own ways:

**The king,** who reign over the stars by ordering them to do what they would anyway.

**The conceited man,** who wants to be admired by everyone.

**The drunkard,** who drinks to forget that he is ashamed of drinking.

**The businessman,** who is always busy counting the stars he is convinced he owns.

**The lamplighter,** who lights and extinguishes the lamp once a minute because he lives in a fast rotating asteroid.

**The geographer,** who makes maps of the world, does not trust things he hasn't seen with his own eyes but have never left his desk.

7.1. Petit Prince        7.2. Businessman        7.3. Fox        7.4. The Garden of Roses

**Fig. 7.** Characters and Scenes from 'Le Petit Prince' (7.1 – 7.4)

The story is rich of famous quotes such as "Grown-ups never understand anything by themselves, and it is tiresome for children to be always and forever explaining things to them". The main character is sometimes very spontaneous and naïve, for instance in one statement he seems to disregard the need to wait for nature "I am very fond of sunsets. Come, let us go look at a sunset now". However The Little Prince is well aware of the importance of emotions and clearly states so when saying: "Here is my secret. It is very simple: One does not see well but with the heart. The essential is invisible to the eye". At other point the character is philosophical: "What makes the desert beautiful," says the little prince, "is that somewhere it hides a well".

Our aim is to use these selected stories as inspiration for the design of cultural computing. However we need first to describe the interaction paradigm we wish to use in the implementation of cultural computing.

## 2  Implementing Cultural Computing

Our approach is to create an interaction based on the cultural values highlighted in these stories. The drawback of this approach is the cultural dependency of the

---

[1] See the work of the philosopher Jacques Derrida.

interaction developed (Nisbett et al., 2001). A westerner would understand and appreciate the implementation of an interaction inspired from 'Alice in Wonderland Adventures' or 'Le Petit Prince', but will be puzzled if s/he was presented with an interaction inspired from the 'Ox story' or 'The Journey to the West'. Similarly, an easterner would appreciate the second set and be confused by the first.

Although the cultural dependency is somewhat a drawback it has many advantages. Cultural computing allows for a much richer experience to be rendered. This is thanks to the complexity and depth of the semantics involved. There is also the advantage of higher bandwidth of information at the interface as symbolic meanings and implicit knowledge can be used. The interface is not limited to explicit messages and meanings. However, there is a challenge in finding culturally rich media that could be used to deliver our proposed system. We propose to rely on Kansei Mediation (KM) as a mean to deliver the necessary media and bandwidth rich interface.

## 2.1 Kansei Mediation

KM is a form of multimedia communication that carries non-verbal, emotional and Kansei information (Nakatsu et al., 2006). It is a combination of Kansei Communication and Kansei Media. In essence it is about exchanging cultural values efficiently and effectively. Kansei Communication is about sharing implicit knowledge such as feelings, emotions and moods. Kansei Media are the channels used to do so, such as voice tone and non-verbal communication. The integration of multiple, multimode and Kansei Media can enable a type of interaction that is neither biased towards cognition, nor biased towards awareness. This is what we call Kansei Mediated Interaction (KMI).

## 2.2 KMI in the Time Domain

Several cognitive functions can be ordered according to their life-span (see Fig. 8). KMI has the potential to stimulate and influence most of these functions. The cognitive functions are: *reflexes*, *sensations*, *thoughts*, *dreams*, *emotions*, *moods*, and *drives*.

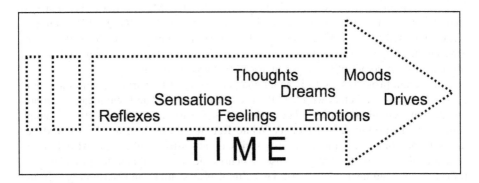

**Fig. 8.** Time Scale of some cognitive functions

These different cognitive functions are linked to different control systems (bold black in Fig. 9) of our body. In turn, these links help us design the right interaction (italic in Fig. 9) through various body parts and control systems. To achieve KMI, one could implement the interaction using a combination of channels and medias (as the examples given to the right of Fig. 9).

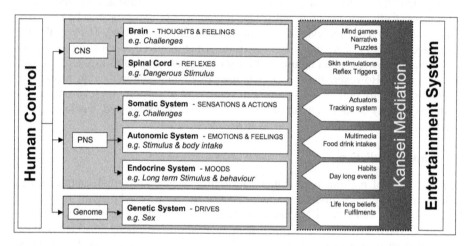

**Fig. 9.** From human control mechanisms to entertainment [CNS: Central Nervous System, PNS: Peripheral Nervous System]

## 2.3   Case Study: Alice in Wonderland

The first interactive, but semi-immersive virtual reality system based on parts of 'Alice's Adventures in Wonderland' was developed at the Entertainment Technology Centre of Carnegie Mellon University. Pierce et al (1999) created a successful virtual experience based on a head-mounted display (HMD) to overcome some or all of the following problems: entering a virtual world is a jarring experience, people do not naturally turn their heads or talk to each other while wearing an HMD, putting on the equipment is hard, and people do not realize when the experience is over. In the Electric Garden at SIGGRAPH 97, they presented the Mad Hatter's Tea Party, a shared virtual environment experienced by more than 1,500 SIGGRAPH attendees. They addressed these HMD-related problems with a combination of back story, see-through head mounted displays, virtual characters, continuity of real and virtual objects, and the layout of the physical and virtual environments.

Our current project ALICE, is an augmented reality (AR) narrative with intelligent agents acting as characters who lead the user through virtual and real locations, moral choices and emotional states. The narrative is a surreal quest, sometimes funny, sometimes disturbing. The character White Rabbit (in our case a robot) introduces himself and joins with the user in a series of absurdist challenges. ALICE is an educational journey towards the user's heart's desire, designed to provoke self-reflection on a number of unconscious cultural issues: logic and reasoning, self and ego, bullying and trusting others; selfish- and selfless-ness; and sublimating pleasure. The user is given the opportunity to occupy and experience any of these mental and

10.1. Stage 1              10.2. Stage 2              10.3. Stage 3

**Fig. 10.** The 3 stages we plan to implement

emotional positions. This will be achieved in line with the Alice in Wonderland plot (albeit shortened).

**Stage-1:** To simulate the 'Down the Rabbit Hole' experience (see Fig. 11), the entrance is a spiral tube slide that ends in the projection cave of stage-2. The spiral tube slide includes visual and audio projections throughout the sliding experience. The rabbit-hole goes straight on like a tunnel, and then dips suddenly down, so that the user has no opportunity to stop him- or herself. Either the well is very deep, or the fall is very slow, for the user has plenty of time as he slides down to look about him and to wonder what is going to happen next.

**Fig. 11.** Alice falling down the rabbit hole

**Stage-2:** The end of stage-1 is inside a cave with four walls of which three are projection walls. Through one of the projection walls the user is able to go through (e.g. based on Fog Screen Technology (2006) or just a mechanical solution) to continue the experience. Inside the cave the user has access to two tangible devices: 'nibble' and 'drink me' (see Fig. 12). Both devices are hanging from the ceiling to control their physical height. With these two devices the user can interact with the environment to adjust the size: shrinking or growing. In case of proper sizing the exit door will be opened to leave the cave. The character 'White Rabbit' in form of a pet robot will accompany the user to provide help. The tangible input devices will have

**Fig. 12.** Two tangible input devices 'Nibble' and 'Drink Me'

an orientation sensor (e.g. VTT's SoapBox or a cheaper replacement) so that the amount of 'drinking' or 'eating' can be measured to control the environment.

**Stage-3:** To talk to the Cheshire Cat a painted wall with a back projection area inside this painting is provided (see Fig. 13). In front of this tree a sensitive floor is laid out. Depended on the position of the user, the reaction of the Cat is different (e.g. visible or disappearing). A particular dialog will challenge the user to reflect on logic and reasoning.

**Fig. 13.** Talking to the Cheshire Cat

**Stage-4:** The next stage of the ALICE experience would be the 'Mad Hatter's Tea Party' in which virtual characters and objects are mixed with real objects and agents. The Helio (2006) display technology will be investigated for projecting the virtual objects on the table. Cavazza et al (2004) describe a new approach to the behaviour of 3D environments that supports the definition of physical processes and interactive phenomena. The work takes as a starting point the traditional event-based architecture that underlies most game engines. These systems discretise the environments' Physics by separating the objects' kinematics from the physical processes corresponding to objects interactions. This property can be used to insert a new behavioural layer, which implements AI-based simulation techniques. They introduce the rationale behind AI-based simulation and the techniques they use for qualitative Physics, as well as a new approach to world behaviour based on the induction of causal impressions. This approach has implications for the definition of complex world behaviour or non-standard physics, as required in creative applications

## 3  Conclusions

In this paper we have attempted to define and explain a novel concept we call Kansei Mediated Interaction (KMI) and we have tried to illustrate an implementation of KMI in entertainment. In our opinion Kansei Mediated Entertainment (KME) is a promising development because it allows for the delivery of both explicitly and implicitly rich experiences. KME is also of relevance nowadays with the acknowledgment of emotions and feelings as important component of our cognitive functions.

We have focused on our current implementation of KME with the project ALICE, however, for the other stories implementation of KME is also feasible. We hereby outline a possible direction for implementation: (1) Ox Herding and Journey to the West: These stories are metaphors. The plot is not based on a principal character performing some actions. These stories are about the discovery of deeper meanings and values for events and other characters. Therefore its implementation is unlike the Alice in Wonderland implementation. It is translated into the interaction iterations akin to interface choreography. (2) Le Petit Prince Adventures relate to the rediscovery of one's lost personality characters when growing from childhood and entering adulthood. The author is inviting us to re-discover ourselves and let the child in every one of us express him/herself again. A possible implementation is in the form of an environment where the interaction is based on play and other children related activities.

Finally, we hope to have raised the awareness of Kansei media and communication in the field of entertainment and demonstrated through our proposed KME of the significant potential a Kansei approach could have on entertainment.

## Acknowledgement

This paper was written as part of a long-term cooperation between the School of Science and Technology, Kwansei Gakuin University, Japan and the Department of Industrial Design, Eindhoven University of Technology, The Netherlands. We are grateful for the sponsoring of Microsoft Research Europe.

## References

Bartneck C, Reichenbach J (2005). Subtle emotional expressions of synthetic characters. *International Journal of Human-Computer Studies*, 62(2), 179-192.
Cavazza M, Hartley S, Lugrin JL, Libardi P, Le Bras M (2004). New Behavioural Approaches for Virtual Environments. *Lecture Notes in Computer Science*, vol. 3166, pp. 23-31.
CCP (2004) Cultural Computing Program, http://www.culturalcomputing.uiuc.edu/
FOGSCREEN (2006), http://www.fogscreen.com/

HELIO (2006) Display, http://www.io2technology.com/

Heiling M (1962). Sensorama Simulator, US Patent 3,050,870.

Kant I (1784). Beantwortung der Frage: Was ist Aufklärung? *Berlinische Monatschrift*, 2, 481-494.

Lough GC (1983). Alice in Wonderland and cognitive development: teaching with examples. *Journal of Adolescence*, 6(4), 305-315.

Nakatsu R, Rauterberg M, Vorderer P (2005). A new framework for entertainment computing: from passive to active experience. *Lecture Notes in Computer Science*, vol. 3711, pp. 1-12.

Nakatsu R, Rauterberg M, Salem B (2006). Forms and theories of communication: from multimedia to Kansei mediation. *Multimedia Systems*, 11(3), 304-312.

Nisbett RE., Peng K., Choi I. & Norenzayan A. (2001). Culture and sSystems of thought: holistic versus analytic cognition. *Psychological Review*, 108(2), 291-310.

Pierce JS, Pausch R, Sturgill CB, Christiansen KD (1999). Designing a successful HMD-based experience. *Presence*, 8(4), pp. 469-473.

Rauterberg M (2004). Positive effects of entertainment technology on human behaviour. In: R. Jacquart (ed.), *Building the Information Society* (pp. 51-58). IFIP, Kluwer Academic Press.

Rauterberg M. (2006, in press). From Personal to Cultural Computing: how to assess a cultural experience. In: Proceedings of the 4th Usability Day (9. Juni 2006), Applied University Vorarlberg, Dornbirn, Austria. Pabst Science Publisher.

Salem B (2005). Commedia Virtuale: from theatre to avatars. *Digital Creativity*, 16(3), 129-139.

Salem B, Rauterberg M (2005a). Aesthetics as a key dimension for designing ubiquitous entertainment systems. In: M. Minoh & N. Tosa (eds.) The 2nd International Workshop on Ubiquitous Home—ubiquitous society and entertainment. (pp. 85-94) NICT Keihanna and Kyoto.

Salem B, Rauterberg M (2005b). Power, Death and Love: a trilogy for entertainment. *Lecture Notes in Computer Science*, vol. 3711, pp. 279-290.

Tosa N, Matsuoka S, Ellis B, Ueda H, Nakatsu R (2005). Cultural Computing with context-aware application: ZENetic Computer. *Lecture Notes in Computer Science*, vol. 3711, pp. 13-23.

The ox herding pictures were taken from the following websites:

Fig 3 http://www.sacred-texts.com/bud/mzb/oxherd.htm,

Fig 4 http://www.hsuyun.org/Dharma/zbohy/VisualArts/OxHerdingPictures/oxher-ding2.html

Fig 5 http://oaks.nvg.org/wm2ra4.html

Fig 6 http://www.donmeh-west.com/tenox.shtml

Fig 10: http://www.buddhanet.net/oxherd10.htm

The Alice in wonderland and the Petit Prince pictures were taken from Wikipedia

# Backseat Playgrounds: Pervasive Storytelling in Vast Location Based Games

John Bichard[1], Liselott Brunnberg[1], Marco Combetto[2], Anton Gustafsson[1],
and Oskar Juhlin[1]

[1] Interactive Institute, P O Box 24 081, SE 104 50 Stockholm
{john.bichard, liselott, anton.gustafsson, oskarj}@tii.se
http://www.tii.se/mobility
[2] Microsoft Research Cambridge UK, Roger Needham Building , 7 J J Thomson Ave, Cambridge CB3 0FB, UK
marcomb@microsoft.com
http://research.microsoft.com/ero/

**Abstract.** We have implemented a conceptual software framework and a story-based game that facilitates generation of rich and vivid narratives in vast geographical areas. An important design challenge in the emergent research area of pervasive gaming is to provide believable environments where game content is matched to the landscape in an evocative and persuasive way. More specifically, our game is designed to generate such an environment tailored to a journey as experienced from the backseat of a car. Therefore, it continuously references common geographical objects, such as houses, forests and churches, in the vicinity within the story; it provides a sequential narrative that fit with the drive; it works over vast areas, and it is possible to interact with the game while looking out of the windows.

## 1  Introduction

In recent years location based experiences and location based pervasive games, where a user's bodily and spatial movement in the physical world is a key element, has increasingly become a research focus. However available applications depend on either constant manual work to make the game fit into new geographical areas [5], [8], [10], [12], or lack location based experience beyond navigation support for chasing [2], [6], [9]. We argue that there is an issue of generating content if pervasive and location based games will scale up beyond the limited experimental setups, which has dominated research so far.

In this paper we investigate enriching pervasive games by providing more narrated elements in the game, as well as scale the game environment through integration with increasingly available geographical information systems. Recent advancements within interactive storytelling are promising [1], [3] [7], [11], [13]. First, these engines can extend the scope of pervasive games, beyond simple chasing games, with more complex interaction. Second, these engines could possibly handle the interaction as it occurs through the players movements through the landscape, as an addition to the more active choices pursued within the narrative experience. Furthermore, GIS data is becoming more widely available and accurate. Available map objects can be used for

R. Harper, M. Rauterberg, M. Combetto (Eds.): ICEC 2006, LNCS 4161, pp. 117–122, 2006.
© IFIP International Federation for Information Processing 2006

reasons other than supporting navigation. They can be used to link the pervasive narrative game with the surrounding environment.

The prototype is designed to provide what we refer to as a "believable environment." In particular we suggest four design characteristics to provide a persuasive inclusion of a journey [4] into a story based pervasive game. First, the story should refer to geographical objects with their everyday meaning. Second, the game needs to scale over vast areas. Third, the application should provide sequential storytelling to make it fit with the journey experience, and finally it should provide interaction support where players can engage in game play and interact with the narrative in various ways at the same time as they are looking out of the car window. In the following, we describe how these requirements have been implemented in the prototype.

## 2   The System

We have implemented a narrative based game, called Backseat Playground on a platform consisting of a PDA; a gyro and a GPS receiver, and a server running on a lap top which connects to the game device over WiFI. The player acts as a manager for field agents. The technologies are utilized to unfold a crime story with supernatural twists, where the actual location of the car is of importance. The game characters reference geographical objects in the vicinity and the player investigates what is happening with the directional microphone and interact with other characters over the phone or the walkie-talkie.

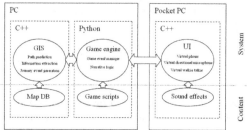

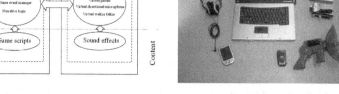

**Fig. 1.** System architecture                     **Fig. 2.** Hardware

### 2.1   User Interaction

The user interaction is built around the idea of having a set of virtual devices, i.e. a mobile cell phone, a walkie talkie and a directional microphone. The cell phone and walkie-talkie both provides a means for the players to keep in contact with the game characters. Both devices use text to speech synthesizing with a number of voices, together with a sound effect system to generate natural incoming phone calls and walkie-talkie calls. The virtual user interface of each of the device is displayed on the pocket pc when the device is active. After a call an options menu can be displayed in order to let the user select between different action in response to the call.

The virtual directional microphone enables us to give the sound an actual location. The player tunes into sounds at different virtual locations by turning the microphone around. The direction of the sound is based on data from the direction sensors together with the GPS location. By monitoring the players' use of the microphone the system will be able to determine which of the sounds the player is listening in to. It generally plays sound effects with local reference, e.g. birds, although it is sometimes used together with the text to speech system to let players listen into conversations.

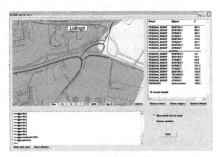

**Fig. 3.** Server path prediction and journey events          **Fig. 4.** Children testing prototype

## 2.2   Game Scripts, Narrative Logic and Game Event Manager

The narrative logic is implemented as a set of story scripts, which each contain a separate part relating to the story world. Each story script contains a tree like structure. The actual path through the tree, i.e. the plot, depends on the player's movements and choices. The narrative logic further ascertains a well paced unfolding of the plot. For example, it keeps track of the tempo between events in the scripts.

The game event manager handles the progression of the game and makes sure different parts of the story are triggered to ensure a meaningful unfolding, as well as an interesting pacing of the narrative. The game event manager first receives a list of roadside objects from the GIS module (see section below) and then asks each story script to rate their current priority to execute according to their perspective of the world. It receives each story scripts internal rating values, rated from 0-100%, and identifies the story script with the highest rate at that moment in time. If the rating is high enough it triggers the story script to proceed with its plot.

## 2.3   GIS Module

We use widely available GIS location data as a basis for the application allowing a fictitious world to be constructed around and within the physical environment. GIS mapping data includes layers of physical objects such as road networks, street signs, buildings and topographic features which can be linked to the game database. The map is processed in a GIS server module in order to predict which objects will occur on the journey, as well as their order and pacing during the upcoming movement through the landscape. The map processing converts the two-dimensional GIS data into a linear series of geographical event that are interpreted by the game event manager. These steps include *prediction of player's paths*; *extraction of visually available information* and *production of journey*.

*Path prediction:* The matching of the narrative to the surrounding geography is done with the calculi of a prediction about how far the car will move in the near future. The prediction is done based on available route options ahead of the vehicle i.e. in the current direction of the vehicle.

The algorithm starts by searching for a road ahead of the current GPS location, by identifying one of the road boundaries. When a path is identified, the algorithm follows it forward until a junction is reached and the road branches. From there onwards, the two different road boundaries will be followed until another branching occurs etc. The algorithm will stop after either one of two threshold values is reached. These values are either reaching the maximum distance of the path from our current location (this value is set to 1000 meters in the implementation) or reaching the maximum number of branch levels of the path (this value is set to two). These values can be dynamically updated to adjust for speed, for example, to allow for a variable window of future events.

The test implementation only provides data on the path to the first branch to the game event manager. However, the path prediction continuously occurs up to two branch levels ahead in the GIS module. This allows for quicker completion of upcoming requested data to the game event manager. The algorithm depends on reliable GIS data. Failures will occur e.g. if a gap occurs in the road side boundaries. To reduce the effects of such problems, the path prediction algorithm will restart and begin a new search for a suitable road on encountering such an error. In the meantime, the system continues running non-location based events.

*Extraction of visually available information:* GIS data contains point objects, line objects and area objects, which represents e.g. houses; roads; forests; elevation curves boundaries. The objects are sorted into different map layers, i.e. files in the data base and marked with different categories of the map supplier's choice. In order to provide an experience where the visual geography has meaning in the narrative, as seen by the player, we need to select the objects available in the map layers that could possibly be seen from the road. Abstract objects, e.g. political borders, are not considered as useful. However, some of visually available objects are only implicitly available in the map information. We then extract such objects e.g. intersections, by use of algorithms customized for that specific object.

The process of selecting layers and processing map information for implicit information is dependent on categories and layering provided by the map manufacturer. In this prototype we use map data from two different manufactures. Altogether we use about 50 different categories of objects and only one algorithm for implicit information extraction.

*Mapping objects to journey experience:* The next step is to combine predicted paths, with the extracted geographical objects, to generate what we define as a journey event list. A journey event is a prediction of an important visual event occurring along the path ahead involving a geographical object. In the current prototype we have so far define three different events i.e. passing right, passing left and crossing. Passing right is defined as the closest point where the distance to the object goes from decreasing to increasing and the object is to the right of the car. Passing left is the same only with the object left of the car. Crossing is the point where the predicted path intersects with a map object.

To further distinguish the visibility of the objects we also predict the distance and direction to it, as well as the frequency in which they appear. The assumption is that unique objects close by in the middle of your field of view are more visually important than others.

## 3   Conclusion

The prototype implement has been tested in a performance test as well as an initial user test. Even if more comprehensive user tests are ongoing, the preliminary results demonstrated that the current implementation provides a game experience according to the concepts described. Thus, the system we designed and implemented meets the requirements defined to build what we refer to as a believable environment in pervasive gaming.

First, it introduces and references to geographical objects with preserved everyday meaning in the story based game. The implementation manages to find GIS data in the vicinity and link that to stories, which were presented to the user. Second, a believable narrative environment should surround the location of the player. It follows that the data should be available along the whole road network and that it should have enough density to provide story experience almost anywhere. The implementation covers an area of around 35 square kilometers (around 41 000 inhabitants), which is per se much larger than other similar narrative environments. Furthermore, the concept is easily scalable if more GIS data is added covering larger geographical areas. Third, the system should match the story to the journey experience, rather than fitting stories to individual locations, to create believable environments. The prototype generates story segments which both made sense in their temporal order as well as their referencing to locations in the story. Finally, the player should mix the interaction with the devices and with the physical surrounding to generate a coherent experience. The implemented user interaction is audio centric, where most of game and narrative features are presented as sounds. Additional interaction through movements is integrated with audio in the form of a directional microphone. The intention has been to allow as much visual focus as possible on the landscape. However, for practical reasons the response to the speech is designed as a selection of options from a list display on the screen, rather than as speech recognition.

Future work will consists of a user evaluation and development of content. We will also investigate the possibilities for user content creation to further improve believability of the environment.

## Acknowledgement

The research was made possible by grants from Microsoft Reseach Cambridge/Intelligents Environments within the area of "Fun, play and creativity". It was also funded by Swedish Foundation for Strategic Research as well as the Swedish Governmental Agency for Innovation Systems.

# References

1. Malaka, R., Schneider, K., Kretschmer, U., Stage-based augmented edutainment, In proceedings of Smart Graphics: 4th International Symposium, SG 2004, Banff, Canada, May, 2004
2. Bell, M., Chalmers, M., Barkhuus, L., Sherwood, S., Brown, B., Rowland, D., Benford, S., Hampshire, A., Capra, M., Interweaving Mobile Games With Everyday Life, In Proceedings of SIG CHI 2006, April, Montreal Canada, ACM
3. Crawford, C., Chris Crawford on interactive storytelling, New Riders, Berkeley, CA, 2005
4. Appleyard, D., Lynch K., Myer R., The view from the road, MIT Press, Massachusetts, 1964
5. Brunnberg, L. and Juhlin, O., Movement and Spatiality in a Gaming Situation - Boosting Mobile Computer Games with the Highway Experience. In Proceedings of Interact'2003 - IFIP TC 13 International Conference on Human-Computer Interaction. IOS Press, pp 407-414.
6. Brunnberg, L. and Juhlin, O. Keep your eyes on the road and your finger on the trigger - Designing for mixed focus of at¬tention in a mobile game for brief encounters. In Proceed¬ings of the 4th International Conference on Pervasive Com¬puting. Springer Verlag.
7. Crawford, C., Chris Crawford on interactive storytelling, New Riders, Berkeley, CA, 2005
8. Crow, D., Pan, P., Kam, L., Davenport, G., M-views: A sys¬tem for location based storytelling, ACM UbiComp 2003, Seattle, WA, 2003
9. Flintham, M., Benford, B., et al.: Where On-line Meets On-The-Streets: Experiences with Mobile Mixed Reality Games. Proceedings of CHI'03, Conference on Human factors in computing systems, Ft. Lauderdale, USA (2003) 569 – 576
10. Kretschmer, U., Coors, V., Spierling, U., Grasbon, D., Schnei¬der, K., Rojas, I., Malaka, R., Meeting the spirit of history, In proceedings of Conference on Virtual reality, archeology, and cultural heritage, Glyfada, Greece 2001
11. Mateas M., Stern A., Façade: An Experiment in Building a Fully-Realized Interactive Drama, Game Developers Confer¬ence, March 2003
12. Nisi, V., Wood, A., G. Davenport, L. Doyle, Hopstory: an interactive, location-based narrative distributed in space and time, In proceedings of Second International Conference, TIDSE 2004, Darmstadt, Germany, June 24-26, 2004.
13. Szilas, N., IDtension: a narrative engine for interactive drama, In proceedings of Technologies for Interactive Digi¬tal Storytelling and Entertainment (TIDSE) Conference, 187-203, 2003.

# Layered Multiple Displays for Immersive and Interactive Digital Contents

Gun A. Lee, Ungyeon Yang, and Wookho Son

Virtual Reality Team, Digital Content Research Division,
Electronics and Telecommunications Research Institute,
Gajeong-dong, Yuseong-gu, Daejeon, 305-700, Republic of Korea
{endovert, uyyang, whson}@etri.re.kr

**Abstract.** In this paper we introduce the concept of 'Layered Multiple Displays (LMD)' for visualizing immersive and interactive digital contents. The LMD platform integrates various display technologies into a unified interaction space by providing natural visualization of three-dimensional virtual spaces, especially in terms of depth perception. Each display component complements one another, providing not only natural visualizations of three dimensional spaces but also personalized point of views. We describe our implementation of a prototype LMD platform with a game application, and discuss about its usability issues, and present future research directions.

**Keywords:** ubiquitous computing, immersive display.

## 1 Introduction

Recently, ubiquitous (a.k.a. pervasive) and wearable computing environments became hot topics in information and communication technology field. Under this new trend, various sensors and new user interfaces are invented and applied to contemporary computing environment, and such newly introduced user interfaces and services are driving the culture and trend of end users' computing experiences. Popularization of various personal computing devices (from desktop computers to mobile smart phones) made people to own multiple computing devices. And while having more than one computing environments, the users came to need integration (and/or synchronization) of services and information between individual devices, so that the users could have consistent experiences throughout their switches between different computing devices. Among many aspects in integrating multiple device interfaces within ubiquitous and wearable computing environments, in this research we especially focus on visual display interfaces.

Among the five modalities of human senses, visual modality is the one that has the biggest weight in our everyday life. Hence, there is no doubt on that a lot of researches have been developing various technologies for visual displays and interfaces. Nowadays, a huge range of visual displays are available in terms of its size and the number of audience supported. Those with huge sizes, such as large projection displays, are used for multitudes of audiences, while those in the midrange (e.g. PC monitors or television sets) support a small group of people. Recently, great

R. Harper, M. Rauterberg, M. Combetto (Eds.): ICEC 2006, LNCS 4161, pp. 123–134, 2006.

advances in mobile devices, such as smart phones and personal digital assistants (PDA), popularized tiny displays held on the users' hands, and even head (or face) mounted displays (HMD or FMD) are ready for getting popularized.

In the near future, where computing environments become ubiquitous and wearable, we can easily suppose that users would need to use multiple visual display interfaces concurrently. Users will carry their own personal visual displays, while there would be a number of public visual displays (such as information kiosks or advertisement displays) available in the surrounding environment. And as users interact with these various displays, we do not suppose that each display will only visualize information individually, but do expect that they will interact with each other, forming an integration of information as well as its visualization. This can be thought of as each visual display interface providing a layer of visualization. And by working together and complementing each other, multiple displays can be integrated into a single information/virtual space. In this paper, we refer to this concept (or configuration) as 'Layered Multiple Displays' or 'LMD' in short.

In the rest of this paper, we first review previous works related to our research topic, and then describe the concept of Layered Multiple Displays in detail with various application scenarios. Next, as a proof of concept, we illustrate our prototype implementation of the LMD platform and its application. And finally, we conclude this paper by discussing usability issues of our new display platform design, and by presenting future research directions.

## 2  Related Works

Many researchers have been working on developing various visualization techniques to overcome certain disadvantages in visual display interfaces.

One of the most well known criteria for evaluating a display system is the field of view (FOV). There have been various efforts to overcome the narrow field of view of display devices. Other than simply making the display surface bigger, various immersive displays have been proposed for providing wide field of view to the user in visualizing immersive virtual environments. One of the most well known display system developed for such purpose is the CAVE [4] system. The CAVE system integrates three to six projection screens into a cube shaped room for immersive visualization. The FOV of this system scales up to omni-directional depending on the number of screens used.

Although projection-based immersive displays have good solution for providing wide field of views, they still have disadvantages with occlusion problems. Since the projection screens are at a certain distance from the user's viewpoint, other physical objects, such as user's hands or interaction devices, may occlude the visualized image. This does not matter when the virtual object visualized on the occluded image is actually farther than the physical object covering the screen. However, when a virtual object is supposed to be visualized in front of a physical object, projection-based display systems normally fails to visualize the image correctly.

Occlusion problems are relatively easier to deal with when using head mounted displays. With opaque head mounted displays, occlusion problems never occur since users are not able to see anything from the real world. Besides, for augmented and mixed reality environments [8], where users see virtual objects registered to the real world space, see-through displays are used. In this case, virtual image is always visualized on top of the real world view even when physical objects are in front. Such incorrect occlusions can be solved by drawing only the certain regions of virtual scene those are in front of physical objects [3][9], and these regions can be decided by depth information of the real world scene [3][5].

Although when the depth information of the real world is available, it is still hard to visualize correct occlusions with optical see-through displays, which provides more natural view of the real world in comparison to video see-through method. Optical see-through displays use half-mirrors to combine the virtual and the real world scenes. The problem is that the transparencies of these mirrors are usually fixed, and hence the users are always able to see certain amount of lights from the real world, preventing full occlusion of the real world view even when it is necessary.

As we can see above, although visual display technology has been advanced a lot through decades, there is no perfect display available yet and each display has its own merits and disadvantages. Under this notion, lately, there were a couple of attempts to use different types of display technologies together and take advantages from each.

Bimber et al. [1] combined hologram image with projection displays to take advantage of high resolution three-dimensional visualization from the hologram and interactivity from projection displays visualizing computer graphics. Winterbottom [11] addressed possibilities of testing newly designed head mounted displays within a fighter plane simulator which uses projection displays for visualizing the virtual environment. Although his purpose was usability test rather than using both displays for visualizing three-dimensional space, he showed the possibilities of using multiple displays in a layered fashion.

## 3 Layered Multiple Displays

### 3.1 Concept

Layered Multiple Displays (LMD) is a set of visual display interfaces registered and synchronized with each other to form and visualize an integrated interaction space to the users (see Fig. 1). We propose LMD as a visual display platform for providing immersive and interactive experiences to the users by visualizing virtual contents in more natural and dynamic fashion. LMDs are especially good for visualizing dynamic three-dimensional (3D) virtual spaces in terms of supporting concurrent visualization of both near body and far environmental virtual spaces.

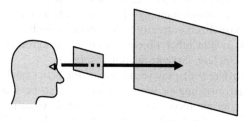

**Fig. 1.** Layered Multiple Displays: users see virtual information space through multiple visual display interfaces

As mentioned formerly, there are no ultimate display technologies available yet, and each display device has its own advantages and disadvantages. With LMD, each visual display interfaces are complemented by one another, using multiple heterogeneous visual displays forming physical/virtual layers of visualization.

Images visualized on a large projection displays easily get occluded by the users' body or other physical user interfaces used together. On the other hand, head mounted displays can visualize virtual images right in front of users' eyes, preventing occlusions by other physical objects. By using these two displays in a LMD configuration, occlusion problems can be resolved by visualizing the virtual objects in between the user's eyes and user's hands on the HMD and other objects on the projection display behind.

Another advantage of using LMD is extending field of views of each single displays. Large projection displays provide wide field of view, while the FOVs of HMDs are relatively narrow. By using it behind the HMD, a large projection display can provide broader peripheral views to the user. On the other hand, although fixed displays (e.g., projection displays) usually have broader geometrical FOV in comparison to HMDs, they still have physical limits in their physical viewing direction. However, HMDs can provide virtually omni-directional view when head tracking is available. Therefore, when a virtual object visualized on the fixed display gets out of the border, it can still be visualized with LMD configurations by transferring the virtual object onto the HMD.

Besides FOV problems, another issue in visualization is to provide correct stereoscopic images in terms of depth focus. Most of the stereo displays (including head mounted displays, stereo monitors and projection displays) provoke depth sensation by visualizing two separate images to each left and right eyes, rendered with certain disparity according to the depth value of the visualized object. Human eyes tilt inward to make a certain convergence to the depth of location in interest according the disparity of the image displayed. However, the accommodation (or focus) is still fixed to the actual display surface (or virtual image plane for HMDs) and this may cause confusions or even cyber sickness to the user. Developing visual displays with adjustable depth of focus is challenging. However until they become available, using proper combinations of displays with different depth of focus in LMD configuration would be helpful to address this problem. Each virtual object could be visualized on an appropriate display layer according to its distance from the user's viewpoint and the depth of focus of the display.

Visualizing stereoscopic images correctly requires knowing the positions of the user's viewpoint. When multiple participants try to see stereoscopic images on fixed displays, other users except the user being head tracked see incorrect stereoscopic images and this causes misunderstanding of 3D geometries. With LMD, those objects that are needed to be visualized correctly in 3D space could be visualized on personal displays (e.g. HMDs), while other objects (such as background environments) are shown on public displays (e.g. large projection displays).

Besides combing different display technologies for better quality of visualization, certain merits such as providing privacy control can also be found by using LMD configuration. LMD configuration can provide separate visualization of public and private (or personal) information using multiple displays. Private information that are needed to be hidden from other participants can be visualized on the user's personal displays, such as HMD or hand held displays, while public information can be visualized on the public display.

Recent researches on multi-participant games show the importance of providing privacy on visual interfaces. Szalavari [10] presented a multi-participant augmented reality game, where the users played a Chinese game 'Mah-Jongg'. In this game, each player held a private virtual display to hide his game blocks from the other players. Recently, Kitamura [6] proposed to use a table display with a display mask for providing public and private display regions. Users were able to see their private information at a certain viewpoint where they can see their private display region through the display mask. These works show managing privacy becomes more important in collaborative computing environments.

In summary, the merits of LMD configuration could be thought in three aspects: providing context consistent integrated visualization space, improving (or complementing) visualization qualities of each displays, and providing privacy controlled visualization in multi-participant applications.

## 3.2  Visual Display Interface Spectrum

Various visual display interfaces used in LMD environment can be categorized into a number of types according to its relative distance from the user's viewpoint (or eyes). Similar to the category made by Bimber et al. [2], here we categorize visual display devices into five types: retinal, head attached, near-body (or hand-held), spatial and environmental displays. Fig. 2 illustrates the relative distance from the user's viewpoint to each type of visual displays.

Retinal displays (http://www.hitl.washington.edu/research/ivrd/) are the most nearest ones to the user's viewpoint. Actually its display surface is the retina itself so that no other displays can visualize images closer than these. Head attached displays are those attached near to users' eyes. Head mounted displays or helmet mounted displays fall into this category of visual displays. Next comes the near-body (or hand-held) displays those are within the near-body space. By the near-body space, we refer to a spatial volume that extends to the distance of hand reach. Hence, near-body displays are usually held or worn by the user. By spatial displays, we refer to those within a distance where human visual sensory can percept depth information according to stereoscopic view. Spatial displays are usually fixed at a certain location in the environment. Finally, the environmental displays are those far beyond from the user's viewpoint.

Display devices in LMD platform can provide either monoscopic or stereoscopic visualizations. With monoscopic visualizations, images are formed on the display surface of the device, hence the visualization range in depth is fixed to the distance between the user's viewpoint and the image plane of the display interface. In the case of providing stereoscopic view, the visualization range in depth becomes a volume covered with max disparity in stereoscopic image. The lower part of Fig. 3 illustrates such ranges for each display types. The ranges are subject to change according to the size of the screen, so that each type of displays has main visualization range marked with solid lines, while they can be extended out to dashed lines with bigger screens.

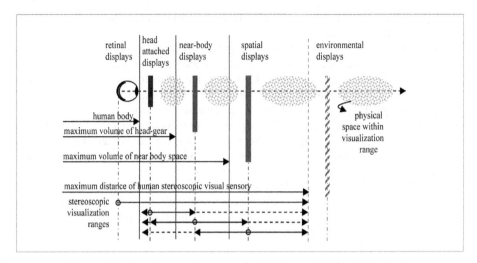

**Fig. 2.** Visual display interface spectrum for Layered Multiple Displays

Although see-through displays are not that common in current visual display markets, display interfaces in LMD configuration are expected to be visually semi-transparent (i.e. optical see-through displays), so that the users could see another display through it. On the other hand, video see-through displays could be another alternative for allowing users to see the scene behind the display interface.

### 3.3  Use Case Scenario

Here we describe a use case scenario of Layered Multiple Displays according to the illustration shown in Fig. 3. In the figure, the three participants are referred as u1, u2 and u3, four visual display interfaces are referred as d1, d2, d3 and d4, and r1 and r2 are real objects within the environment.

The first user (u1) is wearing a head mounted display (d1), while the second user (u2) is holding a hand-held display (d2). The third participant doesn't have his/her own personal device, but still can see the images visualized on the spatial displays (d3 and d4). Fig. 3-(2) shows the visualization range in depth where each display is capable to visualize stereoscopic images (the lines in the middle of the visualization range are the image plane of the display device). Finally, Fig. 3-(3) shows the view frustum and combined view for each user. Note that the first user gets images with correct occlusion by visualizing a pentagon on the HMD (d1) and a circle on the environmental display (d4). Also, the narrow field of view of the first user with the HMD (d1) is extended by the environmental display (d4). The second user (u2) gets correct visualization of the triangle on the spatial display (d3), although the triangle was originally displayed on another spatial display (d4) and crosses its border.

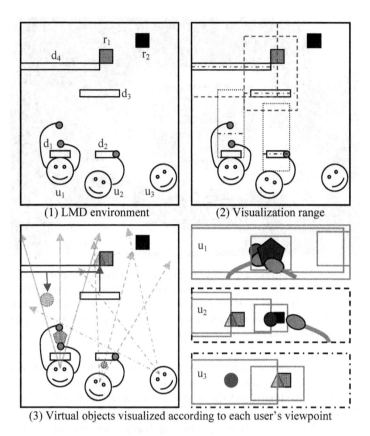

**Fig. 3.** Use case scenario of Layered Multiple Displays (u1-u3: participants, d1-d4: visual display interfaces, r1-r2: real objects)

## 4   Prototype Implementation

As a proof of concept, we implemented a prototype Layered Multiple Displays platform and its game application that provides immersive and interactive experience for multiple participants. We used three visual display interfaces (one monitor and two head mounted displays) for our prototype LMD platform.

The scenario of our prototype LMD game was motivated by a famous movie 'Ghostbusters' (Ivan Reitman, 1984). Within the game, two participants collaborate to find out and capture the ghosts hiding inside a maze (see Fig. 4). One of the participants plays the role of a driver (the left person in Fig. 4) who drives a vehicle with which they navigate through the maze. The other participant plays the role of a hunter (the right person in Fig. 4) who captures the ghosts by shooting them with a proton gun or hitting with a proton saber. Both participants can see the outside view (the maze and the ghosts outside) through the window (which is actually a display monitor) of the vehicle.

**Fig. 4.** The VR Ghostbusters: a prototype game using Layered Multiple Displays. Two participants are collaborating as a driver and a hunter to capture the ghosts hiding inside a maze. Public information (such as 3D visualization of the maze) are visualized on the monitor in front, while personal information (such as the dashboard for the driver and weapons for the hunter) are shown on the head mounted displays.

While watching outside of the vehicle through the monitor, each participant also wears a head mounted display, on which their personal information are visualized. For the driver, the dashboard and the map are shown on his head mounted display; while the hunter can see his weapon on his HMD (Fig. 5 shows personal views of each participant). Notice that the head mounted displays are optical see-through ones so that the users can see the outside world (including the monitor and the other participant as well) along with the graphics visualized on the HMD.

Though the hunter usually shoots a proton gun through the window to capture the ghosts outside, ghosts can also break into the vehicle through the window, popping out from the monitor and hovering in the real world, as shown in Fig. 6. In this case, the ghost is only visible to the hunter, who is considered to be wearing special goggles

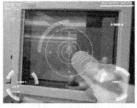

**Fig. 5.** Personal views of each participant: the left picture is the driver's view with a dashboard visualized on the lower right corner, the middle and the right pictures are the view of the hunter using different weapons, a proton gun and a proton saber (the pictures shown are synthesized with a photograph and a screen capture due to difficulties of taking photographs directly through head mounted displays)

**Fig. 6.** A virtual object transfers from one display to another: a virtual ghost which was originally visualized on the monitor (left) popped out into the real world, visualized on the head mounted display (right)

for ghost vision (which is actually the HMD). The hunter needs to change his weapon into a proton saber and try to hit the ghost with it (see the right picture of Fig. 5).

The system was built on a PC platform running Microsoft Windows operating system. Three personal computers were linked through a gigabit Ethernet for communication and synchronization between them. As a virtual reality visualization software toolkit, we used OpenSG (http://www.opensg.org) library which provides functions for manipulating and synchronizing scene graphs over a clustered PCs.

Each PC was equipped with multi-channel 3D graphics accelerator interfaces in order to provide rendered images of the virtual environment for three display devices: a monitor and two head mounted displays. All of these three displays provided their own stereoscopic views.

The CRT monitor (showing 1024x768 resolutions at 85Hz) was equipped with a stereo LCD shutter screen 21SX from NuVision (http://www.nuvision3d.com) which provided frame sequential stereo images through circular-polarizing filters. A pair of polarizing filters was attached in front of the optical see-through HMD so that the user could also see the stereoscopic images displayed on the monitor while wearing it [12]. (We make a note that we used a monitor due to our limited resource. This could be definitely replaced with other stereo display equipments with larger field of view and higher resolutions, such as projection based display systems.)

The head mounted displays from DEOCOM (http://www.deocom.com) provided their own stereoscopic views from multiple channel video input. The HMD supported 1280x1024 resolutions and 45 degrees of diagonal field of view.

Each user was provided with a hand held prop appropriate to his/her role. The driver was provided with a game pad to drive the vehicle, and the hunter was provided with a prop with buttons (actually a wireless mouse) for gun triggering and changing weapons (see Fig. 7). For tracking users' viewpoints and props, we used a motion capture system from Motion Analysis with three Hawk Digital cameras running at 100 frames per second, with sub-millimeter positional accuracy.

Image registration between multiple visual displays is the key problem for making LMD work. To achieve this, first, each display should share the same global coorinate frame in the 3D virtual and physical space. Although we used a single tracking system for all displays, in ubiquitous computing environments, there might be various sensor networks, and the coordinate frame of each tracking sensors might

**Fig. 7.** The head mounted display and props used in the prototype system: upper left is an optical see-through HMD equipped with stereo circular-polarizing filters in its front, lower is a prop with buttons held by the hunter, and on the right is a game pad used by the driver. A set of infrared reflective markers were attached to the devices needed for tracking.

need to be registered. This can be easily achieved by multiplying transformation matrices of each sensor's reference frame to the tracking data.

As the 3D spatial coordinates of each display are aligned, next we need to calibrate the virtual cameras of each display. The virtual cameras of each display in LMD change their intrinsic parameters (i.e. projection matrix) as the user or the display moves, and therefore must be updated every frame. Assuming that the display image planes are planar and rectangular, we represent the virtual camera with an off-axis projection matrix, decided by the user's eye position and the size and pose of the image plane. For many display devices, image planes are identical to the physical display surface, and it is easy to measure their features physically. However, there are also some visual display interfaces, such as HMD, that have virtual image planes different from the physical display element. For this case we referred to the device specifications.

Although after we carefully measured and calibrated the system, still there were some registration errors with few centimeters. However, the registration errors were small enough for our application, showing not much disturbance to the users for playing the game. However, we surely need and are looking forward to improve the registration methods to achieve enough accuracy for general cases, including their use in industrial fields, such as virtual manufacturing and virtual work training. Calibration methods used for optical see-through displays in AR systems might be useful for this purpose.

## 5   Discussion and Future Work

To investigate usability issues in LMD configuration, we are planning for a formal user study. At the moment, we only had chances for informal user tests. After a short use by a couple of test users, we received positive responses of using Layered Multiple Displays in terms of its exciting experience. The users especially liked to see virtual ghosts popping out from the screen, breaking into the real world and hovering around the user. The transition of the virtual object from one display interface to another was good enough to convince users as if the virtual object pops out from the monitor into the real world.

Smoother transition of information and visualization are subjects for improvement. In our current implementation, due to the limitations of the visualization software and communication delays, we use a same copy of scene graphs over different rendering PCs and only switch on and off the virtual ghost nodes to change the display interface on which they are visualized. In order to support general cases of its use in ubiquitous computing environment (as mentioned in section 3), we need to manage and transfer information (such as 3D geometries) between visual interfaces (or computing entities) on demand. This would include managing participants joining in and leaving out from the display platform, and also other security issues in transferring personal information into the shared space.

As we visualized virtual objects on head mounted displays, we found out that rendering dark colored objects on a optical see-through HMD is difficult (since dark colors appear transparent). To overcome this problem, adding another layer of gray level LCD into the optical see-through HMD for shutting off the outside light sources could be useful, as shown in Kiyokawa's work [7]. Besides, we are also considering using video see-through displays with stereo filters in front of video cameras instead of optical see-through ones in this aspect.

## 6 Conclusion

We presented the concept of Layered Multiple Displays that integrates multiple visual display interfaces into one integrated interaction space for visualizing immersive and interactive virtual contents. Visual display interfaces used in LMD configuration complement one another in the aspect of occlusion problem, widening FOV, and varying depth of focus. In addition to providing better quality of visualization, LMD can also provide privacy in multi-participant environments. The prototype implementation of LMD platform and its application showed potentialities of Layered Multiple Displays. With confidence in further researches to solve the problems discussed formerly, we expect Layered Multiple Displays will take an important role as one of the representative visual display platforms in future computing environments where computers become ubiquitous and wearable.

**Acknowledgments.** This paper is a result of the 'Virtual Manufacturing (Intelligent Manufacturing Systems)' research project supported by the Korean Ministry of Information and Communication and Fraunhofer IGD (Germany).

## References

1. Bimber, O., Zeidler, T., Grundhoefer, A., Wetzstein, G., Moehring, M., Knoedel, S., Hahne, U. : Interacting with augmented holograms. SPIE Proceedings of International Conference on Practical Holography XIX, (2005) 41-54
2. Bimber, O. Raskar, R.: Spatial Augmented Reality: Merging Real and Virtual Worlds. A K Peters, Ltd. (2005)
3. Breen, D., Whitaker, R., Rose, E., Tuceryan, M. : Interactive Occlusion and Automatic Object Placement for Augmented Reality. Computer Graphics Forum Vol.15 No.3, (1996) 11-22

4. Cruz-Neira, C., Sadin, D. J., Defanti, T. A. : Surround-screen projection-based virtual reality: the design and implementation of the CAVE. Proceedings of SIGGRAPH '93, (1993) 135-142
5. Hayashi, K., Kato, H., Nishida, S. : Occlusion Detection of Real Objects using Contour Based Stereo Matching. Proceedings of 15th International Conference on Artificial Reality and Telexistence (ICAT2005), (2005) 180-186
6. Kitamura, Y., Osawa, W., Yamaguchi, T., Takemura, H., Kishino, F. : A Display Table for Strategic Collaboration Preserving Private and Public Information. LNCS 3711: ICEC2005, (2005) 167-179
7. Kiyokawa, K., Billinghurst, M., Campbell, B., Woods, E. : An occlusion capable optical see-through head mount display for supporting co-located collaboration. Proceedings of The Second IEEE and ACM International Symposium on Mixed and Augmented Reality, (2003) 133-141
8. Milgram, P., F. Kishino : A Taxonomy of Mixed Reality Visual Displays. IEICE Trans. on Information and Systems (Special Issue on Networked Reality) E77-D(12), (1994) 1321-1329
9. Mulder, J. D. : Realistic Occlusion Effects in Mirror-Based Co-Located Augmented Reality Systems. IEEE Proceedings of International Conference on Virtual Reality, (2005) 203-208
10. Szalavari, Z., Eckstein, E., Gervautz, M. : Collaborative Gaming in Augmented Reality. Proceedings of VRST, (1998) 195-204
11. Winterbottom, M. D., Patterson, R., Pierce, B. J., Covas, C., Winner, J. : The influence of depth of focus on visibility of monocular headmounted display symbology in simulation and training applications. Proceedings of SPIE Helmet- and Head-Mounted Displays X: Technologies and Applications, Vol. 5800, (2005) 65-73
12. Yang, U., Jo, D., Son, W., Kim, H. : Visual Interface for Presenting Multiple Mixed Stereo Image. US Patents, applied no. 11/223066. (2005)

# Design and Implementation of a Fast Integral Image Rendering Method

Bin-Na-Ra Lee[1], Yongjoo Cho[2], Kyoung Shin Park[3], Sung-Wook Min[4],
Joa-Sang Lim[2], Min Cheol Whang[2], and Kang Ryoung Park[2]

[1] Department of Computer Science, Sangmyung University, 7 Hongji-dong, Jongno-gu,
Seoul, 110-743, Republic of Korea
[2] Division of Media Technology, Sangmyung University, 7 Hongji-dong, Jongno-gu, Seoul,
110-743, Republic of Korea
[3] Digital Media Laboratory, Information and Communications University, 517-10
Dogok-dong, Gangnam-gu, Seoul 135-854, Republic of Korea
[4] Optical Image Processing Laboratory, Bradley Department of Electrical and Computer
Engineering, Virginia Tech, Virginia 24061 USA
ycho@smu.ac.kr

**Abstract.** The computer-generated integral imaging system is a way of showing
stereoscopic displays that allows users to see 3D images without wearing any
special glasses. In the integral imaging system, the 3D object information is
stored as elemental images, which are generated by the image mapping method.
This paper reviews the previous image mapping methods, such as PRR (Point
Retracing Rendering), MVR (Multi-Viewpoint Rendering), and PGR (Parallel
Group Rendering). Then, it explains a new image mapping method called VVR,
which shows better performance while generating similar pictures as in MVR.
Finally it mentions process of making the integral imaging system, and analyzes
performance. Then, it discusses some research directions for the future im-
provement.

## 1 Introduction

Virtual Reality (VR) is an interactive multimedia system that provides realistic information visuals and interactivity to users [1]. In most VR systems, stereoscopic displaying method is mostly used in these days because it can be easily implemented and
shows good enough 3D effect than others. However, stereoscopic displays have some
drawbacks. For example, it dose not provide the continuous viewpoint. In other
words, it only gives the depth of image and solidity, but does not provide any volumetric information. Also, users of stereoscopic imaging systems should wear special
glasses to see the three-dimensional images.

Autostereoscopic displays have been improved to overcome the typical drawbacks
of stereoscopic displays by developing and employing new methods, such as multi-
view binocular, volumetric display, and holography [2]. The integral imaging system
is one of the most promising autostereoscopic system because it can provide the full
color image and both vertical and horizontal parallaxes without putting any special
devices on the observers [3]. Moreover, it provides the continuous viewpoint, volumetric information, to users.

R. Harper, M. Rauterberg, M. Combetto (Eds.): ICEC 2006, LNCS 4161, pp. 135–140, 2006.

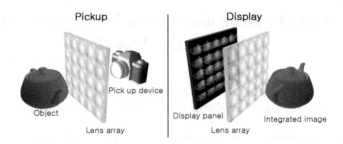

**Fig. 1.** The concept of the Computer Generated (CG) integral imaging system

Fig. 1 presents how the integral imaging system works. As the picture shows, the integral imaging system consists of a pickup and display parts [4]. The pickup part is implemented with the lens array and a pickup device like CCD camera; then, the system captures and stores the three-dimensional information about 3D objects as a set of two-dimensional elemental image. In the display part, the integrated image is shown to users through the lens array; then, users would be able to see the 3D object composed out of the elemental images. Instead of using a real lens array and CCD camera, the pickup part can be replaced with the computer rendering methods, which is often referred as CG (computer generated) image mapping. In this paper, we propose a fast image mapping algorithm called VVR (Viewpoint Vector Rendering). First, this paper explains several previous image mapping methods. Then, it describes the concept, design and implementation of VVR. It also presents the analysis of comparison between VVR with MVR. Finally, future directions of this research will be discussed.

## 2  Previous Image Mapping Algorithms

In the traditional CG integral imaging system, a set of elemental images is drawn pixel by pixel by mapping every point of the 3D object to the elemental images. This method, called PRR (Point Retracing Rendering), is widely used due to its simplicity, but is too slow to be used for real-time graphics applications [5]. The reconstruction process of the 3D integrated image takes longer and longer as the size of the object gets bigger or the number of objects is increased.

A couple of new image mapping methods have been developed to overcome the deficiency of the PRR algorithm, such as Multiple Viewpoint Rendering (MVR) [6] and Parallel Group Rendering (PGR) [7]. MVR imitates the real pickup process of the integral system by using 3D computer graphics technologies. In MVR, elemental images are generated by capturing virtual objects in a 3D space using a virtual camera. The virtual camera is moved by the elemental lens pitch the same as the real CCD camera of the integral imaging system. The advantage of MVR is that it can construct the correct elemental images by following a simple pickup algorithm. It can also use 3D models without any conversion and is not affected by the size of the virtual objects unlike PRR. However, the processing time of generating elemental images takes longer and longer as the number of lenses in the lens array gets increased since it needs to take pictures and renders for each lens of the lens array.

PGR is an algorithm that is designed to overcome the slower performance of other algorithms. In PGR, elemental images are obtained from the imaginary scenes that are observed in a certain direction, which we call the directional scenes. Then, the elemental images are assembled from the pixels of the directional scenes. In PGR, the number of directional scenes is the same as that of the pixels in the elemental lens area, and its directions are corresponded with the viewing vectors from each pixel to the center of the elemental lens. One of the advantages of this method is that the number of elemental lenses does not affect the performance. However, PGR only supports the focused mode, which can show the maximum image depth, while the resolution of the reconstructed images is degraded.

## 3  Design and Implementation of Viewpoint Vector Rendering

In this paper, a new image mapping algorithm called VVR is proposed, which is designed with real-time graphics in mind. VVR's construction process of elemental images is several times faster than MVR, while the quality of the elemental images is competitive to the images generated by MVR. Moreover, the image mapping process of VVR is not degraded as in MVR even when the number of elemental lenses is increased.

### 3.1  Viewpoint Vector Rendering

VVR method is similar to PGR in the way that VVR utilizes the directional scenes and is not affected much when the number of elemental lenses gets increased. However, unlike PGR, which can only be used in the focused mode constructing the integrated images around the lens array, VVR can be used in the focused, real, and virtual mode. Real mode in the integral imaging system means that the integral images are viewable in front of the lens array because the focal length of the lenses is shorter than the length between the display device and the lens array. Virtual mode constructs the integral image behind the lens array because the focal length is longer than the distance between the display and the lens array. As directional scenes are taken in bigger chunks and processed to fit into the smaller elemental images, it requires a little overhead of image processing. However, it is still a few times faster than MVR even if the image processing time is counted when the number of lenses is over certain threshold, which is pretty small and negligible for most integral imaging systems.

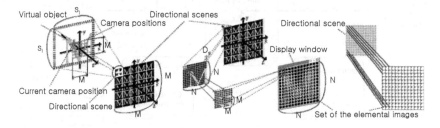

**Fig. 2.** The concept of the CG integral imaging system with VVR

With its faster construction of elemental images and versatility of supporting various stereoscopic modes, VVR shows advantages when it is used for real-time computer graphics than other methods.

Fig. 2 shows VVR process, which creates the set of elemental images with magnification (M) value of 5 (i.e., the number of viewpoint vectors is 5x5), and the number of elemental lenses (N) is 13. The left picture of Fig. 2 shows the pick-up process of the directional scenes, and the center image represents the displaying process. The pick-up part of VVR image mapping process is accomplished by obtaining 5x5 directional scenes. Then, each directional scene is split into 13x13 (169 in total) image segments, which is are distributed to a section of the 13x13 elemental images (see the rightmost picture of Fig. 2). When this process is iterated 25 times for 5x5 directional scenes, the final set of 13x13 elemental images are finally composed and displayed to show the integrated images.

## 3.2  Design and Evaluation of VVR

VVR integral imaging system is implemented using C++ and OpenGL. Fig. 3 shows the architecture of the system. As shown in the picture, VVR integral imaging system is composed of several sub-components, such as control, object, rendering, image mapping and display systems. The control system initializes some required factors for the system and manages the system to run. When it gets started, the system reads several input values of factors, such as N, M, and so on, from a configuration file. Then, it calculates other factors, such as camera positions, the size of a directional scene, the field of view value for the virtual camera, and so on. It also constructs other sub-components of the system and runs the main loop. The object system loads and manages 3D model data to be rendered by the integral imaging system. The rendering system utilizes OpenGL 3D graphics library to generate the directional scenes. It controls the virtual camera by calculating the absolute positions where the camera must be located and take a directional scene of the 3D world. The rendering system creates an image file for each directional scene, which is then manipulated in the

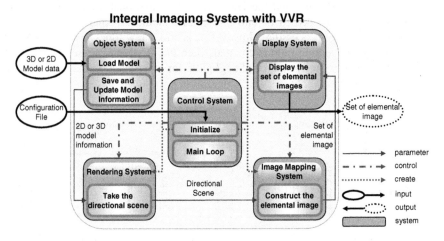

**Fig. 3.** Architecture of the CG integral imaging system with VVR

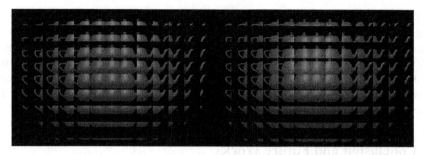

**Fig. 4.** Elemental images of a 3D teapot created using VVR (left) and MVR (right)

image mapping system. The image mapping system processes the slices and replacements of directional scenes, which basically assemble the final set of elemental images. The completed elemental images are then passed to the display system, which draws the images on the screen. When users see the image on the screen through the lens array, users would be able to see the 3D view.

VVR image mapping method is evaluated from two different directions. First, we tried to compare the quality of elemental images generated from both VVR and MVR methods by using the PSNR (Peak Signal to Noise Ratio) test. PSNR is widely used to find out similarity between two images; in general, if the value of PSNR is over 40dB, both images are considered to be almost identical. Fig. 4 shows a set of elemental images generated by VVR and MVR, whose PSNR value was around 50. Some more objects including 2D image planes placed in a 3D world and 3D objects have been examined with PSNR tests and found that the quality of the elemental images was generated by VVR and MVR methods are almost negligible (see Table 1).

**Table 1.** Ths PSNR of elemental image constructed in VVR and the MVR

| MVR vs. VVR | 2D Font | 2D Image | 3D Font | 3D Cow | 3D Teapot |
|---|---|---|---|---|---|
| PSNR | 143.84 | 120.95 | 75.09 | 61.93 | 52.99 |

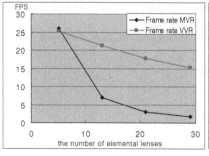
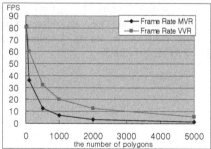

**Fig. 5.** FPS (Frames per seconds) of MVR and VVR

The performance of the construction process of elemental images was also evaluated. To examine the performance, the relationships between the frame rate and the number of lenses and the number of polygons, respectively, were measured for both MVR and VVR. As shown in Fig. 5, when 13x13 lens array (169 lenses in total) was used, VVR showed about 1.5~5 times faster frame rate than MVR. The picture also shows that, in overall, VVR shows better performance than MVR regardless of the number of the lenses or the complexity of the 3D models get increased.

## 4   Conclusion and Future Work

VVR algorithm is a new image mapping algorithm that should be more suitable for real-time graphics applications. Unlike PRR or MVR, VVR usually shows better performance in most cases and is not affected much by the number of lenses or the size of the 3D objects much, while the quality of elemental images are almost identical. Compared to PGR, which could only show the elemental images in the focused mode, VVR can show 3D integral images in either focused or real mode.

As Table 1 shows, when 2D objects (planes) are used with the new algorithm, PSNR values are pretty high, whereas the results get decreased with 3D objects. For the future research, we will try to improve VVR algorithm to get better quality of images by improving the VVR algorithm. We also have plans to increase the frame rate more so that the new method can be used in the interactive environments, such as game or virtual reality worlds.

## References

1. Frederick P. Brooks, Jr, "What's Real About Virtual Reality?" IEEE Computer Graphics & Applications, Nov / Dec, 16 (1999)
2. M. Halle, "Autostereoscopic displays and computer graphics," ACM SIGGRAPH, vol. 31, pp. 58-62 (1997)
3. Takanori Okoshi, "Three-Dimensional Displays," Proceedings of the IEEE, 68, 548 (1980)
4. G. Lippmann "La photographie integrale," Comptes -Rendus 146, pp.446-451 (1908)
5. Yoshihide Igarashi, H. Murata and M. Ueda, "3D display system using a computer generated integral photography," Japan J. Appl. Phys. 17, pp. 1683 (1978)
6. Myunghoon Suk "Enhanced image mapping algorithm for 3D integral imaging display system", Information and Communications University (2005)
7. Ruigang Yang, Xinyu Huang, Shunnan Chen, "Efficient Rendering of Integral Images", SIGGRAPH2005 (2005)

# A Neural Classifier for Anomaly Detection in Magnetic Motion Capture

Iain Miller[1] and Stephen McGlinchey[2]

[1] University of Paisley, Paisley. PA1 2BE, UK
iain.miller@paisley.ac.uk,
[2] stephen.mcglinchey@paisley.ac.uk

**Abstract.** Over recent years, the fall in cost, and increased availability of motion capture equipment has led to an increase in non-specialist companies being able to use motion capture data to guide animation sequences for computer games and other applications.[1] A bottleneck in the animation production process is in the clean-up of capture sessions to remove and/or correct anomalous (unusable) frames and noise. In this paper an investigation is carried out into whether the 2-layer SOM network previously designed [5] and trained on one capture session, can be used to create a neural classifier to be used to classify another separate capture session.

## 1 Introduction

Motion capture is the process of recording the motion of actors and/or objects, and this data is often used in computer games to animate characters and other game objects. The process normally involves tracking sensors or markers that have been placed in key positions on the actor's body, and detecting their locations in three-dimensional space. As the cost of equipment decreases, the realm of Motion Capture is no longer the preserve of specialist companies who take care of all aspects of data capture and post-processing. The task of supplying animation scenes from a motion capture system is now seen as a commodity, and so the focus has started to veer towards processing the output from a capture session as quickly and cheaply as possible. By improving post-processing, motion capture studios can get more useful (and commercial) application out of the capture equipment.

Previous work [4] showed that a statistical method could correctly identify a frame's class 67% of the time, whilst [5] showed that a 2-layer SOM network could produce an output net that grouped classifications together. From this base, the remit of this paper is to investigate the extent to which a network similar to that identified in [5] trained on one set of data could be used to classify data from a different capture session. Other research, such as that in [2], [3] and [6] focuses on the extraction of information from data that is already clean. Currently, it is part of an animators job to clean the raw data from a capture session, and it is this time that we wish to save for the animator.

Positional anomalies in the data come about when the sensors move too close to or too far from the field generators; where the sensors are unable to detect the

R. Harper, M. Rauterberg, M. Combetto (Eds.): ICEC 2006, LNCS 4161, pp. 141–146, 2006.
© IFIP International Federation for Information Processing 2006

field strength accurately or if metallic objects interfere with the magnetic fields and so produce anomalous results. The outcome being sensors reporting their positions that are inverted in the vertical axis or placed at a seemingly random position and breaking the skeleton of the captured article (which can be human, animal or an inanimate object). The next section outlines the structure of the network and the factors involved in designing the classifier.

## 2  Methodology

Data is read in and stored in a separate matrix for each sensor in the session (called nodes from here on). Equation 1 shows one node's data in one frame in the session.

$$n_i(t) = \begin{bmatrix} n_{i1}(t) & n_{i2}(t) & n_{i3}(t) \end{bmatrix} \tag{1}$$

For each node, a one-dimensional SOM is created and initialised (equation 2 with $M$ as the number of neurons in the net). Each SOM is trained for 100 epochs using only the data for its associated node. One epoch uses every frame in the session, fed into the network in a random order.

$$S_i = \begin{bmatrix} s_1 \\ s_2 \\ \vdots \\ s_M \end{bmatrix} = \begin{bmatrix} s_{11} & s_{12} & s_{13} \\ s_{21} & s_{22} & s_{23} \\ & \vdots & \\ s_{M1} & s_{M2} & s_{M3} \end{bmatrix} \tag{2}$$

The Euclidean distance between the input vector and each neuron in a SOM is calculated, and the neuron with the minimum distance being declared the winner (see equation 3, $i$ is the node number and $k$ is the vector element).

$$c_i = \arg \min_{1 \leq j \leq M} \left( \sqrt{\sum_{k=1}^{3} (n_{i_k}(t) - s_{j_k})^2} \right) \tag{3}$$

The weights for the winning neuron are then updated using equation $s'_l = s_l + \alpha h(n_i(t) - s_l)$ with $\alpha$ being the adaptive learning rate ($\alpha = \alpha_0(1 - \frac{tc}{T})$, $T = 100F$, where $F$ is the total number of frames and $tc$ is the training cycle), and $h_1 = e^{\frac{-(j-c_i)^2}{2}}$ is the gaussian neighbourhood function ($j$ and $c_i$ are the indices of the neuron being updated and winning neuron respectively) that modifies the neurons closest to the winner more than those further away.

The outputs from each of these SOMs form the input vector for the second-layer SOM (equation 4). The second-layer SOM is a two-dimensional array of neurons with each neuron having a weight vector of that shown in equation 5. The winner is decided by the minimum Euclidean distance, as in the first-layer SOMs, with the training updates calculated using the same adaptive learning rate and gaussian neighbourhood function $h_2 = e^{\frac{-(R-c_R)^2 - (C-c_C)^2}{2}}$ (with $R$ and

$C$ being the row and column address of the neuron being updated and $c_R$ and $c_C$ the row and column address of the winning neuron).

$$In = \begin{bmatrix} c_1 \\ c_2 \\ \vdots \\ c_M \end{bmatrix} \tag{4}$$

$$v = \begin{bmatrix} w_1 \\ w_2 \\ \vdots \\ w_M \end{bmatrix} \tag{5}$$

## 2.1 Centring Data

The above method does leaves the positional data as it is and does not apply any pre-processing onto it. By leaving the data unaltered, the network can take account for the spatial element of the capture volume. However, when using a test-case to train a neural-classifier, it may be appropriate to remove this spatial element of the data, in order to concentrate the network to train on just the structural element of the capture. To do this, the positional data should be translated to the origin in each frame.

There are several methods of being able to centre the data, e.g. centre of mass, etc. Here, the centre of mass version is used. With this method each node in a frame is given an equal mass and then the geometric centroid of the masses is found using equation 6, but as the masses are all equal this can be simplified to equation 7.

$$\bar{n}(t) = \frac{\sum_{i=1}^{M} m_i n_i(t)'}{\sum_{i=1}^{M} m_i} \tag{6}$$

$$\bar{n}(t) = \begin{bmatrix} \bar{n}_x(t) \\ \bar{n}_y(t) \\ \bar{n}_z(t) \end{bmatrix} = \frac{\sum_{i=1}^{M} n_i(t)'}{M} \tag{7}$$

With $\bar{n}(t)$ giving the coordinates of the centroid. Each node in the captured frame is then translated to the origin in the x- and z- axes towards the origin of the volume space, equation 8.

$$g_i(t) = n_i(t)' - \begin{bmatrix} \bar{n}_x(t) \\ 0 \\ \bar{n}_z(t) \end{bmatrix} \tag{8}$$

The centred data is then used to train the network in exactly the same way as shown in equations 1 to 5, except with $g_i(t)$ replacing $n_i(t)$ in all relevant equations.

## 2.2   Classifier

From previous experiments [5] a network with 41 neurons in each first-layer
SOM and a 21-by-21 SOM for the second-layer gave the most consistent results.
Therefore for these investigations a network with this same structure was trained
and used for classification.

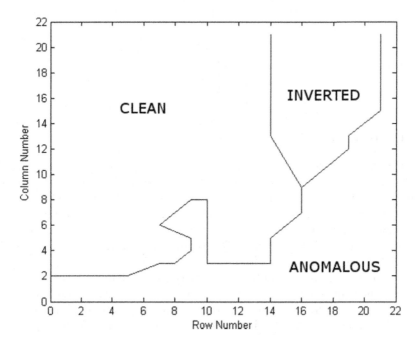

**Fig. 1.** A Graph Showing the Classifier Boundary for a 2-Layer SOM Network trained
with Centred Data

The original outputs of the networks were used to create output classifier
graphs (see figure 1 for an example) and filter. The class boundaries were defined
by a user and the criteria used to decide where to draw the boundary were:

1. The boundary has to go through each Overlapping Point.
2. The boundary should go nearer the "clean" neurons than the "anomalous"
   neurons.
3. In areas of uncertainty, then take the nearest known neurons as reference.
4. The boundary represents the unknown areas

## 3   Results

The classifying networks were trained using a capture session of a single actor
walking around (called Train1 from hereon), that contains two sequences of

anomalous frames sandwiching a series of clean frames, all preceded by a series of frames where the figure is inverted. The networks were then used to classify 5 other files each with different characteristics. File F1 has an identical sensor set up to Train1 with very similar motions and orientations but is less than half the length. File T1 has two series of clean frames alternated with two series of anomalous data, file T2 has a series of clean frames followed by a series of anomalous frames with more clean than anomalous. File T3 is the same as T2 but with more anomalous than clean and File T4 contains only clean frames. Files T1, T2, and T3 all have 2823 frames with similar but not identical sensor setups to Train1 capturing a range of more energetic motions than in Train1. T4 also has 2823 frames, but has similar motions to Train1.

A false positive is where a anomalous or inverted frame is classified as a clean frame, with a false negative if a clean or inverted frame called as a anomalous and a false inverted is when a frame is called as inverted when it should be either clean or anomalous.

As can be seen from tables 1 and 2, for those files with similar motions to those captured in Train1 (files F1 and T4), that the results give us no or very few false readings. However, for file T4 the majority of frames are classified as unknown. On inspection of which neurons are producing these spurious results with the uncentred data 4 neurons have been mislabeled as unknown, when they should have been labeled as clean. With centred data, one neuron has been mislabeled as anomalous when it should have been labeled as unknown and one neuron has

**Table 1.** Table of results for classification using a 2-layer SOM trained with uncentred data

| File | Correct | | | False | | | Unknown |
|------|----------|----------|---------|----------|----------|---------|---------|
| | Positive | Negative | Unknown | Positive | Negative | Unknown | |
| Train1 | 115 | 213 | 46 | 0 | 0 | 0 | 33 |
| F1 | 115 | 37 | 0 | 0 | 0 | 0 | 18 |
| T1 | 299 | 876 | 0 | 393 | 798 | 32 | 425 |
| T2 | 811 | 23 | 0 | 62 | 221 | 0 | 1706 |
| T3 | 474 | 0 | 0 | 0 | 773 | 0 | 1576 |
| T4 | 118 | 0 | 0 | 0 | 0 | 0 | 2705 |

**Table 2.** Table of results for classification using a 2-layer SOM trained with centred data

| File | Correct | | | False | | | Unknown |
|------|----------|----------|---------|----------|----------|---------|---------|
| | Positive | Negative | Unknown | Positive | Negative | Unknown | |
| Train1 | 131 | 225 | 49 | 0 | 0 | 0 | 2 |
| F1 | 129 | 39 | 0 | 2 | 0 | 0 | 0 |
| T1 | 381 | 584 | 0 | 1531 | 107 | 0 | 220 |
| T2 | 2287 | 33 | 0 | 71 | 223 | 2 | 207 |
| T3 | 1261 | 73 | 0 | 1379 | 13 | 3 | 94 |
| T4 | 1074 | 0 | 0 | 0 | 4 | 0 | 1745 |

been labeled as unknown when it should have been labeled as clean. The files where the motions captured are significantly different from Train1 (T1–3) yield poor results, which suggests that it is only possible to use a neural classifier like this on files of similar motions to the trainer file.

## 4    Conclusions

Although it was initially hoped that a file that contained all possible classifications, such as Train1, would be able to create a classifier that could be used on a majority of other files with similar sensor set-ups. This isn't the case but it does show that it is possible to build a classifier that can correctly identify the majority of frames in a separate session with similar set-ups and motions. As was shown, the initial classifier requires a degree of guesswork from the user and so is not at its optimum level, but as further files are tested against the classifier it can be refined further improving performance. There will always be points in a classifier that will produce unknown classifications, due to the existence of overlapping neurons. From the two sets of results it appears on first inspection that centring the data has little effect, but it actually produced an initial classifier that required less refinements than the uncentred data. Part of this will be down to user-guestimates in building the classifier and part due to the centred data-trained network creating a clearer separate in groups of neurons.

To further advance the theory more testing needs to be done with a variety of captured motions, lengths of file and sizes of actors. Furthermore, a trainer file should be created that contains a full range of motions and orientations in itself, rather than in individual files.

## References

1. Geroch, M.: Motion Capture for the Rest of us. Journal of Computing Sciences in Colleges. **19.3** (2004) 157–164
2. Gibson, D., Campbell, N., Dalton, C., Thomas, B.: Extraction of Motion Data from Image Sequences to Assist Animators. Proceedings of the British Machine Vision Conference (2000)
3. Kovar, L., Gleicher, M.: Automated Extraction and Parameterization of Motions in Large Data Sets. ACM Transactions on Graphics, **23.3** (2004) 559–568
4. Miller, I., McGlinchey, S.: Automating the Clean-up Process of Magnetic Motion Capture Systems. Proceedings of the Game Design and Technology Workshop (2005)
5. Miller, I., McGlinchey, S., Chaperot, B.: Anomaly Detection in Magnetic Motion Capture using a 2-Layer SOM network. To Appear in Proceedings of IEEE Conference of Computational Intelligence in Games 2006. (May 2006)
6. Müller, M., Röder, T., Clausen, M.: Efficient Content-Based Retrieval of Motion Capture Data. ACM Transactions on Graphics **24.3** (2005) 677–685

# Multichannel Distribution for Universal Multimedia Access in Home Media Gateways

Frederik De Keukelaere, Davy Van Deursen, and Rik Van de Walle

Multimedia Lab, Ghent University-IBBT,
Sint-Pietersnieuwstraat 41, B-9000 Ghent, Belgium
{frederik.dekeukelaere, davy.vandeursen,
rik.vandewalle}@ugent.be

**Abstract.** Today, people collect their personal multimedia content on home media servers. In addition to consuming their content on TV sets, people are using mobile multimedia players, PCs and even mobile phones. Since those terminals have various capabilities, it is necessary to adapt the content to a more device specific version. For audio, video, and graphics scalable codecs exist which realize this goal. For multimedia presentations no such scalable coding is available. This paper introduces a multichannel distribution system in home media gateways, this implies that a multimedia presentation can to be created once, and consumed on every possible terminal. The introduced multichannel distribution system is realized by combining MPEG-21 technology with existing device specific presentation languages. This results in a device agnostic Digital Item which can be transformed into a device specific presentation. The resulted presentation takes advantage of the full potential of a terminal.

## 1 Introduction

Today, people are using home media servers as their storage for personal multimedia content. By doing this, they create a repository containing all of their favorite songs, pictures, movies, and any combination of them. Due to this augmenting use of personal media, a demand for new ways of consuming media became apparent. This resulted in the development of many new versatile products. Creators of mobile devices are currently building hardware platforms powerful enough to bring the experience of a multimedia application to mobile terminals. Given the capabilities of these new devices, end-users are becoming more and more able to access their personal multimedia content anywhere, at any time.

Accessing multimedia anywhere, anytime, and on any device, is generally known as Universal Multimedia Access (UMA) [1], [2]. To realize this in a home environment, it is necessary to change a home media server into a home media gateway on which content is stored once and consumed using various devices in various circumstances, as presented in Fig. 1. To realize this goal, research is going on in different fields [3], [4] allowing the realization of UMA. This research handles about the multimedia content, not about the presentation. It proposes a scalable presentation format that can be used in a multichannel distribution system.

R. Harper, M. Rauterberg, M. Combetto (Eds.): ICEC 2006, LNCS 4161, pp. 147–152, 2006.
© IFIP International Federation for Information Processing 2006

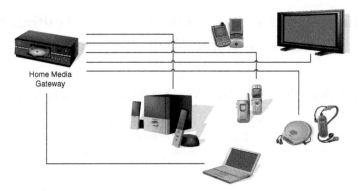

**Fig. 1.** Universal Multimedia Access for Home Media Gateways

## 2  Two Approaches to Multichannel Distribution

When multimedia is provided to a home media gateway nowadays, it is typically designed for one target class of devices. This makes it hard for consumers to use their content on the variety of multimedia devices they typically own. To be able to access the content on their devices, they often need to store several versions of the same content with each version targeted at a different device. In a UMA framework, the ultimate goal is to create, and therefore store, once and afterwards use the content everywhere.

For audio and video data, this problem is solved by the creation of scalable content which can be consumed at different bitrates and resolutions. For multimedia presentations, which are usually a composition of audio, video, text, and graphics, no such scalable coding is available. However, there are at least two possible approaches to realize the UMA goal for multimedia presentations. A first approach is to define one high-level, device agnostic, multimedia presentation and to derive new multimedia presentations for each class of devices from this high-level presentation. The major drawback of this high-level approach is the fact that the full potential of a presentation language, which is usually designed for one specific target device, can not be used. The reason behind this is the fact that in this high-level approach, the multimedia presentation is declared at a device-independent level and transformed to a device-specific level. Because this translation needs to be possible to any device specific language, it is not possible to include device specific information in the high-level presentation. Therefore, it is not possible to make optimal use of device specific functionalities, which results in a generic presentation which might be unacceptable to the end-user.

The second approach, which we will discuss in the rest of this paper, will separate multimedia data (i.e., metadata about audio, video, text, and graphics) from the presentation structure. With this approach we will reuse the multimedia data to the largest extend possible while still being able to optimally use the capabilities of device specific presentation languages. Although this will require new device specific presentation information for each class of devices, it allows the reuse of the multimedia data used in the presentation. While this does not completely realize the

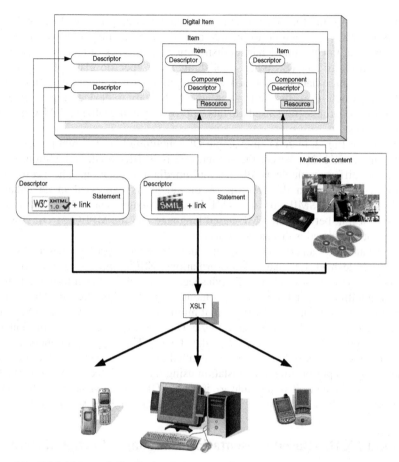

**Fig. 2.** Multichannel distribution in home media gateways using MPEG-21 DIs

true UMA philosophy, it is a first step closer to realizing UMA by allowing the multimedia data to be stored once and to be used in the different presentations for each class of devices.

## 3 Architecture

The main idea behind the second approach is that it is possible to separate multimedia content from its presentation description. To be able to do this, it is necessary to have a declaration format which can describe and organize multimedia content. In MPEG-21 [5], which tries to realize the 'big picture' in the multimedia production, delivery, and consumption chain, such a format is provided in the Digital Item Declaration (DID) [6]. The DID introduces the concept of Digital Items (DIs) which are defined as structured digital objects, with a standard representation, identification, and metadata within the MPEG-21 framework. In this paper, we use the DIs as storage format for multimedia content in a home media gateway. Because of the flexibility of DIs, it is possible to include both the presentation information and the multimedia data. For the multichannel distribution, both types of data are included in separate sections of the DI. When publishing for a specific class of devices, the relevant presentation data is combined with the multimedia content into a multimedia presentation which uses the full potential of the target device. Fig. 2 gives an overview of the architecture used in this approach when realizing UMA in home media gateways.

At the top of Fig. 2, there is an example DI containing two different presentations. The first one is XHTML-based, the second one is SMIL-based. In addition, the DI contains the different elements of the multimedia presentation. The presentation information contained in the Descriptors of the DI is expressed in an enhanced version of XHTML, SMIL, or any XML-based language. The enhancement is the inclusion of a link between an XML-based language and the MPEG-21 DI. How this enhancement is realized is discussed in Sect. 4.

To translate the generic DI structure into a device-specific presentation, an Extensible Stylesheet Language Transformations (XSLT) processor is used. This XSLT processor uses several XSLT stylesheets to combine the information in the presentation with the actual multimedia content. To realize this it resolves the links in the presentation and replaces it by the actual multimedia content. By using XSLT, it is possible to do the translation of the generic DI into a device-specific presentation either at the home media gateway or at the device. The only requirement for this architecture is that an XSLT processor is installed on the device (gateway or end-user terminal) which is performing the translation using the DI and the stylesheets attached to the DI. For example, it is possible to consume DIs with a standard web browser after translating it into HTML using the presentation data and the XSLT stylesheets.

## 4   Linking XML-Based Presentation Languages to Digital Items

To be able to use information stored in a DI within existing XML-based presentation languages, it is necessary to extend presentation languages in such a way that they support linking between them and the DI. This can be realized by the introduction of a new XML element, called Link, which is a placeholder pointing to the actual multimedia content in the DI. There are two possible situations in which linking can be required. The first is a Link pointing to content that needs to be placed in an attribute. The second is a Link pointing to content that needs to be placed between tags. Fig. 3 gives an example of both situations when linking XHTML to MPEG-21 DIs. At the top of the figure, a DI containing the multimedia content is presented. At the bottom of the figure, the two possible situations that require linking are shown: a link for an attribute and a link for data between elements. When a link for an attribute is needed, a placeholder (i.e., 'mpeg21-replacement') is placed in the concerned attribute. This placeholder will be replaced by the actual multimedia content to which the Link element points. Note that although XHTML was used as an example, the introduced linking mechanism can be used for any XML-based language.

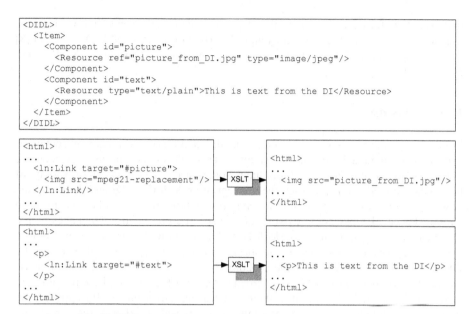

```
<DIDL>
  <Item>
    <Component id="picture">
      <Resource ref="picture_from_DI.jpg" type="image/jpeg"/>
    </Component>
    <Component id="text">
      <Resource type="text/plain">This is text from the DI</Resource>
    </Component>
  </Item>
</DIDL>
```

**Fig. 3.** Linking multimedia content in DIs to presentation languages

## 5 From DID to XiMPF and Back

Since multichannel distribution is getting more and more important for many content providers, the Vlaamse Radio en Televisie (VRT), which is the public Flemish broadcaster, designed a multichannel distribution architecture [7] which is heavily based on the previously discussed architecture. Since they were focusing on their distribution backbones, there were some differences compared to the home media gateway distribution. For example, for storing the multimedia data and the presentation data, they introduced a new storage format called eXtensible Interactive Multimedia Presentation Format (XiMPF). XiMPF is based on MPEG-21 DID, but has proprietary extensions. By applying those extensions to the DID format, it is no longer compliant with MPEG-21 DID.

From an interoperability perspective, this can be considered as a step backwards, since the data stored in XiMPF could only be processed by XiMPF compliant processors. However, the data stored in the XiMPF documents was originally envisaged to only be used in the backbone. Before transmitting the data to the end-user, the XiMPF data was translated into device-specific presentation data, for example, to SMIL. Therefore, the end-user would never notice that the distribution backbone used a proprietary format for storage of its information.

Nevertheless, we are currently living in a world in which multichannel distribution not necessarily happens at the content provider side. For example, in this paper the home media gateway is responsible for realizing the multichannel distribution. Therefore, it is necessary to be able to transport and exchange content which is prepared for multichannel distribution. One way to realize this in an interoperable way, is to provide the content in a standardized format. Content distributors can then understand the format and more easily adapt the content to their distribution channels. For those reasons, the Multimedia Content Distribution Platform (MCDP) project [8] is currently exploring the conversion of the proprietary extensions in XiMPF into MPEG-21 DID.

# 6 Conclusions

In this paper, we discussed how multichannel distribution of multimedia presentations can be realized in a home media gateway. This allows the end-user to consume multimedia presentations stored on their home media gateways on a variety of terminals. To realize this, we used the concept of an MPEG-21 DI and demonstrated how DIs can be used to create multimedia presentations which can be consumed on various devices. By extending existing device specific presentation languages with a Link element, which points to an MPEG-21 DI, we allowed a DI to become device agnostic. Afterwards, this device agnostic DI was transformed into a device specific DI which makes optimal use of the capabilities of a target class of devices. Finally, we shortly discussed how a Flemish broadcaster used the proposed methodology to realize multichannel distribution in their broadcasting environment. By applying the introduced techniques in a home environment, we moved one step closer to realizing a true UMA experience for home media gateways.

# References

1. Perkis, A., Abdeljaoued, Y., Christopoulos, C., Ebrahimi, T., Chicharo, J.: Universal Multimedia Access from Wired and Wireless Systems, Circuits, Systems and Signal Processing, vol. 20, no. 3-4 (2001) 387-402
2. Vetro, A., Christopoulos, C., Ebrahimi, T.: Universal Multimedia Access, IEEE Signal Processing Magazine, vol. 20, no. 2 (2003) 16
3. Mohan, R., Smith, J. R., Li, C. S.: Adapting Multimedia Internet Content for Universal Access, IEEE Transactions on Multimedia, vol. 1, no. 1 (1999) 104-114
4. Vetro, A., Christopoulos, C., Sun, H.: Video transcoding architectures and techniques: An overview, IEEE Signal Processing Magazine, vol. 20, no. 2 (2003) 18-29
5. Burnett, I., Pereira, F.: An introduction to MPEG-21. In: Burnett, I., Pereira, F., Van de Walle, R., Koenen, R. (eds.): The MPEG-21 Book. John Wiley & Sons Ltd, Chichester (2006) 31-68
6. De Keukelaere, F., Van de Walle, R.: Digital Item Declaration and Identification. In: Burnett, I., Pereira, F., Van de Walle, R., Koenen, R. (eds.): The MPEG-21 Book. John Wiley & Sons Ltd, Chichester (2006) 69-116
7. Van Assche, S., Hendrickx, F., Oorts, N., Nachtergaele, L.: Multi-channel publishing of interactive multimedia presentations, Computers & Graphics, vol. 28, no. 2 (2004) 193-206
8. Interdisciplinary institute for BroadBand Technology: Multimedia Content Distribution Platform, http://mcdp.ibbt.be/ (2006)

# Language-Driven Development of Videogames: The &lt;e-Game&gt; Experience*

Pablo Moreno-Ger[1], Iván Martínez-Ortiz[2], José Luis Sierra[1], and Baltasar Fernández-Manjón[1]

[1] Fac. Informática. Universidad Complutense. 28040, Madrid. Spain
{pablom, jlsierra, balta}@fdi.ucm.es
[2] Centro de Estudios Superiores Felipe II. 28300, Aranjuez. Spain
imartinez@cesfelipesegundo.com

**Abstract.** In this paper we describe a language-driven approach to the development of videogames. In our approach the development process starts with the design of a suitable domain-specific language for building games, along with an abstract syntax for the language and its operational semantics. Next an engine supporting the language is built. Finally games are built using the customized language and they are executed using the engine. This approach is exemplified with the &lt;e-Game&gt; project, which delivers the design of a language and the construction of an engine for the documental development of graphical adventure videogames with educational purposes.

**Keywords:** videogames; adventure games; development process; language-driven approach; document-oriented approach; storyboard markup language; game engine; edutainment.

## 1 Introduction

There are fields like edutainment [12], casual gaming [17] or propaganda [26], where rapid development of simple games is required. This development is usually carried out using languages and/or tools specifically tailored to the videogame domain. These languages and tools range from very powerful, but also knowledge-demanding, special-purpose programming languages (e.g. *DIV* [8] and *DarkBasic* [10]) to easy-to-use, but also more limited, authoring systems to be used by non programmers (e.g. *Game Maker* [21]), to scripting solutions based on either general-purpose scripting languages (e.g. *LUA* [11] or *TCL* [20]) or on languages specially tailored to specific videogames.

This search for a good balance between expressive power and simplicity of use and maintenance has also been faced with Language-driven approaches [4, 16]. The specific focus of these approaches is to promote the explicit design and implementation of domain-specific languages [25] as a key feature of the development process. For

---
* The Projects TIN2004-08367-C02-02 and TIN2005-08788-C04-01 and the Regional Government of Madrid (4155/2005) have partially supported this work. Thanks to the CNICE for the game design documents and graphics assets provided.

R. Harper, M. Rauterberg, M. Combetto (Eds.): ICEC 2006, LNCS 4161, pp. 153–164, 2006.

each application domain a suitable language is designed and an interpreter or compiler for such a language is constructed. Being domain-specific, the language can be easily understood and used by the experts in the domain (usually non programmers) in order to *specify* applications in such a domain. Therefore the approach inherits the usability of the production processes based on authoring tools. On the other hand, the approach also provides great flexibility: As long as the design of the languages is an intrinsic activity of the approach, existing languages can be modified and extended and new ones can be created to meet the changing needs of the user community. The main shortcomings of the approach are the costs associated with initial language design and implementation.

The costs associated with language-driven approaches can be amortized in domains where a whole application family (i.e. a set of variants of a single application model) must be produced and maintained [7]. Application families are very frequent in the domain of videogames, where it is possible to distinguish many genres of games, each of them including many common traits that can be abstracted in the design of a domain-specific language or tool. A good example of uniformity is the genre of graphic adventure videogames [13]. In fact, the <e-Game> project provides language-driven methods, techniques and tools for facilitating the production and maintenance of graphical adventure videogames to be applied in education.

In this paper we describe the language-driven approach to the construction of videogames, and we exemplify the different stages of this approach with the experiences gathered from the <e-Game> project. In section 2 we describe the language-driven development approach itself. In section 3 we illustrate this approach with <e-Game>. Finally, section 4 gives the conclusions and lines of future work.

## 2   A Language-Driven Approach to the Development of Videogames

The rationale behind any process aimed at the language-driven construction of videogames is to provide the advantages of using an authoring approach for each particular family of games, while preserving the flexibility provided by using a full featured programming approach. Indeed, the approach must be conceived as providing an authoring tool (the domain-specific language itself) adapted to the specific needs of each domain, and even of each situation. Besides, a feasible approach must keep the costs associated with the design, implementation and maintenance of domain-specific languages within reasonable limits.

For this purpose, an incremental approach can be adopted, extending and modifying both the language and its implementation in order to adapt them to different situations and families of games. The approach that we propose in this paper encourages such an incremental strategy.

Following our previous experiences with the document-oriented approach to the production and maintenance of content-intensive applications [23, 24], we propose the three views shown in Fig 1 for the characterization of this approach. Next subsections give the details.

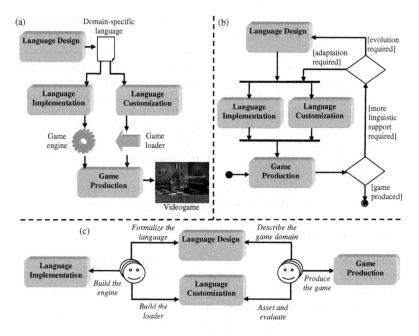

**Fig. 1.** Language-driven approach to the construction of videogames: (a) products and activities view; (b) sequencing view; (c) participants and roles view

## 2.1 Products and Activities

The most characteristic activity in the language-driven approach is the *language design* activity. In this activity a suitable *domain-specific language* is designed for the production of the videogames. For this purpose, the activity addresses two different aspects of the language:

- The language's *abstract syntax*. This syntax can be thought of as the information model representing the data of each sentence in the language that is relevant to the subsequent processing (i.e. translation and/or interpretation) of such a sentence [9]. The focus on abstract syntax when designing a domain-specific language simplifies the other design steps and the implementation activity, since the emphasis is put on processing structured data instead of on raw strings. It also keeps the language and the engine independent from the format finally used during authoring, and therefore facilitates reusing the language in different scenarios by defining suitable concrete (textual or even visual [14]) syntaxes. Finally, for reasonably narrow genres (e.g. the domain of graphic adventures addressed) the resulting languages are usually simple and declarative, which induces simpler abstract syntaxes.
- The language's *operational semantics*. This is a formal and implementation-independent characterization of how games described in the language are executed. Therefore this description sets up the basis for building the game engine. The formalization of this semantics is very useful in anticipating the more obscure aspects of the language's dynamic behaviour without being obfuscated by technological and/or implementation details, and also in allowing rapid prototyping.

The *Language implementation* activity deals in turn with the construction of a *game engine*. This engine will be based on the description of the language produced during language design, and especially on the operational semantics.

Another important activity is *language customization*. In this activity a suitable *concrete syntax* is chosen for the language, and this syntax is actually implemented in terms of a *game loader*. This loader performs a translation of games expressed in a specific syntax into a representation compliant with the abstract syntax, thus allowing their execution using the engine. The activity is very valuable for increasing the usability of the language for different communities. Furthermore, the loader can be turned into a full-featured editing and authoring environment for the domain-specific language provided.

Finally, once the game engine and loader are made available, these artefacts can be used for producing specific *videogames* during the *game production* activity.

## 2.2 Sequencing of the Activities

We promote an incremental process model for the language-driven construction of videogames. In this model languages are not conceived as pre-established, static and unmovable entities, but are dynamic objects that evolve according to the authoring needs that arise during the development of more and more videogames. This evolutive nature alleviates the costs associated with language design and implementation, since these activities can be interleaved with the production of videogames. In addition, it contributes to more usable and affordable languages, since the complexity of the languages is also in accordance with the expressive needs manifested during their application. It avoids the premature inclusion of useless or unnecessarily sophisticated constructs in the languages.

Sequencing of the activities in our approach is in accordance with this pragmatic posture. As depicted in Fig 1b, new development iterations start when new games must be developed or existing ones modified or extended. These production stages can be interrupted in order to refine the game engine and/or the concrete syntax and the associated game loader, in order to introduce a completely new concrete syntax together with the associated loader, or in order to resolve a lack of expressiveness in the current language. This latter situation supposes undertaking a new language design activity, followed by the corresponding implementation and customization of the newly defined features.

## 2.3 Participants and Their Roles

Our approach explicitly involves two different communities of participants in the development process: *game experts* and *developers*. Game experts group the experts in the different aspects involved in the development of a videogame not directly related to programming (e.g. storyboard writing, graphical design, musical composition, design of the game-play, etc.). Developers in turn represent experts in the different aspects related to programming and software development. This separation of roles, which is taken from our previous experiences with the aforementioned document-oriented approach, is mandatory for a successful application of the approach, although the separation itself is not a novelty in the videogame industry.

In the Language-driven approach, the main responsibility of domain experts is during game production, because they will be the main stakeholders who are in charge of producing the videogames using the language and supporting tools available (the engine and the loader). In turn, the main responsibility for developers is during the language implementation activity, where they build the game engine. The other activities (language design and customization) require active collaboration between experts and developers. During language design, experts must collaborate in order to let developers formulate the right language. For this purpose, developers can use well-known domain analysis methods [2] tailored to the particular domain of videogames. In addition, narrowing the game genre and using rapid prototyping based on the language's operational semantics can help in harmonizing this collaboration. Finally, during language customization experts help developers to define suitable syntaxes. Once the syntax is stable, the construction of game loaders is a routine task that can be tackled by using standard techniques and tools in compiler construction [1] or standard linguistic frameworks like those alluded to in [25].

# 3 The <e-Game> Project

<e-Game> is a project oriented to the provision of means for the authoring and the deployment of graphic adventure videogames with educational purposes [15, 18]. This project was conducted under the language-driven directives described in the previous section. In this section we detail the consecution of the project in terms of the products yielded by such a language-driven approach.

## 3.1 The <e-Game> Language: Abstract Syntax and Operational Semantics

During the design of the <e-Game> domain-specific language we chose a characterization of the domain of graphic adventure videogames guided by the instructional uses envisioned [13]. As a result of an initial domain analysis we depicted the main features of the games to be built:

- Adventures occur in a world made of *scenes*. Typical examples of scenes might be a bedroom, a tavern or a street. Scenes have *exits* that lead to other scenes. Besides, some of these scenes are *cutscenes*: fixed scenarios that can be used to include special events in the game flow (e.g. playing a videoclip).
- The player is represented inside the game world by an avatar that plays the leading role in the adventure and navigates the different scenes as commanded by the player.
- The world is populated by *characters*. The player maintains *conversations* with such characters. Conversations follow the model of multiple-choice dialog structures organized as a tree with the player's possible answers as nodes that open new sub-conversations.
- The scenes can contain several *objects*. Good examples of objects might be an axe, a sword, a key or a chest. The player is allowed to perform several types of actions with the objects: he/she can *grab* objects and add them to its personal *object inventory*, *use* objects in his/her inventory with other objects, and *give* inventoried objects to some characters.

| Information item | Intended meaning |
|---|---|
| \<scene,*s*\> | *s* is a scene. |
| \<cutscene,*cs*\> | *cs* is a cutscene. |
| \<start,*s*\> | Scene or cutscene *s* is the game's starting point. |
| \<next-scene,*cs,ns,c,*es\> | If condition *c* holds, once the cutscene *cs* is finished, it is possible to enter *ns* and get *es* as effects. |
| \<next-scene,*s,i,ns,c,*es\> | If condition *c* holds, it is possible to go from scene *s* to *ns* by traversing the exit number *i* and to achieve *es* as effects. |
| \<object,*s,o,c*\> | Object *o* is visible in the scene *s* provided that *c* holds. |
| \<grab,*o,c,*es\> | If condition *c* holds, object *o* can be grabbed. The effect is the achievement of *es*. |
| \<use-with,*o*$_s$, *o*$_t$,*c,*es\> | Object *o* can be given to character *ch* when condition *c* holds. Then effects *es* are achieved. |
| \<give-to,*o*, *ch* ,*c,*es\> | Object *o*$_s$ can be combined with object *o*$_t$ provided that condition *c* holds. Then the effects *es* are achieved. |
| \<character,*s,ch,c*\> | Character *ch* is visible in scene *s* provided that *c* holds. |
| \<conversation,*ch,conv,c*\> | The conversation *conv* can be maintained with character *ch* when condition *c* holds. |

**Fig. 2.** Main types of information items that constitute the abstract syntax for the \<e-Game\> language

- Games include a declarative notion of *state*, which is mainly based on boolean propositional variables called *flags*. Flags can be used to describe the conditions that the player must have previously achieved in order to be allowed to carry out an action in a game, such as to see an object, activate an exit or initiate a conversation with a character. When a flag holds, it is said to be *active*. Otherwise, it is said to be *inactive*. Conditions will be expressed as *conjunctive normal forms* on the flags (i.e. as sequences of alternatives made of elementary activation and deactivation conditions).
- Finally, the different actions undertaken by the player can produce several *effects*. These effects can be of different types: (i) activation of a flag; (ii) consumption of an object in the inventory as a consequence of combining it with another or giving it to a character; (iii) speech uttered by a character when he/she receives an object; and (iv) triggering a cutscene. Notice that in \<e-Game\> it is not possible to *deactivate* flags. Intuitively, a flag represents an achievement, which cannot be unachieved.

The abstract syntax for an \<e-Game\> language able to express these features can be easily characterized as set of tuples, which will be called \<e-Game\> *information items*. In Fig 2 the main types of information items comprised by this abstract syntax are summarized (for the sake of simplicity we omit information items used for presentational purposes, such as for instance the coordinates and the dimensions of an exit, or the external assets required to render a character). In these items, conditions are further represented as ordered pairs \<*f*+,*f*-\>, where *f*+ is the set of flags that must be active, and *f*- the set of those that must be inactive. In turn, effects are represented as a list of tuples representing the individual effects (e.g. \<activate,*f*\> for activating the flag *f*). Lists themselves are represented either by \<\> (in case of the empty list) or by *<e,l>* (in case of a list with head *e* and with rest *l*). Finally, conversations are represented as lists of tuples with the basic conversation steps. Option lists in the conversation are represented as lists of pairs of the form *<o,conv>*, where *o* is the text of the option and *conv* is the sub-conversation that follows. In Fig 3 the representation of a fragment of a conversation using this abstract syntax is depicted. This conversation concerns a simple educational game about safety regulations at work.

```
<conversation, Foreman,
            <<speak-char, "Well José, did you measure the
                          scaffold">,
            <<response,
             <<"No sir, not yet",
               <<speak-char, "And what are you waiting for, boy?">,
               <<speak-player, "At once, sir">,
               <end-conversation,<>>>>>,
             <<"Yes sir, it's ready",
               <<speak-char, "And...">,
               <<response,
               ... >,
            {{SecondTaskInitiated, UsedMeasureTapeScaffold},∅}>
```

**Fig. 3.** A fragment of conversation represented in the abstract syntax of the <e-Game> language

This abstract syntax, although reasonably readable, is not intended to be used by authors directly. It sacrifices clarity for a representation that allows a reasonably straightforward definition of its formal operational semantics. The operational semantics for the <e-Game> language is specified using the style of *structural operational semantics*, a common method of specifying the operational semantics of artificial computer languages [19, 22].

In Fig 4 we show some of the semantic rules for the <e-Game> language that formalize the behaviour associated with conversations. In such rules, expressions of the form $\vdash \Phi$ are used to introduce both generic set-theoretical statements that must hold and <e-Game> specific predicates that are readily translated into such kind of statements (such *translation* is addressed by other semantic rules). In turn $s_0 \rightarrow s_1$ is used for denoting a basic transition between execution states. Such states are represented as 5-tuples with the form $<\theta,G,\sigma,in,out>$ where: (i) $\theta$ is a set of attribute-values pairs which represent the *control state* of the execution; (ii) $G$ is the set of information items that represents the game; (iii) $\sigma$ is the *game state*, which contains a pair for the active flags and another one for the objects in the inventory; (iv) *in* is an *input stream* that contains the commands representing the player's interactions; and (v) *out* is an *output stream* where the commands for producing the game's presentation are written.

The notation of both the abstract syntax and the operational semantics is oriented to allowing a relatively effortless implementation of the <e-Game> engine and facilitating prototyping processes [5]. As we will see later, the abstract syntax can be customized to a more usable language with a lower cognitive overload for authors.

$$\frac{\vdash \text{is-in}(\theta,s) \ ;; \ \vdash \text{is-in-scene}(G,\sigma,s,ch) \ ;; \ \vdash \langle \text{conversation},ch,conv,c \rangle \in G \ ;; \vdash \text{holds}(c,\sigma)}{\langle \theta,G,\sigma,\langle\langle \text{talk-to},ch\rangle,in\rangle,out\rangle \to \langle \text{ctrl-talking}(s,ch,conv),G,\sigma,in,\langle out,\langle \text{do-talk-to},ch\rangle\rangle\rangle} \text{ init-conv}$$

$$\frac{\vdash \text{is-talking}(\theta,\langle\langle \text{speak-player},m\rangle,conv\rangle)}{\langle \theta,G,\sigma,in,out\rangle \to \langle \theta_{conv} := conv,G,\sigma,in,\langle out,\langle \text{do-speak-player},m\rangle\rangle\rangle} \text{ speak-player2}$$

$$\frac{\vdash \text{is-talking}(\theta,\langle\langle \text{speak-char},m\rangle,conv\rangle)}{\langle \theta,G,\sigma,in,out\rangle \to \langle \theta_{conv} := conv,G,\sigma,in,\langle out,\langle \text{do-speak-char},\theta_{char},m\rangle\rangle\rangle} \text{ speak-char2}$$

$$\frac{\vdash \text{is-talking}(\theta,\langle\langle \text{options},os\rangle,\langle\rangle\rangle)}{\langle \theta,G,\sigma,in,out\rangle \to \langle \text{ctrl-goto-choosing}(\theta,os),G,\sigma,in,\langle out,\langle \text{do-choosing},os\rangle\rangle\rangle} \text{ choosing1}$$

$$\frac{\vdash \text{is-choosing}(\theta,os) \ ;; \ \vdash \langle o,conv \rangle \in os}{\langle \theta,G,\sigma,\langle\langle \text{select},o\rangle,in\rangle,out\rangle \to \langle \text{ctrl-goto-talking}(\theta,conv),G,\sigma,in,\langle out,\langle \text{do-choosen},o\rangle\rangle\rangle} \text{ choosing2}$$

$$\frac{\vdash \text{is-talking}(\theta,\langle \text{go-back},\langle\rangle\rangle)}{\langle \theta,G,\sigma,in,out\rangle \to \langle \theta_{ctrl} := choosing,G,\sigma,in,\langle out,\langle \text{do-going-back},\theta_{options}\rangle\rangle\rangle} \text{ going-back}$$

$$\frac{\vdash \text{is-talking}(\theta,\langle\langle \text{end-conversation},es\rangle,\langle\rangle\rangle)}{\langle \theta,G,\sigma,in,out\rangle \to \langle \text{ctrl-app-effects}(es,\text{ctrl-in}(\theta_{scene})),G,\sigma,in,\langle out,\text{do-end-conv}\rangle\rangle} \text{ ending-conv}$$

**Fig. 4.** <e-Game>'s semantics rules associated with conversations

## 3.2 The <e-Game> Engine

The architecture of the <e-Game> engine is depicted in Fig. 5. The design of this architecture was driven by the operational semantics of the <e-Game> language. According to this architecture, the engine is comprised of the following elements:

- A *component repository*. This repository contains a set of *game components*, which can be adequately selected and assembled to create the final videogame. There are two kinds of game components: *control rules*, which roughly correspond to the semantic rules of the <e-Game> operational semantics, and *GUI components*, which implement interaction and presentation services to support the final presentation layer of the videogame.
- The *game controller*, which encodes the operational behaviour of the engine. This controller can be customized with an appropriate set of control rules, and it includes a *control driver* that implements the selection and application strategies for such rules.
- The *user interface*, which takes care of the basic interactions with the player and of the presentation of the game. This interface is customized with a suitable collection of GUI components, and its behaviour is controlled by a pre-established *GUI shell*.
- *Input* and *output streams* that connect the controller and the user interface.
- A *game generator*. This artifact processes the game's information items, selects the appropriate game components, and registers them in the core and user interface of the engine. This component is in turn architected with an extensible set of *configuration rules*.

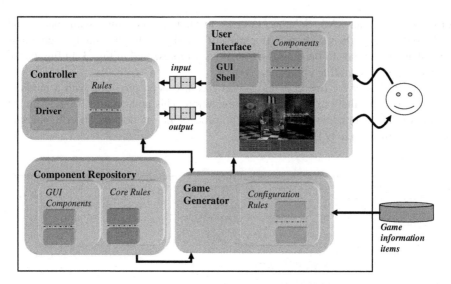

**Fig. 5.** Architecture of the <e-Game> engine

This architecture is modular enough to accommodate evolutions in the <e-Game> language, as we realised at earlier design stages of this language.

### 3.3 The <e-Game> Language as a Descriptive Markup Language for Game Storyboards

We have customized the <e-Game> abstract language to yield a XML-based descriptive markup language [3, 6] that can be used to directly mark up the game storyboards. This customization facilitates the production and maintenance of the graphic adventure videogames for game writers. Indeed, being descriptive and mirroring the structure of the storyboards, the language is easily understandable to game writers, which can use it to make the structure of their storyboards explicit. Besides, the markup can also be used to refer to the art assets required to display the different game components. These assets can be provided by another community of experts (the artists).

As a consequence of markup-based customization, a collaboration model for the development of graphical adventure videogames arises, which is based on our previous work on the document-oriented approach. The development process is ruled by game writers, although it also involves the other participants (including artists and developers) in a rational way. According to this model, game writers prepare the storyboards in plain English and then they mark them up with the <e-Game> markup language. In this process they can be advised by developers regarding the most abstract aspects of the language (e.g. specification of conditions), and also by artists regarding the aspects related to the art assets (e.g. coordinates and other presentational information). In Fig. 6a we depict the concrete syntax for describing conversations (we use XML DTDs notations for the sake of brevity, although the syntax is actually formalized using an XML Schema, in order to facilitate its future maintenance and evolution). In Fig. 6b we show a fragment of storyboard for the safety regulations game that corresponds to the conversation already represented in Fig. 3. In Fig. 6c we show the result of marking up this fragment.

The game loader for this concrete syntax has also been provided with a modular architecture to facilitate its extension and evolution. This architecture is based on the model for the incremental construction of processors for domain-specific markup languages described in [24].

```
(a) <!ELEMENT conversation (%dialogue;, %continuation;)>   (b) F: Well José, have you
    <!ATTLIST conversation id ID #REQUIRED>                         measured the scaffold?
    <!ENTITY % dialogue "(speak-char|speak-player)*">          ->J: No sir, not yet
    <!ENTITY % continuation "(response|end-conversation)*">     F: And what are you
    <!ELEMENT response (option)+>                                         waiting for,
    <!ELEMENT option (speak-player,%dialogue;,                                 boy?
                    (%continuation;|go-back))>                 J: At once, sir
    <!ELEMENT go-back EMPTY>                                  ->J: Yes sir, it's ready
    <!ELEMENT end-conversation (effects?)>                      F: And...

(c) <conversation id="CompleteSecondTask">
      <speak-char>Well José, did you measure the scaffold?</speak-char>
      <response>
        <option>
          <speak-player>No sir, not yet</speak-player>
          <speak-char>And what are you waiting for, boy?</speak-char>
          <speak-player>At once, sir</speak-player>
          <end-conversation/>
        </option>
        <option>
          <speak-player>Yes sir, it's ready</speak-player>
          <speak-char>And...</speak-char> (...)
```

**Fig. 6.** (a) Formalization of the markup for conversations; (b) a fragment of conversation in a storyboard; (c) markup of the fragment in (b)

### 3.4   Production of Videogames with <e-Game>

Until now we have applied <e-Game> in the development of some educational videogames about safety regulations and work risks prevention (Fig. 7a), and also in several experiences carried out in collaboration with the CNICE, the Spanish National Center of Information and Educative Communication, the biggest repository of educational games in Spain (Fig. 7b). These experiences consisted of reusing the instructional design and art assets of the videogames corresponding to a *History of Music* course provided by the CNICE. During these experiences we substantially improved the different products in <e-Game>, realizing the benefits of the incremental language-driven approach. We also realized that game writers could easily learn and dominate the operational and presentational aspects of the language to the point of maintaining <e-Game> documents on their own. When they reach the adequate level of proficiency, they can proceed with little support from the other participants (developers and artists).

**Fig. 7.** (a) Snapshot of the safety regulations videogame; (b) Snapshot for *Hall of the Kings*, a little educative game developed by reusing assets provided by CNICE

## 4 Conclusions and Future Work

In this paper, we have presented a language-driven approach to the development of videogames. This approach promotes the incremental definition of domain-specific languages in order to deal with the particular features of each family of videogames. We have successfully experienced the feasibility of the approach with <e-Game>, a project for the development of graphic adventures with an instructional purpose. On the negative side we must highlight the costs associated with the design, implementation and customization of the languages. We must also indicate as a drawback the highly specialized skills required of developers, who must have rather specialized skills regarding language design and implementation technologies.

We are currently further improving <e-Game> by exploring alternative (visual) concrete syntaxes. We also want to extend the language to explore alternative conversation models. As future work we are planning to apply <e-Game> to alternative domains other than the educational (e.g. advertising and diffusion of ideas). We also want to apply the language-driven approach to other game domains with educational purposes, like interactive fiction or interactive simulation.

## References

1. Aho, A., Sethi, R., and Ullman, J.D., Compilers: Principles, Techniques and Tools. Adisson-Wesley (1986).
2. Arango, G., Domain-Analysis: From Art Form to Engineering Discipline. ACM SIGSOFT Notes. Vol. 14(3). (1989).
3. Bray, T., Paoli, J., Sperberg-McQueen, C.M., and Maler, E. Extensible Markup Language (XML) 1.0. W3C Recommendation (2000) Available: www.w3c.org March 27th, 2006.
4. Clark, T.E., Sammut, P., and Willans, J. An eXecutable Metamodelling Facility for Domain Specific Language Design, in The 4th OOPSLA Workshop on Domain-Specific Modeling. Vancouver, Canada (2004).
5. Clément, D., Despeyroux, J., Despeyroux, T., Hascoet, L., and Kahn, G., Natural Semantics on the Computer, in Rapport de Recherche N 416. INRIA Sophia Antipolis: Valbonne, France (1985).

6. Coombs, J.H., Renear, A.H., and DeRose, S.J., Markup Systems and the Future of Scholarly Text Processing. Communications of the ACM. Vol. 30(11). (1987) 933-947.
7. Coplien, D., Hoffman, D., and Weiss, D., Commonality and Variability in Software Engineering. IEEE Software. Vol. 15(6). (1998) 37-45.
8. DIV Community Website. Available from: http://www.divsite.net March 27th, 2006.
9. Friedman, D., Wand, M., and Haynes, C.T., Essentials of Programming Languages Second Edition. MIT Press (2001).
10. Harbour, J. and Smith, J., Beginner's Guide to DarkBasic Game Programming. Premier Press (2003).
11. Ierusalimschy, R., Figueirido, L.H., and Celes Filho, W., LUA-An Extensible Extension Language. Software Practice & Experience. Vol. 26(5). (1996) 635-652.
12. Jenkins, H., Klopfer, E., Squire, K., and Tan, P., Entering the Education Arcade. ACM Computers in Entertainment. Vol. 1(1). (2003).
13. Ju, E. and Wagner, C., Personal computer adventure games: Their structure, principles and applicability for training. The Database for Advances in Information Systems. Vol. 28(2). (1997) 78-92.
14. Marriott, K., Meyer, B., and Wittenburg, K.B.A., Survey of Visual Language Specification and Recognition, in K. Marriot and B. Meyer (eds), Visual Language Theory. Springer-Verlag. (1999).
15. Martinez-Ortiz, I., Moreno-Ger, P., Sierra, J.L., and Fernández-Manjón, B. Production and Maintenance of Content Intensive Videogames: A Document-Oriented Approach, in International Conference on Information Technology: New Generations (ITNG 2006). Las Vegas, NV, USA: IEEE Society Press (2006).
16. Mauw, S., Wiersma, W.T., and Willemse, T.A.C., Language-driven System Design. Int. J. of Software Engineering and Knowledge Engineering. Vol. 14(6). (2004) 625-664.
17. Mills, G. Casual Games. International Game Developers Association White Paper (2005) Available from: http://www.igda.org/casual/IGDA_CasualGames_Whitepaper_2005.pdf March 27th, 2006.
18. Moreno-Ger, P., Martinez-Ortiz, I., and Fernández-Manjón, B. The <e-Game> project: Facilitating the Development of Educational Adventure Games, in Cognition and Exploratory Learning in the Digital age (CELDA 2005). Porto, Portugal (2005).
19. Mosses, P.D., Modular Structural Operational Semantics. Journal of Logic and Algebraic Programming. Vol. 60-61. (2004) 195-228.
20. Ousterhout, J.K., Scripting: Higher Level Programming for the 21st Century. IEEE Computer. Vol. 31(3). (1998) 23-30.
21. Overmars, M., Teaching Computer Science through Game Design. IEEE Computer. Vol. 37(4). (2004) 81-83.
22. Plotkin, G.D., A Structural Approach to Operational Semantics, in Tech. Report DAIMI FN-19. Computer Science Dept. Aarhus University (1981).
23. Sierra, J.L., Fernández-Manjón, B., Fernández-Valmayor, A., and Navarro, A., Document Oriented Development of Content-Intensive Applications. International Journal of Software Engineering and Knowledge Engineering. Vol. 15(6). (2005) 975-993.
24. Sierra, J.L., Navarro, A., Fernández-Manjón, B., and Fernández-Valmayor, A., Incremental Definition and Operationalization of Domain-Specific Markup Languages in ADDS. ACM SIGPLAN Notices. Vol. 40(12). (2005) 28-37.
25. Van Deursen, A., Klint, P., and Visser, J., Domain-Specific Languages: An Annotated Bibliography. ACM SIGPLAN Notices. Vol. 35(6). (2000) 26-36.
26. Water Cooler Games Web Site. 2006; Available from: http://www.watercoolergames.org March 27th, 2006.

# Architecture of an Authoring System to Support the Creation of Interactive Contents

Kozi Miyazaki[1,2], Yurika Nagai[1], Anne-Gwenn Bosser[1], and Ryohei Nakatsu[1,2]

[1] Kwansei Gakuin University, School of Science and Technology
2-1 Gakuen, Sanda 669-1337, Japan
miyazaki@nirvana.ne.jp, annegwenn@gmail.com,
nakatsu@ksc.kwansei.ac.jp
[2] Nirvana Technology
Keihanna Plaza Lab Wing
1-7 Hikaridai, Seika-cho, Soraku-gun, Kyoto 619-0237, Japan
http://www.nirvana.ne.jp/

**Abstract.** Since three-dimensional computer graphics (3D-CG) technology and interaction technology should be applied to e-learning as well as games, people must be able to easily create interactive contents based on 3D-CG, even if they are not 3D-CG professionals. In this paper, we propose a support system for creating interactive contents that runs on MS Windows and uses Direct X as the file format. By describing a script using two kinds of script files prepared by the system, a content creator can easily create 3D-CG scenes and can also control interactions between a user and the system. As an example of content creation, we present and explain interactive content in which users can enter the virtual world of classic Japanese tales and experience the story development of various types of classic tales for the first time.

## 1 Introduction

Recently, extremely rapid progress has been made in computer graphics (CG) technology for game machines and computers. This development has been particularly noticeable in the expression capability and special effects technology for three-dimensional (3D) computer graphics, and now it is finally becoming possible to generate images that look highly realistic. Because of this progress, it is now possible to virtually generate various kinds of objects in the real world, and such technologies are being widely applied to video games and simulations. At the same time, however, it is becoming increasingly difficult and time-consuming to develop/create various types of software or content related to CG. For example, to create new games that include 3D-CG, first we have to prepare a virtual 3D space, 3D computer characters, and rules of various actions for this 3D world. Such tasks require a lot of effort and time. In addition, this type of work needs a wide variety of in-depth knowledge, such as sophisticated programming skills and comprehensive understanding of calculation techniques for 3D space and modeling techniques for 3D computer characters. Therefore, in this area non-professionals face various barriers to develop entire systems from scratch.

R. Harper, M. Rauterberg, M. Combetto (Eds.): ICEC 2006, LNCS 4161, pp. 165–174, 2006.
© IFIP International Federation for Information Processing 2006

Based on the above considerations, we want to simplify the development of games and/or contents using 3D-CG, especially for non-professionals. Focusing on the creation of contents using 3D-CG, we have begun to develop an authoring system whose most significant feature is that we have prepared and installed various types of 3D-CG-handling functions in it, and we have also made it possible for users to handle these functions easily using high-level commands. In our authoring system it is possible to handle a simple script language. As a result, even if users lack the specific skills required for 3D-CG creation, with this script language they can still create 3D-CG contents and 3D characters relatively easily. Furthermore, since this system will simplify contents creation, it can be applied to various fields of interest. For example, game creators could easily develop game prototypes by this system and carry out preliminary evaluations of the game.

In the case of e-learning, several platforms are already available, but the problem of how to create new contents suitable for e-learning remains. So far, most e-learning contents are character-based, and only a few include interactive functions; thus the creation of interactive contents promises to become crucial in the near future. One purpose of the system presented in this paper is to help contents creators of e-learning create interactive contents more easily.

In this paper we describe the authoring system we are studying and developing. First, we explain the system's concept and provide an overview of it, followed by a detailed description of its architecture. Finally, we show several examples of how users can develop interactive contents with it.

## 2 Related Work

One representative interactive contents is Role Playing Games (RPGs), which is a genre of video games where users enjoy various story developments by controlling their characters. One of the most important issues for RPGs is how to control the development of interactive stories that have been actively studied under the name of "Interactive Storytelling" [1][2][3][4][5][6][7]. Although there are various kinds of small variations for story development, basically for RPGs the overall storyline is carefully designed beforehand and controlled to lead users through it. On the other hand, in the case of interactive storytelling, the key issues include the generation of autonomous interactive characters and also the emergence of storylines based on interactions between virtual characters and users and also among virtual characters. This is surely the final target of interactive storytelling. Society consists of people with autonomous capabilities, and based on interactions among people various everyday events occur: in other words, story. The problem with present interactive storytelling is that, since the generation of sophisticated autonomous characters is so complicated, it is difficult to maintain the consistency of the generated story for more than several minutes [8]. For games and e-learning users are expected to interact with the system for a certain duration, probably for hours. Therefore, for these applications, it is more realistic to develop a narrative based on a plot prepared beforehand. If a great amount of story variation must be generated, our idea is to generate a story by connecting various kinds of short stories called 'plots.' In this case there must be an authoring system with which content creators, even non experts in computer graphics or animation techniques, could easily develop interactive contents. Based on this simple consideration, we started to develop an authoring system for the creation of interactive contents.

## 3   Concept and Overview of the Authoring System

### 3.1   Concept of Story Generation

Here the basic concept of story generation is described. A story consists of a concatenation of short stories called plots. In linear stories such as novels and movies, plots are connected based on fixed storylines. On the other hand, in interactive storytelling, a plot to be connected to a previously developed storyline is based on the interaction between users and the system (Fig. 1). If a large number of plots are prepared as a plot database and the system can watch the process of story development and extract an appropriate plot from the database, an immense number of story variations could be generated. The selection process of adequate plots and combining plots to maintain story consistency are of great importance and difficulty. In this paper we focus on the generation of storyline by connecting plots one by one, as we believe that this is the key function of an authoring system.

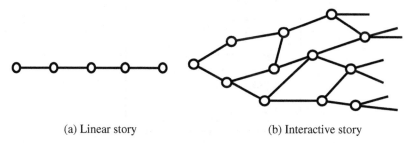

(a) Linear story                              (b) Interactive story

**Fig. 1.** Linear story vs. interactive story

### 3.2   Concept of Authoring System

Our first prototype authoring system supplied two major benefits: one for contents viewers and one for contents creators. For contents viewers, they can enter a 3D world created by the system and walk through it. Also, they can experience various events in the 3D world through interactions with the 3D characters who inhabit it. For contents creators, by preparing 3D characters and describing scripts of the script file, they can create any kind of interactive contents or event contents that employ these 3D characters and 3D backgrounds.

We carefully considered and prepared the contents/software development environment of this system and adopted Windows as its basic OS and Microsoft Visual C++ for the software development. To generate 3D scenes and play music, we use Direct X and Direct X SDK (software development kit), respectively. The data file format for 3D models is the X file format normally used for Direct X. Since X file format is standard for Direct X, its generality makes it superior to other file formats.

### 3.3  System Construction

In our authoring system, there are two kinds of files: object (Object.txt) and script (Script.txt). The system generates interactive narrative by interpreting these files.

Objext.txt: A text file used for the basic definition and setting of 3D objects.

Script.txt: A text file that defines the generation of each scene, the actions of each character, and the interactions between users and the characters and also among characters.

Detailed explanations of the functions of these files will be described in section 4. In this section, the basic mechanism of story is described. The control of interactive story development is basically described and achieved by Script.txt. The file consists of a set of plot scripts each of which corresponds to a plot described in 3.1. Each plot script begins with START and concludes with END, as shown in Fig. 2, where PLOT X is the name of the plot script. Also utilizing GOTO mechanism, control is handed from one plot script to another based on interaction results. By utilizing this basic mechanism, the storyline can proceed from plot to plot, thus achieving interactive story generation.

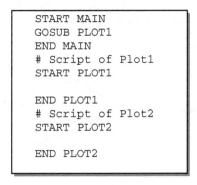

```
START MAIN
GOSUB PLOT1
END MAIN
# Script of Plot1
START PLOT1

END PLOT1
# Script of Plot2
START PLOT2

END PLOT2
```

**Fig. 2.** Basic structure of "Script.txt."

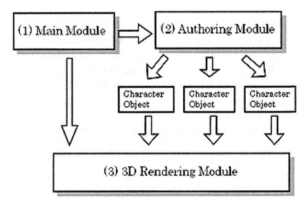

**Fig. 3.** System configuration

The system mainly consists of three modules: a main, an authoring, and a rendering for 3D rendering. Figure 3 illustrates the construction of the system. The main module manages the overall process and thus controls the entire application. The authoring module manages the script and the data flow. It also controls each independent object that corresponds to each character. Furthermore, that module manages interactions. The rendering module manages the information for the rendering process and also controls the creation of 3D models.

## 4 Contents Creation

As described in section 3, in this authoring system, contents can be created using Object.txt and Script.txt. Now the details of the contents and functions of these files will be described.

### 4.1 Object.txt

This file is used to define 3D objects. It can treat multiple X files by grouping them and treating them as one 3D object. For one X file data (mesh data), three types operations can be carried out: rotation, parallel shift, and size change. These operations can also be simultaneously performed for multiple X files. An example of the description of Object.txt is shown in Fig. 4.

In Fig. 4, X files corresponding to house and ground models are read from the data storage, and by integrating them, the background 3D object is defined. In the authoring system, this integrated object is named [Background01] and referred to at the time of script processing, 3D rendering, and so on.

```
// Countryside
BACKGLOUND_01 {
// House
LOAD_MESH( "cottage01.x" );
MESH_SCALE( 1.2 );

// Ground
LOAD_MESH( "ground01.x" );
MESH_ROTATION(    0.0,    0.0,
0.0 );
MESH_SCALE( 1.0 );
}
```

**Fig. 4.** A description sample of "Ojbect.txt."

### 4.2 Script.txt

This file is used to define the interactions, motions, and conversations of each character. Basically, a sequence of statements is interpreted and carried out according to its order. In addition to this basic control mechanism, just as for the functions of C language or the subroutines of BASIC language, it is possible to describe a script as a module and to call any module at any time. Furthermore, as one type of flow control, branch processing that uses [IF] can be carried out. When a script is described and separated by [START] and [END], it is treated as one module corresponding to a plot script, and a group of these modules controls all processing. [START MAIN] denotes an entry point, and processing starts from this module, corresponding to the "main ()" in C language. Also, several variables such as character strings, integers, and real numbers can be handled by this system, which can carry out simple numerical calculations among these variables. The character string after [#] is treated as a comment and is neither interpreted nor processed.

**Table 1.** Commands and their functions

| Statements | Function |
|---|---|
| GOSUB | Call another plot script. |
| GOTO | Jump to the specified plot script. |
| IF, ELSE, END_IF | Same function as C/C++ |
| EYE_POSITION | Specify the eye position. |
| EYE_DIRECTION | Specify the eye direction. |
| RENDERING_ON | Show a 3D object. |
| RENDERING_OFF | Hide a 3D object. |
| INPUT | Input user's string. |
| MSG | Show a message. |
| STRING | Show a narration message |
| SET_BOUNDERING_RADIUS | Specify a radius for collision detection |
| SET_INTERACTION | Jump to the specified plot script based on the collision detection |
| MOVE | Move a 3D object according to the specified shift and rotation |
| ANIMATION_START | Start an animation of 3D object using the specified animation data |

Table 1 presents examples of basic commands and their functions. In the present version only a small number of basic functions have been prepared to achieve interactive contents. Future versions, however, will include many additional convenient functions and image effects.

GOSUB is a function to summon a specified plot script. On the other hand, GOTO jumps to that specified plot script. By combining these functions it is possible to describe story development based on the concatenation of plot script. Also it is possible to describe sub story development within a plot script. EYE_POSITION and

```
START MAIN
GOSUB INIT
END MAIN
# script of Interactive comm.
START HUMAN_SCRIPT
$count = $count + 1
BACKGROUND_COLOR   128 0 0
IF $count > 1 THEN
@mes = $count
@mes   =   @mes   +   "times   you
visited."
MSG @mes
ELSE
MSG "Hello!(^o^)"
END_IF
WAIT 0.5
END HUMAN_SCRIPT
```

**Fig. 5.** A description sample of "Script.txt."

EYE_DIRECTION are used to specify the position and direction of the eye's perspective or the camera. RENDERING_ON and RENDERING_OFF are used for showing a 3D object or hiding it from the display. INUT is used to obtain an input from a user. So far only key input is allowed but input based on speech/image recognition is planned. By combining the IF, GOSUB, and GO_TO functions, control can be handed to any plot script based on interaction results. STRING is a function to show a message identical to MSG. As STRING can display a message of various character sizes and colors, it is mostly used to display narration messages. MOVE is used to move a 3D object according to specified shift and rotation. ANIMATION_START is used to start animation using specified animation data. By combining these commands, any kind of animation for a 3D object is fairly easily achieved. Figure 5 illustrates an example of a description of Script.txt.

## 5   Example of Contents Creation

One significant characteristic of the proposed authoring system is that content creators, even schoolteachers or e-learning content creators who are not CG technique experts, can fairly easily create new interactive contents. Utilizing these contents, children can be expected to experience the world of old tales or historical events. People used to learn how to do with other people, some of whom are not good guys, by listening to old tales told by their parents or grandparents. Also people learned the basic mechanisms of how our society is managed and how to adopt themselves to it. Therefore, we think that one good application of the authoring system is the generation of interactive tales. Below are the functions the system is expected to achieve.

*Function that generate classic tales as animation:
*Function that allows users to join the development of a tale story by interaction with the characters in the tale's world.
*Function to generate new tales based on a mixture of classic tales.
We carried out an experiment to achieve the above functions by selecting five representative classic Japanese tales. For these five stories, we carried out the following processes:
*Segmented each story into a set of short plots and generated a plot database
*Generated CG models necessary to generate scenes and objects for all plots
*Generated animation data necessary to generate actions and events that occur in each plot
The details of each process will be described below.

## 5.1  Plot Database Generation

Each of the five classic Japanese tales was analyzed and segmented into a series of short stories called plots. Each tale consisted of about 30 to 40 plots, and the total number of plots that consisted of five tales is 180. Then the description of each plot was abstracted. For example, "Momotaro left his home to kill monsters" became "A left B to do C." By doing this, it became possible to merge similar plots. Also this allows plots from two different tales to be combined. After combining similar plots based on this abstract process, the total number of plots was halved to 90. Each of these plots was then converted into a plot script including wide variations expected to occur based on interactions.

## 5.2  CG Database Generation

Then we investigated the number and types of CG models necessary to generate each of the plots in the plot database. There are basically two types of CG models to be prepared. One is characters, animals, and sometimes static objects that are expected to interact with users. The other type is static objects that do not interact with users and that are considered background. By combining similar objects and backgrounds, the total number of CG models is reduced to one third of the original numbers. In the experiments carried out here, we only prepared the fewest number of CG models. In such real applications as education software, however, it would be preferable to prepare as many variations as possible for one CG object to increase the software's appeal.

## 5.3  Evaluation of Authoring System

After the above preparation processes, it is necessary to carry out story generation. As each plot is expressed abstractly, each user is asked to make correspondences between each character, object, and CG model. The following system function was confirmed in experiments.

### Generation of Animation

It was confirmed that all five classic Japanese tales were generated as an animated movie by concatenating plots according to the original story. It was found that adding a small variation to the animation gave users a fresh feeling each time they observed the animation. Figure 6 illustrates one variation created by the system.

**Interactive Story Development**
Our system still lacks a function that automatically selects a plot to be connected to the already developed storyline. This time, therefore, we carefully prepared various plot concatenations beforehand, and by monitoring story development, decided which plot to select. Automatic plot selection and connection is a future research theme. At the same time real-time manual development of interactive story, as in the movie "Truman Show," is also an interesting research theme.

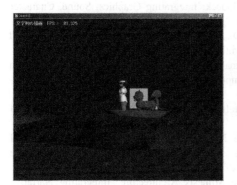

**Fig. 6.** An example of a scene generation

# 6   Conclusion

In this paper we proposed an authoring system to help people create new contents and described the details of the system's construction and functions. Although in such applications as games and e-learning, various types of 3D interactive contents are required, to date the creation of interactive contents continues to consume much time and effort. The system we have proposed and developed is the first prototype with the potential to reduce the time and labor required for producing interactive content. As a result, even users who lack sufficient 3D-CG knowledge or techniques will be able to create 3D-CG interactive contents using this system.

This system features potential for use in a variety of applications. In history, for example, education using only textbooks is often boring and difficult to provide students with a realistic sense of historical events. This system, however, will enable teachers themselves to create interactive contents for history lessons. Another merit of this system is that, since it adopts Direct X as a computer graphics module, we can use the latest 3D rendering environment.

Several issues require further study. The first is the addition of input devices, visual effects, and sound effects. In the present version, interaction between computer characters and users only operates by using character input/output. To make the system more realistic, it is desirable to adopt speech recognition/synthesis for interaction between computer characters and users. Also, utilizing a camera image of a user, carrying out image processing, and then inputting that image processing result into the system would improve the user interface. Furthermore, to make the interaction in virtual space more immersive, various image and sound effects must be added to the system. It is also necessary to evaluate the system. We are planning to create several historical interactive contents that allow user interaction with the system and obtain feedback using questionnaires. Such evaluation would clarify the weaknesses of our system.

## References

1. Swartout, W. et al., 2001. Toward the Holodeck: Integrating Graphics, Sound, Character and Story. Proceedings of the Autonomous Agents 2001 Conference.
2. Hayes-Roth, B., van Gent, R. and Huber, D., 1997. Acting in Character. In R. Trappel and P. Petta (Eds.), Creating Personalities for Synthetic Actors. Berlin, New York, Springer.
3. Bickmore, T., and Cassell, J., 1999. Small Talk and Conversational Storytelling in Embodied Interface Agents. AAAI Fall Symposium. "Narrarive Intelligence," November 5-7, Cape Cod, MA.
4. Mateas, M. and Stern, A., 2000. Socially Intelligent Agents: The Human in the Loop. AAAI Fall Symposium.
5. Young, R.M., 2000. Creating Interactive Narrative Structures: The Potential for AI Approaches. AAAI Spring Symposium in Artificial Intelligence and Interactive Entertainment, AAAI Press.
6. Young, R.M., 2001. An Overview of the Mimesis Architecture: Integrating Narrative Control into a Gaming Environment. AAAI Spring Symposium in Artificial Intelligence and Interactive Entertainment, AAAI Press.
7. Cavazza, M. Charles, F. and Mead, S.J., 2001. AI-based Animation for Interactive Storytelling. Proceedings of Computer Animation, IEEE Computer Society Press.
8. Charles, F. and Cavazza, M., 2004. Exploring Scalability of Character-based Storytelling. Proceedings of ACM AAMAS'04.

# Applying Direct Manipulation Interfaces to Customizing Player Character Behaviour

Marco Gillies

Department of Computer Science, University College London,
Malet Place, London WC1E 6BT, UK
m.gillies@cs.ucl.ac.uk
http://www.cs.ucl.ac.uk/staff/m.gillies

**Abstract.** The ability customize a players avatar (their graphical representation) is one of the most popular features of online games and graphical chat environments. Though customizing appearance is a common ability in most games, creating tools for customizing a character's behaviour is still a difficult problem. We propose a methodology, based on direct manipulation, that allows players to specify the type of behaviour they would like in a given context. This methodology is iterative, with the player performing a number of different customizations in different contexts. Players are also able to continue customizing their character during play, with commands that can have long term and permanent effects.

## 1 Introduction

Avatars are a vital part of any online game. The graphical representation of a player is the essential element that presents their persona to the rest of the community. Players can develop a deep bond and association with their avatar. For this reason, creators of online games have dedicated a lot of attention to the appearance and animation of avatars. It has also recently been pointed out[29] that allowing avatars some autonomous behaviour can greatly enhance their realism, for example by giving them complex body language that would be too difficult for a player to control in real time. This autonomous behaviour allows the avatar to produce appropriate responses to the behaviour of other players without the player having to control every movement, for example, looking at another player's avatar when they talk. If a player is to truly form a bond with their avatar then they must be able to customize it to create the persona they want to project, this is one of the most popular features of on-line worlds[6]. Current games largely restrict customization to graphical appearance, however, if an avatar is to present a consistent persona it should also be possible to customize their behaviour to make it consistent with their appearance.

Creating user-friendly tools for customizing characters is a challenging problem. When customizing the appearance of a character the player can pretty much see the whole effect of their changes in a single view, maybe having to rotate the view occasionally. However, autonomous behaviour involves responding to different events in the world and therefore requires the character to respond very differently in different contexts. This means that a player cannot simply judge whether they have created the

R. Harper, M. Rauterberg, M. Combetto (Eds.): ICEC 2006, LNCS 4161, pp. 175–186, 2006.
© IFIP International Federation for Information Processing 2006

character they want by quickly looking at a single view, or even a moderately sized sequence of views. What is needed is an iterative process of refinement of a character. We propose a methodology that involves iterative design of a character. Players may design their characters before joining a game by editing their behaviour in a number of different contexts. However, they can also refine the behaviour while playing using real-time customization.

Another problem with customizing behaviour is that autonomous behaviour systems are typically controlled by a large number parameters. The effect of these parameters on behaviour can be complex and, as described above, highly dependent on context. This means that directly editing these parameters can be highly unintuitive for players. To solve this problem we take inspiration from the highly successful "Direct Manipulation" paradigm of human computer interaction. Direct manipulation enables people to interact with software by directly editing the end result rather than the internal parameters that produce this result. Our methodology allows players to directly specify the behaviour that the characters should produce in a given context, while the software infers appropriate parameters. Typically specifying behaviour in a single context underconstrains the values of parameters. This means that players must edit behaviour in a number of different contexts, however, doing so in all possible contexts would be very time consuming, if possible at all, certainly not something that can be required of people playing games in their leisure time. This leads us back to the need for an iterative methodology that allows players to specify just as much as they feel they need at a given time, while allowing them to refine the behaviour at a given time.

## 2 Related Work

This work builds on a long tradition of character animation. The lower level aspects focus on body animation in which there has been a lot of success with techniques that manipulate pre-existing motion data, for example that of Gleicher[10,20], Lee and Shin[14] or Popović and Witkin[31]. However, we are more interested in higher level aspects of behaviour control. This is a field that brings together artificial intelligence and graphics to simulate character behaviour. Research in this area was started by Reynolds[26] whose work on simulating birds' flocking behaviour has been very influential. Further important contributions include the work of Badler et al. on animated humans[1]; Tu and Terzopolous' work on simulating fishes[27]; Blumberg and Galyean's "Silas T. Dog"[3], Perlin and Goldberg's "IMPROV" system[23] and the work of Gratch, Johnson and Marsella[12,19]. We mostly deal with non-verbal communication, which is a major sub-field of behaviour simulation with a long research history including the work of Cassell and her group[4,5,29]; Pelachaud and Poggi[22] and Guye-Vuillème et al. [11]. The two types of behaviour we are using are gesture which has been studied by Cassell et al.[4] and posture which has been studied by Cassell et al. [5] and by Bécheiraz and Thalmann[2]. Vihljàlmsson[28] has applied this type of autonomous non-verbal behaviour to avatars for on-line games.

Most of the work described above deals with the algorithms for simulating behaviour rather than tools for designing behaviour. Of the work on tools, most has focused on using markup languages to specify the behaviour of characters and avatars, for example the APML language[7]. However, though markup languages are an important step towards making it easier to specify behaviour they are a long way from the usability of graphical tools. There have also been tools for designing the content of behaviour, for example designing gestures[11], however, these tools do not address the autonomous aspects, i.e. how to decide which behaviour to perform in a given context. Del Bimbo and Vicario[8] have worked on specifying autonomous behaviour by example, but their work was restricted to vehicles and was not applied to human-like characters. Pyandath and Marsella[25] use a linear inference system to infer parameters of a Partially Observable Markov Decision Process used for multi-agent systems. This inference system is similar to ours, however, they do not discuss user interfaces. In the field of robotics Scerri and Ydrén[21] have produced user friendly tools for specifying robot behaviour. They use a multi-layered approach, with programming tools to design the main sections of the behaviour and graphical tools to customise the behaviour. They were working with soccer playing robots and used a graphical tool based on a coach's tactical diagrams to customise their behaviour. Their multi-layered approach has influenced much of the discussion below. Our own approach to specifying behaviour has been influenced by work on direct manipulation tools for editing other graphical objects, for example the work on free form deformations by Hsu, Hughes and Kaufman[30] and Gain[13].

## 3   Method Overview

As described in the introduction we are proposing an iterative methodology for customising and refining the behaviour of a character. A player starts by selecting a context and viewing the character's behaviour in this context. They may change this behaviour by selecting from a menu of possible actions (which can be combined and blended together). This choice of behaviour is used to determine a suitable choice of parameters for the character. The parameters must be such that they will produce the chosen behaviour in the given context. It is likely that many different sets of parameters will produce the same behaviour in that one context so the effect of choosing behaviour is not to identify a single set of parameters but to put a number of constraints on the possible parameter values. These constraints are solved using linear programming to produce a set of parameters. After choosing behaviour in a single context the system is likely to be highly under-constrained, and the parameters chosen might not be appropriate in different contexts. The player must, therefore, repeat the processes, putting the character in a number of different contexts. Each time a new behaviour is chosen for a new context more constraints are added and the whole set of constraints are solved for. As the number of contexts is potentially very large the player should not be expected to edit every single context or to completely finish the process of editing their character before starting play. Instead they should be able to update the character to correct any behaviour they find to be wrong during play. Players can do this by returning to the original custommnisation tool after a session of play, but this looses some of the immediacy of correcting a problem as it occurs. We therefore provide a second interface, which allows players to continue customising during play in a way that is integrated with the real time control methods.

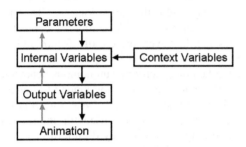

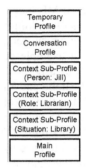

**Fig. 1.** An overview of the behaviour generation process. The black arrows show the behaviour generation process and the grey arrows show the inference process that determines parameters from animation.

**Fig. 2.** The profiles stack containing a number of loaded contextual profiles

## 4  Behaviour Generation

The Demeanour architecture is used to generate behaviour for our avatars[17,18], figure 1 shows the behaviour generation method. The basic components of the behaviour system are parameters and variables. Parameters vary between characters and are the element that determines the difference in behaviour between different avatars. Examples might be, how friendly an avatar is or how often it nods when listening to another avatar. Variables, on the other hand, changes with different contexts. Some variables, context variables, are determined solely by external contextual factors, for example the behaviour of other characters. Parameters and variables are combined together to create new, internal variables, which represent the current state of the avatar, for example, whether it is angry or whether it likes the avatar it is talking to.

Some variables are used as outputs that driven the animation system. There are two mains ways of combining parameters and variables. The first is by addition and multiplication, which is often used to combine context variables with weighting parameters. Variables and parameters can also be combined by if-then-else rules that set the value of a variable to that of one of two option variables depending on the value of a boolean condition variable:

$$x = x_1 \quad if \quad x_c = a$$
$$= x_2 \quad \quad otherwise$$

The animated behaviour is generated using a set of basic pieces of motion, each of which represents and action such as a gesture. The basic motions are interpolated using a quaternion weighted sum technique similar to Johnson's[15]. Each weight is determined by the value of an output parameter. Many motions can be continuously interpolated, e.g. leaning forward, however, others are more all-or-nothing, for example it makes no sense to cross your arms 50%. Therefore some motions are classed as discrete and can only have weights of 0 or 1. In this case the corresponding variable is thresholded so that values over 0.5 give a weight of 1.

# 5  Profiles

The behaviour of avatars can be controlled by using profiles[16]. A profile is a set of parameter values that are loaded together. Profiles are used as a means of customising a character, with the profile determining the behaviour of a character. They can also provide contextual variation, with different profiles being loaded in different contexts (see [16] for more details), and for regulating real time interaction, as described in section 6. This means an avatar will have a number of profiles loaded at any given time. They are stored in a stack as shown in figure 2. The base of the stack is always the main profile that contains the context independent customisations of a character, as described in section 5. Above this, a number of context dependent profiles are loaded. At the top are two profiles that are used to store results of user interaction, the temporary and conversation profiles, as described in section 6. When a new context profile is loaded it is added above all the previously loaded profiles in the stack but below the temporary and conversation profiles. Profiles higher up the stack will override profiles lower in the stack, so recently loaded profiles override older ones and user input overrides other profiles.

# 6  Off-Line Customisation

This initial stage of customization will happen before the player starts playing the game through a first off-line editing state. The player can select contexts in which to view their avatars behaviour and then edit that behaviour. The behaviour is edited by selecting from a menu of actions such as gestures and head nodding. Action can either be discrete (you are either doing them or you are not, e.g. crossing your arms) or continuous (you can do them to a greater or lesser degree, e.g. leaning backward). The interface contains buttons which can select discrete actions and sliders to vary the degree of continuous actions. The user interface is shown in figure 3. The user first sets the context for a behaviour, which is itself expressed as discrete or continuous variables that are edited by buttons and sliders. The user may then view the resulting animation and if they are unhappy with it they may go to an editing screen to change the animation. When they are happy with this they submit the animation. The resulting set of actions is used to generate a number of linear constraints which are then solved for to updated the parameters of the avatar, as described in section 8. The player can then repeat the process by choosing an new context and editing the behaviour if it is not suitable. Figure 3 gives an example of a sequence of edits.

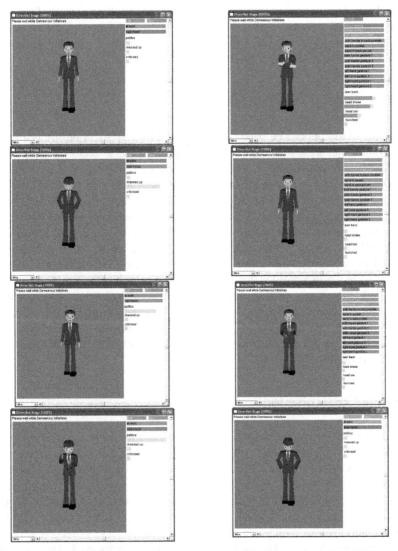

**Fig. 3.** A sequence of edits using the tool from the action based specification example. The the user initially specifies context (in this case that the avatar is in a bad mood). The initial behaviour (image 1, left to right, top to bottom) is neutral as there have been no edits (for clarity, in these examples neutral behaviour is merely a constant rest posture). The user then specifies some hostile behaviour and submits it (2). The system has set the general hostile parameter so the avatar produces hostile behaviour in a new context (3). The user removes this behaviour to specify a neutral context (4), thus reducing the contexts in which hostile behaviour is produced, so in the next context (a political discussion) neutral behaviour is generated (5). The user adds gesturing and submits (6). The final two images show results after these edits, the avatar in a bad mood discussing politics produces both gesturing and hostile behaviour (7). The final image has the same context as the original edit, showing that the same type of behaviour (hostile) is successfully reproduced, but that the exact behaviour is different (8).)

# 7   Real Time Customisation

The problem with using off-line customization for something as context dependent as character behaviour is that, after editing, the player cannot be sure that their avatar will behave as they want it too in all context. Even after a relatively long period of customization, they are likely to find incorrect behaviour when they actually use the avatar during play. For this reason we propose that players should also be able to continue customizing their character during play. This means that the initial effort is reduced, allowing players to start playing the game quickly. It also means that customization and correction of errors are situated in play so that players are able to specify the real behaviour they want at that time, rather than specifying behaviour for a hypothetical situation. It is likely to be easier for a user to know what behaviour is appropriate when actually engaged in a conversation than to think about it abstractly during an off-line customisation step.

Demeanour also contains a real-time control system where users can determine the affective state of their character through a number of commands as described in Gillies, Crabtree and Ballin[17]. So as to minimize the effort of controlling a character the control system should be well integrated with the rest of the game controls. As we are looking at conversational behaviour we have produced a control system that is integrated with the type of text-chat interface that is commonly used in on-line games (shown in figure 4). As well as typing the text that they are speaking players can also enter textual commands that control the behaviour of a character. These might be emoticons, e.g. :-) , which can control high level parameters such as the mood of a character, but they can also be direct requests for a particular action, enclosed in asterisks, e.g. *arms crossed*. When a player enters this command their avatar performs the action, but the action is also used to infer appropriate parameter for the character. A set of constraints is generated as described in section 8, these constraints are added to those from previous customizations, and solved for to generate new parameters.

When a player enters a command it not clear how long they intend a change of state to last, for example an increase in friendliness might have a very short scope, just the length of the current utterance or it might indicate a permanent positive attitude to the person being talked to. Demeanour uses character profiles to allow users to choose between four different scopes for a change of state:

- Temporary changes lasting for a limited period, disappearing after a time out.
- Changes lasting for the whole length of the current conversations
- Permanent changes to the attitude toward the conversational partner
- Permanent changes to the character's main profile.

Initially, when a player types a command that changes a parameter value, it is stored in temporary profile. This temporary profile is deleted after a short period of time and all the edits it contains are deleted. Thus the default scope for edits is that they are temporary. However, when a temporary profile is present (i.e. after the user sends a command) a button appears in the text chat interface allowing the user to save the profile. If the user clicks this button the temporary profile is saved into a conversation profile (as shown in figure 2), which has a longer scope lasting for the entire conversation. When temporary edits are saved into the conversation profile they are merged.

At the end of the conversation the user can merge the resulting edits into a permanent profile that is used in all future interactions. This can be to the character's main profile which controls its behaviour and is the chief method of customising a character. Users can also merge the conversation profile into a contextual profile for their conversational partner, thus developing the relationship between the characters during interaction.

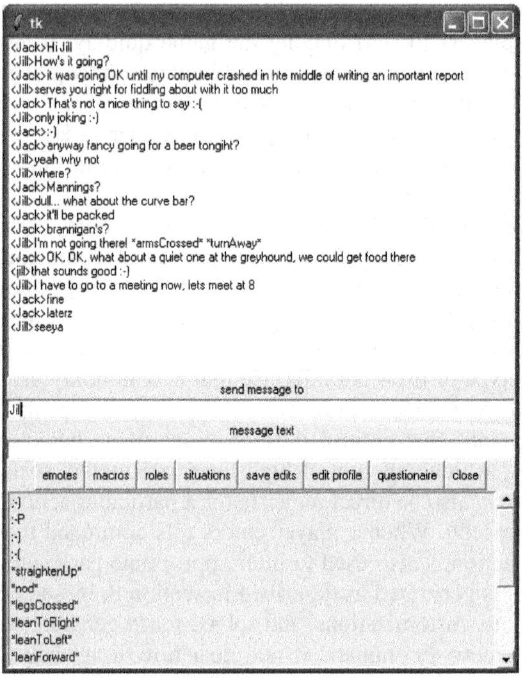

**Fig. 4.** The text chat interface

# 8 Inferring Parameters from Behaviour

The main technical requirement for this user interface is the ability to use a number of examples of behaviour to generate constraints which are then solved for a suitable set of parameter values for the avatar's behaviour. To be more exact, each example is a tuple $<a_i,c_i>$ containing a context for behaviour $c_i$ and an animation specified by the user $a_i$, which is the behaviour of the avatar in that context. The output of the method is a set of parameters. Each example tuple provides a constraint on the possible values of the parameters. We must solve for these constraints using a method that makes it simple to add new constraints, as the editing methods is iterative users will continually be solving and adding new constraints. The method must also be fast enough to solve in real time, if the tools is to be usable. This is simplified by the fact that the parameters and variables are combined together using linear summation, meaning that all relationships between variables, and therefore constraints are linear. This allows us to use Linear Programming[24] to solve for the constraints. Linear programming mimimizes a linear expression subject to to a number of linear equality and inequality constraints:

$$\sum c_i x_i \ subject\ to \quad \sum d_i y_i = 0$$
$$\sum e_i x_i \geq 0$$

where the $x,y,z$ are variables and the $c,d,e$ are constant coefficients. We form constraints from the characters behaviour and internal parameters as described in the next sections. We then minimize the sum of all parameters values using a simplex linear programming method[24]. This minimization solves for the parameters while keeping their values as low as possible (to avoid extreme behaviour).

## 8.1  Constraints from Action Specifications

As described in section 6, the action-ased interface allows user to specify the avatar's behaviour using buttons and sliders to give weights for each action (0 or 1 in the case of discrete actions). When a animation is submitted these weights are used to form linear constraints. For a continuous motion the weight of the motion $(w_i)$ should be equal to the corresponding output variable $(v_i)$ so we add the constraint $v_i - w_i = 0$. In the case of discrete actions we are less certain: if the $w_i$ is 0 we know that $v_i$ is less than 0.5, otherwise it is greater, so we add an inequality constraint:

$$v_i - 0.5 \quad \leq 0\ if \quad w_i = 0$$
$$\geq 0 \quad w_i = 1$$

## 8.2  Constraints from Internal Variables

With this initial set of constraint we then start to form new constraints based on internal variables and parameters. Any variable will depend on other variables and parameters. A variable $v_1$ depends on another variable $v_2$ if $v_2$ is used to calculated $v_1$ via addition and multiplication, $v_2$ is a condition or option in an if-then-else rule that is used to calculate $v_1$, or $v_1$ depdends on a third variable that recursively depends on $v_2$. If a variable only depends on context variables and not parameters it has a constant value in a given context so it is a *known* $(k_i)$ variable in the current constraint. Parameters, and variables that depend on parameters, are *unknowns* $(u_i)$. We must form constraints on all unknowns. We start with the constraints that are given by the animations, each of these contain at least one output variable. Each variable $v$ may take one of 4 forms. If it is a parameter it is an unknown and no further constraints are added. If it is a constraint variable it is a known and has a constant value (this is not allowed for an output variable). If it depends on other variables and parameters by addition and multiplication we add a linear constraint. To ensure that it is soluble we ensure that in each multiplication, only one term is an unknown. Thus the equation for the variable is of the form:

$$v = \sum_i \left( u_i \prod_j k_j \right)$$

We can evaluate all knowns to calculate the coefficients of each unknown and rearrange to get a constraint:

$$\sum_i c_i u_i + c_0 - v = 0$$

If the variable depends on other variables by an if-then-else rule the condition variable is a known so we can evaluate it and know which the option variable $v_i$ that $v$ depends on, we can just add a constraint $v - v_i = 0$. The newly added constraints will have introduced new variables, and we recursively add new constraints for these until we are only left with knowns and parameters, at which point we perform the minimization as described above.

## 9  Conclusion

This paper has proposed a methodology for customizing avatars in on-line games. This methodology is based on Direct Manipulation in that players choose the concrete behaviour that they want their character to perform in a given context and linear programming is used to infer an appropriate set of parameters for the character from the chosen behaviour. This methodology is readily extensible to both off-line customization, and real-time customization during play. The second feature allows players to gradually adapt their character and to customize their character in a way that is situated in play. We are currently planning a user trial involving long term use of the system to evaluate its effectiveness.

We have used linear programming as it is a fast inference method. This means that it is usable in an interactive interface such as the one we are proposing, and remains usable for our real-time customization method. However, using linear programming does limit our behaviour systems to linear ones, which can limit the complexity of the behaviour produced. With the type of interface we propose, there is always likely to be a trade off between complexity behaviour and speed of inference, but more work is needed to determine the ideal balance, and therefore an appropriate inference method. More complex machine learning models, such as neural networks or Bayesian networks can give more powerful results at a greater computational cost. An even more powerful method would be to use an arbitrary parameterised algorithm to generate behaviour and then use a numerical optimisation method to determine parameter value. This would be extremely flexible but may well by computationally intractable.

It is also important to compare our method with other interface styles. We have also experimented with a reinforcement learning method in which users do not directly specify behaviour, instead they judge behaviour that is suggested by the system[9]. Our feeling, after initial experimentation, is that the task of judging behaviour is easier for an untrained user than specifying behaviour, but that reinforcement learning involves the user viewing a very large number of behaviours to produce a good result, which may make it impractical. We will conduct user trials to understand the issues better.

## Acknowledgements

This work was sponsored by BT plc. I would like to thank the former members of the BT Radical Multimedia Lab for their help and support on this work, in particular

Amada Oldroyd (in particular for the use of her avatars), Jon Sutton (for his advice on on-line chat worlds), Daniel Ballin and Barry Crabtree. I would also like to thank the members Virtual Environments and Computer Graphics Group at University College London, and in particular Mel Slater.

# References

1. Badler, N., Philips, C., and Webber, B.: Simulating Humans: Computer Graphics, Animation and Control Oxford University Press (1993)
2. Bécheiraz, P. and Thalmann, D.: A Model of Nonverbal Communication and Interpersonal Relationship Between Virtual Actors In: Proceedings of the Computer Animation '96 IEEE Computer Society Press (1996) 58-67
3. Blumberg, B. and Galyean, T.: Multi-Level Direction of Autonomous Creatures for Real-Time Virtual Environments In: ACM SIGGRAPH (1995) 47-54
4. Cassell, J., Bickmore, T., Campbell, L., Chang, K., Vilhjálmsson, H., and Yan, H.: Embodiment in Conversational Interfaces: Rea In: ACM SIGCHI ACM Press (1999) 520-527
5. Cassell, J., Vilhjálmsson, H. H., and Bickmore, T.: BEAT: the behavior expression animation toolkit In: ACM SIGGRAPH (2001) 477-486
6. Cheng, L., Farnham, S., and Stone, I.: Lessons Learned: Building and Deploying Virtual Environments (2002)
7. DeCarolis, B., Pelachaud, C., Poggi, I., and Steedman, M.: APML, a markup language for believable behaviour generation (2004) 65-87
8. Del Bimbo, Alberto and Vicario, Enrico: Specification by-Example of Virtual Agents' Behavior IEEE transactions on visualtization and Computer Graphics 1:4(1995) 350-360
9. Friedman, D. and Gillies, M.: Teaching Characters How to Use Body Language In: Intelligent Virtual Agents (2005)
10. Gleicher, Michael: Motion Editing with Space Time Constraints In: symposium on interactive 3D graphics (1997) 139-148
11. Guye-Vuilléme, A., T.K.Capin, I.S.Pandzic, Magnenat-Thalmann, N., and D.Thalmann: Non-verbal Communication Interface for Collaborative Virtual Environments The Virtual Reality Journal 4)(1999) 49-59
12. J.Gratch and S.Marsella: Tears and Fears: Modeling emotions and emotional behaviors in synthetic agents In: 5th International Conference on Autonomous Agents (2006)
13. James, Gain: Enhancing spatial deformation for virtual sculpting (2000)
14. Jehee, Lee and Sung, Yong Shin: A Hierarchical Approach to Interactive Motion Editing for Human-like Figures In: ACM SIGGRAPH (1999) 39-48
15. Johnson, M. P.: Exploiting Quaternions to Support Expressive Interactive Character Motion (2003)
16. M.Gillies, I.B.Crabtree, and D.Ballin: Customisation and Context for Expressive Behaviour in the Broadband World BT Technology Journal 22:2(1-4-2004) 7-17
17. Marco, Gillies, Barry, Crabtree, and Daniel, Ballin: Expressive characters and a text chat interface In: Patrick, Olivier and Ruth, Aylett (ed): AISB workshop on Language, Speech and Gesture for Expressive Characters (2004)
18. Marco, Gillies and Daniel, Ballin: Integrating autonomous behavior and user control for believable agents In: Third international joint conference on Autonomous Agents and Multi-Agent Systems (2004)
19. Marsella, S. C., Johnson, W. L., and LaBore, C.: Interactive Pedagogical Drama In: the proceedings of the 4th international Conference on Autonomous Agents (2000) 301-308

20. Michael, Gleicher: Comparing Constraint-Based Motion Editing Methods Graphical Models :63(2001) 107-134
21. Paul, Scerri and Johan, Ydrén: End User Specification of RoboCup Teams (2000)
22. Pelachaud, C. and Poggi, I.: Subtleties of facial expressions in embodied agents Journal of Visualization and Computer Animation. 13(2002) 287-300
23. Perlin, K. and Goldberg, A.: IMPROV: A System for Scripting Interactive Actors in Virtual Worlds In: Proceedings of SIGGRAPH 96 ACM SIGGRAPH / Addison Wesley (1996) 205-216
24. Press, W. H., Flannery, B. P., Teukolsky, S. A., and Vetterling, W. T.: Numerical Recipes in C Cambridge University Press (1992)
25. Pynadath, D. V. and Marsella, S. C.: Fitting and Compilation of Multiagent Models through Piecewise Linear Functions In: the International Conference on Autonomous Agents and Multi Agent Systems (2004) 1197-1204
26. Reynolds, Craig W.: Flocks, Herds, and Schools: A Distributed Behavioral Model In: ACM SIGGRAPH (1987) 25-33
27. Tu, X. and Terzopoulos, D.: Artificial Fishes: Physics, Locomotion, Perception, Behavior In: ACM SIGGRAPH (1994) 43-49
28. Vilhjalmsson, H.: Animating Conversation in Online Games In: M.Rauterberg (ed): Entertainment Computing ICEC Springer (2004) 139-150
29. Vilhjálmsson, H. H. and Cassell, J.: BodyChat: Autonomous Communicative Behaviors in Avatars In: second ACM international conference on autonomous agents (1998)
30. William, M. Hsu, John, F. Hughes, and Henry, Kaufman: Direct manipulation of free-form deformations In: Proceedings of the 19th ACM SIGGRAPH annual conference on Computer graphics and interactive techniques ACM Press (1992) 177-184
31. Zoran, Popovi and Andrew, Witkin: Physically Based Motion Transformation In: ACM SIGGRAPH (1999) 11-20

# Programmable Vertex Processing Unit for Mobile Game Development

Tae-Young Kim[1], Kyoung-Su Oh[2], Byeong-Seok Shin[3], and CheolSu Lim[1]

[1] Dept. of Computer Engineering, Seokyeong University 136-704 Seoul, Korea
[2] Dept. of Media, Soongsil University 156-743 Seoul, Korea
[3] Dept. of Computer Engineering, Inha University 402-751 Inchon, Korea
tykim@skuniv.ac.kr, oks@ssu.ac.kr, bsshin@inha.ac.kr,
cslim@skuniv.ac.kr

**Abstract.** Programmable vertex processing unit increases flexibility and enables customizations of transformation and lighting in the graphics pipeline. Because most embedded systems such as mobile phones and PDA's have only the fixed-function pipeline, various special effects essential in development of realistic 3D games are not provided. We designed and implemented a programmable vertex processing unit for mobile devices based on the OpenGL ES 2.0 specification. It can be used as a development platform for 3D mobile games. Also, assembly instruction set and encoding scheme are examples of standard interface to high-level shading languages.

## 1 Introduction

In last a few decades, much research has been done to enhance the functionality and efficiency of graphics hardware [1]. One of them is the programmable graphics pipeline, which provides a programmer with the full control of the vertex and fragment processes. Various special effects which were impossible with the fixed pipeline can be implemented [2][3]. The vertex processing in the programmable pipeline does not use the fixed-function T&L (Transformation & Lighting) but a vertex program written by a programmer. As a result, this enables us to make realistic 3D games.

Unfortunately, most embedded systems such as mobile phones and PDA's only have fixed-function pipeline. Although some mobile 3D game consoles equip with specially designed programmable units, they require a lot of computing resource. Since they are subset of GPU's for desktop PC, they cannot be applied to generic mobile phones or PDA's. Therefore, we have designed and implemented a programmable vertex processing unit for the mobile devices.

Our vertex processing unit is designed based on the OpenGL ES 2.0 [4] and GL_ARB_vertex_program [5]. The GL_ARB_vertex_program is the specification of assembly shading language for programmable graphics processor in the general computing systems. OpenGL ES is a graphics APIs standard for the embedded systems, which specifies graphics APIs and high level shading language for the programmable vertex and fragment programs [6]. But it does not include low-level specification of the shading language [7]. We modified GL_ARB_vertex_program assembly language to fully support OpenGL ES 2.0. We defined some instructions and substituted an

R. Harper, M. Rauterberg, M. Combetto (Eds.): ICEC 2006, LNCS 4161, pp. 187–192, 2006.
© IFIP International Federation for Information Processing 2006

instruction with several other primitive instructions to encode/decode an instruction efficiently. Since it provides high-order flexibility to simple mobile devices, we can use them as mobile 3D game consoles. Also, our instruction design and operand encoding scheme can be used as an interface standard between low-level and high-level shader language.

In Sect. 2 we present the structure of our vertex processing unit. Instruction set design and encoding schemes are explained in Sect. 3. Implementation and results are in the next section. Lastly, we summarize and conclude our work.

## 2   Architecture of Vertex Processing Unit

A vertex program is a sequence of vector operations that determines how a set of program parameters and per-vertex input parameters are transformed to a set of per-vertex result parameters. Fig. 1 shows the architecture of our vertex processing unit.

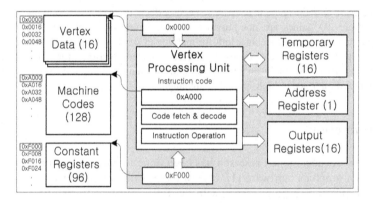

**Fig. 1.** Architecture of our vertex processing unit. It consists of seven components.

- **Machine code:** (Up to 128) binary codes to be executed in vertex processing unit.
- **Vertex Processing Unit:** A processing engine that fetches, decodes and operates each machine code.
- **Vertex data:** A set of 16 read-only registers containing 4-component floating point vector. Each register represents position, colors, normal of vertex.
- **Constant Registers:** A set of 96 read-only registers. It stores parameters such as matrices, lighting parameters and constants required by vertex programs.
- **Temporary Registers:** A set of 16 readable and writable registers to hold temporary results that can be read or written during the execution of a vertex program.
- **Address Register:** A register containing an integer used as an index to perform indirect accesses to constant data during the execution of a vertex program.
- **Output Registers:** A set of 16 write-only registers to hold the final results of a vertex program. They are passed to the remaining graphics pipelines.

## 3   Instruction Set and Encoding Scheme

We define 28 primitive instructions and 3 macro instructions based on the operation processing method, as shown tables 1. Since macro instruction means an instruction that can be replaced by a series of primitive instructions, each one is translated into multiple primitive instructions in assembling time. In table 1, the instructions in shadowed entries are additional instructions which are not included in the GL_ARB_vertex_program instruction set. We added them in order to implement the macro instructions as shown in table 1 (below).

**Table 1.** Primitive instructions and macro instructions used in our implementation

| Instruction | Description | Instruction | Description |
|---|---|---|---|
| ARL | Address register load | DPH | Homogenous dot product |
| MOV | Move | DP3 | 3-component dot product |
| ABS | Absolute | DP4 | 4-component dot product |
| FLR | Floor | clamp | Clamp |
| FRC | Fraction | Mulz | Multiply on z |
| SWZ | Extended swizzle | MAD | Multiply and add |
| ADD | Addition | EXP | Exponential base 2(approximate) |
| MUL | Multiply | LOG | Logarithm base 2(approximate) |
| DST | Distance vector | EX2 | Exponential base 2 |
| XPD | Cross product | LG2 | Logarithm base 2 |
| MAX | Maximum | RCP | Reciprocal |
| MIN | Minimum | RSQ | Reciprocal square root |
| SGE | Set on greater or equal than | rEX2 | Exponential base 2(rough) |
| SLT | Set on less than | rLG2 | Logarithm base 2(rougn) |

| macro | description | macro | description | macro | description |
|---|---|---|---|---|---|
| LIT | : Light coefficients<br><br>LIT f, a, b<br>clamp  tmp, a.0, b<br>rLG2  tmp.w, tmp.w<br>MUL  tmp.w, tmp.w, tmp.y<br>rEX2  tmp.w, temp.w<br>Mulz  f, tmp.1xz1, tmp.w | POW | : Power (f = a^b)<br><br>POW f, a, b<br>LG2  tmp, a<br>MUL  tmp, tmp, b<br>EX2  f, tmp | SUB | : Subtraction<br>: (f = a – b)<br><br>SUB f, a, b<br>ADD  f, a, -b |

Fig. 2 shows the 64bit machine code structure, which is composed of an opcode, a destination operand, and up to 3 source operands. The low bit fields [$4^{th}$ ~ $18^{th}$ bit] can be used as a source operand ($Src_2$) field or an extended swizzle field. They are recognized as a source operand field in MAD instruction, and as an extended swizzle field in other cases. MAD is the only instruction having three source operands.

The opcode has 6 bits, so it is possible up to 64 instructions. The destination operand field (register type, index, and mask) has 9 bits. Each bit is translated as follows:

```
T (1bit) : type      / 0 (Temporary register)
                     / 1 (Output register)
index (4bits) : register index (0~15)
mask (4bits) : mask flag for each component
```

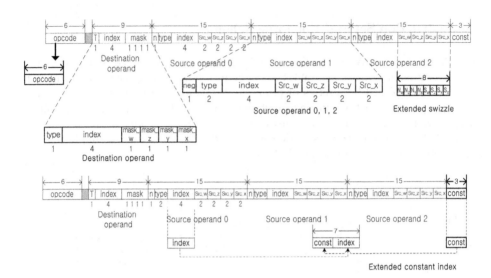

**Fig. 2.** Machine instruction format : An opcode field, a destination operand field, source operand fields, extended swizzle field, and extended constant index field

The source field (register type, index, and swizzle information) has 15 bits. Each bit is translated as follows:

neg(1bit): negation flag
type(2bits): type  / 00(Temporary register)
                    / 01(Vertex data)
                    / 10(Constant register, absolute addressing)
                    / 11(Constant register, relative addressing)
index (4bits): register index (0~15)
Src_?(2bits): component swizzle / 00(x component) 01(y component)
                               / 10(z component)  11(w component)

The extended swizzle field has additional swizzle information of source operand 0. With swizzle information, four components of source operand 0 can be negated or changed with other components value, zero or one. For example, if the swizzle suffix is ".yzzx" and the specified source register value is contains {2,8,9,0}, the swizzled operand used by the instruction is {8,9,9,2}.

Colr.{-}[01xyzw] {-}[01xyzw] {-}[01xyzw] {-}[01xyzw]

PARAM Colr = {5, 6, 7, 8};
TEMP Tmp1, Tmp2;
SWZ Tmp1, Colr.xy01;   // Tmp1 = { 5, 6, 0, 1};
SWZ Tmp2, Colr.-x-yz1; // Tmp2 = {-5,-6,7, 1};

In this field, $N_?$ and $S_?$ mean negation and zero or one value flags for each component. The extended index field has 3 bits, which is used for indexing the location of constant register. Totally, 7 bits indexing is possible with the 4 bits in the source operand field and the 3 bits in the extended constant index field.

## 4  Implementation and Results

We implemented our programmable vertex processing unit in software emulation. Our implementation can be used to emulate mobile game applications including vertex programs. We tested the performance of our work on a desktop PC with 4.3 GHz Pentium processor and ATI Radeon 9800 XT graphics card.

To test our vertex processing unit, we implemented the OpenGL ES 2.0 APIs related with vertex processing. Using the APIs, vertex data are stored and passed to our vertex processing unit. A vertex program is assembled into machine codes and they are passed to the vertex processing unit through our APIs. The vertex processing unit calculates the position and the color of each vertex by fetching, decoding, and executing the machine codes. The outputs of our vertex processing unit are sent to the OpenGL graphics pipeline installed in our computer via the original OpenGL APIs.

The arithmetic unit in our vertex processing unit supports 24 bit floating point format which satisfies the requirement of the OpenGL ES 2.0. We tested three vertex programs as shown in Fig.3.

**Fig. 3.** Test vertex programs, left: Normal value, middle: Cook-Torrance illumination, right: Environment map. All programs use same model whose vertex count is 6,984.

**Table 2.** Frame rate accoding to the number of instructions

|                              | sample 1 | sample 2 | sample 3 |
|------------------------------|----------|----------|----------|
| Number of assembly commands  | 6        | 31       | 21       |
| fps                          | 61.79    | 17.54    | 26.2     |

**Fig. 4.** A screen shot of mobile game implemented with our vertex processing unit (left) and a hardware prototype of target system using FPGA (right)

We compared an image rendered by our system with an image rendered by pure OpenGL on PC. We found little differences that cannot be recognized with naked eye. Comparison of frame rates among test programs is shown in table 3. We can see that the frame rate is inversely proportional to the number of assembly commands.

# 5  Conclusion

We design and implement a programmable vertex processing unit for the mobile environments based on the OpenGL ES 2.0 specification. Since the final draft of OpenGL ES 2.0 came out about September 2005, it is hard to find software or hardware implementation based on the specification. We present the architecture and instruction format of vertex processing unit. And we define 28 primitive instructions and 3 macro instructions based on the operation processing method. Our implementation and test results show that error is negligible and the performance is inversely proportional to the number of vertices and the number of instructions in the vertex program as we expected. At present we have only implemented the vertex processing unit. However, the fragment processing unit is also under development and the both units will be implemented as H/W chip.

# Acknowledgement

This work was supported by the Ministry of Culture & Tourism and KOCCA under the Culture and Content Technology Research Center (CTRC) Support Program.

# References

1. James D. F., Andries van D., Steven K. F., John F. H.:Computer Graphics: Principles and Practice in C Addison-Wesley Professional, Boston (2005)
2. Matt, P., Randima, F.:GPU GEMS 2. Addison-Wesley Professional, Boston (2005)
3. Michael M., Stefenus D. T., Tiberiu P., Bryan C., Kevin M.:Shader algebra, Transaction on Graphics, Vol 23, ACM Press, Newyork (2004)
4. OpenGL ES 2.0 specification. Available at http://www.khronos.org/opengles/2_X/
5. OpenGL ARB Vertex program specification. Available at http://oss.sgi.com/projects/ogl-sample/registry/ARB/vertex_ program.txt
6. OpenGL ARB Fragment program specification. Available at http://oss.sgi.com/projects/ogl-sample/registry/ARB/fragment_ program.txt
7. Randi J. R.: OpenGL Shading Language, Addison Wesley, Boston (2004)

# Vision-Based Real-Time Camera Matchmoving with a Known Marker

Bum-Jong Lee, Jong-Seung Park, and Mee Young Sung

Dept. of Computer Science & Engineering, University of Incheon,
177 Dohwa-dong, Nam-gu, Incheon, 402-749, Republic of Korea
{leeyanga, jong, mysung}@incheon.ac.kr

**Abstract.** A primary requirement for practical augmented reality systems is a method of accurate and reliable camera tracking. In this paper, we propose a fast and stable camera matchmoving method aimed for real-time augmented reality application. A known marker is used for the fast detection and tracking of feature points. From the feature tracking of one of three different types of markers on a single frame, we estimate the camera position and translation parameters. The entire pose estimation process is linear and initial estimates are not required. As an application of the proposed method, we implemented a video augmentation system that replaces the marker in the image frames with a virtual 3D graphical object during the marker tracking. Experimental results showed that the proposed camera tracking method is robust and fast enough to interactive video-based applications.

## 1 Introduction

Tracking the camera pose using images it acquires while the camera is moving in unknown environments is considered as an important problem in image analysis. During the recent two decades, many research works have focused on vision-based camera tracking. Most representative approaches can be classified into two categories: fiducial marker-based approaches and feature-based approaches. The feature-based approaches exploit geometric constraints arising from the automatic selection and tracking of appropriate point features [1]. An example is the planar-surface tracking method which tracks a manually specified planar region and computes the planar homography to align the real and virtual coordinate systems [2]. The fiducial marker-based approaches rely upon the presence of known fiducial markers or a certain calibration object in the given environment [3].

Though feature-based approaches do not assume any known geometric objects, they require sets of corner matches over an image sequence for the pose estimation, which means the methods are designed to operate in a batch off-line mode. However, most augmented reality applications require the camera pose in online mode to project computer generated 3D graphics models into the real world view in real-time. Hence, utilization of a fiducial marker is a natural choice for the fast feature tracking as well as for the computation of initial camera pose.

The projective camera model or the affine camera model is frequently used in computer vision algorithms. The projective model has eleven degree of freedoms and

R. Harper, M. Rauterberg, M. Combetto (Eds.): ICEC 2006, LNCS 4161, pp. 193–204, 2006.
© IFIP International Federation for Information Processing 2006

it is unnecessarily complex for many applications. There are non-linear relationships for the camera model parameters and iterative least-squares minimization must be used to improve the solution for the cost of a great amount of time. Since the camera tracking for an augmented reality application must be fast enough to handle real-time interactions, appropriate restrictions on the camera model should be introduced as long as the approximation is not far from the optimal solution.

This paper describes a stable real-time marker-based camera tracking method for augmented reality systems working in unknown environments. We propose a fast linear camera matchmoving algorithm that the initial estimates are not required.

## 2   Simplified Camera Model for Linear Approximation

Assume an arbitrary point $\mathbf{x}$ in the 3D scene space is projected to an image point $\mathbf{m}$ where all points are represented by the homogeneous form. The projection of a point $\mathbf{x}=[x\ y\ z\ 1]^T$ into the image point $\mathbf{m}=[u\ v\ 1]^T$ is presented by a projection equation of the form $\lambda\mathbf{m}=\mathbf{Px}$ where $\lambda$ is an arbitrary scalar constant. The 3×4 matrix $\mathbf{P}$, called the projection matrix, specifies how each 3D point is mapped to an image point.

When the transformation between the world space and the camera space is Euclidean, the projection matrix of the perspective camera model can be decomposed into two matrices and a vector of the form $\mathbf{P}=\mathbf{K}[\mathbf{R}|\mathbf{t}]$. The 3×3 matrix $\mathbf{K}$, called the camera calibration matrix, encodes all the intrinsic parameters. The matrix $\mathbf{R}$ and the vector $\mathbf{t}$ encode the pose of the object with respect to the camera. The calibration matrix has four intrinsic parameters: the focal length in two image directions ($f_x$ and $f_y$) and the coordinates of principal point ($p_x$ and $p_y$). The matrix $\mathbf{R}=[\mathbf{r}_x\ \mathbf{r}_y\ \mathbf{r}_z]^T$ is a 3×3 orthonormal matrix and $\mathbf{t}=[t_x\ t_y\ t_z]^T$ is a 3×1 vector. $\mathbf{R}$ and $\mathbf{t}$ represent the relative rotation translation between the model and the camera. The intrinsic parameters are unknown but, in most cases, they are constant or smoothly varying. The intrinsic parameters are determined through on the fly calibration performed prior to the pose recovery. Assume that the four intrinsic parameters encoded in $\mathbf{K}$ are known a priori. In a moment, we let $\mathbf{K}$ be an identity matrix only for simplicity purposes.

In the perspective model, the relations between image coordinates ($u$ and $v$) and model coordinates ($x$, $y$ and $z$) are expressed by non-linear equations. By imposing some restrictions on the projection matrix $\mathbf{P}$, linearized approximations of the perspective model are possible. A well-known linearized approximation of the perspective camera model is the weak-perspective model [4]. The weak-perspective model can be used instead of the perspective model when the dimensions of the object are relatively small compared to the distance between the object and the camera. In the weak-perspective model, all object points lie on a plane parallel to the image plane and passing through $\mathbf{x}_c$, the centroid of the object points. Hence, all object points have the same depth: $z_c=(\mathbf{x}_c-\mathbf{t})\cdot\mathbf{r}_z$.

The projection equations for an object point $\mathbf{x}$ to an image point $\mathbf{m}$ are:
$$u=(1/z_c)(\mathbf{r}_x\cdot(\mathbf{x}-\mathbf{t})),\ v=(1/z_c)(\mathbf{r}_y\cdot(\mathbf{x}-\mathbf{t})).$$
Assume $\mathbf{x}_c=0$, then $z_c=-\mathbf{t}\cdot\mathbf{r}_z$ and it leads the projection equations:

$$u=\check{\mathbf{r}}_x\cdot\mathbf{x}+x_c/z_c,\ v=\check{\mathbf{r}}_y\cdot\mathbf{x}+y_c/z_c \qquad (1)$$

where $\check{\mathbf{r}}_x=\mathbf{r}_x/z_c$, $\check{\mathbf{r}}_y=\mathbf{r}_y/z_c$, $x_c=-\mathbf{t}\cdot\mathbf{r}_x$, and $y_c=-\mathbf{t}\cdot\mathbf{r}_y$.

The equation (1) corresponds to an orthogonal projection of each model point into a plane passing the origin of the object space and parallel to the image plane, followed by a uniform scaling by the factor $(1/z_c)$. The equation (1) can be solved by the orthographic factorization method [5] with constraints $|\check{\mathbf{r}}_x|=|\check{\mathbf{r}}_y|=1$ and $\check{\mathbf{r}}_x \cdot \check{\mathbf{r}}_y=0$. Once $\check{\mathbf{r}}_x$ and $\check{\mathbf{r}}_y$ are obtained, the motion parameters $\mathbf{r}_x$ and $\mathbf{r}_y$ can be computed by normalizing $\check{\mathbf{r}}_x$ and $\check{\mathbf{r}}_y$, i.e., $\mathbf{r}_x=\check{\mathbf{r}}_x/|\check{\mathbf{r}}_x|$ and $\mathbf{r}_y=\check{\mathbf{r}}_y/|\check{\mathbf{r}}_y|$, and the translation along the optical axis is computed by $z_c=1/|\check{\mathbf{r}}_x|$.

Though camera pose estimation for coplanar points is also available [6], known methods using a closed form pose solution for coplanar points are not robust. We use a known marker in camera tracking mainly for the fast detection and tracking of feature points.

## 3   Camera Tracking Under Scaled-Orthographic Projection

The weak-perspective model approximates the perspective projection by assuming that all the object points are roughly at the same distance from the camera. The situation becomes true if the distance between the object and the camera is much greater than the size of the object.

We assume that the depths of all points of the object are roughly at the same depth. All depths of the object points can be set to the depth of a specific object point, called a reference point. Let $\mathbf{x}_0$ be such a reference point in the object and all other points have roughly same depth denoted by $z_0$. We consider the reference point $\mathbf{x}_0$ is the origin of the object space and all other coordinates of the object points are defined relative to the reference point. Consider the point $\mathbf{x}_i$ and its image $\mathbf{m}_i=[u_i \ v_i \ 1]^T$, which is the scaled orthographic projection of $\mathbf{x}_i$. From the equation (1), the relation can be written:

$$\check{\mathbf{r}}_x \cdot \mathbf{x}_i = u_i - u_0, \ \check{\mathbf{r}}_y \cdot \mathbf{x}_i = v_i - v_0 \qquad (2)$$

where $\check{\mathbf{r}}_x=\mathbf{r}_x/z_0$, $\check{\mathbf{r}}_y=\mathbf{r}_y/z_0$, $u_0=-\mathbf{t}\cdot\mathbf{r}_x/z_0$, $v_0=-\mathbf{t}\cdot\mathbf{r}_y/z_0$, and $\mathbf{m}_0=[u_0 \ v_0 \ 1]^T$ is the image of the reference point $\mathbf{x}_0$. Since the object points are already known and their image coordinates $\mathbf{m}_i$ $(0 \le i < N)$ are available, the equations (2) are linear with respect to the unknowns $\check{\mathbf{r}}_x$ and $\check{\mathbf{r}}_y$.

### 3.1   Linear Approximation

For the $N-1$ object points $(\mathbf{x}_1,...,\mathbf{x}_{N-1})$ and their image coordinates $(\mathbf{m}_1,...,\mathbf{m}_{N-1})$, we construct a linear system using equation (2) by introducing the $(N-1)\times3$ argument matrix $\mathbf{A}$, the $(N-1)$-vector $\mathbf{u}$, the $(N-1)$-vector $\mathbf{v}$:

$$\mathbf{A}=[\mathbf{x}'_1 \ \mathbf{x}'_2 \ ... \ \mathbf{x}'_{N-1}]^T, \ \mathbf{u}=[u'_1 \ u'_2 \ ... \ u'_{N-1}]^T, \ \mathbf{v}=[v'_1 \ v'_2 \ ... \ v'_{N-1}]^T$$

where $\mathbf{x}'_i=\mathbf{x}_i-\mathbf{x}_0$, $u'_i=u_i-u_0$, and $v'_i=v_i-v_0$. All the coordinates are given by column vectors in non-homogeneous form. The unknowns $\check{\mathbf{r}}_x$ and $\check{\mathbf{r}}_y$ can be obtained by solving the two linear least squares problems:

$$\mathbf{A}\check{\mathbf{r}}_x=\mathbf{u} \text{ and } \mathbf{A}\check{\mathbf{r}}_y=\mathbf{v}. \qquad (3)$$

The solution is easily obtained using the singular value decomposition (SVD). The parameters $\mathbf{r}_x$ and $\mathbf{r}_y$ are computed by normalizing $\check{\mathbf{r}}_x$ and $\check{\mathbf{r}}_y$.

### 3.2 Iterative Refinement

Once the unknowns $\mathbf{r}_x$ and $\mathbf{r}_y$ have been computed, more exact values can be obtained by an iterative algorithm. Dementhon [7] showed that the relation of the perspective image coordinates ($u_i$ and $v_i$) and the scaled orthographic image coordinates ($u_i^{''}$ and $v_i^{''}$) can be expressed by:

$$u_i^{''}=u_i+\alpha_i u_i, \; v_i^{''}=v_i+\alpha_i v_i$$

in which $\alpha_i$ is defined as $\alpha_i=\mathbf{r}_z \cdot \mathbf{x}_i/z_0$ where $\mathbf{r}_z=\mathbf{r}_x \times \mathbf{r}_y$. Hence, in the equations (2), we can replace $u_i$ and $v_i$ with $u_i^{''}$ and $v_i^{''}$ and we obtain:

$$\check{\mathbf{r}}_x \cdot \mathbf{x}_i=(1+\alpha_i)u_i-u_0, \; \check{\mathbf{r}}_y \cdot \mathbf{x}_i=(1+\alpha_i)v_i-v_0 . \tag{4}$$

Once we have obtained initial estimates of $\check{\mathbf{r}}_x$ and $\check{\mathbf{r}}_y$, we can compute $\alpha_i$ for each $\mathbf{x}_i$. Hence, the equations (4) are linear with the unknowns, $\check{\mathbf{r}}_x$ and $\check{\mathbf{r}}_y$. The term $\alpha_i$ is the $z$-coordinate of $\mathbf{x}_i$ in the object space, divided by the distance of the reference point from the camera. Since the ratio of object size to $z_0$ is small, $\alpha_i$ is also small, which means only several iterations may be enough for the approximation.

## 4   Fast Pose Estimation Using a Known Geometric Marker

Assume the $N$ object points $\mathbf{x}_0, \mathbf{x}_1, ... \mathbf{x}_{N-1}$ are observed in a frame and their image coordinates are given by $\mathbf{m}_0, \mathbf{m}_1, ... \mathbf{m}_{N-1}$ in a single frame. All the points are given by column vectors in non-homogeneous form. We automatically choose the most preferable reference point which minimizes the depth variation. The camera intrinsic parameters $p_x$, $p_y$, $f_x$, and $f_y$ are also used for the better pose estimation. The overall steps of the algorithm are as follows:

- Step 1: Choose a reference point $\mathbf{x}_k$ satisfying $\arg\min_k \sum_i (z_i-z_k)^2$ where $z_i$ is the $z$-coordinate of $\mathbf{x}_i$.
- Step 2: Translate all the input object points by $-\mathbf{x}_k$ so that the reference point $\mathbf{x}_k$ becomes the origin of object space. Also, translate all the input image points by $[-p_x \; -p_y]^T$ so that the location of principal point becomes the origin of image space.
- Step 3: Using object points $\mathbf{x}_i$ and their corresponding image points $\mathbf{m}_i$ ($i=1,...,N-1$), build the $(N-1)\times3$ argument matrix $\mathbf{A}$, the $(N-1)$-vector $\mathbf{u}$, and the $(N-1)$-vector $\mathbf{v}$ shown in equation (3). Set $\mathbf{u}_t$ and $\mathbf{v}_t$ by $\mathbf{u}_t=\mathbf{u}$ and $\mathbf{v}_t=\mathbf{v}$.
- Step 4: Solve the two linear least squares problems, $\mathbf{A}\check{\mathbf{r}}_x=\mathbf{u}_t$ and $\mathbf{A}\check{\mathbf{r}}_y=\mathbf{v}_t$, for the unknowns $\check{\mathbf{r}}_x$ and $\check{\mathbf{r}}_y$. The solution is easily obtained using the singular value decomposition (SVD).
- Step 5: Compute $z_k$ by $z_k=2f_xf_y/(f_y|\check{\mathbf{r}}_x|+f_x|\check{\mathbf{r}}_y|)$ where $f_x$ and $f_y$ are the camera focal lengths by the $x$- and $y$-axis. Compute $\mathbf{r}_x$ and $\mathbf{r}_y$ by $\mathbf{r}_x=\check{\mathbf{r}}_x/|\check{\mathbf{r}}_x|$ and $\mathbf{r}_y=\check{\mathbf{r}}_y/|\check{\mathbf{r}}_y|$.
- Step 6: Compute $\alpha_i$ by $\alpha_i=\mathbf{r}_z \cdot \mathbf{x}_i/z_k$ where $\mathbf{r}_z=\mathbf{r}_x \times \mathbf{r}_y$. If $\alpha_i$ is nearly same to the previous one, stop the iteration.
- Step 7: Update $\mathbf{u}_t$ and $\mathbf{v}_t$ by $\mathbf{u}_t=(1+\alpha_i)\mathbf{u}$ and $\mathbf{v}_t=(1+\alpha_i)\mathbf{v}$. Go to Step 4.

The rotation matrix $\mathbf{R}$ is the arrangement of the three orthonormal vectors: $\mathbf{R}=[\mathbf{r}_x \ \mathbf{r}_y \ \mathbf{r}_z]^T$. The translation vector $\mathbf{t}$ is the vector from the origin of the camera space to the reference point. Hence, once we found $\check{\mathbf{r}}_x$ and $\check{\mathbf{r}}_y$, the depth of the reference point $z_k$ is computed by $z_k=2f_xf_y/(f_y|\check{\mathbf{r}}_x|+f_x|\check{\mathbf{r}}_y|)$. Then, the translation $\mathbf{t}$ is obtained by $\mathbf{t}=[z_k u_k/f_x, \ z_k v_k/f_y, \ 2/(|\check{\mathbf{r}}_x|+|\check{\mathbf{r}}_y|)]^T$.

If at least three points are available other than $\mathbf{x}_k$ and not every point is on the same plane, the matrix $\mathbf{A}$ in equation (3) has rank 3 and the over-determined linear system in Step 4 can be solved. On the other hand, if all the object points are on a single plane, the matrix $\mathbf{A}$ has rank 2 and the linear system in equation (3) is ill-conditioned. For such rank deficient cases, the SVD-based method is a better choice among several least squares method then the Cholesky factorization method or the QR decomposition method. For the rank-deficient cases, the Cholesky method will fail and the QR decomposition method is unstable.

## 5   Experimental Results

To demonstrate the effectiveness of the proposed method we implemented the camera pose tracking system that relies on known marker tracking from a real video stream. The 3D coordinates of the marker are assumed to be known and are fixed in the program codes. For each frame, the feature points for the marker have been identified after converting the image frame to a binary image.

**Fig. 1.** A calibration pattern and its detected corners

To recover the accurate shape geometry, it is required to know the camera intrinsic parameters, the focal lengths for two axes and the coordinates of the principal point. In our implementation, we equipped the system to deal with on-line camera calibration for convenience purpose only. The calibration algorithm is well described in [8]. When the system enters the calibration mode, the system monitors a grid pattern and it starts to accumulate detected grid pattern corners. When the grid pattern is found more than four frames the camera parameters are calculated.

As an example, we tested on a sequence of 768×512 image frames containing a 4×5 grid pattern as shown in Fig. 1. The computed focal lengths and principal point coordinates are as follows: $f_x=1034.96$, $f_y=1024.62$, $p_x=360.79$, $p_y=204.29$.

**Fig. 2.** Three different types of known markers: *Cube*, *TwoSidedMarker*, and *ARMarker*

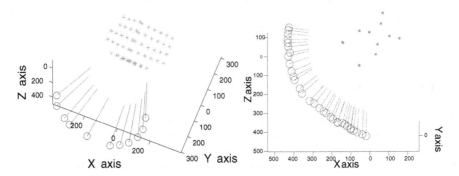

**Fig. 3.** Camera tracking results from two video frames each containing a known marker (*Cube* and *TwoSidedMarker* in Fig. 2)

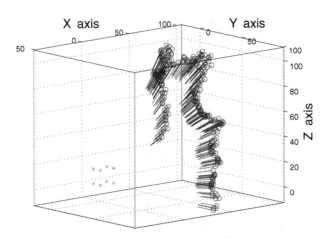

**Fig. 4.** Camera matchmoving for 507 frames using marker *Cube*

For each frame, the camera pose for the current frame is calculated using the tracked feature points on a marker from a single frame. The implemented system can recognize three types of markers (*Cube*, *TwoSidedMarker*, and *ARMarker*) as shown in Fig. 2. The continuous marker tracking and re-initialization are robust and also not sensitive to illumination changes. Fig. 3 shows the camera tracking results (recovered marker points and the camera pose trajectory). Fig. 4 shows a camera trajectory for a long sequence. The camera positions and orientations for the frames are shown relative to the marker points.

We compared the estimation accuracy of the proposed method with the linear scaled orthographic method (SOP) [9] and the iterative scaled orthographic method (POSIT) [7]. Using the estimated camera pose parameters, we projected 3D points onto the frames and compared the distances between the image features, which are shown in Fig. 5. The projection error is under 2 pixels in most cases and it is less than that of SOP or POSIT. The comparison of accuracy is shown in Fig. 6. We measured the error variation according to the relative distance of the marker from the camera divided by the marker radius, which is shown in Fig. 6(a). The average reprojection error is also measured when the scene point depth variation relative to the reference point increases, which is shown in Fig. 6(b). We found the proposed method is fast, stable, and versatile for various point distributions and various camera distances from a marker.

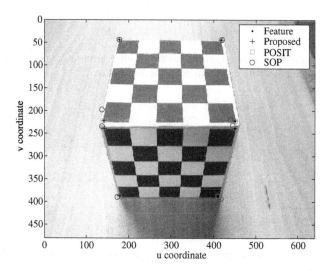

**Fig. 5.** Comparison of reprojected points

**Table 1.** Accuracy and computing time with respect to marker types

| Marker type | #frame | #feature points | avg accuracy(pixel) | Time(ms) |
|---|---|---|---|---|
| *CubeSparse* | 1000 | 5 | 1.64 | 1.73 |
| *TwoSidedMarker* | 500 | 16 | 0.815 | 1.986 |
| *ARMarker* | 300 | 4 | 0.435 | 1.672 |
| *CubeDense* | 700 | 72 | 0.327 | 2.113 |

Fig. 7 shows the stability of the camera pose estimation. The camera was moved very slowly and smoothly during 60 frames. The camera rotation parameters and translation parameters are stable along the frame sequence without serious oscillation.

Fig. 8 shows the comparison of stability of the proposed method with other methods. The proposed method was stable when the number of feature points varies (See Fig. 8(a)). Since the proposed method is based on a single frame, any error from previous frames does not affect future frames (See Fig. 8(b)).

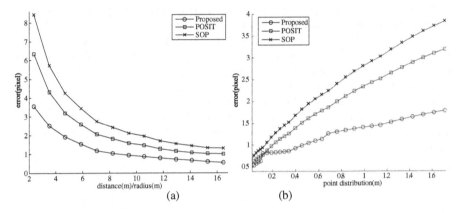

**Fig. 6.** Comparison of accuracy: (a) error variation with respect to the relative distance of the marker, (b) error variation with respect to the point distribution

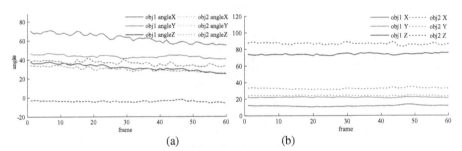

**Fig. 7.** The stability of camera pose parameters: (a) rotation parameters and (b) translation parameters

The computation time for the proposed camera tracking method was measured. On a Pentium 4 (2.6GHz) computer, the processing speed is about 27 frames per second including all steps of the system such as frame acquisition, marker detection, feature extraction, pose estimation, and 3D rendering. The camera pose estimation process roughly takes 4 ms and 8 ms, respectively, and its speed is fast enough to be ignored for real-time augmented reality applications. Fig. 9 shows the camera pose computing time of the proposed method together with other methods. The camera pose estimation stage of the proposed method consumes about 1.8 ms CPU time per frame and, moreover, the number of points hardly increases the processing time.

Our method has also been applied to coplanar cases. We compared the results with ARToolKit method [10] which can estimate relative camera pose from a single rectangular marker. Although ARToolKit is fast and interactive, we found several critical problems exist in ARToolKit. First, the error of image corners of the marker rectangle critically increases errors. Second, when the camera moves away too much from the marker the marker detection step fails frequently. The proposed method is relatively more stable in most cases. The comparison of accuracy is shown in Fig. 10.

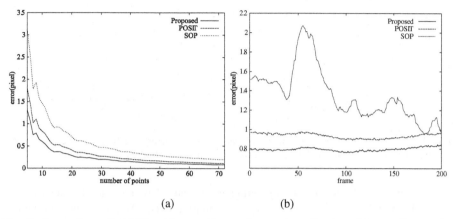

(a)                                    (b)

**Fig. 8.** Comparison of stability: (a) according to the number of points, (b) according to the frame moving

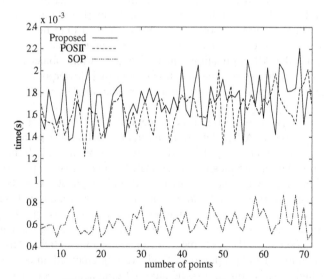

**Fig. 9.** Comparison of the computing time

We have measured the accuracy and computing time with respect to different type of markers. We compared four different types of markers: *CubeSparse*, *TwoSidedMarker*, *ARMarker*, and *CubeDense* (See Table 1). Note that *CubeSparse* and *CubeDense* correspond to the same marker (*Cube* in Fig. 2) but they utilize different number of feature points on the marker.

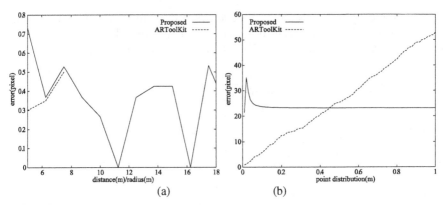

**Fig. 10.** Comparison of accuracy for coplanar cases: (a) error variation with respect to the relative distance of the marker, (b) error variation with respect to the point distribution

The time is proportional to the number of feature points and the accuracy is inversely proportional to the number of feature points. Overall numerical values indicate that the type of markers does not affect the pose accuracy critically.

We implemented an interactive augmented reality system and tested camera tracking with real video frames. From a video stream, an image frame is captured and the known marker is detected in the frame. From the marker features, we estimate the camera pose. Then, we project some 3D graphical object onto the frame and render the projected virtual object together with the original input frame.

Fig. 11 shows the AR application which inserts a virtual object into a live video stream. The upper figure shows the insertion of a virtual flowerpot at the cube marker position. The lower figure shows the tracked planar marker is replaced by a wall clock.

This article has presented a real-time camera pose estimation method assuming a known marker is visible. A fast detection and tracking of marker points is possible by assuming a known marker. From the marker tracking from a single frame, the camera position and translation parameters are estimated using a linear approximation. The pose estimation process is fast enough to real-time applications since entire pose estimation process is linear and initial estimates are not required. Compared with previous fast camera pose estimation methods, the camera pose accuracy is greatly improved without paying extra computing time. Another advantage is that it can cope with a planar marker since the SVD method can handle rank deficient cases.

As an application of the proposed method, we implemented an augmented reality application which inserts computer-generated 3D graphical objects into a live-action video stream of unmodeled real scenes. Using the recovered camera pose parameters, the marker in the image frames is replaced by a virtual 3D graphical object during the marker tracking from a video stream. Experimental results showed that the proposed camera tracking method is robust and fast enough to interactive video-based applications.

As future work, it would be preferable to extend the type of markers so that it accepts general primitives. Another possible direction concerns the use of features on a planar patch without using any known markers.

(a)

(b)

**Fig. 11.** An augmented reality application to insert virtual objects into a video stream: (a) using *Cube* maker, (b) using planar *ARMarker*

**Acknowledgments.** This work was supported in part by grant No. RTI05-03-01 from the Regional Technology Innovation Program of the Ministry of Commerce, Industry and Energy(MOCIE) and in part by the Brain Korea 21 Project in 2006.

# References

1. Gibson, S., Cook, J., Howard, T., Hubbold, R., Oram, D.: Accurate camera calibration for off-line, video-based augmented reality. In: Proceedings of International Symposium on Mixed and Augmented Reality (ISMAR 2002). (2002) 37-46
2. Simon, G., Fitzgibbon, A., Zisserman, A.: Markerless tracking using planar structures in the scene. In: Proceedings of IEEE and ACM International Symposium on Augmented Reality (ISAR 2000). (2000) 120-128

3. Kutulakos, K.N., Vallino, J.R.: Calibration-free augmented reality. IEEE Transactions on Visualization and Computer Graphics 4 (1998) 1-20
4. Carceroni, R., Brown, C.: Numerical method for model-based pose recovery (1997)
5. Tomasi, C., Kanade, T.: Shape and motion from image streams under orthography: A factorization approach. International Journal of Computer Vision 9 (1992) 137-154
6. Oberkampf, D., DeMenthon, D.F., Davis, L.S.: Iterative pose estimation using coplanar feature points. Comput. Vis. Image Underst. 63 (1996) 495-511
7. Dementhon, D., Davis, L.: Model-based object pose in 25 lines of code. International Journal of Computer Vision 15 (1995) 123-141
8. Zhang, Z.: A flexible new technique for camera calibration. IEEE Transactions on Pattern Analysis and Machine Intelligence 22 (2000) 1330-1334
9. Poelman, C., Kanade, T.: A paraperspective factorization method for shape and motion recovery. IEEE T-PAMI 19 (1997) 206-218
10. Kato, H., Billinghurst, M., Poupyrev, I., K., Tachibana, K.I.: Virtual object manipulation on a table-top AR environment. In: Proceedings of the International Symposium on Augmented Reality (ISAR 2000). (2000) 111-119

# OHAJIKI Interface: Flicking Gesture Recognition with a High-Speed Camera

Toshiki Sato, Kentaro Fukuchi, and Hideki Koike

Graduate School of Information Systems,
The University of Electro-Communications Chofu-shi, Tokyo, Japan 182-8585
{den, fukuchi, koike}@vogue.is.uec.ac.jp

**Abstract.** This paper describes a novel interaction technique that recognizes a finger flicking gesture for power adjustment input for a sports game, such as golf swing or hitting. Our system measures speed of the finger motion and direction of the gesture by using a high-speed camera and a high frame rate image processing technique. By using this system, users can adjust power and angle intuitively. We developed a 3D golf game using this interaction technique to provide an intuitive golf swing input.

## 1 Introduction

Conventional interfaces of power adjustment for video games employ common controllers (e.g. game pad) or dedicated input devices. For example, in a golf game, the player presses a button of a controller several times to shoot. Typically the pressure power on the button is ignored. However, the feeling from this action is very different from an actual golf swing. Since it is preferred that a video game provides a real and intuitive interaction, this input is not desirable.

Finger flicking, by the way, is a very familiar action to us, as anyone who had played marbles or flicked coins on a table.[1]

We consider that finger flicking has the same property with golf swing or hitting in respect of action that hits something to a distance. Hence, we propose to use the finger flicking for power adjustment, which can be useful for video games.

## 2 Related Works

There are two well-known finger tracking techniques. One uses special equipments or sensors, while the other uses a vision based recognition technique.

Data glove is a well-known glove-shaped input device for finger tracking. A data glove detects motion of the hand and the fingers, and it is used to recognize or record manual gestures, but a user has to put a sensor device on his hand that can act as an obstacle in the gesture.

Gokturk and Sibert introduced a finger mounted pointing device based on infrared sensing technique[1]. With the device, a user can point to a position in a display directly with his finger, but mounting a device on a finger is uncomfortable for the user. Besides, it restricts his hand motion physically.

---

[1] In Japan, playing marbles, or "Ohajiki", is a popular game with children.

R. Harper, M. Rauterberg, M. Combetto (Eds.): ICEC 2006, LNCS 4161, pp. 205–210, 2006.
© IFIP International Federation for Information Processing 2006

By contrast, a vision based interaction technique can recognize a user's motion without using any special equipments or sensors, therefore the user can interact with the computer intuitively. Oka et al developed a real-time finger tracking system, which can detect positions of hands and fingertips[2].

However, most of vision-based finger tracking system has the same problems that are a tracking latency caused by the cost of image analysis and low scan rate of camera (30 frames per second). Because of that, those systems cannot track fast motion of fingers, such as finger flicking.

## 3   Vision Based Finger Flicking Recognition

### 3.1   Finger Flicking Motion

Finger flicking is a motion of hitting a small object with a quick motion of a forefinger or midfinger. This motion can be seen in our daily life (e.g. playing marbles or flicking a coin).

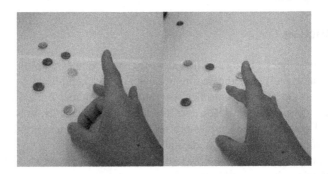

**Fig. 1.** Finger flicking: at first put a forefinger or mid finger on a thumb and add power to the finger (left), then release the finger (right)

Controlling the power on the finger enables to adjust the impact force of the flicking. Besides, its direction can be adjusted by changing the relative position or angle of the hand to the object.

This kind of motion can be found in various situations, such as hitting or kicking. In fact, we can find finger flicking motions in many kids plays, such as "finger flicking football". Therefore, we consider that finger flicking can be used as an intuitive input method of power in terms of using real force to control.

In addition, finger flicking is safer than a real action with a golf club or bat for home use, and it saves space. Besides, because it is familiar to us, it is unnecessary to learn how to do it.

### 3.2   Design Principle

It is difficult to put some sensors on a finger to track the quick motion of finger flicking gesture, because the size of the sensor is limited to the size of the finger and it may be different among users. Besides, because the motion is very quick, the sensor has to be fitted to a finger tightly, and its size and weight should be as small and light as possible.

For that reason, we used a vision based recognition technique to track finger flicking motion and measure the position and direction of a hand. We hypothesized that the power of the finger flicking can be recognized by measuring the speed of the finger motion which can be tracked by vision based techniques. However, its accuracy and scan rate are worse than the result by the hardware based recognition typically, because of the low frame rate of the camera. Because of that, it was difficult to track a quick motion by a camera. To solve this problem, we have employed a high-speed camera and developed a high throughput image processing system to track a quick finger motion.

# 4   Implementation

Figure 2 shows the hardware structure of our system. An image from the camera is processed by the image processing PC, and the results are sent to the application PC via Ethernet.

## 4.1   Finger Flicking Recognition

In a finger flicking gesture, while a flicking motion is done in very short time, positioning and directing are performed in relatively longer time. Therefore, the high-speed image processing is only required during a very short period of a flicking gesture. For that reason, our system consists of some recognition phases and each phase uses an optimal recognition mode. When the system tracks a quick motion, it scans the image in maximum speed of the camera with a simple image processing technique, while it uses rich image processing techniques with low scan rate when it is unnecessary.

We employed Point Grey Research's high-speed camera, Dragonfly Express, which has several scan modes and it can increase the scan rate by limiting the scan range. The size of an image, camera scan rate and image processing frame rate in each recognition phase is shown in the table below.

**Table 1.** Frame rate for each phase of recognition

| Phase | Image Size | Frame rate | Scan rate |
|---|---|---|---|
| stance detection | 640 × 480 | 200 fps | 160 fps |
| window setting | 320 × 240 | 320 fps | 130 fps |
| fingertip detection | 100 × 80 | 450 fps | 450 fps |

## 4.2   Processes of Motion Recognition

The gesture recognition process consists of following three phases.

1. Hand detection phase
   At first, the system scans the table to find whether a user is going to flick with his finger or not. To recognize the gesture, the system detects a user's stance of flicking. We defined this stance that it makes a small circle region by a thumb and

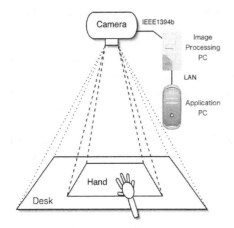

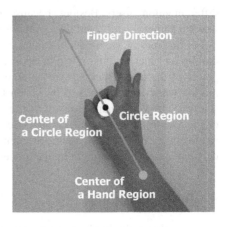

**Fig. 2.** System overview                    **Fig. 3.** A stance of finger flicking

a flicking finger as seen in figure 3. The system detects this small circle region using a background subtraction and a region extraction process. When the region is detected, the system goes into the next phase.

2. Search window setting phase

   Next, the system sets a search window that detects a flicked finger. The size of this window is smaller than the original camera view used in previous phase, to increase scan rate of the camera and reduce the computational cost of the following image processing phase. The finger is tracked only in this window.

   The position of the windows is set according to the position and the angle of the user's hand. To set the window correctly, its position is determined in the following way: it sets the search window on the position shown in the figure 4 whose initial position is calculated from the positions of the circle region and the hand region. Then, it slides the window towards the circle region until the window conflicts with the hand region. Finally the window is set on this position.

   At the same time, the direction of the hand is calculated from the line between the center of the hand region and the circle region. When the user keeps his hand still for a while, the system goes to the next phase.

3. Fingertip Detection Phase

   The system changes its view to the search window and tracks the finger motion inside the view. This process uses background subtraction and template matching that uses a small circle-shaped template to detect a fingertip. When the fingertip runs out from the camera view, the system stops tracking and calculates the velocity of the finger from the result.

4. Result Calculation Phase

   The velocity of the finger is calculated by the following steps: let $T$ be a length of time (msec) from the first detection of a finger to the last, and $L_n$ represents the distance in pixels between positions of fingers of $n$ and $n + 1$, and N is the number of detected fingertips. The velocity of the finger $V$ (pixels/msec) is calculated as

$$V = \frac{\sum_{i=1}^{N-1} L_i}{T}$$

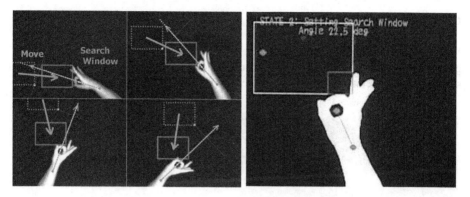

**Fig. 4.** Search window setting image(left), and the screen shot(right)

## 5 Evaluation

We ran an experimental evaluation to test that our system could recognize the power of the finger flicking. We should note that we did not measure the actual impact power of the finger flicking. Instead, we had four subjects to flick with their fingers five times with five grades of power, from "weakest" to "strongest". Figure 5 shows the result of the test. As seen in the graph, our system could distinguish those five grades of power. But the number of detected fingertips was 20–40 at the first (weakest) flicking, 10–14 at the second, 5–10 at the third, 4–9 at the forth, 2–4 times at the fifth (strongest). In this simple tracking, the result depends on the scan rate of the camera. Therefore, the precision of the result could decrease if a flicking speed is too fast. To solve this problem, we conclude that we should use a camera which has a higher scan rate to track the motion of a fingertip certainly, or to use a mathematical model of finger movement to estimate the speed precisely.

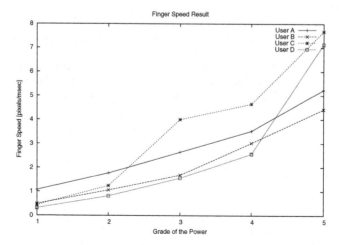

**Fig. 5.** The result of the evaluation test. The horizontal axis represents the grade of the power, and the vertical axis shows the measured velocity of the finger (pixels/msec).

# 6    Application

We developed a simple 3D golf game that a player can shoot a ball by a finger flicking gesture. A player controls the direction of a shot by moving his hand on the input surface, and then controls the power of the shot by finger flicking.

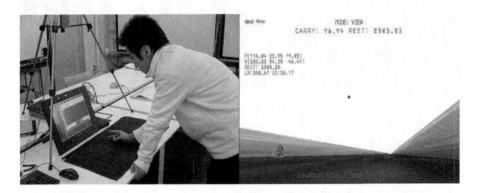

**Fig. 6.** A user playing the 3D golf game (left) and a screenshot of the game (right)

# 7    Conclusion

We introduced a finger flicking gesture recognition technique and the result from the evaluation test demonstrated that our system works sufficiently. At this time the estimation of the finger power is not accurate enough. We plan to evaluate the estimation closely.

# References

1. Mehmet Gokturk and John L. Sibert, "An Analysis of the Index Finger as a Pointing Device", ACM CHI99 Conference Companion, May 1999.
2. K. Oka, Y. Sato, and H. Koike, "Real-time Tracking of Multiple Fingertips and Gesture Recognition for Augmented Desk Interface Systems" in Proc. of 2002 IEEE International Conference on Automatic Face and Gesture Recognition (FG 2002), May 2002.

# The Smart Dice Cup: A Radio Controlled Sentient Interaction Device

Carsten Magerkurth, Timo Engelke, and Carsten Röcker

Fraunhofer IPSI, AMBIENTE – Smart Environments of the Future
D-64293 Darmstadt, Germany
{magerkurth, engelke, roecker}@ipsi.fhg.de

**Abstract.** In this paper, we present the Smart Dice Cup, a novel interaction device aimed at gaming applications in smart home environments. The Smart Dice Cup is used in a similar way as a traditional leather dice cup to generate random numbers. Integrated accelerometers relate the shaking of the device to the resulting rolls of the dice. In addition to an autonomous stand-alone mode, where the Smart Dice Cup serves as self-sustained gaming system, the device is also capable of communicating with its surrounding environment serving as an input device for other pervasive gaming applications.

## 1 Introduction

There is a growing trend in the computer gaming research community to augment traditional video games with aspects from the real world, e.g. [1], [2], [6]. These hybrid or pervasive games combine the virtual nature of traditional video games with physical and social context, thus creating immersive gaming experiences that pervade the boundaries of virtual, physical and social domains [4].

We have been active in the field of pervasive tabletop games that take place in smart home environments and provide tangible interfaces that borrow interaction techniques from traditional board games (see fig. 1). The central idea is to combine the advantageous elements of traditional board games and computer entertainment technologies [3]. Board games emphasize the direct interaction between human players. They sit together around the same table, facing each other at an intimate distance. Their close face-to-face interaction integrates discussion, laughing, and all kinds of non-verbal communication hints creating a rich social situation. Complementarily, playing computer games introduces many highly interesting possibilities that enhance the playing experience. Game presentation is enriched with audio and visual support and game content is limited only by the imagination of the developers. The drawback of computer games, however, is the lack of social interaction in a face-to-face setting, since the players' notion of each other is mostly conveyed by screen and keyboard. To combine the strengths of both game types and to provide interaction metaphors appropriate for face-to-face group situations, it is a promising approach to augment the proven tangible interfaces from traditional board games [8] with unobtrusive pervasive computing technology.

R. Harper, M. Rauterberg, M. Combetto (Eds.): ICEC 2006, LNCS 4161, pp. 211–216, 2006.
© IFIP International Federation for Information Processing 2006

## 2   The Smart Dice Cup

Dice are crucially important components of a wide range of games. They are used for creating variations in the game flow. By rolling dice, an element of chance is introduced to an otherwise static and deterministic flow of game actions. The chance in the dice, however, is not equal to the generation of a random number. Rolling dice involves both a physical act and skill (some people and some dice roll better results than others) as well as a social mechanism to supervise and control the physical act, because cheating is a common phenomenon associated with this particular way of adding variability to games. Hence, rolling dice is a very interesting example of a gaming interface that is particularly suitable for a computer augmented realization.

**Fig. 1.** A pervasive tabletop game with the Smart Dice Cup being in use

In order not to lose the physical and social aspects of rolling dice by simply creating random numbers in a computer application, we tried to preserve the multi-faceted nature of dice-rolling in our computer adaptation. Due to the size and feasibility problems associated with augmenting individual dice with respective sensor technology, we integrated multiple dice into one single smart artifact.

### 2.1   Interaction Design

The interaction with the device was designed to be as similar to a traditional dice cup as possible. To generate random numbers, the device is lifted, shaken, put on a plain surface upside down, and then finally lifted again to see the results. However, in contrast to traditional dice, the sum of the spots is not counted from the physical dice after being tossed on the surface of the table. Instead, the spots are displayed via light emitting diodes (LEDs) on the surface of the dice cup's top.

Shaking the device also emits a sound mimicking the sound of shaking a traditional dice box, although the integrated sound hardware does hardly deliver sound of acceptable quality. Since the smart dice cup is capable of communicating with the environment via radio transmission, it is more preferable to let another sound source outside the device perform the respective audio output. In addition to the basic interface of shaking, dropping and turning the device, there is also a conventional button interface with a graphical display integrated in the top surface of the dice cup as shown in figure 2. The button interface is used for advanced configuration of the device when it is in autonomous mode and no other interface such as a respective GUI application (running on a nearby PC) is available or when single dice are to be "held" or "released", i.e. when they are to be included or excluded from tossing.

Each of the five dice displayed on the surface of the dice cup consists of seven red LEDs that represent the spots of the respective die. Whenever the device is shaken, the respective light patterns change in accordance to the tossed result. A small green LED is used to indicate whether the respective die is held or released, i.e. if its face changes when the device is shaken. To toggle between holding and releasing a die, a small button is associated with each die that turns the respective green LED on or off with each press, thus ensuring an intuitive way of changing the individual held states by providing visual feedback and adhering to the Gestalt law of proximity regarding the button layout.

**Fig. 2.** The user interface of the Smart Dice Cup

The graphical display features two lines of eight characters each and is used for any optional interaction with the user beyond the scope of mere dice rolling. It is accompanied by two buttons on the left and right of it labeled "SELECT" and "OK" that allow for simple dialog navigation with "SELECT" cycling through a list of menu options and "OK" confirming the respective choices. The dice cup software currently includes a simple state machine that toggles between several menu states such as "Free Play" (the default state in which the device is used for tossing only or "Game" (allowing to chose one of currently two built-in mini games) or "Options". The device can be turned off and on and put into a remote controlled mode with a respective three-state-switch above the graphical display. The remote controlled mode allows the device to be controlled from the environment via radio transmission as discussed in the following section.

## 2.2 Operating Modes

The Smart Dice Box was designed to function both as an autonomous smart artifact that performs its functions independent of the environment and as an interaction device that offers its services to other instances (software applications, smart artifacts etc) in the vicinity of the smart home environment. For the stand alone operating mode, the device's integrated memory and the built-in games offer added value compared to a traditional dice box. For instance, it replaces pen and paper when games like e.g. Yahtzee are played that require the counting of individual results. In fact, a similar game (the Counter Game) is currently implemented on the device, albeit simpler than its original.

When the dice cup is brought to a smart environment, it can be put into a remote controlled mode in which it is both able to receive commands from the environment and to convey back information about its own state. As illustrated in figure 3, an application in the environment can utilize the information from the device and create a respective virtual counterpart.

**Fig. 3.** The physical device and its virtual counterpart

This virtual counterpart interprets and displays the device's radio signals conveying both the orientation/ shaking status measured by accelerometers and the current spots on the virtual dice. To visualize the received dice box data, a 3D view of the dice box is rendered illustrating the orientation (whether the device is upside down) and the presumed vertical position. The spots of the dice are visualized as respective bitmaps and an optional sound output of dice being shaken can be generated. The application is furthermore capable of transmitting the received dice data to other software components in a pervasive games setup, so that the dice cup can be exploited as a central tangible input device for any kind of pervasive game.

In the same way as data can be read from the device, the dice cup can also be remotely controlled including individual dice being held or released. Furthermore, additional functions that are not available on the device interface are exposed for the remote software. This includes setting the sides of individual dice and showing messages on the graphical display. It is also possible to change the random number generation on the device with the introduction of so called "luck dice".

This "luck dice" concept relates to the way the random numbers are generated. The seed of the random number generator on the device is initialized with the data from the accelerometers integrated in the cup that measure the shaking of the device. This allows for modeling an important aspect of the physical act of rolling dice: Should a person be able to shake a traditional dice cup two times in exactly the same way, she would roll exactly the same results. The corresponding is true for the Smart Dice Cup, although in reality nobody should be capable of doing this with any of the two devices. Depending on the range of respective transformations of the accelerometer data, one could however investigate in how far the sensor data can be blurred or otherwise modified to allow for perceivable influences of the physical act of shaking and the respective results.

In a remote controlled operating mode, the dice cup allows for tweaking the amount of "luck" a person has by performing additional rolls with respective "luck dice". This is an interesting twist to the traditional realization of luck as a trait, in which a player rolls against an arbitrary luck criterion of differing magnitude. By introducing luck dice, the spots rolled correspond directly to the result instead of being valid only in combination with an external criterion. Each luck die associated with the rolling of a target die has a 50% chance to affect the result of the target, if it does, a second roll is performed and the higher result becomes the target.

## 2.3  Technical Realization

The core of the Smart Dice Cup consists of a Smart-Its particle computer equipped with additional LC displays, LEDs and switches. Such a particle is "a platform for rapid prototyping of Ubiquitous and Pervasive Computing environments, for Ad-Hoc (Sensor) Networks, Wearable Computers, Home Automation and Ambient Intelligence Environments. The platform consists of ready-to-run hardware components, software applications and libraries for the hardware and a set of development tools for rapid prototyping" [7].

The Smart-Its particle platform is built around two independent boards, a core board that consists mainly of processing and communication hardware and basic output components and a sensor board containing a separate processing unit, various sensors and actuators. In the case of the Smart Dice Cup, these were accelerometers, other sensors include light, humidity, temperature, or force/ pressure. Figure 4 shows the internals of the device.

**Fig. 4.** The internals of the Smart Dicebox

The random number generator implemented is a Mersenne Twister [5] that is freely available as portable C-code. It has become a popular algorithm, since it passed the relevant, stringent statistical tests and is still comparable to other modern random number generators in terms of speed, hence making it a suitable algorithm for an embedded microcontroller such as the PIC16F876 used with the particle platform integrated inside the dice cup.

## 2.4  Next Steps

To demonstrate and explore the benefits of the Smart Dice Cup and other related interaction devices in a rather complex pervasive gaming application, we are currently developing a "Dungeons & Dragons" style tabletop roleplaying game called "Caves & Creatures" that makes extensive use of the device. Next to the integration of RFID augmented playing cards that represent items, weapons, armor, etc. and a physical game board that is used for positioning and moving game characters, the Smart Dice Cup will be the single most important pervasive interaction device, because rolling dice is a central component of any tabletop roleplaying game. Until we will have the game running and ready to test in a controlled experimental setting, our own preliminary observations using the dice cup are very positive, for the user interaction is really as intuitive as with a traditional dice cup. The benefits of not having to worry about the link between the physical act of rolling dice and informing a computer application about it are obvious. Finally, the capability of operating the device in a standalone mode promotes its use also outside the laboratory.

The work presented here is part of the Amigo integrated project of the European Commission in the Sixth Framework Programme under contract number IST 004182.

# References

1. Benford, S., Magerkurth, C., Ljungstrand, P. (2005) Bridging the Physical and Digital in Pervasive Gaming. In Communications of the ACM, March 2005, vol. 48. No. 3. Pages 54-57.
2. Ciger, J., Gutierrez, M., Vexo, F., Thalmann, D. (2003). The magic wand. 19th Spring Conference on Computer Graphics (Budmerice, Slovakia, April 24 - 26, 2003). L. Szirmay-Kalos, Ed. SCCG '03. ACM Press, New York, NY, 119-124.
3. Cheok, A. D., Yang, X., Ying, Z. Z., Billinghurst, M., Kato, H. (2002) Touch-Space: Mixed Reality Game Space Based on Ubiquitous, Tangible, and Social Computing. In Personal and Ubiquitous Computing (2002), 6: 430-44
4. Magerkurth, C., Cheok, A.D., Mandryk, R.L., Nilsen, T. (2005): Pervasive Games. In: ACM Computers in Entertainment, Vol. 3, No. 3, July 2005.
5. Matsumoto, M. and Nishimura, T. (1998). Mersenne twister: a 623-dimensionally equidistributed uniform pseudo-random number generator. ACM Trans. Model. Comput. Simul. 8, 1 (Jan. 1998), 3-30.
6. Rauterberg, M., Mauch, T., Stebler, R. (1996). The Digital Playing Desk: a Case Study for Augmented Reality. 5th IEEE Workshop on Robot and Human Communication, Tsukuba, Japan, 410-415.
7. Smart Its particle Website: http://particle.teco.edu/
8. Ullmer, B., Ishii, H. (2000). Emerging frameworks for tangible user interfaces. IBM Systems Journal, 39(3):915–931.

# Learning About Cultural Heritage by Playing Geogames

Peter Kiefer, Sebastian Matyas, and Christoph Schlieder

Laboratory for Semantic Information Technology
Otto-Friedrich-University Bamberg
96045 Bamberg, Germany
{peter.kiefer, sebastian.matyas,
christoph.schlieder}@wiai.uni-bamberg.de

**Abstract.** Context-aware and location-based information systems with conventional or AR visualization are a well-proven means for enhancing the experience of a tourist visiting a cultural heritage site. A less explored way for achieving immersion in the spatial environment is provided by location-based games which offer the additional advantage of being entertaining. In this paper we describe a subclass of location-based games, Geogames, which are characterized by a specific spatio-temporal structuring of the game events. We show that the spatio-temporal structuring permits to easily integrate educational content into the course of the game, making Geogames an ideal medium for edutainment. We report on our experiences with using the game GeoTicTacToe for teaching school children. Furthermore, we present a didactical workflow and four example didactical patterns that permit to exploit the edutainment potential of Geogames. The outcome of two empirical case studies indicates that enriching Geogames with educational content does not take the fun out of the game.

## 1 Introduction

Although the traditional CD-based audio guide is still in use in many museums and cultural heritage sites, progress in computing has opened up other and better ways to satisfy the information needs of the visitor, namely context-aware and location-based information systems (e.g. Cheverst et al. 2000). The visitor's experience can be further enhanced by perceptual immersion in an artificial environment. Virtual reality permits the user to experience a heritage site or object which is far away or does not exist any longer (e.g. Gaitatzes et al. 2001). Other research aims at designing augmented-reality guides for on-site exploration of cultural heritage such as the Archeoguide system installed as a prototype at the archeological site of Olympia, Greece (Vlahakis et al. 2002). Augmented-reality in this context not only enables a user to perceive the (virtually enhanced) cultural object itself, but at the same time allows to apprehend the embedding of the object in its environment, e.g. to feel the sun and the wind at the site of Olympia.

This total immersion into the environment is also one key success factor of location-based games, i.e. games played on mobile devices using localization technology. In contrast to traditional computer or console gaming, these games require players to move in a real world gaming area, thus implying the locomotion and the physical effort characteristic of any sportive activity. Location-based games may be supported

R. Harper, M. Rauterberg, M. Combetto (Eds.): ICEC 2006, LNCS 4161, pp. 217–228, 2006.
© IFIP International Federation for Information Processing 2006

by computation-intensive technology like augmented-reality (e.g. ARQuake, Thomas et al. 2000), but the vast majority of location-based games has requirements for computational resources that can be satisfied by personal digital assistants or even simple GPS handhelds (e.g. Geocaching). What makes those games entertaining is in the first place an interesting game concept that coordinates the actions of players in an intelligent and challenging way. A major reason for enjoying location-based games is their embedding in a real world setting: instead of staying at home and diving into a virtual world, these games get the players involved in exploring an urban environment.

In this paper we discuss the usage of a certain class of location-based games called Geogames in an edutainment context, namely for the learning about built heritage in an urban environment. Geogames are a potentially infinite class of games that arise from mapping classic board games to geographic space (Schlieder et al., 2006). As our running example we will use the GeoTicTacToe game played in the historic centre of Bamberg, a UNESCO world heritage site. We explain why certain properties inherent in every Geogame make this class of games an ideal medium for the presentation of cultural heritage. A didactical workflow and four didactical patterns for the mediation of knowledge about cultural heritage are described. A first case study conducted in cooperation with the Heritage Documentation Centre of the City of Bamberg studies the appeal of Geogames to school children. A second case study in the city of Coburg confirms the main finding: integrating educational content into a Geogame does not eliminate its entertaining aspect.

The rest of this paper is structured as follows: in section 2 we shortly summarize the Geogames framework and introduce the Geogame GeoTicTacToe. Section 3 explains how to use Geogames for the presentation of cultural heritage. A didactical workflow and didactical patterns are shown. Our preliminary case studies are described in section 4, while in the last section we discuss related work, with special emphasis on the field of mobile edutainment, and give an insight on future research issues.

## 2  Geogames

The Geogames framework describes a special class of location-based games, which are created with the metaphor of classic board games being mapped to the real world. Thus, board positions which were relevant on the original game board are now assigned a geographic coordinate (*locations*). For taking their turns, *players* are required to move between these locations and pick up, dispose or change *resources* which are distributed over the locations. Resources may be real objects or virtual resources only displayed on the mobile device which players carry with them. Although real world game boards may be of any size, for the rest of this paper we will assume city sized game boards. All players are moving concurrently, so that the turn-taking restriction of the original board game is lifted making Geogames interesting from a game theoretical point of view. For a formal definition of Geogames see Schlieder et al. (2006).

A transition of classic board games into location-based games, named spatialization, provides a rich pool of challenging games, if one major problem is being solved: in the line of Nicklas et al. (2001) we detect that "lifting turn-based restrictions can make a game unfair". Consider a location-based variant of TicTacToe displayed in figure 1: like in the classic board game, two players, X and O, are trying to place three marks, X or O, in a row, a column or one of the two diagonals to win the game. Furthermore, we determine for the right hand side of figure 1 that player X moves faster than player O. Without turn-based restrictions this leads to a simple winning strategy for player X and lets the game deteriorate to a non-challenging race: Player X can simply run from location 1 over 4 to 7 without player O having any chance to hinder him from winning the game.

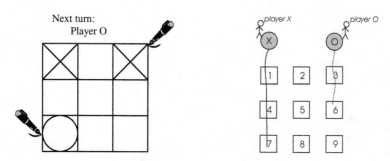

**Fig. 1.** Board game Tic Tac Toe (left) and the spatialized version GeoTicTacToe (right)

Designing fair and challenging Geogames is not a trivial task. A Geogame is considered *challenging*, if it equally demands the players' acting and reasoning skills to win the game. Consequently, neither a pure chase game nor a live version of chess would fulfil this definition. To balance a Geogame between a pure racing game and a pure strategy game, a surprisingly simple solution is proposed: a game designer must include a *synchronization time interval (syncTime)* in his rule set. Players now must wait at a location until the syncTime is over before they can move again. Depending on the length of the synchronisation time interval the game can be tuned between the two mentioned extremes. The syncTime parameter must be chosen individually for each Geogame to keep it challenging. With the Geogames tool (Kiefer and Matyas, 2005) a game designer can compute the syncTime parameter for every constellation of locations and speed differences of the players, making adjustments to new game boards an easy task.

The syncTime approach allows a game designer the free choice of geographic footprints, because locations on a real world city game board will probably never be arranged in a regular 3x3 square like that on the right hand side of figure 1. Road networks, hills, parks and other obstacles will make some coordinates impossible and additionally hinder players from moving in air-line distances. Figure 2 shows an example game board in the UNESCO world heritage city of Bamberg: the free choice of geographic footprints allows the game designer to assign the nine locations to cultural points of interest like the cathedral or the historic city hall. Even for a distorted game board like this, the Geogames tool will compute an appropriate value for the syncTime parameter.

In the line with findings of Schwabe et al. (2005a), Geogames should preferably be played in teams of two or three players, resulting in a deeper gaming experience than being played alone, so "player X" in our examples may consist of three players

220 P. Kiefer, S. Matyas, and C. Schlieder

moving together as a team. The possibility to play with virtual resources will prevent harm from sensible cultural heritage sites, like e.g. medieval buildings and other protected sites.

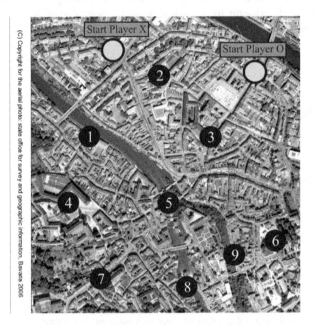

| 1 | beautiful view ("little Venice") |
|---|---|
| 2 | statue of Botero (contemporary art) |
| 3 | church St. Martin |
| 4 | cathedral |
| 5 | historic city hall |
| 6 | statue and theatre of E.T.A. Hoffmann |
| 7 | church "Obere Pfarre" |
| 8 | millers' bridge |
| 9 | historic craftsmen buildings |

**Fig. 2.** GeoTicTacToe game board in the UNESCO world heritage city of Bamberg

## 3  Presenting Cultural Heritage

The syncTime interval in Geogames does not necessarily have to be implemented directly as idle wait time, but can also be integrated indirectly through other game elements. Think, for example, of solving mini games before moving on or searching for elements hidden on the real-world game board, e.g. for an RFID to set a game field. Another solution we propose in this paper is the embedding of educational content into the syncTime interval. With the wait time being an integral part of the game rules of Geogames, fun, entertainment and the educational content seamlessly merge to create a true edutainment experience.

In the following we will subsume under the term educational content or learning any kind of knowledge mediation from simple fact learning, like in Meisenberger and Nischelwitzer (2004), to communicating background information on cultural heritage sites, or even a deeper understanding of an epoch or architectural style. An important subtask in our case study was not only the presentation of cultural heritage, but also to communicate the idea of the UNESCO world heritage list (http://whc.unesco.org/en/list/). After the game, the participants should be able to answer questions like "What are the criteria for a site being nominated for the list? Which specific criteria were relevant for the city of Bamberg? How can we see these criteria in the building in front of us?"

The combination of the game conceptual perspective and the didactical perspective is illustrated in Fig. 3. On the one hand we find the game concept responsible for the entertainment aspect, on the other side a didactical concept covers the educational aspect. Although both define their own goals, they melt together when used in combination with a location-based game, e.g. a Geogame like GeoTicTacToe. The rules of the game should assure that a win can either be achieved by superior strategy or by superior knowledge to keep players motivated for learning. For instance, we decided for GeoTicTacToe that in the case of a draw situation the player with more correct answers will be the winner. In general, the overall winner should be determined as a combination of "winning by board game rules" and "winning by superior knowledge".

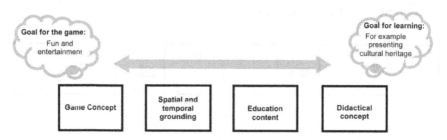

**Fig. 3.** Combining location-based games and education

Coming from the didactical perspective, educational content has to be developed and adjusted for mobile devices. In section 3.2 we describe some recommendable patterns that can be followed for the communication of cultural heritage, which can also be easily adjusted to different educational content. From the game conceptual perspective, Geogames imply two key features, making them especially useful for presenting cultural heritage sites and communicating the cultural heritage idea:

*Spatial grounding:* Players of a Geogame have to wait the syncTime interval at various discrete locations to set a virtual marker (X or O). We fill this wait time with educational content specific for the respective location, ranging from simple questions about facts (like on the edification of the cathedral of Bamberg) to transfer questions (like on the recognition of a baroque facade). This connects the knowledge to learn with a real world place the players actually visit, making the knowledge livelier and consequently more memorable. In section 1 we called this effect "immersion into the environment" when describing the augmented reality system Archeoguide. In our case of Bamberg a player could for instance physically experience the distance between a medieval bishop with the cathedral and a palace on the hill, and the normal craftsmen who were working down at the river. The spatial grounding is particularly effective if players have to gather information actively at the location, e.g. by asking the man at the cash desk of a museum or reading an information panel on a medieval building.

*Temporal grounding*: Closely connected to the spatial grounding of the educational content, players do also acquire and learn the location specific knowledge at the same time they are resided at that location on the real world game board. This means that getting and experiencing the knowledge are not separated in time, but happen simultaneously.

The spatial and temporal grounding include the configuration of the real world game board to locations of interest for the game, in our example cultural heritage sites (see Fig. 2). The same is the case with the educational content, which has to be adjusted to the overall context the game is taking place and the locations chosen for the real world game board. Because the used didactical concept is crucial for any kind of knowledge mediation we further divided this process in three sub phases.

### 3.1 Didactical Workflow

To achieve a maximum learning effect on the side of the participants, we use three phases for knowledge mediation (see Fig. 4).

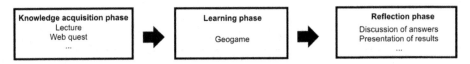

**Fig. 4.** Phases of the didactical workflow

Before the actual start of the game (knowledge acquisition phase), the participants are offered the possibility to gather the knowledge he or she will need in the second phase (learning phase). In our current setting we work in close collaboration with teachers, cultural scientists and monument conservators, who prefer knowledge transfer over traditional lectures. Other possibilities for this phase include self learning techniques like (guided) web quests, learning videos or self-playing PowerPoint presentations. The positive aspect of a lecture is that the lecturer can easily adapt the style of the presentation depending on the reactions of the actual audience during the lecture, like in our case a group of high school pupils who live in Bamberg and already know the city. On the other hand this is no practicable solution for a general tourist context, where a considerable amount of visitors should be able to play the game spontaneously. In this case we propose the Geogame to be played after one of those guided city tours frequently attended by tourists. A quicker and more game play oriented solution would be to integrate all the background information into the intro of the game, like playing a short video clip on the mobile device.

In the second phase the participants play the Geogame. Figure 5 illustrates the game flow in principle: players begin the game at predefined starting locations at the same time (see Fig. 2) and are then free to move to an arbitrary location on the game board. When arriving at a location, the mobile device displays the associated educational content, in this case a simple multiple choice question. Players have time at least the duration of syncTime to figure out the answer – either by pure knowledge from the first phase, or by gathering the information on site (or by a combination of both). After answering the question and when syncTime has passed, the players are free to move on to the next location.

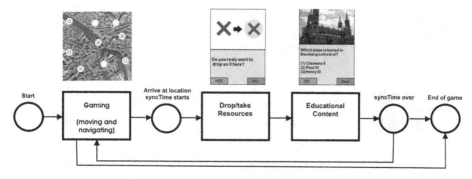

**Fig. 5.** Game flow of a Geogame

Because of the game rules of Tic Tac Toe, a player can arrive at a maximum of six different locations in the course of one GeoTicTacToe game. This is the case when one team wins at the last free location of the game board and the other team only managed to go to three location in that time. More common is the case that the game ends in a draw, leading to an arrived location share of five to four. Additionally, a player cannot visit a location, if the other player has already set an X or O there. This leads to a situation in which not all questions were presented to both players in the second phase. To provide all knowledge equally to all players, they meet after the game in a reflection phase where they have the possibility to discuss and present the answers and experiences with the other players, thus learning new knowledge about places they have not been to. In a tourist context it would certainly be quite unsatisfactory not having had the possibility to visit all important sights, but a Geogame could in this case be played as an add-on after a guided city tour.

### 3.2  Didactical Patterns for Knowledge Mediation

As we have seen so far, Geogames provide a unique way for communicating world heritage and deepen the learning situation for the information corresponding to it. To fully use the potential of this new knowledge mediation form we discovered four didactical patterns, which we use for instance in our Geogame GeoTicTacToe. Although there are surely more patterns possible, we found that particularly these four support the spatial and temporal grounding of Geogames.

*Fact pattern:* The simplest pattern is posing questions on hard facts, like "Which pope is buried in Bamberg cathedral?" or "Which of the following religious orders had a settlement in Bamberg?" This kind of knowledge is most appropriate to be presented in form of multiple choice questions (Fig. 6). In addition it is also a good method to encourage the players to get in contact with local people and ask for the correct answers.

*Geographic coherence pattern:* This pattern fosters a better understanding and experiencing of (cultural) geographic coherences. Figure 6 shows an example of this pattern. Here the centre of Bamberg is separated in three main parts, the Theuerstadt, the island town and the episcopal town. A player who is standing up the hill in episcopal town with a good view on the whole city can be asked to identify the other parts by looking around the scenery. Just using a simple fact pattern on this subject would surely not create such an experience.

Geographic coherence pattern    Present-past pattern    Pattern recognition pattern    Fact pattern

**Fig. 6.** Four didactical patterns for communicating cultural heritage

*Present-Past pattern:* With the multimedia possibilities of a mobile device, knowledge about past conditions can be illustrated visually at significant locations on the game board (Fig. 6). A player could for instance be displayed a photo of a district taken during the Second World War and be asked to describe the differences to nowadays' situation.

*Pattern recognition pattern:* The knowledge acquisition phase preceding the actual game also allows posing transfer questions and more enhanced learning tasks in the game. For example "use the digital camera of your phone to take pictures of all baroque-specific style elements of the church in front of you!" (Fig. 6).

## 4 Fun and Learning with Geogames: Two Case Studies

The two empirical case studies we conducted up to now had the goal to evaluate how the integration of the educational aspect would have an impact on the fun factor of the Geogame GeoTicTacToe. There were in total three games, one at the 22nd of February 2006 in cooperation with the Documentation Centre World Heritage of the city of Bamberg to communicate the idea of the UNESCO world heritage list. Two further games were organized for a Girls' Day on the 1st of March 2006 at the University of Applied Science in Coburg.

At both occasions the identical version of the game was used – identical except for the educational content.

### 4.1 UNESCO World Heritage Game in Bamberg

In this first case study the participants were school children from a local school in Bamberg. A total number of six children were competing in two teams, one team of three girls and one team of three boys. All of them were between 15 and 16 years old. The game was captured on video and a questionnaire was handed out in the discussion phase which could be taken home and sent back for the evaluation.

**Table 1.** Items and answers of the first case study concerning the fun aspect

| Question | Answer |
|---|---|
| *How did you like the game play in general? State your personal experience:* | It was very interesting and fun. |
| | It was a lot of fun, because the game did not only take place on paper but in the whole city. |
| | It was interesting and fun. Indirectly also a confirmation of my athletic abilities. But winter is not a good time for this game: cold fingers. |
| | Interesting, versatile, diversified. Physically demanding. Simple game brought in an exciting context. |
| | Good. |
| *Do you want to play Geogames once more in the future?* | Yes (four times) |
| | Yes, if there were more "scenarios" (game boards). Playing with always the same game board would get boring in the end |

One questionnaire was not returned. The questionnaire was constructed with open questions. Because of this and the preliminary nature of this case study, Table 1 shows only the items most relevant for the evaluation of the fun factor of the game and summarizes the given answers.

## 4.2 Teaching Girls About GPS

In our second case study, a total of 11 girls of the age from 10 to 14 attended. We split them into two groups, so that a maximum of three girls were in one team in a game. This left us with a distribution of six girls in the first run and five in the second. Because this time the educational context was GPS functionality, unfortunately we did

**Table 2.** Rating of the fun aspect of GeoTicTacToe

| | M | SD |
|---|---|---|
| The game was much fun. | 4.4 | 0.6 |
| Today I have learned something interesting about GPS | 4.2 | 0.7 |
| GeoTicTacToe has deepened my knowledge about GPS | 4.5 | 0.7 |

| Questions | Answers |
|---|---|
| *Would you want to play GeoTicTacToe once more in the future?* | Yes (11 times) |
| *What is more fun for you:* | |
| *1.) Normal computer games* | 4 times |
| *2.) I do not know; I have not played computer games* | 3 times |
| *3.) A location-based game like GeoTicTacToe* | 4 times<br>(3 times selected in combination with another option) |

not have a spatial and temporal grounding of the questions, so that the educational aspect was only evaluated with subjective questions. Besides for open questions, we used a five point Likert scale in this questionnaire. Possible answers ranged from 1 = totally decline to 5 = totally agree. The questionnaire was presented to the participants after the discussion phase. Table 2 shows the ratings as well as additional relevant items and answers of the questionnaire. Again video material was captured.

### 4.3 Discussion of the Results

Our collected data in combination with the captured video material clearly indicates the fun potential of Geogames in the edutainment context. Aside from complaining about the weather conditions (case study 1) all given answers were positive. The pupils of case study 1 also mentioned correctly that the physical abilities are one major feature of GeoTicTacToe, as being fast is necessary to win a Geogame. Here the video material shows some nice examples of a race situation between the two rivalling teams. This is also the case for the strategic elements in Geogames: lively discussions about the next move can be observed between the team members. There were also discussions on the correct answers for the questions. This strengthens results mentioned in Schwabe et al. (2005) that playing a location-based game in teams contributes to the immersion into the game.

Taking the ratings of case study 2 into account, our proposed edutainment workflow is in the first place fun to play and we also got no negative feedback about the integration of the educational content in GeoTicTacToe. The participants in all case studies suggested that they want to replay the game or similar Geogames, further fortifying the thesis that integrating educational content in Geogames does not reduce the fun factor of these games. One participant of case study 2 even made the suggestions that *"this will be surely the next killer-application for tourists"*.

Although the positive answers about the learning effect indicate the worth of our presented didactical workflow, there is clearly more sophisticated research necessary to strengthen this thesis. Such an evaluation would have to compare the learning effects of our Geogame approach with that of traditional forms of knowledge mediation. In our specific case, a control group comparable to the gaming group would need to be taught the same educational content with a classic guided tourist tour or a school lecture. Some weeks after the experiment, one group who has played the game and the control group would be tested about the educational content to evaluate the long-term learning effect. Up to now, our test groups did not have enough participants for such an experiment. Comparable experiments on mobile and location-based learning (e.g. Schwabe and Göth, 2005b) had the same problems in gathering an appropriate amount of participants for the evaluation.

## 5  Related Work and Future Research

Using our proposed didactical concept in combination with a Geogame like GeoTicTacToe can greatly enhance the presentation of cultural heritage. Furthermore, we presented four didactical patterns which let the players experience the various aspects of cultural heritage sites from different perspectives.

We also confirmed the findings of Facer et al. (2004) that learning with a location-based game adds more fun to the learning experience. In contrast to our approach, in Savannah players are part of a simulation: they are role-playing youngster lions in the savannah, rather than playing a real competitive game like GeoTicTacToe. The necessity of speed in GeoTicTacToe to be competitive with the adversary adds extra fun, especially for young people, while at the same time the syncTime assures enough time for experiencing and learning. Another issue about Savannah is portability: a Geogame like GeoTicTacToe very easily fits to almost every learning situation, while it would take much more effort to change the Savannah simulation to e.g. a "GPS simulation game". However, it is possible to create location-based games with role-playing elements which are also an instance of the Geogames class (with resources, players and locations); think of a game in a medieval city where each team incorporates one medieval population group (knights, priests, craftsmen, farmers), and changes gold pieces, goods or weapons to occupy strategically or economically important locations.

Schwabe and Göth (2005b) apply their MobileGame in the orientation days for new students at the University of Zurich. The MobileGame is a simple catch game where three groups hunt each other and simultaneously try to solve different tasks, like finding specific buildings or meeting a certain person. This game is not embedded in a whole didactical concept like Savannah or Geogames. The reported learning gains (also in Schwabe et al., 2005a) with this kind of edutainment game are therefore only minor ones.

Mobile learning, like the mobile learning engine from Meisenberger and Nischelwitzer (2004), allows users to carry their multimedia learning content with them wherever they go. However, they lack the spatial and temporal grounding of Geogames as well as the whole entertainment aspect.

Plenty of literature on computer game-based learning exists, for example Prensky (2001), which fortify the positive aspects of merging the motivational effects of playing games with the intellectual demanding aspects of learning. As in the case of pure mobile learning, stationary computer games do not inherit spatial and temporal grounding of the educational content.

Our future research includes a more sophisticated evaluation of the educational part of our proposed didactical workflow in combination with additional games in the following months. Furthermore, we want to transfer the whole concept to other contexts than cultural heritage, which allow a spatial and temporal grounding of the educational content. In these new fields of application more didactical patterns should surely be provided. Another question would be if the proposed edutainment application and workflow generates long-term learning effects.

# References

Cheverst, K., Davies, N., Friday, A., Mitchell K. (2000) Experiences of Developing and Deploying a Context-Aware Tourist Guide: The Lancaster GUIDE Project, Mobicom'00, Boston, U.S.

Facer, K., Joiner, R., Stanton, D., Reid, J., Hull, R., Kirk, D. (2004): Savannah: mobile gaming and learning? Journal of Computer Assisted Learning, 20, pp. 399-409

Gaitatzes, A., Christopoulos, D., Roussou, M. (2001) Reviving the past: Cultural Heritage meets Virtual Reality, VAST2001: Virtual Reality, Archaeology, and Cultural Heritage, November 2001

Kiefer, P., Matyas, S. (2005): The Geogames Tool: Balancing spatio-temporal design parameters in location-based games. In Mehdi and Gough (Eds.), Conference on Computer Games (CGAMES 2005), Angoulême, France

Meisenberger, M., Nischelwitzer, A. K. (2004): The mobile learning engine (MLE) – a mobile, computer-aided, multimedia-based learning application. In: ultimedia Applications in Education (MApEC), Graz

Nicklas, D., Pfisterer, C., Mitschang, B. (2001): Towards Location-based Games. In: Loo Wai Sing et al. (Eds): Applications and Development of Computer Games in the 21st Century: ADCOG 21; Hongkong Special Administrative Region, China

Schlieder, C., Kiefer, P., Matyas S. (2006): Geogames - Designing Location-based Games from Classic Board Games, IEEE Intelligent Systems, Special Issue on Intelligent Technologies for Interactive Entertainment (accepted, to appear in September 2006)

Schwabe, G., Göth, C. (2005a): Mobile Learning with a Mobile Game: Design and Motivational Effects. Journal of Computer Assisted Learning, Vol. 21, 2005, pp. 204-216

Schwabe, G., Göth, C., Frohberg, D. (2005b): Does Team Size Matter in Mobile Learning? International Conference on Mobile Business 2005

Prensky M. (2001): Digital Game-Based Learning. McGraw-Hill, New York.

Thomas, B., Close, B., Donoghue, J., Squires, J., De Bondi, P., Morris, M., Piekarski, W. (2000) ARQuake: An outdoor/indoor augmented reality first person application. Proceedings of the Fourth International Symposium on Wearable Computers (ISWC'00), Atlanta, Georgia

Vlahakis, V., Ioannidis, N., Karigiannis, J., Tsotros, M., Gounaris, M., Stricker, D., Gleue, T., Daehne, P., Almeida, L. (2002) Archeoguide: An Augmented Reality Guide for Archaeological Sites, IEEE Computer Graphics and Applications, vol. 22, no. 5, pp. 52-60, Sept/Oct, 2002

# Dynamic Binding Is the Name of the Game*

Marco A. Gómez-Martín, Pedro P. Gómez-Martín,
and Pedro A. González-Calero

Dep. Sistemas Informáticos y Programación
Universidad Complutense de Madrid, Spain
{marcoa, pedrop}@fdi.ucm.es, pedro@sip.ucm.es

**Abstract.** This paper presents a tutoring system aimed at teaching how to compile Java into the language of the Java Virtual Machine, and, at the same time, promotes a better understanding of the underlying mechanisms of object-oriented programming. The interaction with the systems takes the form of a 3D videogame where the student must compete to provide the right machine instructions, collect resources needed by the instructions and use her knowledge about Java compilation to find the best strategy.

## 1 Introduction

In 1970, Carbonell publicizes its classical paper about the integration of artificial intelligence techniques in computer assisted instruction [2]. This application would be later known as *Intelligent Tutoring Systems* (ITSs) [7]. During the last decades, much effort has been made to enhance these systems using different pedagogical approaches. One particularly widespread is based in the constructivist approach [4], that put emphasis on the learner's active role while they acquire new concepts.

Learning-by-doing method [6] is based on these theories. The apprentice approach has been used for ages, and today has been extrapolated to ITSs. More and more systems provides an habitable 3D environment [1]. Learners are represented in that environment by an avatar that they guide through the virtual world. The student has to make their avatar perform actions to solve the current problem the system has posed.

However, those systems focus on the learning factor, and often are boring applications that the student uses because they have to. On the other hand, computer users are more and more engaged to entertainment software. Players are immersed in microworlds, becoming part of the environment. When the game design, story and appearance are good enough, users can spend a huge amount of time using them. Mixing up both areas, ITSs and games, results in what is known as *game-based learning* or *game-based teaching* [5].

Related to these kind of systems, over the last few years, we have been developing JV$^2$M, a system to teach how to compile Java code, in particular, which kind of target instructions has to generate the compiler of Java [3]. The

* Supported by the Spanish Ministry of Education & Science (TIN2005-09382-C02-01).

R. Harper, M. Rauterberg, M. Combetto (Eds.): ICEC 2006, LNCS 4161, pp. 229–232, 2006.

application presents a virtual world where the student controls an avatar that executes the action they order to resolve the exercise.

## 2    JV²M, a System to Teach to Compile

Usually, compiler subjects are quite hard due to the strong formal knowledge required to understand how these program work. However, if both source and object languages are known, the *translation* is, in fact, quite intuitive.

For some years we have been developing JV²M, an application where students are faced to Java programs that must be translated to JVM assembler code. Users have to make this translation by themselves, using their intuitive knowledge about the source code semantic and the JVM internals.

Being JVM a *software machine*, some of its instructions have a quite high abstraction level. In that sense, some of them are designed to implement very specific characteristics of the object oriented programming, like dynamic binding. In that sense, pupils not only learn the translation process, but also practise these object orientation concepts.

The aim is the user generating the object code for the exercise. This could be done just written it down. But in this way, the complete process would be quite boring. Instead of that, our system recreates a game atmosphere, showing a 3D virtual world where the action develops. The environments has a special room where the compilation takes place. But, before entering in there, user must go around all over the place collecting resources (such as operands) needed for this translation. Apart of the 3D environment, the program has more typical game ingredients like time limit, enemies, and other strategy aspects.

As said before, some JVM instructions are quite pedagogically interesting for object orientation. Instead of just *compile them* in the special room, student must *execute them* in order to practise the runtime aspects of the object–oriented programming. In this sense, the most significant JVM instruction is `invokevirtual` used to call a method using dynamic binding.

The environment is enriched with JAVY, an avatar that helps the student about the compilation process. This character has information about each exercise and the general aspects of the translation in order to adapt his explanation to the user knowledge.

## 3    Sample Exercise

As an example of execution of the system, we will describe an exercise, to show the kind of Java programs we are thinking of. We will also detail the kind of JVM instructions the user has to face.

The exercise is a typical example in object oriented programming. It has an abstract class `Figure`, with a single `public abstract` method, `getArea` that returns a `double`. Two concrete classes inherit from it: `Circle` and `Square`, with their particular constructors: the `Square`'s one receives the edge's longitude and store it in an object's attribute, and the `Circle`'s one receives its radius. The

```
public class Circle                 public class Exercise {
        extends Figure {
                                      public static void main(
    Circle (double radius) {              String params[]) {
        _radius = radius;
    }                                         Figure f1;
                                              Figure f2;
    public double getArea() {                 double total;
        return _radius * PI;
    }                                         f1 = new Circle(10);
                                              f2 = new Square(10);
    protected double _radius;                 total = f1.getArea();
    protected final double                    total += f2.getArea();
        PI = 3.1415926535898;             } // main

} // class Circle                    } // class Exercise
```

**Fig. 1.** Code example

exercise is completed with a `main` function in a fourth class, that creates two
figures, and calculates the sum of both areas. Figure 1 shows the Java code of
two classes: `Circle` and `Exercise`.

The exercise does not pursue a perfect object oriented design. For example,
`Figure` class should be an interface instead of an abstract class. Besides, `PI`
attribute should be static or, even better, `Circle` class should use `Math.PI`.

However, this example introduces a lot of interesting concepts that the learner
has to practice. The content creator (tutor) has to decide, based on their experience, how many concepts include in each exercise for the user to face.

In this concrete code, the student has to practice arithmetical expressions
(sum and multiplication), attribute access and object construction. But, above
all, the main goal of the example is dynamic binding. During the exercise resolution, the student has to think about the *execution* of the JVM `invokevirtual`
instruction. When the program counter reaches `f1.getArea()`, the student has
to realize that, though Java code seems to say that the method `Figure.getArea`
has to be called (due to the *static type* of the `f1` variable, they have to find out
its *execution type* to call the correct method.

Figure 2 shows the environment with part of the compiled code for this exercise. All the operands in the instructions (for example `Figure.getArea` in
instruction 23) are the *resources* the student must look for before entering in
the compilation room. This enforces the user to think about the translation
while she is playing the level in the rest of the spaceship. Instructions 23 and 29
in the `main` code are the `invokevirtual` mentioned previously. Although they
are both the same instruction in the object code, their executions are different
because the runtime type of the references they affect are distinct.

```
class Exercise
Method void main (String [] args )
...
23: invokevirtual [Figure.getArea()]
26: dstore_3
27: dload_3
28: aload_2
29: invokevirtual [Figure.getArea()]
```

**Fig. 2.** Application snapshot with object code

## 4    Conclusions

After a few years developing $JV^2M$, a system to teach how Java code is executed in the Java Virtual Machine using game-based teaching strategies, we are now in a position of been able to face users to real exercises.

This paper shows a description of the system and describes an scenario of execution. In particular, we list the Java code of an exercise that face the student with concepts such as attribute access, object construction, inheritance and dynamic binding.

## References

1. W. H. Bares, L. S. Zettlemoyer, and J. C. Lester. Habitable 3D learning environments for situated learning. In *ITS '98: Proceedings of the 4th International Conference on Intelligent Tutoring Systems*, pages 76–85, London, UK, 1998. Springer.
2. J. R. Carbonell. AI in CAI: an artificial intelligence approach to computer-assisted instruction. *IEEE Transactions on Man-Machine Systems*, 11(4):190–202, 1970.
3. M. A. Gómez-Martín, P. P. Gómez-Martín, and P. A. González-Calero. Game-driven intelligent tutoring systems. In *Entertainment Computing - ICEC 2004, Third International Conference*, Lecture Notes in Computer Science, pages 108–113. Springer, 2004.
4. J. Piaget. *The Construction of Reality in the Child*. New York: Basic Books, 1955.
5. M. Prensky. *Digital Game-Based Learning*. McGraw-Hill, 2004.
6. R. Schank and C. Clearyv. *Engines for Education*. Lawrence Erlbaum Associates, Hillsdale, NJ, 1994.
7. D. H. Sleeman and J. S. Brown, editors. *Intelligent Tutoring Systems*. Academic Press, London, 1982.

# Lessons Learned from Designing a Virtual Heritage Entertainment Application for Interactive Education

Kyoung Shin Park[1], Yongjoo Cho[2], and Soyon Park[3]

[1] Digital Media Laboratory, Information and Communications University,
517-10 Dogok-dong, Gangnam-gu, Seoul 135-854, Korea
park@icu.ac.kr
[2] Division of Media Technology, Sangmyung University,
7 Hongji-dong, Jongno-gu, Seoul 110-743, Korea
ycho@smu.ac.kr
[3] Department of Media Art, Jeonju University,
1200 Hyoja-dong, Wansan-gu, Jeonju, Korea
hohopark@hotmail.com

**Abstract.** Digital Koguryo is a virtual reality reconstruction of a Koguryo mural tumulus, Anak No. 3, designed to help educate visitors in the cultural background and life style of the ancient Koguryo. The focus of Digital Koguryo was to give users an interactive, entertaining experience and to feel engaged in the activity of finding the life aspects of the Koguryo culture and enjoy the spectacle of historical events. This paper presents the findings and lessons learned from the development and public demonstration of Digital Koguryo in the creation of a virtual heritage.

**Keywords:** VR, Cultural Heritage, Edutainment, Interactive Education.

## 1 Introduction

Research in virtual reality and cultural heritage has shown a considerable growth in recent years. Virtual heritage applications employ the immersive virtual reality technology to recreate or interpret cultural heritage artifacts as they are today or as they might have been in the past. It gives users access to digital reconstruction of cultural heritage that would normally be inaccessible due to the location or the fragile condition of the artifacts. It also provides the opportunity to visit historical sites with no archeological remains or the excitement of reliving historical events. However, the majority of virtual heritage applications are archeological reconstructions of past cultural artifacts for digital preservation and restoration, which have been more concerned with the accurate restorations of original appearance [3].

Cultural heritage is particularly valuable for studies of ancient society, culture, and history. It contains all the data such as pictures and materials of architectural structure, cultural setting, artifacts and people. It is an excellent first use material in understanding ancient cultures. Therefore, it is important that the designers develop the applications that will enable visitors to learn cultural perceptions and understand the meaning of local cultural activities and stories behind the historical artifacts.

R. Harper, M. Rauterberg, M. Combetto (Eds.): ICEC 2006, LNCS 4161, pp. 233–238, 2006.
© IFIP International Federation for Information Processing 2006

Recently the designers have considered adding user interactivity (or activity) to increase user engagement in the virtual heritage environment. Examples include using actor dialogues [5], game-like interfaces [1, 2], and storytelling through user feedbacks [4].

Digital Koguryo is a virtual heritage application that reconstructs the Koguryo mural tumulus, Anak No. 3. The Anak No. 3 Tumulus is a large stone-built multi-chamber structure with mural paintings drawn on its walls and ceilings. Koguryo mural paintings illustrate the life and historical events of the Koguryo civilization and details of the customs special in the ancient Korea. They are rich in color and tone, and still retain their distinct colors even after fifteen hundred years. The goal of the Digital Koguryo project is to help visitors learn and discuss the culture and customs of Koguryo. Digital Koguryo has been demonstrated to the general public in a variety of art and technical exhibitions.

It is a challenging process to create virtual heritage environments that are both engaging and educational. In this paper, we present the findings and lessons learned from the development and public demonstration of Digital Koguryo. It will show the design and implementation of Digital Koguryo, with an emphasis on interactivity. It will then discuss some of the important practical issues involved in the design and public demonstration of virtual heritage applications to increase user engagement.

## 2  Digital Koguryo

Koguryo (37 BC – 668 AD) is one of the three kingdoms of ancient Korea. The cultural background of Koguryo is revealed to have been of considerable complexity with various layers of artistic, religious and cultural influences upon its neighboring countries. There are thousands of Koguryo tombs spread out in North Korea and China of which, so far, only a hundred have been discovered to have wall paintings. Among the mural tumuli, the Anak No. 3 is the oldest and the biggest so far discovered. It is located in Anak-gun, Hwanghae-province, North Korea, and it is not open to the public due to its current fragile conditions. North Korean scholars claim it is the tomb of King Gugugwon.

Digital Koguryo recreates the fifteen hundreds-year old mural paintings in dynamic three dimensional computer graphics and animations. It is designed to create an interactive learning environment that can enrich user understanding of the past and to comprehensively present the history, life, and values of Koguryo cultural heritage. In Digital Koguryo, the game begins when the players enter at the front entrance of the tomb. The players can explore the painted chambers and corridors as they exist at the present time. As the players move closer to the paintings, the two dimensional painted figures become life-sized three dimensional characters, giving narrations about cultural artifacts, and interactively ask and answer questions on the context of the paintings.

Digital Koguryo is designed to run on a passive stereoscopic virtual reality system that is built using the passive stereoscopic polarization filters attached on two low-cost LCD/DLP projectors, a polarization-preserving screen, and a PC rendering the virtual world scene. Users wear a polarizing glass to see the immersive three-dimensional content. They can navigate and interact with the virtual environment

**Fig. 1.** A demonstration of Digital Koguryo in the CAVE (on the left) and on the passive stereoscopic virtual reality system (on the middle), and the players are surrounded by the mural paintings printed on the walls in the exhibition room (on the right)

using a wand or a joystick. Audio is enabled through the use of loudspeakers to give narrations. Digital Koguryo also run on a fully immersive CAVE virtual reality system. Fig 1 shows a large number of people who've participated in Digital Koguryo experience, which was demonstrated at the opening reception in the Center of Digital Ocean Virtual Environment (on the left image), at the SCIART 2004 (on the middle), and at the Game Expo 2004 (on the right) in Korea.

## 3  Game Design

Digital Koguryo is a collaborative effort between multidisciplinary research teams including archeologists, artists, and computer scientists in the creation of educational and exhibition contents of the Koguryo cultural heritage. In the design of Digital Koguryo, we wanted to create an interactive and entertaining virtual environment which enable users to feel engaged in the activity of finding cultural artifacts and enjoy the spectacle of the past historical events. Hence, we employed game-like design to improve user's cultural experience for interactive learning. This approach is similar to 3D adventure games that use popular culture as a game setting in a sense that they also cater to teaching history by playing. However, we were more focused on effectively conveying historical materials in Digital Koguryo.

### 3.1  Learning Materials and Scenario-Based Game Design

The Koguryo mural tombs are historical relics, which had a big influence on the painting and architectural development of eastern culture in the medieval ages. In the absence of contemporary historical texts from the Koguryo kingdom, the mural paintings are valuable resources for understanding Koguryo's life and spirit. In Anak No. 3, the mural paintings depict the portraits of a king and a queen in the left chamber, everyday life and culture of Koguryo society in the right chamber (such as, a woman cooking in the kitchen, using a tread mill, drawing water from a well, the three-legged crow, horses and carriages standing on a stable, etc), a musical performance in the inner middle chamber, and a long procession featuring as many as two hundred warriors in the corridor. Fig. 2 shows the architectural structure and the three-dimensional models reconstructed from the mural paintings as experienced in Digital Koguryo.

**Fig. 2.** The reconstructed 3D model of the tomb structure (on the left), and the carriage in the right chamber (on the middle), and the foot soldier in the corridor (on the right)

It is quite a challenging task to recreate the Anak No. 3 Tumulus in virtual reality because little is known about the detail structure of the tomb and its mural paintings. It is not possible to take measurements of the tomb nor can it be photographed due to its current location. So, a variety of resources were used to collect information, such as old documents, slides, old photographs, books, a TV documentary, and a multimedia CDROM. This is then assorted by architecture, people, domestic animals, historical relics, and other ornaments to build the database.

We developed the 2D scenario-based animations and 3D reconstructed models for historical relics to convey the learning materials in a more effective manner. To this end, there are about ten items hidden behind the mural paintings in the virtual tomb. This includes a king's crown 'Baeklakwan', a queen clothing, a cooking pot, a carriage, a trumpeter, a Korean lute 'Geomoongo', a walking solder, a metal shield, a Korean ancient harmonica 'So', and a drum for pairs. We wanted to encourage our visitors to carefully investigate the mural paintings and direct them to recognize historical relics shown in the paintings. As the players move closer to the paintings, they will receive a riddle to find the 3D reconstructed models matched to the items shown in the paintings. When they solve the riddle, they will then see a 2D animation depicting an historical episode – for example, the 2D kitchen animation shows a woman cooking, a pot boiling, the three-legged cow flying away from the roof of the kitchen to the sky, etc. They may also see some animations automatically triggered by their proximity to the murals, such as Korean traditional exercise 'Taegen.'

### 3.2 Digital Restoration of 2D Mural Painting Images and 3D Models

The existing surfaces of the original mural paintings are damaged in various places, and do not provide enough detail. Therefore, we had to perform a digital restoration of the 2D mural painting images to create the texture maps for Digital Koguryo. The artists scanned the photographs taken from the murals and the books, created the illustrations for the base to reconstruct the restored image. They then corrected for color, hue, and intensity of the digital images and filled the abrasion parts. This process is based on the historical research and documents on the polygenetic natural dyes of Koguryo and how the colors would change with moisture and how the texture of the painted walls would interfere with the colors.

We then digitally restored the Anak No. 3 tomb as if it existed today, such as the interior and exterior architectural structure and the mural paintings using the 2D restored images. We also created the 3D reconstructed models of historical relics that are identical to the excavated objects, which were used for the riddles that were given to the visitors. We also developed the scenario-based 2D animations to portray the Koguryo cultural spectacle which cannot easily be rendered in real-time using 3D modeling.

### 3.3  VR Interaction and Surrounding Interior Design

We used a high-level VR toolkit called Ygdrasil (YG) [6] to construct the virtual environment and user interaction in Digital Koguryo. Ygdrasil is a set of C++ classes designed to simplify the construction of behaviors for virtual objects using re-usable components; and on sharing the state of an environment through a distributed scene graph mechanism. In the public exhibition, we provided a game joystick as a primary user interface. By using the familiar game interface, most people can easily navigate and select items in the virtual environment, except for the narrow corridors due to its lack of finer control. For example, some people tried to move or rotate in this corridor which made them get stuck in the walls.

We also had to consider the design of the surroundings to assist in immersion in the virtual environment. Digital Koguryo was first shown in an art exhibition installed in a room painted white. This made the room look rather empty. To better blend the exhibition room with the virtual environment and to make it look more like a tomb, we adjusted the illumination dimmer by covering the lights with Korean traditional paper. We then put the mural paintings printed on a long strip of silkscreen on the walls surrounding the VR display, so that users would feel as if they entered an ancient mural tomb. Many people said that they were delighted by the prints on the walls which helped to draw their attention to the virtual environment.

## 4  Issues and Lessons Learned from Design and Demonstration

Virtual heritage environments are a promising medium for interactive education but it is still difficult to construct due to limited historical documents and resources, and requiring close collaboration between multiple designers, and various kinds of conflict resolutions between these designers. In the design of Digital Koguryo, geographically distributed, multidisciplinary researchers (such as archeologists, artists, and computer scientists) had worked closely together for over six months from initial planning to final deployment. One of the main problems we encountered was in trying to compromise over the desire of building accurate digital reconstruction and rendering performance for real-time, interactive virtual reality experiences, such as reducing the size of 3D models and 2D texture images. Hence, we had to meet several times online or offline to adjust the models, interaction design, and other technical details.

In the demonstration, we found that visitors wanted tactile feedback on virtual objects. We also found that the 3D models reconstructed as the exact replications of original form seemed to cause problems. The long procession mural painting (while it is the most important mural paintings in the Anak No. 3) is located in the narrow corridor, and some people seemed to have difficulty in navigating this corridor and observing the animation at the same time. Moreover, we did not provide a navigational aid (such as, a map with the item locations) in Digital Koguryo thinking the tomb small enough, but it resulted in some people missing some of the important lesson– e.g., the horn riddle nearby the entrance, the inner chamber riddle, and three riddles with the long procession mural painting.

## 5   Conclusion

The Digital Koguryo project was a collaborative effort among multidisciplinary researchers in the creation of a VR cultural heritage entertainment environment for interactive cultural and historical education. In Digital Koguryo, we have employed a game-like design to improve user engagement, to better give a rich sense of cultural learning experience. Game is a familiar medium to users, and they can better engage in tasks in the game environment. In Digital Koguryo, the players walk through the chambers and interact with the mural paintings inside the tomb. As they move closer to the paintings, they are given a riddle about the cultural artifacts drawn on the painting and must choose from possible answers.

In the development and public demonstration, we learned that the virtual heritage environment with interactivity encouraged users to be more immersed and engaged in cultural experience. However, we also learned the need for blended surroundings during demonstrations and a need for developing other user interface such as a tactile feedback to give richer sense of the VR experience. We will continue to explore more ways in providing an interactive, entertaining, and educating experience for the visitors to help them better immerse in the past cultural perspectives.

## References

1. Abaci, T., Bondeli, R., Ciger, J., Clavien, M., Erol, F., Gutierrez, M., Noverraz, S., Renault, O., Vexo, F., Thalmann, D., Magic Wand and the Enigma of the Sphinx, Computers & Graphics, 28, pp. 477-484, 2004.
2. Gaitatzes, A., Christopoulos, D., Roussou, M., Reviving the Past: Cultural Heritage Meets Virtual Reality. In Proc. of Virtual Reality, Archaeology and Cultural Heritage 2001, pp.103-110.
3. Ikeuchi, K., Nakazawa, A., Hasegawa, K, Ohishi, T., The Great Buddha Project: Modeling Cultural Heritage for VR Systems through Observation, In Proc. of International Symposium on Mixed and Augmented Reality 2003.
4. Lee, Y., Oh, S., Woo, W., A Context-Based Storytelling with a Responsive Multimedia System, In Proc. of Virtual Storytelling 2005, pp.12-21.
5. Park, K., Leigh, J., Johnson, A., How Humanities Students Cope with the Technologies of Virtual Harlem, Works and Days 37/38, 19 (1&2), pp. 79-97, 2001.
6. Pape, D., Anstey, J., Carter, B., Leigh, J., Roussou, M., Rotlock, T., Virtual Heritage at iGrid 2000, In Proc. of INET2001, Stockholm, Sweden, June 5-8, 2001.

# A Dynamic Load Balancing for Massive Multiplayer Online Game Server

Jungyoul Lim, Jaeyong Chung, Jinryong Kim, and Kwanghyun Shim

Digital Content Research Division
Electronics and Telecommunications Research Institute
Daejeon, Korea
{astroid, jaydream, jessekim, shimkh}@etri.re.kr

**Abstract.** On-line games are becoming more popular lately as the Internet becomes popular, game platforms become diverse and a ubiquitous game environment is supported. Therefore, distributed game server technology is required to support large numbers of concurrent game users simultaneously. Especially, while game users are playing games, many unpredictable problems can arise, such as a certain server handles more server loads than recommended because many game users crowded into a specific region of a game world. These kinds of situations can lead to whole game server instability. In this paper, global dynamic load balancing model and distributed MMOG(Massive Multiplayer Online Game) server architecture are proposed to apply our load balancing algorithm. Many different experiments were carried out to test for efficiency. Also an example of applying real MMOG application to our research work is shown.

## 1 Introduction

On-line games are becoming more popular lately as the Internet becomes popular, game platforms become diverse and a ubiquitous game environment is supported. Furthermore, as multi-platform game technology, which allows one game to be played in a different platform simultaneously, advances, development of distributed game server technology is required to support large numbers of concurrent game users safely. MMOG(Massive Multiplayer Online Game), in which large number of users play a game in the same game world, is a big genre of heavy server loads because of game event handling, NPC(Non Player Character) control and persistency in game world management. Generally, MMOG distributed game server system is used to handle large numbers of game users, and to provide the necessary consistency to provide game users the same feeling of the same game world, the biggest computational power and network bandwidth is used [1].

In reality, in on-line games, when a certain server load becomes very big to the other servers by an unpredictable case, caused by many gamers crowded in a specific region of a game world, the whole server can become unstable. This can cause response time delay, game server instability etc. and results in an undesirable situation to maintain consistency. In this case, many different ways of load balancing can solve these problems [1][9][10]. A global load balancing technique which minimizes the

R. Harper, M. Rauterberg, M. Combetto (Eds.): ICEC 2006, LNCS 4161, pp. 239–249, 2006.
© IFIP International Federation for Information Processing 2006

load discrepancy by monitoring the whole load and a local load balancing technique which distributes the load to the nearest server using threshold values are researched for a dynamic load balancing technique[2][4][11].

In this paper, to support very large numbers of simultaneous game users, we propose a hierarchical structured distributed server architecture, and global a dynamic load balancing model. The rest of this paper is organized as follows: Section 2 explains MMOG game server system building method for dynamic load balancing; Section 3 defines a dynamic load balancing model which can be applied to a distributed server. Section 4 shows the formation of suggested distributed server architecture and a dynamic load balancing model test is carried out. This shows an example of a real application applied to this system. Finally, section 5 concludes with our results and discusses shortcomings.

## 2   Distributed MMOG Server System

### 2.1   Server Architecture

Because in Distributed MMOG Server multiple game servers support one game, it is important to distribute the game load effectively to maximize efficiency. Generally after splitting each game server into regional groups, game users belonging to a split area and NPC (Non Player Character) are handled. MMOG Server load is proportionate to the user numbers belonging to the split area.

As illustrated in Fig.1, to form Distributed MMOG Server the following are necessary: World Server distributes and manages a game world; Zone Server handles game processes in a given game space; Login Server authenticates users who participate in the same game. Also, a Gateway Server is required, which handles internal server changes such as server's regional processing area change flexibly by controlling the network communication between User and server.

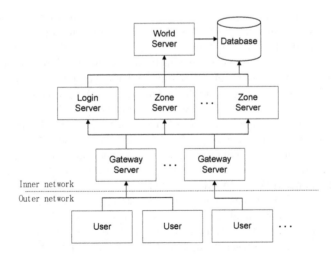

**Fig. 1.** MMOG structure that has three network layers

World Server divides game spaces by the number of Zone Servers. It uses a re-dividing method of dividing the divided areas again after dividing into a maximum number of 4 game spaces. It is managed to quad tree type. Fig.2 shows the splitting order of game spaces and allocated processing areas according to connecting orders of Zone Server.

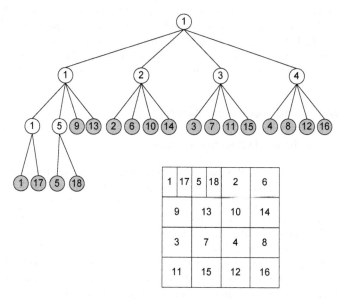

**Fig. 2.** Game space divided by the connecting order of Zone Server and management of quad tree

| Cell(0,0) | Cell(0,1) | Cell(0,2) | Cell(0,3) | Cell(0,4) | Cell(0,5) |
|---|---|---|---|---|---|
| Cell(1,0) | Cell(1,1) | Cell(1,2) | Cell(1,3) | Cell(1,4) | Cell(1,5) |
| Cell(2,0) | Cell(2,1) | Cell(2,2) | Cell(2,3) | Cell(2,4) | Cell(2,5) |
| Cell(3,0) | Cell(3,1) | Cell(3,2) | Cell(3,3) | Cell(3,4) | Cell(3,5) |
| Cell(4,0) | Cell(4,1) | Cell(4,2) | Cell(4,3) | Cell(4,4) | Cell(4,5) |

**Fig. 3.** The interest area of avatar A is a game space divided into 30 cells (the circle formed at the center of A is the Visual field and the 9 shaded cells are the Interest area)

## 2.2 Division and Management of Game Space

Users in MMOG participate in a game after choosing an avatar that represents itself, and while playing a game it sends its information or receives other characters' information through communication to the server. Because the MMOG Server restricts each avatar to exchange information to avatars within an AOI (Area Of Interest) it reduces severe network load and the total amount of network transmission [10][12][13]. For distributed processing of game space form a game world to regular defined size cell. If the cell size is set up to the same size of AOI radius of an avatar, the AOI of an avatar is defined to be a collection of 9 cells that consists of a cell that it belongs to and cells that are adjacent to it as shown in figure 3.

# 3 Dynamic Load Balancing Model

## 3.1 Characteristics of MMOG Server Load

The purpose of Dynamic load balancing is to minimize the load differences by evenly controlling the loads between servers by real time monitoring and analyzing the state of the game server. For real time analysis of the server load, first it is important to understand the critical factors that affect the server load of MMOG Server.

For real time analysis of the server load, first it is important to understand the critical factors that affect the server load of MMOG Server.

Firstly, the process loads in the server, which are known as the W(work load), due to the management and process of entities. Secondly, C(communication load) due to the interaction of entities in boundary regions in multiple servers.

Lastly, M(management load) due to domain management in the virtual worlds.[1,3]. Management load is not directly related to the numbers of users. It is a default load generated by the allocated game space and is a very small load compared to the work load and communication load. The boundary domains should be remained in straight line so that an average communication load can be minimized in boundary domains.

Work load and management load of MMOG Server load is generated definitely and proportionally according to the numbers of users and scale of the server area, but the communication load is varied by how the boundary area is defined.

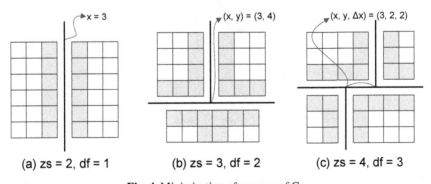

(a) zs = 2, df = 1          (b) zs = 3, df = 2          (c) zs = 4, df = 3

**Fig. 4.** Minimization of average of C

Consequently, this statement indicates a method for minimizing average of $C$, which is a primary factor of loads in communications with other servers under the statement of "distribution of entities in virtual world is unpredictable." If we assume that distribution of entities in virtual world is uniform, then $C$ can be minimized when the boundary between partition regions is maintained in straight line and such characteristic improves an application efficiency of managing technique and dynamic load balancing model in virtual world. Fig.4 illustrates the case of 2 to 4 of partitions in virtual world.

## 3.2  Server Load Definition

As defined in 3.1, through work load, communication load and management load, $i^{th}$ server load $L_i$ can be

$$L_i = aW_i + bC_i + cM_i \text{ with } a + b + c = 1.$$ (1)

In this Formulas, the terms $a$, $b$, and $c$ are weight factors $W_i$, $C_i$, $M_i$, respectively and their sum must be 1. Through using Formulas.1, we are able to acquire a process efficiency enhancement such as an enhancement of server's response time if we maintain the managing region of a server as an optimized state. The dynamic load balancing model for enhancing the process efficiency of a server can be defined by applying reflexive 4-partitioning method in the previous section. If we divide the virtual worlds using 4-partitioning method, we get reflexive load balancing for 4 partitioned regions in maximum. If dynamic load balancing for maximum 4 existing partitioned regions is defined, an efficient model is also defined without consideration of size of virtual

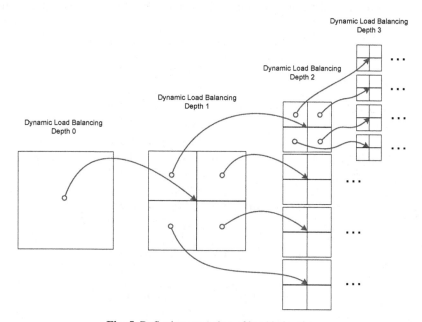

**Fig. 5.** Reflexive operation of load balancing

world or number of servers. Fig.5 illustrates reflexive operation for dynamic load balancing in reflexive 4 partitioning method. In dynamic load balancing, it is started with *Depth 0, Depth1, … , Depth n*, reflexively, and optimized load deviation in each depth uniforms the load deviation in between servers.

Because finding an optimized server processing region is to maintain each partition with uniform loads, this can be restate that minimization of standard deviation in load of the partition in $i^{th}$ server $L_i$ . Thus, if we set the number of partition in a specific depth as $d$ $(\leq 4)$ and an average of load $L_{ik}$ in $k^{th}$ partition as $L_k^*$ , then standard load deviation $SD_k$ for each partition is

$$SD_k = \sqrt{\sum_{i=1}^{d} (L_{ik} - L_k^*)^2 / d} \quad with \ d \ (\leq 4) \tag{2}$$

At this time, $k^*$ can be obtained by minimizing SD.

$$\min( SD_k ) = SD_{k^*} = \sqrt{\sum_{i=1}^{d} (L_{ik^*} - L_{k^*}^*)^2 / d} \tag{3}$$

### 3.3 Simplified Load Searching Technique

For actual implementation for such dynamic load balancing model, the load deviation of entire virtual world is inspected and then the partition $k^*$ is found using Formulas.3. However, it is difficult to instantly find optimized partition $k^*$ when the virtual

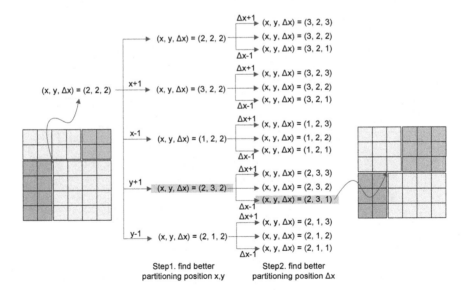

Step1. find better partitioning position x,y        Step2. find better partitioning position Δx

**Fig. 6.** Simplified load searching technique

world is getting larger. Thus, we believe that application of optimized partition searching techniques that sequentially searches for next optimized partition based on current partition will enhance the application possibility and processing efficiency of proposed dynamic load balancing model [4]. Fig.6 illustrates a Simplified load searching technique based on our idea.

## 4 Experimental Result

In this section, we present experiment for the dynamic load balancing architecture that includes both the distributed MMOG server architecture in section 2 and the dynamic load balancing model in section 3. We used 25 x 25(cell) sized game world and distributed 5000 virtual clients in a uniform distribution, a skewed distribution, and a cluster distribution respectively [7]. We carried out the experiment with the following conditions.

Because most of Distributed MMOG Server load occurred at network process, management load is ignored by setting c=0 in Formula.1.

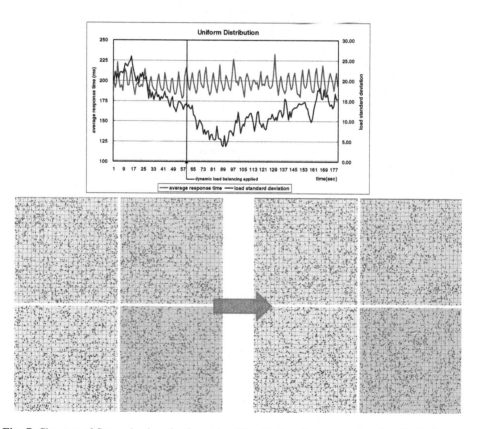

**Fig. 7.** Changes of Server load evaluation value (blue line) and response time (red line) when users are distributed uniformly

Work load and communication load is defined as the number of network transmissions created by one avatar. So, when the Gateway Server undertakes network broadcasting, the work load is defined by the number of users within split areas.

Also, the communication load is the total number of existing servers (excluding the server that itself exists in) within AOI of each avatar. Therefore, $a=0.5$, $b=0.5$, and we experimented $i^{th}$ server load as Formula.4.

$$L_i = 0.5 \times W_i + 0.5 \times C_i \qquad (4)$$

## 4.1 Uniform Distribution

With uniform distribution, the measured server load decreased to a narrow range from the point when dynamic load balancing was applied, but the server response time that shows real game server performance was increased by a narrow range or showed a similar level. The result of this experiment shows that dynamic load balancing can even increase the server load in a condition where users are distributed uniformly.

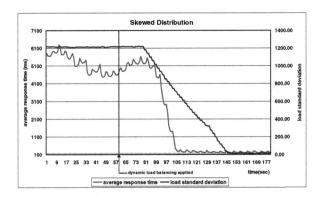

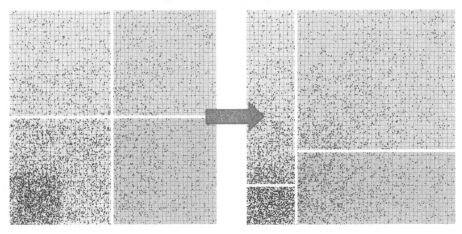

**Fig. 8.** Changes of Server load evaluation value (blue line) and response time (red line) when users are in a skewed distribution

## 4.2  Skewed Distribution

With skewed distribution, the measured server load decreased by a large range from the point where dynamic load balancing was applied, and the server response time also decreased by a narrow range. It means that dynamic load balancing improves general server performance when users are concentrated in a specific game space. Skewed distribution of Game clients is often seen in real game situation.

## 4.3  Clustered Distribution

The clustered distribution case showed that server load evaluation value and server response time decreased at the same time, which means that these results were similar to the skewed distribution case. Especially, estimated load evaluation value and response time can be verified that dynamic load balancing model shows better performance with a skewed distribution than a clustered distribution. The results of this experiment indicate that, with a real MMOG game, this research can be applied efficiently in a situation where game users were frequently crowded in one area.

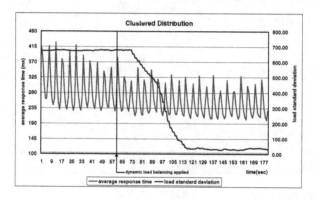

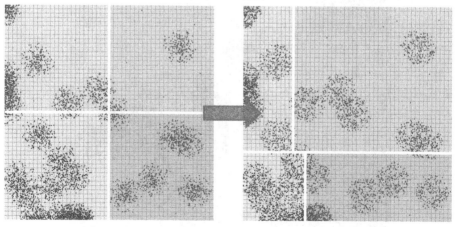

**Fig. 9.** Changes of Server load evaluation value (blue line) and response time (red line) when users are in a clustered distribution

# 5   Conclusion

In this paper we present the dynamic load balancing architecture which includes both distributed MMOG server system and dynamic load balancing model. This research was applied to real MMOG game and verified server performance through the simulation of a manifold situation that used massive virtual clients. As shown in the experiment's results, the server system efficiency was increased when game clients were in a skewed or clustered distribution in a game world that is similar to a real game situation, and our server architecture supported server load balancing efficiently which changed in real time. Also, as shown in Fig.10, this research was verified by applying the research products to a commercial game product.

**Fig. 10.** Applied images in Elma (commercial on-line MMOG game contents)

However, although the simplified load searching technique in section 3.3 decreased loads concerned to searching optimized world partition, it sometimes exposed the problem of abnormal partition result for local optimization problem. Nevertheless, the positive results of our experiments show that the load balancing architecture applied to real MMOG server and can also expand its effect to general networked virtual environment such as military training, business etc. In future work, we will improve a real-time load searching technique and apply various shapes of cell such as a brick or hexagon.

## Acknowledgement

The work presented in this paper has been supported in part by the Korea Ministry of Information and Communication's project: Development of Next-Generation Online Game S/W Technology.

## References

1. J. Lui, M. Chan : An Efficient Partitioning Algorithm for Distributed Virtual Environment Systems. IEEE Transaction on Parallel and Distributed Systems(2002)
2. Ta Nguyen, Binh D, Suiping Zhou: A Dynamic Load Sharing Algorithm for Massively Multiplayer Online Games. ICON(2003)131-136
3. J.C.S. Lui, M.F. Chan., K.Y.So., T.S. Tam: Balancing Workload and Communication Cost for a Distributed Virtual Environment. Fourth International Workshop on Multimedia Information Systems(1998)
4. D.Min, E. Choi., Donghoon Lee., B. Park: A Load Balancing Algorithm for a Distributed Multimedia Game Server Architecture: Proceedings of IEEE International Conference on Multimedia Computing and Systems(1999)882-886
5. Beatrice Ng, A. Si, R. Lau, F. Li: A Multi-Server Architecture for Distributed Virtual Walkthrough. ACM VRST(2002)163-170
6. Weyten L, De Pauw W: Quad list quad trees: a geometrical data structure with improved performance for large region queries. IEEE Transactions on Computer-Aided Design of Integrated Circuits and Systems(1989)Volume 8, Issue 3, 229-233
7. YungWoo Jung, et al: VENUS: The Online Game Simulator using Massively Virtual Clients. Lecture Notes in Computer Science, Springer-Verlag(2005) Volume 3398
8. Hunjoo Lee, Taejoon Park: Design and Implementation of an Online 3D Game Engine. Lecture Notes in Computer Science(2004) Volume 3044
9. Microforte: Bigworld game engine. http://www.bigworldgames.com/
10. 10.Emergent: Gamebryo game engine. http://www.emergent.net/
11. Jung Youl Lim, Jin Ryong Kim, Kwang Hyun Shim: A Dynamic Load Balancing Model For Networked Virtual Environment Systems Using an Efficient Boundary Partition Management.IEEE The 8th International Conference on Advanced Communication Technology(2006)
12. Bjorn Knutsson, Honghui Lu, Wei Xu, and Bryan Hopkins: Peer-to peer support for massively multiplayer games, INFOCOM (2004)
13. Stefan Fiedler, Michael Wallner, Michael Weber: A communication architecture for massive multiplayer games. The 1st workshop on Network and system support for games (2002)

# My Photos Are My Bullets - Using Camera as the Primary Means of Player-to-Player Interaction in a Mobile Multiplayer Game

Riku Suomela and Ari Koivisto

Nokia Research Center, P.O.Box 100,
FIN-33721 Tampere, Finland
{riku.suomela, ari.m.koivisto}@nokia.com

**Abstract.** Camera is becoming more common in mobile phones and it is commonly used for exchanging photos between people. The photos could be used for other purposes as well, such as gaming. This paper presents Assassin, a mobile multiplayer game using camera and photos as the main form of player-to-player interaction. The goal in the game is to catch other players in the game without them noticing this. The game is meant to be running in the background of the people's main activity, such as a working day, and not be played intensively all the time. The game was evaluated with 29 persons in four games organized during the participants' working days. The results suggest the camera is a very suitable game mechanics for gaming, and the participants in general did not find the game to be a violation of their privacy.

## 1 Introduction

Mobile phones with cameras have recently become widely used devices for taking and sharing photos. Photos are taken for private use, or they are shared with friends via the mobile networks using MMS or similar technologies. The camera is becoming a standard feature in mobile phones, and for example Nokia estimated that in 2005 the mobile industry shipped a total of 340 million camera phones [1], which has rapidly increased when compared to 90 million units sold in 2003.

Mobile gaming has been part of mobile phones for a longer time. Preinstalled games have been in mobile phones for over a decade, and new games can be downloaded over the air. Technologies, such as J2ME, allow one application to be run on many devices and downloadable Java games form a very large industry.

Mobile games often use the joystick as the main interaction device, but the joystick is of varying quality in different phones. The camera, however, relies less on the joystick, since taking a photo usually requires only a single press of a button. Camera and photos could offer an easy way to make games that work well in many devices.

Some examples exist that combine mobile gaming and the use of camera in mobile phones. Siemens SX1 mobile phone had a bundled game called Mozzies, which augments the video feed of the camera with bugs that the player needs to shoot. Another example is the Mobile Maze [2], where the player controls a ball and steers it by tilting the phone.

R. Harper, M. Rauterberg, M. Combetto (Eds.): ICEC 2006, LNCS 4161, pp. 250–261, 2006.

In this paper we present Assassin, a mobile multiplayer game that uses the camera as the main form of player-to-player interaction. The camera is used as it is normally used, that is, taking photos of other people (or players in this case). The idea of the game is to take photos of other players, without them noticing this. The photos are then sent to the target player, who then awards points if they are in the photo. The photos are sent to the target player only, to avoid the problem of stalking that naturally arises in a game that tries to catch people unaware. However, this game is meant to be played in a group of friends, so there should not be a situation where the players feel stalked at. In addition, all players have subscribed to the game, and they are aware of the rules, and that they are being stalked at.

We arranged four games, where we studied the game, players, the environment and the technical implementation. The four games had a total of 29 players at their workplace in a normal working day. The results suggest, that the game is fun to play, but takes the players minds of the work. Privacy was not seen as a problem by the majority of players, and the technical implementation could be improved.

The paper is organized as follows. First we look at previous work done in mobile, and camera gaming. After that, we present Assassin in detail, followed by the experiments that we have conducted and technical analysis. Finally we conclude the work and present our future plans for using camera in games.

## 1.1  Related Gaming

Assassin has common features with many different games. Mozzies that was already mentioned uses the camera in a single player mobile phone game. Eyetoy [3] is one of the most well known games using camera. Eyetoy is a console game that uses the player movement as game input.

Pirates! [4] is one game with many common points to Assassin. In Pirates!, the players could locate other ships in the real world, that were controlled by other players. In the game, the players needed to be in the range of the hardware in order to interact, and direct line of sight was not enough.

Augmented Reality (AR) often uses video camera for aligning the real and virtual worlds. ARQuake [5] is a good example of an AR game, in which the players try to hunt down monsters projected onto the real world. ARToolKit [6] has been ported to standard mobile phones [7] which open up possibilities for video AR applications in mobile phones.

Laser tag [8] is a very popular game that is played with laser weapons in the real world. This game is very close to Assassin, although Assassin is meant to integrate seamlessly into a normal day, and not require any extra equipment than what people normally have.

The First Person Shooters (FPS), such as the Quake series [9], and first-person sneakers, such as Thief [10], found in the PC and console world are the digital equivalents of real world FPS games. Assassin uses exactly the same setup, but with the higher resolution of the real world.

## 2  Assassin the Game

In Assassin, the player's goal is to take photos of other players so that the target does not notice this. The concept has many similarities to other games and applications. The first person sneakers are one example, picture messaging is another, and Killer – a game of assassination [11] is third. Killer is a live role-playing game, where all gaming happens in the real world. Assassin is meant to be a fun game that is played with friends to add something special to a meeting of friends, a working day, or any other social situation where people are occasionally meeting each other.

Assassin is meant to be a game that is constantly running, but not constantly played. In a normal working day, co-workers often meet during the day either planned, or unplanned, and these working days could be augmented with a casual game. The game can be played in any other social setting as well, and the game pace should automatically adapt to the number of these meetings. The more often people meet, the more photos are taken and vice versa. A study on camera phone use [12] suggested that a common social reason for image capture was to enrich a mutual experience between the people who were present. Assassin is designed to enrich such a situation.

### 2.1  Design

Although the game rules seem to support stalking, it is limited to people who are playing and are aware of this. The photos cannot be sent to any other player, except the target player, and the photos cannot be sent to anyone outside the game. The photos taken in a single game are strictly exchanged between players, so everyone knows who has taken the photo, and everyone knows who the possible photo takers are, when joining a game are.

Another design consideration was whether the game should notify players on assassination attempts, when the players are idle in the game. By idle we mean the players are actively doing their normal daily activities, such as work. We chose not to use any notifications and let the players decide when they playing. This means, that whenever players are in the game, they may receive all assassination attempts to their phone, but when their game client is turned off, there is no notifications (e.g. SMSes) about the attempts. The normal daily lives of the people should not be interrupted, and this approach lets the people decide when they are playing. The players can still monitor other players in the real world, but the digital device does not offer any help.

In Assassin, the players play themselves, that is, there is no virtual character that is being controlled. Each person has a virtual representation, but purely for targeting and point scoring reasons. The real world is the game arena, and real people are the game characters.

In the game, the players first create a profile of themselves. This profile contains their name, game icon, motto, and a photo of themselves. Only the name is compulsory, as this is how the target is selected. Motto is just for fun, in case players want to browse other players in the game. The icon is used on the UI next to the player name, but it is not necessary in the game. The photo is meant to remind the players who this person is, but the game does not work really well unless the players know each other beforehand. If players need to constantly browse the faces of other players, they are most likely losing since it becomes difficult to track and target opponents.

## 2.2  Game Mechanics: Attack, Defense, and Judge

The assassin main UI consists of three screens, as seen in Fig. 1. The first one contains the main actions (Attack/Defend), the second one the current game status, and the third one the chat screen for non hostile interaction. The game UI is made as simple as possible, since taking photos should be as easy as possible. Players can browse the player information in the game status view.

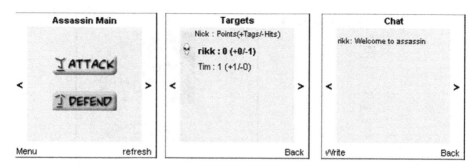

**Fig. 1.** The three main UIs of Assassin. The main functionality is attack and defense, and in addition the player can monitor the current status of the game and chat with other players.

In Assassin, the players have two actions: attack, and defend, and they also need to be the judges in the game. **Attacking** consists of taking a photo, selecting which target(s) are in the photo, and sending the photo for the target(s) for judgment. The photos are the bullets in the game, and the target selection is seen In Fig. 2.

**Defending** is a press of a button, that stops any attempt being made at you for three minutes, and it is meant for players who see someone making an attempt at them. This happens in the game, but there are other ways to defend in the real world, if players so agree. One possibility is to indicate in the photo that the attacker has been noticed, by for example using a rule: "when my hand is in front of my face in the photo, do not award a point".

Players are **judging** when they receive a photo taken presumably of them. In this case, the judge decides, whether he/she is in the photo and awards a point for the attacker. This judgment option relies on player's honesty. Players can choose not to award points even on good shots, if they so decide. There are other options to do the judgment, like peer review where any other player in game decides if a point should be awarded. However, the option of sending the photo to target is chosen for privacy. The game emphasizes, that the targets photo is the property of the target him/herself, not meant for distribution to others. An example judgment UI is seen in Fig. 2.

## 2.3  Implementation

The game is implemented with the Multi-User Publishing Environment (MUPE) [13]. MUPE is a client server application platform that supports end-user published content, as the name suggests. In Assassin, all content is end user generated. Player characters, player-to-player interaction, and point awarding are all end-user generated.

All instances of Assassin games are in a single server. The game contains a game lobby, where players can start new instances games. The games can be password protected to allow only friends to join. The Assassin server can contain as many games as possible, and the server should scale to very large number of game instances, since the game is a slow update game, with only occasional data transactions from players. The only data transmissions between client and server are photo UI download and updates, and photo uploads when attacking and download when judging.

**Fig. 2.** The attacker selects the opponent, and the photo is sent to the target for judgment

The data traffic should be always kept at the lowest possible level, in connected mobile games. In Assassin, this means keeping the size of the photos at a minimum. Even though there is megapixel or better resolution cameras in the current mobile phones, the mobile phone screen does not support such high resolutions. Due to this, we keep the image size in assassin at 110x82 pixels.

## 3  Experiments

The game has been played in four controlled games in the actual real world situation the game is meant to be played. The games had five to eight players in each, and the games have been played in different environments. The first game was organized in our company's premises, with eight participants who each worked in an office not shared with other players (1 was in open office space). The second and third games each had eight players all in a small building with open office space shared with other players. The last game was organized in a university, with five members of a department, each in their private room.

In all games, all players knew each other beforehand. In total, 29 persons started to play the game, and actually 27 players played the game. None of the players had played the game beforehand. Two players were too busy during the course of the game to play at all. Our main focus in the tests was on the battle system, that is, is it fun to use the camera as the main game mechanics in player-to-player interaction. In addition, we studied how the game integrates to a normal day, what are the privacy implications and how well the game was implemented. The players were awarded a movie ticket (value 8€) for participation.

In total, the number of participants was even larger. We had agreed to arrange a session in an information technology company, but the company policy stopped us from entering. Taking photos in the company premises was forbidden, and the tests had to be cancelled. Still, this is a very valuable result, as one in five tests were forbidden by company policies. This will be a serious obstacle in the future for games based on taking photos.

## 3.1  Setup and Instructions

All games were played in a similar fashion. At the start of the game, instructions to play the game were given. The participants were instructed to:

1. Create a player character using your own name as the name of the character.
2. Join a practice game.
3. Take a photo, and attack another player with it.
4. Judge the attacks they received.
5. Leave the practice game, and go back to the lobby room.

There were no difficulties in understanding how the game system works, and all players learned the game mechanics easily on the setup phase, and there was no need for assistance at a later stage. The problems were with occasional technological problems in the setup phase or during the actual tests.

After these preliminary steps were taken, players joined the actual game. Before the start of the game, players had a truce of few minutes, during which the players were instructed not to give points on attacks.

There was no observation of players by the test organizers, as this would have been impossible to setup. The organizers merely sat on a predefined location, and acted as technical assistance in case there were technical difficulties in the game.

The games were played with equipment provided by us. The first game was played with four different devices: Nokia models 6600, 7610, N70, and N90. The rest of the games were played with one Nokia N70 device, and the rest were Nokia 6600 models.

## 3.2  Rules

All games were played until a player got ten successful attacks. During the first game, the defense system provided by the game was found to be too slow. Pressing a defense button was sometimes seen as too slow, if the phone was in ones pocket and another player was well positioned.

To test another setup, the second and third games were played with defense in the real world, that is, in addition to the defense button in the UI, the players were instructed to place their hand in front of their face when taking a photo. If the players received such a photo, they were instructed not to give points. In the fourth and final game the players were given a choice before the game between the two defense systems, and they chose to use the hand in front of the face.

## 3.3  Experiment Results – The Effect of the Environment

The four games played revealed a lot of interesting facts about the game, and how the environment in which the game is played affects the game. The first game, which was played in an office where each player had their own room, was the longest lasting approximately two hours and forty minutes. In this game, two players were so busy with their work that they did not play the game at all during this time, as they felt other work was much more important. These players thought they still had time to play the game later, but they did not play before were told the game is over.

In the second and third game the players at least partially shared the same working space. The game tempo was very fast, since the players felt they could not stay in the same place as another player was constantly seeing them. The second game lasted 50 minutes, and the third 20 minutes. All the players were shooting constantly until the end of the game, and no-one did any other work during this time.

The same result could also be seen in the first game, when the players went for a coffee break. At one point, there were four players in the coffee room at the same time, and they were unable to take coffee since they were constantly aiming at each other and hiding behind corners. The situation ended in a truce that was declared by the players themselves.

The fourth game had five players of the same department in a university. Each player did not share the same working space with the other players, and the game lasted two hours. This game was very similar to the first game. The players also declared a truce when entering the coffee room. This implies the game is really happening in the real world, and the players understand the rules are purely set by themselves. The key figures of the games are summarized in the following table 1.

**Table 1.** Summary of the key facts in each of the four games

| Game | Participants | Duration of game | Environments |
|------|--------------|------------------|--------------|
| 1 | 8 | 2h 40 minutes | All in separate rooms |
| 2 | 8 | 50 minutes | Players worked in the same room |
| 3 | 8 | 20 minutes | Players worked in the same room |
| 4 | 5 | 2h | All in separate rooms |

## 3.4 Questionnaires

All participants in all games were asked to fill in a questionnaire with questions on their background, and about the game. With the questionnaire, we wanted to find answers to questions about the game system, on technical problems, game experience, and privacy.

The four games played had a total of 29 players, out of which 27 players played the game, and 25 players answered the questionnaire. Two players were not eligible to answer the game, since they did not play the game at all, and two players failed to submit their answers in time. From those who answered, 19 were males (77%) and 6 were females (23%). The average age of the players was 23, and two were native English speaking and the rest had Finnish as the mother tongue. The necessary UI consisted of two main buttons (attack and defense), and a simple question "Is it you in the photo" with Yes and No buttons, the language skills were irrelevant in this test. No-one reported of any language problems.

The main prerequisite questions concerned the photos, and sending photos to friends. The participants generally liked taking photos, since the average answer in a scale of one (definitely no) to five (definitely yes) gave an average of 3.9, and only one person answered no, and none definitely no. Participants were less keen on sending these photos to their friends, since the question "I think it is fun to send photos to friends" got an average of 2.9, the most common answer being "no". The problem is not in the difficulty, since the question "It is too difficult to send the photos" got an average of 1.9, the most common answer being "definitely no", and no-one answering "definitely yes". These answers indicate that taking photos and sending them to friends could be enhanced somehow, and in this paper we study how games could enhance the exchange of photos. Some key questions in the questionnaire relating to this paper are seen in Table 2.

**Table 2.** The key questions from the full questionnaire, and the average and median of answers

|     | Question (answer 1 definitely no ... 5 definitely yes) | Avg | Med |
|-----|--------------------------------------------------------|-----|-----|
| Q1  | I liked the way the battle was made in game (photos)   | 4.0 | 4   |
| Q2  | If such a game were integrated to a phone, I would play it | 3.6 | 4 |
| Q3  | I think it was fun to battle with others               | 4.2 | 4   |
| Q4  | Considering only the battle system, I would play this game again | 4.2 | 4 |
| Q5  | If you think about the entire game, I would play it again | 3.8 | 4 |
| Q6  | Playing the game was fun                               | 4.2 | 4   |
| Q7  | The game provided additional fun to a working day      | 4.1 | 4   |
| Q8  | The game hampered my working day                       | 3.5 | 4   |
| Q9  | Working hampered my gaming                             | 3.3 | 3.5 |
| Q10 | People, who were not part of the game provided a fun addition | 3.3 | 4 |
| Q11 | I was wary all the time                                | 3.5 | 4   |
| Q12 | I think the game violates my privacy                   | 2.0 | 2   |
| Q13 | The battle system supports stalking others             | 3.8 | 4   |
| Q14 | It was easy to take a photo of an opponent             | 3.1 | 3   |
| Q15 | The UI worked well                                     | 2.5 | 2   |
| Q16 | The UI was fast enough to be used while in battle      | 2.0 | 2   |
| Q17 | When judging, was it easy to recognize yourself?       | 2.8 | 3   |
| Q18 | The game functioned flawlessly                         | 2.4 | 2   |
| Q19 | Fighting with others was social                        | 4.4 | 4   |
| Q20 | I think other players cheated                          | 2   | 2   |

The first main theme in the questionnaire relates to the game mechanics, that is, is it fun to use camera as the main form of interaction in the game. The player responses were very positive, as seen in the first six questions Q1-Q6. The questionnaire suggested that the technical implementation of the game was not optimal, since the questions relating to the using photos in game (Q1, Q3, Q4) had a higher average than those relating to the actual game implementation (Q2, Q5).

The second theme we wanted to study was how the game integrates to a normal working day. This game was not meant to be an intense experience, that is played constantly, but rather have it run in the background of your normal daily routines. The five questions (Q7-Q11) find answers to how the game related to a normal working day. One should note that the first game had two players virtually unable to play due to their workload, and thus we did not include their answers in the analysis. With them, the game was not at all compatible with their normal daily routine. Questions Q7 suggests that the game lightened up a normal working day. Q8 and Q9 suggest that work was affected by the game, and vice versa, which is more related to which the person finds more interesting. As the games were played in a normal working environment, there were more non players than there were players. Q10 gives positive feedback on such a setting, but this question is too vague and requires further study in more detail. Q11 relates also to privacy, but it suggests people's attention is diverged away from their normal daily routines, since they are more aware of other people and players around them.

The third theme in such a game is privacy. Since other players are followed constantly, this is a really serious issue in the game, but question Q12 gives very positive results in this regard. Only two players answered definitely yes, and two yes, which means the vast majority of the players did not find the game offending. One player commented: "How could it, all players joined voluntarily." Players agreed that the game supports stalking (Q13), but as one player stated in comments:"You must sneak to do well".

The fourth part of the questionnaire (Q14-Q18) concerned the implementation of the game, and this got the worst feedback from the participants. Especially the UI was considered to be a problem. This is mostly a problem of the network bandwidth. Although we kept the image sizes to a minimum it still takes time to upload images to a server over a normal wireless connection.

There were two important questions that do not fall under these categories. First, the social aspect (Q19) of the game is highly important, since the game happens in the real world. The game was meant to support the existing social networks already available in groups, and the game succeeds in this regard. Only one player was definitely sure that someone cheated (Q20), although cheating in the game was possible. One player reported taking a photo of a photo of the player, which is cheating.

### 3.5  Player Comments

We asked the players to give freeform comments relating to all questions, or anything else in the game. Some comments proposed very good improvements to the game, some focused on technical problems, and some to the gaming experience.

One obvious fault found in the first game was the easy targets. Some players were playing the game not very intensively, and thus were easy prey for the hunters. To counter this, one player suggested a game form in which players can gain points only once for each other player. In this game, the first player to take a good photo of each other player first wins.

The second and third groups were annoyed by the fact that the game was over so fast. They proposed that only one photo per hour (or other fixed time) could be taken, in order to allow playing the game casually even if working on the same open office space. This could add another layer of excitement to the game, and should be considered seriously.

The fourth group thought there could have been more players, since they were only five players. One player was teaching a student group for a part of the game, and was easy prey for the other players. One player also suggested a delay for taking the pictures, as also proposed in the previous group.

## 4   Technical Performances

Connected mobile games always cost money. Data is being moved over a wireless cell network, and this often has a price tag directly proportional to transferred bytes. Assassin was designed to move as little data as possible.

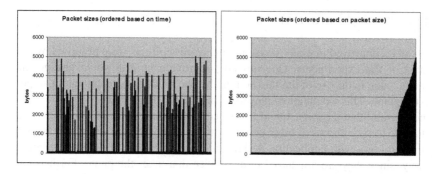

**Fig. 3.** Data upload traffic in the game during game 1

Data traffic for each player consists of downloaded and uploaded data. Both were analyzed from test games of Assassin. From analysis, we can see that the traffic consists of large number of small requests to the server and few big ones when images are uploaded onto the server. These requests are illustrated in Fig. 3., first over time and then ordered by size to show the portions of messages of different sizes. 89% of the sent requests are small ones, while remaining 11% include an image upload. Overall median request size was 91 bytes, while largest single request was nearly five kilobytes in size. Summing these requests up for each player of Assassin, average upload traffic per player was 24 kilobytes during the test game session, where amounts varied between 4 and 69 kilobytes based on player's activeness in the game.

Download data includes the same images that others have uploaded, as well as more application data as game UIs are downloaded. Excluding the image downloads, median download package size was 738 bytes, where largest package was nearly five

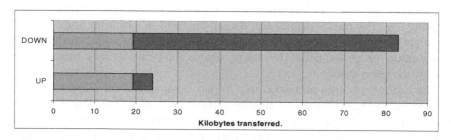

**Fig. 4.** Average data uploads per player. Images take about 19 kilobytes per player, and the rest is application logic.

kilobytes. This traffic summed up per player resulted in average download of 64 kilobytes, plus the image downloads which averages to about 19 kilobytes per player,bringing grand total to 83 kilobytes per player, as seen in Fig 4. . Again, player activity affects this a lot, as download amounts between players varied from 7 to 217 kilobytes, plus image downloads.

## 5  Discussion and Future Work

Assassin can be improved in many ways, and many possibilities were proposed by the participants of the experiments. One obvious improvement that would change the tactics in the game is the use of digital zoom in the phone, that is, implements a sniper scope to the game. This would allow players to better stay unnoticed.

It is not certain, that the game could be played in all countries. It is forbidden or at least not polite to take photos of other people without telling them about this. Assassin tackles this problem with application design. In Assassin photos are not taken in the normal way, since they are not stored in the device that takes the photo. Further, the photos are sent to the target, who does not store the photo either. Only subscribed players are part of the game, no other can receive the photos taken in the game. We do not consider the game to be a violation of privacy more than the normal camera is. Any technology can be abused, if so desired, and Assassin only works inside a group, to not encourage misuse.

Photos can be used in many other ways in gaming, and we are implementing other camera games that do not take photos of other people. The four games also provided us a lot of further data in the form of user comments, which we will be analyzing next.

## 6  Conclusions

This paper presented assassin, a mobile multiplayer game that uses camera as the main form of player-to-player interaction. The game is constantly running, but it is only played whenever the players meet, and thus should adapt to the social rhythm of a normal day. The more players meet, the more opportunities there is for playing.

The game was tested in four games with in a varying environment during a normal working day. The results suggest that the environment in which the game is played has a great affect on how the game is played. The number of social meetings had a direct effect on opportunities for taking photos, and this directly impacted how quickly the game ended.

The camera was seen as a good way to play a game, and the players were very pleased with using the camera as the main form of interaction. The game did not integrate perfectly with a normal working day, since the game took sometimes too much time and did not allow players to concentrate on their main task that was work. Some improvements were suggested, such as limiting how often players can attack. Privacy was not seen as a problem, and the implementation got the most critique.

## Acknowledgements

We like to thank Kai Bergström, Tero Järvensivu, Johanna Mäkinen, Henna Vainiola, Kristiina Palomäki and Kenneth Aro for an excellent implementation on Assassin.

## References

1. Nokia. The mobile device market. Available online at http://www.nokia.com/link?cid= EDITORIAL_803
2. Bucolo, S., Billinghurst, M., and Sickinger, D. 2005. Mobile maze: a comparison of camera based mobile game human interfaces. In Proceedings of the 7th international Conference on Human Computer interaction with Mobile Devices & Services. MobileHCI '05, vol. 111. ACM Press, New York, NY, 329-330.
3. Sony. 2003. Eyetoy. Available online at http://www.eyetoy.com
4. Björk, S., Falk, J. , Hansson, R. , and Ljungstrand., P. 2001. Pirates! – using the physical world as a game board. In Proceedings of the Human-Computer Interaction INTERACT'01, 2001, 423-430.
5. B. Thomas, B. Close, J. Donoghue, J. Squires, P. D. Bondi, and W. Piekarski. First person indoor/outdoor augmented reality application: Arquake. Personal Ubiquitous Computing, 6(1):75–86, 2002.
6. ARToolKit. Available online at: http://www.hitl.washington.edu/artoolkit/
7. Henrysson, A. and Ollila, M. 2004. UMAR: Ubiquitous Mobile Augmented Reality. In Proceedings of the 3rd international Conference on Mobile and Ubiquitous Multimedia. MUM '04, vol. 83. ACM Press, New York, NY, 41-45.
8. Laser Tag. Available online at: http://www.lasertag.org/
9. Id software. Quake series. Available online at: http://www.idsoftware.com/
10. Eidos Inc. Thief 3. Available online at: http://www.thief3.com/
11. S. Jackson. Killer – the game of assassination. Available online at: http://www.sjgames.com/killer/
12. Kindberg, T., Spasojevic, M., Fleck, R., and Sellen, A. 2005. The Ubiquitous Camera: An In-Depth Study of Camera Phone Use. *IEEE Pervasive Computing* 4, 2 (Apr. 2005), 42-50.
13. Suomela, R., Räsänen, E., Koivisto, A., and Mattila, J. 2004. Open-Source Game Development with the Multi-user Publishing Environment (MUPE) Application Platform. In proceedings of the Third International Conference on entertainment Computing (Eindhoven, The Netherlands, September 1-3, 2004). ICEC 2004. Lecture Notes in Computer Science. Springer-Verlag GmbH.

# Enjoyment or Engagement? Role of Social Interaction in Playing Massively Mulitplayer Online Role-Playing Games (MMORPGS)

Vivian Hsueh-Hua Chen[1], Henry Been-Lirn Duh[2], Priscilla Siew Koon Phuah[1], and Diana Zi Yan Lam[1]

[1] 31 Nanyang Link, School of Communication and Information, Nanyang Technological University, Singapore, 637718
{chenhh, S8315167F, S8323234}@ntu.edu.sg
[2] 50 Nanyang Avenue, Center for Human Factors and Ergonomics
Nanyang Technological University, Singapore
mblduh@ntu.edu.sg

**Abstract.** Based on data collected through 40 in-depth interviews, it is found that (a) the balance between perceived challenges and skills, and (b) the types of in-game social interactions can both facilitate and impede the enjoyment of game playing. Through these two factors, a conclusive link was also found between game enjoyments and a gamer's engagement level. Engaged gamers experience optimal enjoyment more frequently and value the importance of social interactions more than non-engaged gamers. In addition, game enjoyment can be enhanced through game design and it can also be adversely affected by real world contextual factors and technical difficulties. More importantly, the study underlines the importance of social interaction. Social interaction is the key factor that determines the level of engagement of gamers. For engaged gamers, social interaction is essential in this gaming experience. For non-engaged gamers, social interaction is not important and they have little tolerance of negative social interaction within the game.

**Keywords:** MMORPG, engagement, enjoyment.

## 1 Introduction

Enjoyment is a complex experience, and it likely reflects the intersection of a variety of factors, including cognitive, affective, social and physiological elements [7]. Previous studies on enjoyment [7] typically explored the enjoyment of traditional media, such as books, music, film and television viewing. They overlooked the uprising new media, computer games. Poole [10] argues that games are finally becoming accepted as a mature medium for entertainment. Online game is an extremely successful new medium with arguably the greatest significance for the everyday consumption of new media [8]. The current study investigates entertainment, enjoyment and engagement of playing Massively Mulitplayer Online Role-playing Games (MMORPGs).

R. Harper, M. Rauterberg, M. Combetto (Eds.): ICEC 2006, LNCS 4161, pp. 262–267, 2006.

## 1.1  Current Research Trend

Current literatures on MMORPGs address three main aspects: the structural aspects of the game, the effects and impacts of gaming, and the gamers. Studies focus on the game features and the structural aspects of games sought to find out the preferred elements of the game [2]. However, these studies only elaborated on the features preferred, without considering why gamers were using these features and how they affected the enjoyment of the game itself.

Studies focus on the effects of gaming explore both possible positive [5] and negative [1] impacts of gaming. Negative effects include violence, aggression, and addiction [14]. Besides investigating the negative impact of gaming, positive effects of video gaming have also been examined. Green and Bavelier [5] found that non players trained on an action video game show marked improvement in their perceptual and motor skills compared to their pre-training abilities.

Studies focused on gamers have typically focused on gamers' motivations [4] [8]. One common reason that ran across all the studies is the social interaction that gamers have within the game. The challenge and competition that the game poses is another important motivation. Other factors include the ability for gamers to immerse or escape into the fantasy world that the game provides. Some studies focusing on the gamer themselves have developed player typologies and explored the profile of the online gamer [14], while others studied the virtual communities that gamers have forged within the gaming world of MMORPGs [3] [12]. Other studies differentiated gamers according to their engagement level with online games. However, the reasons behind such different levels of engagement have not yet been explored. This study therefore focuses on gamers' enjoyment and engagement of playing MMORPGs.

## 1.2  Enjoyment of MMORPG

Several key factors influence the enjoyment of MMORPG: Social interaction, the ratio between gamers' skills and the difficulty of the game, and anti-enjoyment factors.

Social interaction in MMORPGs forms an intrinsic part of game play, as compared to other computer or online game genres such as adventure games. This social aspect of MMORPGs, referring to the ability of gamers to construct friendships, build communities and engage in social interactions in the virtual world, is often stated as one of the reasons for the increasing popularity of MMORPGs [4] [8].

Previous studies have also utilized the conceptual framework of Flow Theory to gain a better understanding of games [2] [10] [13]. Flow theory addresses the relationship between the skills of the player and the difficulty of the game. Dimensions include: apathy, anxiety, flow and relaxation. However, none of the studies explored the enjoyment of playing games while recognizing and emphasizing the importance of social interactions within the game

Past research also fails to address factors that disrupt the flow and enjoyment of gaming. Studies have shown that gamers who have experienced flow are more likely to be addicted [2]. By finding out the factors that would obstruct game flow, the link between sustained game play and enjoyment could be exploited, and excessive gaming controlled.

### 1.3  Research Focus

To summarize, the enjoyment and engagement of playing MMORPGs provides an important, overriding explanation for why people continue to play games. Enjoyment has been found to be a factor that determines media usage [4]. However, previous research focused only on motivations, [4] [8], and overlooked the concept of enjoyment and engagement, as well as the circumstances promoting it. Therefore, the present study addresses three research questions: What makes the experience of playing MMORPGs enjoyable? How do the factors influencing enjoyment explain a gamer's level of engagement? What are the factors that disrupt MMORPG enjoyment?

## 2  Methodology

Semi-structured interviews were conducted to provide a holistic account of the participants' gaming experiences. Forty participants (20 each for non-engaged and engaged gamers), 31 male and 9 female, age 14 to 27, were subsequently selected for in-depth interview. Non-engaged gamers spend an average of 10 to 12 hours per week on online gaming, while engaged gamers spend an average of 35 to 37 hours per week on online gaming. The MMORPGs they played are Maple Story, World of Warcraft, Ragnarok Online, Conquer Online, City of Heroes, Guild Wars, Goonzu and MU Online.

Interview questions were formulated based on the theoretical framework of flow theory and in-game social interactions. All interviews were then transcribed verbatim and analyzed using constant comparison method [7].

## 3  Results

Enjoyment of playing MMORPGs is influenced by a variety of factors. It is found that both the ratio of challenge to skills and the types of social interactions one has within the game can both enhance and disrupt the gaming experience.

Figure 1 shows how each factor affects enjoyment, as well as the level of engagement with the game.

### 3.1  Factors Facilitating Game Enjoyment

Factors that promote enjoyment include the experiential states of flow (where perceived challenge equals perceived skills and both are higher than an individual's subjective mean) and relaxation (where skills are perceived as greater than challenges), game design and positive social interactions. Positive social interaction include behaviors such as prosocial behavior, collaboration, and inter-mingling.

### 3.2  Factors Impeding Game Enjoyment

Other factors that disrupt enjoyment include the experiential states of apathy (where perceived challenge equals perceived skills but both are lower than an individual's subjective mean) and anxiety (where perceived challenges are greater than skills), real

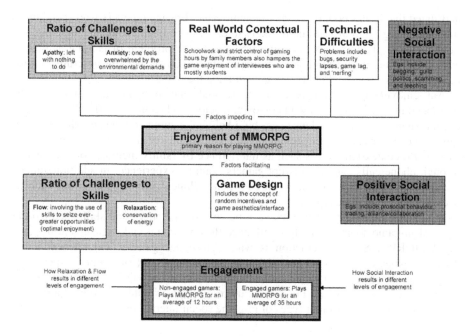

**Fig. 1.** Factors Facilitating and Impeding Game Enjoyment

world contextual factors, technical difficulties, as well as negative social interactions. Negative social interactions include behaviors such as begging, bullying, scamming, guild politics and leeching.

## 4   Discussion and Conclusion

Social interaction within MMORPGs is of paramount importance, influencing both the enjoyment and the level of engagement that a gamer has. The enjoyment that gamers derive from the game is affected by the level of skills and challenges perceived by the gamer, positive social interactions and the game design. When the level of skills and challenge as perceived by the gamer is higher than the subjective mean, the experiential state of flow/deep enjoyment is achieved within the game. Game enjoyment can also be derived from the experiential state of relaxation where skills are perceived to be much higher than the level of challenges. Enjoyment is greatly enhanced when the game provides opportunities for pleasurable social interactions such as grouping and socializing, resulting in the formation of social ties. A reinforcing stimulus is built into the game design, through the random nature of drops and rewards. This built up of anticipation for future rewards as gamers are never sure when the next essential item will be dropped, adds on to their enjoyment and tempts gamers to game even further.

Especially important is the link between social interaction and engagement. Non-engaged gamers found social interaction a waste of time and a hindrance to their game play. Conversely all engaged gamers valued social interactions within the game and stated that it was both important and enjoyable. Engaged gamers who spend more time and energy in game are more likely to experience flow. However, high engagement of game playing does not necessary lead to the problem of gaming addiction. This may be due to self-regulation exercised by the gamers who purposefully control their gaming habit even though they are enjoying the game.

Anti-enjoyment factors include the experiential states of apathy and anxiety, negative social interactions, real world contextual factors and technical difficulties. Apathy occurs when skills and challenges are both below the subjective mean, while anxiety sets in when the challenges presented are too difficult for the gamers to deal with. Real world contextual factors such as interference by family members or disturbance through phone calls can also disrupt gamers' gaming experience. In addition, enjoyment of the game is also compromised when technical problems crop up, such as hacking, bugs and game lag.

In conclusion, a) the balance between perceived challenges and skills, and (b) the types of in-game social interaction influence the enjoyment and engagement of playing MMORPG. Social interaction is what determines gamers' engagement level. Engaged gamers view social interaction as an essential part of gaming experience. Non-engaged gamers do not value social interaction and have little tolerance for negative social interaction within the game. Future research should aim to gain a holistic understanding of the different types of in-game social interaction.

# References

1. Anderson, C., & Bushman, B. J. (2001). Effects of violent video games on aggressive behaviour, aggressive cognition, aggressive effect, physiological arousal and prosocial behaviour: A meta-analytic review of the scientific literature. Psychological Science, 12, 353-359.
2. Choi, D., & Kim, J. (2004). Why people continue to play online games: In search of critical design factors to increase customer loyalty to online contents. CyberPsychology & Behavior, 7(1), 11-34.
3. Ducheneaut, N., & Moore, R. J. (2004, November). The social side of gaming: A study of interaction patterns in a MMORPG. Paper presented at the Proceedings of Computer Supported Cooperative Work (CSCW) 2004, Chicago, Illinois, USA.
4. Friedl, M. (2003). Online game interactivity theory. Hingham, Massachusetts: Charles River Media, Inc.
5. Green, C. S., & Bavelier, D. (2003). Action video game modifies visual selective attention. Nature, 423, 534-537.
6. Griffiths, M. (2000). Does Internet and computer "addiction" exist? Some case study evidence. CyberPsychology & Behavior, 3(2), 211-218.
7. Lincoln, Y. S., & Guba, E. G. (1985). Naturalistic inquiry. Beverly Hills, California: Sage Publications.
8. Lister, M., Dovey, J., Giddings, S., Grant, I., & Kelly, K. (2003). New media: A critical introduction. New York: Routledge.
9. Oliver, M. B., & Nabi, R. L. (2004). Exploring the concept of media enjoyment: An introduction to the special issue. Communication Theory, 14(4), 285-287.
10. Poole, S. (2000). Trigger happy: The inner life of videogames. London: Fourth Estate.
11. Rouse, R. (2001). Game design: Theory & practice. Plano, Texas: Wordware Publishing Inc.

12. Schiesel, S. (2005, September 2). Conqueror in a war of virtual worlds. New York Times, 1.
13. Sherry, J. L. (2004). Flow and media enjoyment. Communication Theory, 14(4), 328-347.
14. Sherry, J. L. (2004). The effects of violent video games on aggression: A meta-analysis. Human Communication Research, 27, 409-431.
15. Smith, M. A., Farnham, S. D., & Drucker, S. M. (2000). The social life of small graphical chat spaces. Paper presented at the Proceedings of the Special Interest Group on Computer-Human Interaction (SIGCHI) Conference, The Hague, The Netherlands.
16. Sweetser, P., & Wyeth, P. (2005). GameFlow: A model for evaluating player enjoyment in games. ACM Computers in Entertainment, 3(3), 3A.
17. Whang, L. S. & Chang, G. (2004). Lifestyles of virtual world residents: Living in the online game "lineage". CyberPsychology and Behavior, 7, 592-600.

# On-Line Motion Style Transfer

Xiaomao Wu[1], Lizhuang Ma[1], Can Zheng[1], Yanyun Chen[2], and Ke-Sen Huang[3]

[1] Department of Computer Science & Engineering, Shanghai Jiao Tong University
No. 800, Dongchuan Road, Shanghai 200240, P. R. China
wu.xiaomao@gmail.com, ma-lz@cs.sjtu.edu.cn, z_oasis@sjtu.edu.cn
[2] Microsoft Research Asia
No. 49, Zhichun Road, Haidian District, Beijing 100080, P. R. China
yachen@microsoft.com
[3] Department of Computer Science
National Tsing Hua University
101, Kuang Fu Rd, Sec.2
HsingChu, Taiwan 300 R.O.C.
kesen.huang@gmail.com

**Abstract.** Motion capture techniques play an important role in computer animation. Because the cost of motion capture data is relatively high and the virtual environment changes frequently in actual applications, researchers in this area focus their work on developing algorithms for editing the capture motion data, and synthesizing new motions from available motion database. Although abundant work has been done on motion editing and synthesis, few of them obviously take motion styles into consideration. Meanwhile, existing style editing algorithms either need an obvious definition of "style", or need a time-consuming training process. In this paper, we propose a fast and convenient algorithm for human-motion style editing. We define the style of motion as statistic properties of mean and standard variance of joint quaternions in 4D unit sphere space. The proposed algorithm can transfer the style of a motion to another by transferring these properties. Experiment results demonstrate that our approach has the advantages of fast execution, low memory occupation, and easy implementation. It can be widely applied to various real-time entertainment-computing applications, such as gaming and digital movie producing.

**Keywords:** motion editing, motion style, style transfer, quaternion mean and variance.

## 1 Introduction

Motion capture techniques have been widely adopted in digital movie producing, gaming and other digital entertainment applications. Creating animations with motion capture techniques commonly consists of the following three steps: First, acquire 3D motion data from real actors or actress with available commercial motion capture devices. Second, map the acquired data onto virtual characters. Finally, edit and fine-tune the mapped motion until satisfactory results are obtained. Compared with traditional keyframing techniques and procedure-based methods, motion capture techniques provide a more reliable and convenient way for creating realistic character animation.

R. Harper, M. Rauterberg, M. Combetto (Eds.): ICEC 2006, LNCS 4161, pp. 268–279, 2006.
© IFIP International Federation for Information Processing 2006

The key issue with motion capture techniques is: how to process the captured motion data so that it can satisfy the constraints of specific applications. Abundant work has been done on this issue. We can classify them into two categories: motion editing and motion synthesis. Among those works, few of them take motion style into consideration, despite that motion style is an important issue for motion editing and synthesis. Meanwhile, existing motion style editing approaches either rely on procedural definition of the motion styles [1, 2, 3], or explicit input of style parameters of the user [2, 3], or even a model-training process [4, 5].

In this paper, we propose a new on-line algorithm for motion style transfer. The proposed algorithm does not need any user's input, or expensive training process. The basic idea of the proposed algorithm is to encode motion style in a statistic distribution model, and transfer the style of one motion to another by transferring the according model parameters. As illustrated in Fig. 1, the proposed approach in this paper can transfer the style of the reference motion $\mathcal{M}_r$ to the source motion $\mathcal{M}_s$, resulting in a new motion $\mathcal{M}_t$ which preserves the motion details of $\mathcal{M}_s$ and inherits the style of $\mathcal{M}_r$. For example, we can transfer the "stride" style from a stride-working motion $\mathcal{M}_r$ to a normal running motion $\mathcal{M}_s$, resulting a new "stride running" motion $\mathcal{M}_t$.

Among the existing motion style editing approaches, Hsu et al.'s [5] work is most related to ours. Our work differs from theirs in the following aspects: First, Hsu et al. use two motions (one basic motion and one motion with style) for defining a motion style, while we use only one motion and abstract the style directly from that motion. This difference is very similar to the difference between the work of Reinhard [6]'s and of Hertzmann [7]'s in the field of image processing. Another difference between our work and Hsu's is that their method use time-consuming N4SID algorithm to train a LTI (linear time identification) model. Our approach does not need this process, thus can transfer the style from one motion to another on the fly.

## 2   Related Work

Many techniques have been proposed for modifying captured motion data so that it can meet different requirements of actual applications. In general, these techniques can be classified into two categories: motion editing and motion synthesis. Here we only review motion editing techniques because it is more related to our work.

Spline fitting [8, 9], signal processing [10] and constrained optimization [11, 12, 13] have been successfully applied to motion editing. Although these methods are useful for editing kinematic and dynamic properties of motions, they do not explicitly take motion style into consideration.

Among the motion editing techniques, motion retargetting mainly focuses on designing a mapping function which can be used to map the motion of a figure to another one who has identical skeleton topology but different segment length [14, 15, 16], or even has different skeleton topology [17, 18] as the first one. Our work differs from them in that their work focus on processing kinematic and dynamic constraints when retargetting a motion of a character to another, while our work concentrates on transferring the style from one motion to another. Meanwhile, motion retargetting techniques treat style and motion as a whole, and do not treat the style of motion separately. Our method separates style from motion, and treats style and motion details as two different layers.

Comparing to motion editing techniques, few work have been done for motion style editing. Amaya et al. [1] introduce an algorithm which can transform the emotion of a motion to another. Unuma et al. [2] successfully use Fourier series expansions of the motion data sets to do expansion, smooth transition, interpolation, and even extrapolation between different types of motions. Brand et al. [4]'s style machine can be trained to create motions with different styles. Urtasun et al. [3] propose an algorithm which can be used to change the style of a motion by projecting it onto a PCA space generated by pre-existing motion data. More recently, Hsu et al. [5] use linear space identification analysis to obtain a style translation model between two motions.

Style editing is also explored by researchers in the filed of image processing. Two representative image style transfer approaches are respectively proposed by Reinhard et al. [6] and Hertzmann et al. [7]. Our work is inspired by Reinhard's work [6] which has obtained convincing results for transferring the color characteristics of one image onto another with an efficient statistical analysis.

## 3   Overview

The overview of our approach is illustrated in Fig. 1. The goal of our approach is to transfer the style of the reference motion $\mathcal{M}_r$ to the source motion $\mathcal{M}_s$, producing a target motion $\mathcal{M}_t$. The target motion can preserve the details of the source motion and can inherit the style of the reference motion. The style transfer pipeline works as follows: First, $\mathcal{M}_s$ and $\mathcal{M}_r$ are input directly into the time warping module to setup frame correspondence. Then, the time-warped motions are fed into the statistic style transfer module for style transferring. In the post-processing stage, we apply a reverse-time-warping to the target motion $\mathcal{M}_t$ and then remove artifacts such as footskate which is introduced during the style translation process. After that, we can obtain the target motion that inherits the style of the reference motion and preserve the details of the source motion.

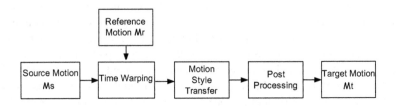

**Fig. 1.** Overview of our approach

## 4   Time Warping

The frame correspondences are vitally important for motion style transfer. Without proper frame correspondence, unnatural results may be produced. We use the IMW (iterative motion warping) algorithm proposed by Hsu et al. [5], because it performs better then other proposed DTW (dynamic time warping) algorithms when dealing with stylistically different motions.

The IMW algorithm process one DOF (degree of freedom) each time. Suppose the frame numbers of the source motion $\mathcal{M}_s$ and the reference motion $\mathcal{M}_r$ are $N_s$ and $N_r$ respectively. We further suppose that $N_s < N_r$. When $N_s \geq N_r$, we only need to exchange the position of $\mathbf{S}$ and $\mathbf{r}$ in equation 1. The IMW algorithm aims at minimizing the following energy equation:

$$E(\mathbf{a}, \mathbf{b}, \mathbf{W}) = \|\mathbf{W}(\mathbf{Sa} + \mathbf{b}) - \mathbf{r}\|^2 + \|\mathbf{Fa}\|^2 + \|\mathbf{Fb}\|^2 + \|\mathbf{Gb}\|^2 \qquad (1)$$

Here, $\mathbf{S}$ is a diag($s$), whose diagnose elements contains one DOF data of $\mathcal{M}_s$. $\mathbf{W}$ is a *warp matrix* used to perform a nonuniform time warp. The terms $\|\mathbf{Fa}\|^2$ and $\|\mathbf{Gb}\|^2$ measure the smoothness of $\mathbf{a}$ and $\mathbf{b}$. $\mathbf{F}$ and $\mathbf{G}$ provide weighted finite-difference approximations to the first derivative of $\mathbf{a}$ and $\mathbf{b}$.

The IMW algorithm works as following:

First, initialize $\mathbf{a} = 1$ and $\mathbf{b} = 0$.

Second, calculate matrix $\mathbf{W}$ with dynamic time warping, i. e., solve the following linear equation:

$$\min_{\mathbf{W}} \|\mathbf{Wp} - \mathbf{q}\|^2 = \min_{w} \left\| \begin{bmatrix} l_{w1} & & & \\ & l_{w2} & & \\ & & \ddots & \\ & & & l_{wN_s} \end{bmatrix} \mathbf{p} - \mathbf{q} \right\|^2 \qquad (2)$$

where $\mathbf{p} = \mathbf{Sa} + \mathbf{b}$ and $\mathbf{q} = \mathbf{r}$.

Third, solve scale vector $\mathbf{a}$ and offset vector $\mathbf{b}$ with the following equation which is transformed from equation 1:

$$\begin{bmatrix} \mathbf{S}^T \mathbf{W}^T \mathbf{WS} + \mathbf{F}^T \mathbf{F} & \mathbf{S}^T \mathbf{W}^T \mathbf{W} \\ \mathbf{W}^T \mathbf{WS} & \mathbf{W}^T \mathbf{W} + \mathbf{G}^T \mathbf{G} \end{bmatrix} \begin{bmatrix} \mathbf{a} \\ \mathbf{b} \end{bmatrix} = \begin{bmatrix} \mathbf{S}^T \mathbf{W}^T \mathbf{r} \\ \mathbf{W}^T \mathbf{r} \end{bmatrix} \qquad (3)$$

The above steps are performed iteratively until the change of $\mathbf{a}$ and $\mathbf{b}$ between two consecutive iteration is below a pre-defined threshold. For more detailed description of the IMW algorithm, please refer to the original paper [5].

## 5    Statistic Style Transfer

In this section, we first introduce the representation of the motion and the statistic components which will be utilized for designing the style transfer pipeline. And then, we introduce the style transfer algorithm for the root joint, followed by a detailed description of the style transfer algorithm in the Euclidean space and in the 4D quaternion space. For convenience and clarity of description, we only discuss one joint in this section. Other joints can be processed in the same way, except that the root joint should be considered separately because it contains global translation components.

### 5.1    Motion Representation and Style Definition

A motion can be denoted by $\mathbf{m}(t) = (\mathbf{p}(t), \mathbf{q}^1(t), ..., \mathbf{q}^n(t))^T$, where $\mathbf{p}(t) \in \mathbb{R}^3$ and $\mathbf{q}^1(t) \in \mathbb{S}^3$ represent the translation and rotation of the root joint. $\mathbf{q}^i(t) \in \mathbb{S}^3$ denotes the rotation of the $i$-th joint for $2 \leq i \leq n$.

In the research community of image processing, Reighar et al. [6] define the style of an image as the mean and standard variance of color components in a linearized color space $l\alpha\beta$, and has successfully transfer the style of an image to another by transferring the mean and standard variance of color components in this space. Inspired by Reighar's work, we also use mean and standard variance to represent the style of a motion. In the remaining part of this paper, we briefly describe "standard variance" as "variance". With this representation, motion style can be transferred by modifying the mean and variance of the source motion $\mathcal{M}_s$ according to that of the reference motion $\mathcal{M}_r$. However, our experiment results demonstrate that straightforwardly apply the style transfer algorithm to Euler angles produces poor results, while applying the algorithm to quaternion domain can give us smooth results. And since the mean and variance have no unified meanings for quaternions, we give our definition of quaternion mean and variance in Section 5.4.

In our implementation, we assume that each joint is independent of the others, following [10, 8, 5]. While doing the style transfer, we translate one joint at a time. All joints are passed through the style transfer stage one by one.

## 5.2  Transfer for the Root Joint

We treat the root joint separately because it encodes a transformation with respect to the global coordinate system. The translation part of the root joint is translated separately for each dimension. Because motion style is invariant to ground plane translation, we encode the translation of the root joint of each frame in its previous frame [5, 19]. We first calculate the mean and variance of the translations of the root joints of the source motion $\mathcal{M}_s$ and the reference motion $\mathcal{M}_r$ respectively, and then transfer each of the three translation DOFs as:

$$\mathbf{p}_t^i = \sigma_r/\sigma_s \cdot (\mathbf{p}_s^i - \bar{\mathbf{p}}_s) + \bar{\mathbf{p}}_r, 1 \leq i \leq N_s \qquad (4)$$

where $N_s$ is the frame number of $\mathcal{M}_s$ after time warping. $\mathbf{p}_s^i$ and $\mathbf{p}_t^i$ denote the $i$-th DOF of the root joint of $\mathcal{M}_s$ and $\mathcal{M}_t$. $\bar{\mathbf{p}}_s$ and $\bar{\mathbf{p}}_r$ denote the mean of the root joint angle of $\mathcal{M}_s$ and $\mathcal{M}_t$. $\sigma_s$ and $\sigma_r$ denote the variance of the root joint of $\mathcal{M}_s$ and $\mathcal{M}_t$, respectively. The vertical rotation is preserved by encoding the root orientation in the previous frame, as suggested by Kovar [19] and Hsu [5].

## 5.3  Transfer with Euler Angles

Transfer with Euler angles is straightforward. Our algorithm transfers each DOF individually. Specifically, let $\bar{\theta}_s$ and $\sigma_s$ denote the mean and variance of the source motion $\mathcal{M}_s$, and $\bar{\theta}_r$ and $\sigma_r$ denote the mean and variance of the reference motion $\mathcal{M}_r$. The transferred angle is calculated as

$$\theta_t = \sigma_r/\sigma_s \cdot (\theta_s - \bar{\theta}_s) + \bar{\theta}_r \qquad (5)$$

where $\theta_t$ represents the transferred angle of the target motion $\mathcal{M}_t$.

Our experiments demonstrate that style transfer with Euler angles does not produce smooth results in most cases (Fig. 2), because interpolation of Euler angles may result in poor rotations [20].

**Fig. 2.** Style translation with Euler angles produces unnatural results, shown in red

### 5.4 Transfer with Quaternions

Representing rotations and orientations by quaternions is widely adopted in computer animation as it is free of gimbal lock and has good interpolation behavior [21, 22, 23, 9]. Quaternion is also an ideal representation for our style transfer operation. However, we should carefully choose the meaning of "mean" and "variance" in quaternion space. Although quaternions can be linearly interpolated and we can define the mean with linear interpolation. This definition will result in inconsistent velocities [24]. By using a recursive definition based on the sphere linear interpolation ($Slerp$) [21], we can obtain a well defined centroid, or the mean of a sequence of quaternions. Meanwhile, we define the distance between two quaternions on the 4-D hypersphere, and use this definition to derive the variance of quaternions.

**Mean and Variance of Quaternions.** Let $\mathbf{q}_i$ for $0 \leq i \leq n$ denotes a sequence of $n$ quaternions. The mean of $\mathbf{q}_i$s can be recursively defined as:

$$\bar{\mathbf{q}}_n = \begin{cases} \mathbf{q}_1 \ , for \ n = 1 \\ Slerp(\frac{1}{2}, \mathbf{q}_1, \mathbf{q}_2), for \ n = 2 \\ Slerp(\frac{n-1}{n}, \bar{\mathbf{q}}_{n-1}, \mathbf{q}_n), for \ n \geq 3 \end{cases} \tag{6}$$

Here, $Slerp$ is a sphere linear interpolation function [21] which can be defined by: $Slerp(t, \mathbf{q}_1, \mathbf{q}_2) = \frac{\sin(1-t)\theta}{\sin\theta}\mathbf{q}_1 + \frac{\sin u\theta}{\sin\theta}\mathbf{q}_2, \theta = \cos^{-1}(\mathbf{q}_1 \cdot \mathbf{q}_2)$. When doing $Slerp$ between two quaternions $\mathbf{q}_1$ and $\mathbf{q}_2$ during the mean calculation process, one should make sure that the angle between $\mathbf{q}_1$ and $\mathbf{q}_2$ are not larger than $\frac{\pi}{2}$ for consistent representation. This can be done by checking the sign of the dot product of two quaternions $d = \mathbf{q}_1 \cdot \mathbf{q}_2$. If $d < 0$, we reverse the sign of $\mathbf{q}_1$, because $\mathbf{q}_1$ and $-\mathbf{q}_1$ represent the same rotation.

We should mention that besides this definition, other definitions can also be adopted for calculating the mean of quaternions, because mean is a special case of weighted sum. We use the above definition because it is simple and efficient, and can produce reasonable results. Other more rigorous methods exist, such as global linearization [23] and functional optimization [25]. Those algorithms follow more rigorous definition of mean of quaternions, but are more computationally expensive. We have found that equation 6 works well in all of our experiments.

The variance of quaternions is defined similar to its definition for real numbers, except that the distance is defined in $\mathbb{S}^3$ as: $dist(\mathbf{q}_1, \mathbf{q}_2) = ||log(\mathbf{q}_1^{-1}, \mathbf{q}_2)||$. The variances of quaternion sequence of the joint of the source and reference motion, denoted by $\sigma_s$ and $\sigma_t$, are calculated under this definition.

**Transfer Algorithm.** With the definition of mean and variance of quaternion, we can calculate the mean and variance of the source motion, denoted by $\bar{\mathbf{q}}_s$ and $\sigma_s$, and that of the reference motion, denoted by $\bar{\mathbf{q}}_r$ and $\sigma_r$.

The first step of motion style transfer is to transfer the mean of the reference motion to the source motion. This can be implemented by applying a $\mathbf{q}^T$ transformation (Fig. 3). $\mathbf{q}^T$ is defined by: $\mathbf{q}^T = (\bar{\mathbf{q}}_s)^{-1} * \bar{\mathbf{q}}_r$.

By applying transformation $\mathbf{q}^T$ to all the quaternion sequence of the source motion $\mathcal{M}_s$, we can obtain the aligned version of quaternions whose mean is equal to that of the reference motion $\mathcal{M}_r$.

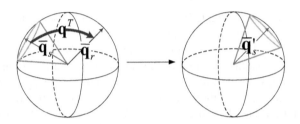

**Fig. 3.** The mean of the joint quaternions of the source motion, denoted by $\bar{\mathbf{q}}_s$, is aligned with that of the reference motion $\bar{\mathbf{q}}_r$ by applying a transform $\mathbf{q}^T$

Finally, we scale the variance of the joint of the source motion according to that of the reference motion by the following equation:

$$\mathbf{q}_t^i = Slerp(\frac{\sigma_r}{\sigma_s}, \bar{\mathbf{q}}_r, \mathbf{q}_s^{i'}) \tag{7}$$

where $\mathbf{q}_s^{i'}$ and $\mathbf{q}_t^i$ are the $i$-th quaternion of the joint of the source motion $\mathcal{M}_s$ and the target motion $\mathcal{M}_t$.

## 6   Post-processing

The purpose of post-process stage is to reverse the time warping effect and process kinematic constraints.

In the reverse-time-warping step, we apply a $Slerp$ for the adjusted frames, in order to bring back the normal timing.

In the kinematic constraints processing step, we apply the footskate cleanup algorithm proposed by Kovar et al. [26] to $\mathcal{M}_t$ in order to obtain correct and smooth results. The footskate cleanup algorithm works as follows: First, the position of each footplant constraint is calculated. For each constrained frame, compute the ankle's global positions and orientations. Then we determine where the root should be placed. For each constrained ankle, adjust the leg so the ankle meets the configurations found previously. Finally, we filter the motion in order to obtain smooth results. Readers are referred to the original paper [26] for detailed description.

# 7    Results

We have tested our algorithm on several captured motion pairs in order to demonstrate its validity and efficiency. All the motion clips are obtained from CMU motion capture library [27].

In the first example, we transfer the "hobble" style of a walk motion to a normal walk motion (Fig. 4), producing a new "hobble walk" motion. In the second example, we transfer the "stealthy" style of a walk motion to a normal walk motion (Fig. 5), producing a new "stealthy walk" motion. In the third example, we transfer "stride" style of a walk motion to a running motion, producing a "stride running" motion (Fig. 6). In the fourth example, we transfer the "jaunty" style of a walk motion to a running motion, producing a "jaunty running" motion (Fig. 7).

All the experiments were done on a Pentium 4 2.8G PC with 1.5GB memory. The computation time are listed in Table 1. The memory usage is negligible, because we

**Fig. 4.** Transfer the "hobble" style of a walking motion (middle) to another walking motion (top) produces a new "hobble walking" motion (bottom)

**Table 1.** The running time of the main steps for four examples in our experiment

| Process (source-reference) | Frame number (source-reference) | Time warping (milliseconds) | Transfer time (milliseconds) | Post-processing time (milliseconds) |
|---|---|---|---|---|
| Normal walk - Hobble walk | 427-400 | 900 | 21 | 80 |
| Normal walk - Stealthy walk | 277-410 | 600 | 17 | 61 |
| Normal running - Stride walk | 135-302 | 300 | 10 | 22 |
| Normal running - Jaunty walk | 135-450 | 400 | 13 | 25 |

**Fig. 5.** Transfer the "stealthy" style of a walking motion (middle) to another walking motion (top) produces a new "stealthy walking" motion (bottom)

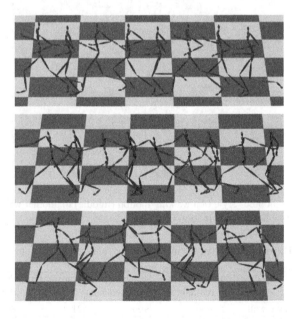

**Fig. 6.** Transfer a "stride" style of a walking motion (middle) to a running motion (top) produces a "stride running" motion (bottom)

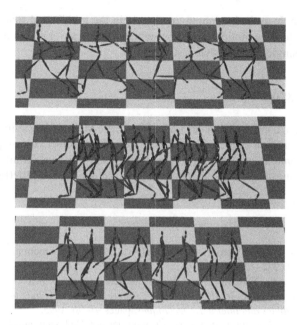

**Fig. 7.** Transfer the "jaunty" style of a walking motion (middle) to a running motion (top) produces a "jaunty running" motion (bottom)

only need to additionally store the time-warping parameters and the mean and variance of the source and reference motion during the style transfer process.

According to the experimental results, our approach runs very fast, occupies negligible memory, which makes it suitable for real-time motion editing applications.

## 8    Conclusion and Discussion

In this paper, we propose a fast and memory efficient algorithm for transferring the style of a motion to another motion. Comparing to existing style transfer approaches, our approach is simple to implement, runs very fast and occupies negligible memory, making it suitable for interactive applications.

Compared with the state-of-the-art work of Hsu's [5], our approach is more suitable for fast prototyping. One may argue that when the training process has been carried out with N4SID, Hsu's LTI model can achieve very fast transfer speed. But the training the LTI model is a time-consuming time, and if the training data is not enough, i. e., the frame number is relatively small, one may not obtain satisfactory results. Meanwhile, the N4SID model is sensitive to input parameters. This could be a problem with inexperienced users. Our approach do not depends on any user input, and can run automatically, with rather fast speed.

Currently, our approach can not be applied to transfer style between figures that do not have identical structures. Existing motion retargetting algorithms [18, 28] may be helpful for solving this problem. Meanwhile, when the reference has several different styles, e. g. hobble at the beginning then stride in the middle and stealthily run at the end, then the reference motion should be segmented into several segments so that each segment has a single distinguishable style.

## Acknowledgements

We would like to thank the Graphics Lab. of Carnegie Mellon University for generously providing their motion capture data on their web. This project was supported by Supported by National Science Fund for Creative Research Groups (grant No. 60521002) and National Natural Science Foundation of China (grant No. 60373070 and 60573147).

## References

1. Kenji Amaya, Armin Bruderlin, and Tom Calvert. Emotion from motion. In *Graphics Interface '96*, pages 222–229, 1996.
2. Munetoshi Unuma, Ken Anjyo, and Ryozo Takeuchi. Fourier principles for emotion-based human figure animation. In *SIGGRAPH '95: Proceedings of the 22nd annual conference on Computer graphics and interactive techniques*, pages 91–96, 1995.
3. Raquel Urtasun, Pascal Glardon, Ronan Boulic, Daniel Thalmann, and Pascal Fua. Style-based motion synthesis. *Computer Graphics Forum*, 23(4):799–812, 2004.
4. Matthew Brand and Aaron Hertzmann. Style machines. In *SIGGRAPH '00: Proceedings of the 27th annual conference on Computer graphics and interactive techniques*, pages 183–192, 2000.
5. Eugene Hsu, Kari Pulli, and Jovan Popović. Style translation for human motion. *ACM Trans. Graph.*, 24(3):1082–1089, July 2005.
6. Erik Reinhard, Michael Ashikhmin, Bruce Gooch, and Peter Shirley. Color transfer between images. *IEEE Computer Graphics and Applications*, 21(5):34–41, Sep.-Oct. 2001.
7. Aaron Hertzmann, Charles E. Jacobs, Nuria Oliver, Brian Curless, and David H. Salesin. Image analogies. In *SIGGRAPH '01: Proceedings of the 28th annual conference on Computer graphics and interactive techniques*, pages 327–340, 2001.
8. Andrew Witkin and Zoran Popović. Motion warping. In *SIGGRAPH '95: Proceedings of the 22nd annual conference on Computer graphics and interactive techniques*, pages 105–108, 1995.
9. Jehee Lee and Sung Yong Shin. A hierarchical approach to interactive motion editing for human-like figures. In *SIGGRAPH '99: Proceedings of the 26th annual conference on Computer graphics and interactive techniques*, pages 39–48, 1999.
10. Armin Bruderlin and Lance Williams. Motion signal processing. In *SIGGRAPH '95: Proceedings of the 22nd annual conference on Computer graphics and interactive techniques*, pages 97–104, 1995.
11. Charles Rose, Brian Guenter, Bobby Bodenheimer, and Michael F. Cohen. Efficient generation of motion transitions using spacetime constraints. In *SIGGRAPH '96: Proceedings of the 23rd annual conference on Computer graphics and interactive techniques*, pages 147–154, 1996.
12. Michael Gleicher. Motion editing with spacetime constraints. In *SI3D '97: Proceedings of the 1997 symposium on Interactive 3D graphics*, pages 139–148, 1997.
13. Anthony C. Fang and Nancy S. Pollard. Efficient synthesis of physically valid human motion. *ACM Trans. Graph.*, 22(3):417–426, 2003.

14. Michael Gleicher. Retargetting motion to new characters. In *SIGGRAPH '98: Proceedings of the 25th annual conference on Computer graphics and interactive techniques*, pages 33–42, 1998.
15. Kwang-Jin Choi and Hyeong-Seok Ko. Online motion retargetting. *Journal of Visualization and Computer Animation*, 11(5):223–235, 2000.
16. Hyun Joon Shin, Jehee Lee, Sung Yong Shin, and Michael Gleicher. Computer puppetry: An importance-based approach. *ACM Trans. Graph.*, 20(2):67–94, 2001.
17. Jean-Sébastien Monzani, Paolo Baerlocher, Ronan Boulic, and Daniel Thalmann. Using an intermediate skeleton and inverse kinematics for motion retargeting. *Compuuter Graphics Forum (Eurographics 2000)*, 19(3), 2000.
18. Min Je Park and Sung Yong Shin. Example-based motion cloning. *Journal of Computer Animation and Virtual Worlds*, 15(3-4):245–257, 2004.
19. Lucas Kovar and Michael Gleicher. Flexible automatic motion blending with registration curves. In *SCA '03: Proceedings of the 2003 ACM SIGGRAPH/Eurographics symposium on Computer animation*, pages 214–224, 2003.
20. F. Sebastian Grassia. Practical parameterization of rotations using the exponential map. *Journal of graphics tools*, 3(3):29–48, 1998.
21. Ken Shoemake. Animating rotation with quaternion curves. In *SIGGRAPH '85: Proceedings of the 12th annual conference on Computer graphics and interactive techniques*, pages 245–254, 1985.
22. Jehee Lee and Sung Yong Shin. A coordinate-invariant approach to multiresolution motion analysis. *Graphical Models*, 63(2):87–105, March 2001.
23. Sang Il Park, Hyun Joon Shin, and Sung Yong Shin. On-line locomotion generation based on motion blending. In *SCA '02: Proceedings of the 2002 ACM SIGGRAPH/Eurographics symposium on Computer animation*, pages 105–111, 2002.
24. Erik B. Dam, Martin Koch, and Martin Lillholm. Quaternions, interpolation and animation. *DIKU technical report 98/5*, 1998.
25. Samuel R. Buss and Jay P. Fillmore. Spherical averages and applications to spherical splines and interpolation. *ACM Trans. Graph.*, 20(2):95–126, 2001.
26. Lucas Kovar, John Schreiner, and Michael Gleicher. Footskate cleanup for motion capture editing. In *SCA '02: Proceedings of the 2002 ACM SIGGRAPH/Eurographics symposium on Computer animation*, pages 97–104, 2002.
27. CMU graphics lab motion capture database. *http://mocap.cs.cmu.edu/*.
28. Maher Moakher. Means and averaging in the group of rotations. *SIAM Journal on Matrix Analysis and Applications*, 24(1):1–16, 2002.

# Dynamic Skinning for Popping Dance

HongJung Son and JungHyun Han*

Game Research Center, College of Information and Communications,
Korea University, Seoul, Korea
hj79337@gmail.com, jhan@korea.ac.kr

**Abstract.** This paper presents an efficient technique to enhance the realism of character animation by adding muscle dynamics. Focusing on the isometric contraction of muscles, the proposed algorithm takes normal mesh and clenched mesh, and uses the disparity between them to simulate the skin vibration. The skin simulation algorithm is integrated with an example-based skinning, and shows real-time performance. The proposed approach proves to be useful for animating popping dance.

**Keywords:** character animation, skinning, mesh deformation.

## 1 Introduction

Skin movement plays a key role in computer animation. The dominant approach to skin animation has been Linear Blend Skinning(LBS)[5]. The LBS algorithm is fast enough to be processed in real-time, is widely used among computer artists, and is also widely supported by commercial applications. However, binding the skin to the bones restricts dynamic effects caused by muscle movement, which is important to make realistic animation. Our goal is to simulate the dynamic skin caused by muscle movement.

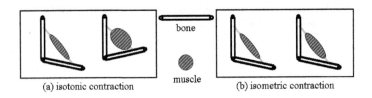

(a) isotonic contraction     (b) isometric contraction

**Fig. 1.** Muscle contraction

The factors that bring changes to skin include bones, muscles, tendon, fat, etc. With respect to muscles, anatomists distinguish between two types of muscle contraction[1]: *isotonic* and *isometric*, as shown in Fig. 1. Upon isotonic contraction, the belly changes shape, often bulging, while the total length of the muscle diminishes so that the bones to which the muscle is attached are pulled

---

* Corresponding author.

R. Harper, M. Rauterberg, M. Combetto (Eds.): ICEC 2006, LNCS 4161, pp. 280–285, 2006.
© IFIP International Federation for Information Processing 2006

towards each other. Upon isometric contraction, the shape of the belly also alters because of the tension in the muscle but the length of the muscle does not change, and therefore no skeletal motion is produced.

The dynamic skin effect caused by the isometric contraction of muscles can be easily found in *popping dance*, where one pumps up the muscles on purpose to bulge muscles. This paper focuses on the isometric contraction to add dynamic effect to the skin, and presents an algorithm for simulating popping dance.

## 2    Related Work and Background

The skinning algorithm is notorious for its failings including *collapsing joint* and *candy-wrapper* problems. A representative effort to resolve the problems is *example-based skinning*, which uses a set of examples typically made by designers [4,5,7,11]. There have been attempts to add dynamic effect to the character skin since Chadwick *et al.*[2]. Turner and Thalmann[10] and Wilhelms and Gelder[12] used an elastic surface to represent a deformable skin layer. James and Pai[3] pre-computed modal analysis of dynamic elastic models and combined vibration modes in real-time using graphics hardware. While this technique gives a physical realism for animation, it requires the animator to have advanced physics knowledge to set up the finite element simulation and to provide a volumetric mesh for the model.

Fig. 2-(a) illustrates a muscle's twitch upon isometric contraction[9]. The time-to-peak denoted by $t_1$ leads to instant *bulging* of muscle. Fig. 2-(b) shows cross sections of human arm, where a complex structure of the muscles can be found. Such a complex structure leads to *skin vibration* when muscles bulge altogether. Skin vibration can be easily found in popping dance. Fig. 3 shows snapshots of skin vibration for a fixed skeletal configuration.

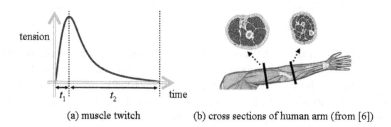

(a) muscle twitch                (b) cross sections of human arm (from [6])

**Fig. 2.** Properties of human muscle

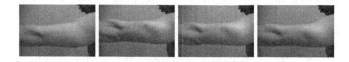

**Fig. 3.** Skin vibration examples from video

## 3    Skin Vibration and Its Integration with Skinning

To capture the popping effect, two meshes are taken as input from the designer, as shown in Fig. 4. One is *normal mesh* of a character, and the other is the mesh with isometric contraction, which we call *clenched mesh*. When one pumps up the muscles, all vertices of the normal mesh are supposed to move to the surface of the clenched mesh, i.e. the *goal position* of a vertex is set to the corresponding vertex position in the clenched mesh.

**Fig. 4.** Normal and clenched meshes

For simulating the skin vibration, a modified version of the integration scheme proposed by [8], which guarantees unconditionally stable simulation, is used to calculate the velocity($v$) and position($x$) of a vertex $i$ with time $t$ and time step $h$:

$$v_i(t + h) = (1 - \alpha)v_i(t) + \alpha\frac{g_i(t) - x_i(t)}{h} \tag{1}$$

$$x_i(t + h) = x_i(t) + hv_i(t + h) \tag{2}$$

where $\alpha=(0\ldots 1]$ simulates the *stiffness* of a skin vertex, and $g$ denotes the goal position toward which the vertex is pulled. Given two vertices, $x(t)$ and $g(t)$, the iterative scheme yields the following update rule:

$$\begin{bmatrix} v(t + h) \\ x(t + h) \end{bmatrix} = \begin{bmatrix} 1 - \alpha & -\alpha/h \\ (1 - \alpha)h & 1 - \alpha \end{bmatrix} \begin{bmatrix} v(t) \\ x(t) \end{bmatrix} + \begin{bmatrix} \alpha g(t)/h \\ \alpha g(t) \end{bmatrix}$$

The first term on the right hand side is the system matrix. Its eigenvalues are $1 - \alpha \pm i\sqrt{\alpha(1 - \alpha)}$, and the magnitude of both eigenvalues is $1 - \alpha$. If $\alpha=1$, the vertex instantly adheres to the goal position, i.e. there is no vibration. If $\alpha < 1$, the vertex sequentially translates towards the goal position. With accumulated translations, the vertex may pass by the goal position. Then, it retreats. When such a back-and-forth move is repeated, the vibration effect is achieved near the goal position.

Fig. 5 visualizes the skin vibration or popping effect. The horizontal bold line segments marked by 'vertex position in clenched mesh' represent the goal positions, and the curved graph traces the vertex movement.

Most of skeletal muscles in the limbs are long *fusiform* muscles[1]. The biceps and triceps in Fig. 6-(a) are good examples. When the muscles are pumped up, the central parts experience more vibration effect than the parts near the tendon. It can be simulated by assigning different stiffness values to vertices. Given two example meshes (normal and clenched meshes), the distances are

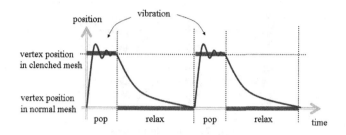

**Fig. 5.** Skin popping

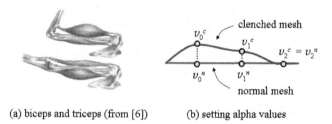

(a) biceps and triceps (from [6])     (b) setting alpha values

**Fig. 6.** Setting stiffness values

computed for all pairs of corresponding vertices. Suppose that the maximum distance is $dist_{max}$. For the $i$-th vertex in the normal mesh with distance $dist_i$, its stiffness $\alpha_i$ is computed as follows:

$$\alpha_i = (\alpha_{min} - 1) \times \frac{dist_i}{dist_{max}} + 1 \tag{3}$$

where $\alpha_{min}$ is the minimum stiffness (between 0 and 1) set by the animator. Fig. 6-(b) shows examples. For vertex $v_0$, $dist_0=dist_{max}$ and therefore $\alpha_0=\alpha_{min}$. Vertex $v_0$ is assigned the minimum stiffness, and experiences the most vibration. For all other vertices, the stiffness values are greater than $\alpha_{min}$, which results in faster convergence. The extreme case is found in $v_2$, where $dist_2=0$ and $\alpha_2=1$.

Note that, when one relaxes the muscles, the normal mesh is used to set up the goal positions. As visualized in Fig. 5, the skin surface smoothly moves from the clenched mesh to the normal mesh without vibration. Such a monotonically decreasing curve can be simulated as follows:

$$x_i(t + h) = x_i(t) + \beta(g_i(t) - x_i(t))h \tag{4}$$

where $\beta$ is a scalar value between 0 and 1. The bigger $\beta$ is, the more sharply the curve decreases. When the distance to the goal position becomes less than a threshold, the vertex is clamped to the goal position of the normal mesh.

The proposed algorithm works as a secondary animation for LBS, and is added to the result of LBS. However, they cannot be separated because the translation vector for popping effect should be determined considering the bone configuration in LBS especially for the joint part of a character. Example-based

**Fig. 7.** Example meshes

skinning algorithm can resolve the problem. As shown in Fig. 7, three pairs of example meshes are used. A pair is per a distinct bone configuration. The normal meshes are illustrated in the upper row, and the clenched meshes are in the lower. The sparse data interpolation technique[5] is applied both to the normal mesh group and to the clenched mesh group, and the results are fed into the proposed dynamic skin simulation algorithm.

## 4   Implementation

The proposed approach has been implemented in 3.6GHz Intel CPU and 2GB RAM. Fig. 8 compares the skinning results with and without dynamic skin effect. The character has 4,380 vertices, and is animated at 60 FPS on average when integrated with the sparse data interpolation technique for skinning.

**Fig. 8.** Results

## 5   Conclusion

This paper presents an efficient technique to enhance the realism of character animation by adding muscle dynamics. Aiming at real-time animation of popping dance, the proposed algorithm takes normal mesh and clenched mesh, and uses the disparity between them to simulate the skin vibration. The skin simulation algorithm is neatly integrated with an example-based skinning. The experimental results show the feasibility of animating the dynamic skin effect in real-time.

## Acknowledgements

This research was supported by the Ministry of Information and Communication, Korea under the Information Technology Research Center support program supervised by the Institute of Information Technology Assessment, IITA-2005(C1090-0501-0019).

# References

1. Aubel, A.: Anatomically-based human body deformations. Ph.D Thesis No. 2573, EPFL. (2002)
2. Chadwick, J. E., Haumann, D. R., Parent, R. E.: Layered construction for deformable animated characters. ACM Computer Graphics. **23** (1989) 243–252
3. James, D. L., Pai, D. K.: DyRT: Dynamic response textures for real time deformation simulation with graphics hardware. ACM Transactions on Graphics. **21** (2002) 582–585
4. Kry, P. G., James, D. L., Pai, D. K.:Eigenskin: Real time large deformation character skinning in hardware. In ACM SIGGRAPH Symposium on Computer Animation. (2002) 153–160
5. Lewis, J. P., Cordner, M., Fong, N.: Pose space deformations: A unified approach to shape interpoalation and skeleton-driven deformation. In Proceedings of ACM SIGGRAPH. (2000) 165–172
6. Macintosh, B. R., Gardiner, P. F., McComas, A. J.: Skeletal Muscle - Form and function. Human Kinetics Press. (2005)
7. Mohr, A., Gleicher, M.: Building Efficient, Accruate Character Skins from Examples. ACM Transactions on Graphics. **22** (2003) 562–568
8. Muller, M., Heidelberger, B., Teschner, M. Gross, M.: Meshless Deformations Based on Shape Matching. ACM Transactions on Graphics. **24** (2005) 471–478
9. Phillips, C. A., Repperger, D. W., Neidhard-Doll, A. T., Reynolds, D. B., Biomimetic model of skeletal muscle isometric contraction. I. An energetic viscoelastic model for the skeletal muscle isometric force twitch. Computers in Biology and Medicine. **34** (2004) 307–322
10. Turner, R., Thalmann, D.: The elastic surface layer model for animated character construction. In Proceedings of Computer Graphics International. (1993) 399–412
11. Wang, X., Phillips, C.: Multi-weight enveloping : Least-squares aproximation techniques for skin animation. ACM SIGGRAPH Symposium on Computer Animation. (2002) 129-138
12. Wlhelms, J., Gelder, A. V.: Anatomically based modeling. ACM Computer graphics. (1997) 173–180

# Discovery of Online Game User Relationship Based on Co-occurrence of Words

Ruck Thawonmas*, Yuki Konno, and Kohei Tsuda

Intelligent Computer Entertainment Laboratory
Department of Human and Computer Intelligence, Ritsumeikan University
Kusatsu, Shiga, 525-8577, Japan
ruck@ci.ritsumei.ac.jp

**Abstract.** Understanding of users is an important key to keep an online game fascinating to them. In this paper, we discuss a heuristic that associates relationship between users with co-occurrence of words uttered by them in a given period. An experiment is conducted using Ragnarok Online logs in the client-side of one human subject, which confirms the effectiveness of the proposed method based on this heuristic.

## 1 Introduction

The MMOG (Massively Multiplayer Online Game) industry is one of the fastest growing industries. The Themis Group estimated in one of their white papers [1] that worldwide revenues of MMOGs will rise from 1.30 Billion USD in 2004 to 4.10 Billion USD in 2008, and to 9 Billion USD in 2014.

In MMOGs, social relationship among players is naturally formed. For MMOG companies, it is important to discover such relationship in order to maintain a good community. This is because being in a good community usually makes players addicted to the game.

Communications in MMOGs are mainly based on chat. In the research field called social network analysis, the strength of relationship between members of a group can be analyzed through their communications [2]. This is usually done by asking the question "who do you communicate with?" to group members.

Automatic approaches also exist for identifying conversation chatters. For example, PieSpy [3] uses heuristics such as addresses mentioned in messages as well as consecutive messages from only two users. The performance analysis of PieSpy, however, has not been studied and reported in the literature.

Another approach proposed in [4] is based on the assumption that users who utter messages in a same interval are interacting with one another. In this approach, time is divided into multiple slots, and users are grouped into clusters

---

* The author was supported in part by Ritsumeikan University's **Kyoto Art and Entertainment Innovation Research**, a project of the 21$^{st}$ Century Center of Excellence Program funded by Ministry of Education, Culture, Sports, Science and Technology, Japan; and by Grant-in-Aid for Scientific Research (C), Number 16500091, the Japan Society for Promotion of Science.

R. Harper, M. Rauterberg, M. Combetto (Eds.): ICEC 2006, LNCS 4161, pp. 286–291, 2006.

**Fig. 1.** A screen shot of an avatar chat where word co-occurrence is seen

based on input features extracted by singular value decomposition (SVD) from their co-occurrence in each slot. Due to not considering discussion topics, the approach has arguably low performance in discovering conversation chatter pairs, as shown in [4], when multiple discussions are on-going concurrently by many chatter groups.

## 2    User Relationship Based on Co-occurrence of Words

The aim of our study is to examine a new heuristic for use in conjunction with the heuristics mentioned above. We focus on discussion topics. Our heuristic is that if chatters utter messages that contain common words in a particular period, they are participating in a same discussion and thus are communicating to one another. In other words, this heuristic is based on co-occurrence of words uttered by different users in a given period. Figure 1 shows a screen shot of an avatar chat, where there exists one common word, those surrounded by the box, muttered by multiple chatters who are talking to each other.

To implement our heuristic, a list data structure is employed for each user. Each list contains up to $W$ different meaningful words uttered by its user. The definition of meaningful words is given in the next section; henceforth, we simply use word(s) for meaningful word(s), unless stated otherwise. In addition, words whose span $\geq \tau$ are removed from the list. If a message is uttered by a user, each word in the message is first tagged with a present time stamp and is then operated as follows:

- If the user's list does not already contain it and is not full, the new word of interest will be placed in the list.
- If the user's list does not already contain it but is full, the word with the oldest time stamp in the list will be replaced by the new word of interest.
- If the user's list already contains it, the time stamp of the word of interest in the list will be updated.

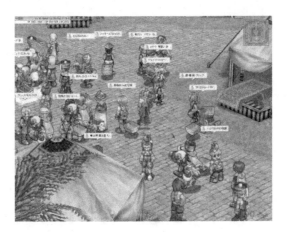

**Fig. 2.** A screen shot of Ragnarok Online used in the experiment

Now we describe how to compute user relationship based on our heuristic. Let $t$, $S(t)$, and $L(t)$ denote the message number, the sender of message $t$, and one of the listeners of this message, respectively. In addition, let $\omega_{L(t)}$ and $\gamma_t$ represent the set of words in the word list of $L(t)$ and the set of words in message $t$, respectively. The increase in the relationship of $L(t)$ toward $S(t)$ due to message $t$, $\delta_{L(t),S(t)}$, is defined as follows:

$$\delta_{L(t),S(t)} = \frac{|\ \omega_{L(t)} \cap \gamma_t\ |}{W} \tag{1}$$

For a period of $n$ messages, the total increase in the relationship of user $A$ toward user $B$, $T_{A,B}$, is computed as follows:

$$T_{A,B} = \sum_{t=1}^{n} I_{A,B}(t), \tag{2}$$

where $I_{A,B}(t) = \delta_{L(t),S(t)}$ if $A = L(t)$ and $B = S(t)$; otherwise, $I_{A,B}(t) = 0$.

For this period, the mutual relationship between users $A$ and $B$, $M_{A,B}$ or $M_{B,A}$, is given as follows:

$$M_{A,B} = M_{B,A} = T_{A,B} + T_{B,A} \tag{3}$$

## 3    Experiment

To examine its effectiveness, we tested the proposed method with chat logs of one subject who is a user of Ragnarok Online (RO) [5], a popular Korean online game in Japan whose screen shot [6] is shown in Fig. 2. These logs were obtained over a period of six months at the subject's PC, and they contained about sixty thousand messages.

There are four chat modes in RO, namely, normal chat, party chat, guild chat, and whisper chat, described as follows:

**Table 1.** Rankings in the relationship between the subject and his most favorite five user characters by the subject himself, by co-occurrence of words (proposed method), and by the number of messages

| No. | subject himself | co-occurrence of words | number of messages |
|-----|-----------------|------------------------|--------------------|
| 1 | A | A | E |
| 2 | B | B | A |
| 3 | C | - | - |
| 4 | D | D | B |
| 5 | E | C | - |
| 6 | - | E | - |
| 7 | - | - | - |
| 8 | - | - | - |
| 9 | - | - | D |
| 10 | - | - | - |
| 11 | - | - | - |
| 12 | - | - | - |
| 13 | - | - | - |
| 14 | - | - | - |
| 15 | - | - | C |

- In the normal chat mode, a user of interest can chat with other users who are within the chat range defined by RO.
- In the party chat mode, a user of interest can chat with other users who have formed a party for a particular mission with him.
- In the guild chat mode, a user of interest can chat with other members of a guild where he belongs.
- In the whisper chat mode, a user of interest can secretly chat with particular users.

In our study, in order to test the generalization ability of the proposed method, we did not distinguish chat messages based on their modes. In addition, we did not take into account whisper-mode messages because sending messages in the whisper chat mode of a user do not remain in client-side logs.

For the proposed method, meaningful words were both noun-type words and unknown-type words that are parsed and categorized by ChaSen [7], a morphological parser for the Japanese language. Unknown-type words are words not registered in the word database of ChaSen. They are important because they represent slang words or RO oriented special worlds. However, unknown-type words consisting of too few or too many characters are usually from looters; as a result, only those with the length between two and twenty characters were considered meaningful words in this experiment[1].

---

[1] From the authors' experience, most of the unknown-type words with one character are symbols with no meaning, and those with more than twenty characters are usually URL addresses of sites whose contents are not related to the game.

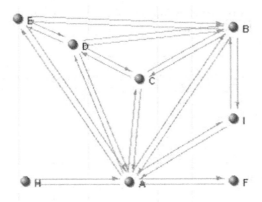

**Fig. 3.** An example of a social network of game users

The subject was asked to rank the most favorite five other user characters. This ranking is shown in the second column of Table 1, where user character names are represented by aliases. The third column of this table shows the ranking of these five user characters by the proposed method (eqn. 3), where the valid span of each word, $\tau$, and the maximum number of words in the list, $W$, were set to 10 minutes and 100 words, respectively. In the last column of the table, the ranking by another method is shown that ranked user characters according to the number of their messages in the subject's logs. This table indicates that the proposed method is more accurate than its counterpart.

## 4    Conclusions and Future Work

We have proposed the method that discovers the relationship between chatters based on co-occurrence of words in their massages. For the RO logs of the subject in the experiment, the proposed method has the result comparable to the result given by the subject himself.

The proposed method is applicable also to chat logs in the server-side, from which social networks of all game users can be constructed, as shown in Fig. 3. This network information can be exploited for obtaining high user satisfaction. One example is that of providing more in-game social activities or events to users with close relationship. Another possible application is that of detecting looters. In addition, if one wants to know more about action behavior of a group of related users, a visualization technique discussed in [8] can be applied to a group of interest.

We do not claim, however, that the proposed method based on word co-occurrence is always better than those in [3] and [4]. In fact, as our future work, we plan to find an effective strategy that combines all of these heuristics for practical use.

# References

1. Alexander, K., Bartle, R., Castronova, E., Costikyan, G., Hayter, J., Kurz, T., Manachi, D., Smith, J.: The Themis Report 2004 – Preview. (2004) `http://www.themis-group.com/uploads/Themis%20Report%202004%20-%20Preview.pdf`
2. McCarty, C.: Social Network Analysis. BEBR Research Report (2003) `http://www.bebr.ufl.edu/Articles/SNA_Encyclopedia_Entry.pdf`
3. Mutton, P.: Inferring and Visualizing Social Networks on Internet Relay Chat. Proc. Eighth International Conference on Information Visualisation (IV'04) (2004) 35–43
4. Çamtepe C., Krishnamoorthy, M., Yener, B.: A Tool for Internet Chatroom Surveillance. Lecture Notes in Computer Science. Chen, H., Moore, R., Zeng, D., Leavitt, J. (eds.) **3073** (Second Symposium on Intelligence and Security Informatics, ISI 2004) 252–265
5. Ragnarok Online Japan. `http://www.ragnarokonline.jp/`
6. Ragnarok Online Gallery. `http://game.goo.ne.jp/contents/oexgallery/Ragnarok/gallery3.html`
7. ChaSen: A morphological parser for the Japanese language. `http://chasen.naist.jp/hiki/ChaSen/`
8. Thawonmas, R., Hata, K.: Aggregation of Action Symbol Subsequences for Discovery of Online-Game Player Characteristics Using KeyGraph. Lecture Notes in Computer Science. Fumio Kishino et al. (eds.) **3711** (Proc. of IFIP 4th International Conference on Entertainment Computing, ICEC 2005) 126–135

# Mobile Phone Gaming (A Follow-Up Survey of the Mobile Phone Gaming Sector and Its Users)

Tobias Fritsch, Hartmut Ritter, and Jochen Schiller

Freie Universität Berlin, Technical Computer Science Workgroup, Takustrass 9,
14195 Berlin, Germany
{fritsch, hritter, schiller}@inf.fu-berlin.de

**Abstract.** Over the last decade the importance of network games has seen a tremendous growth. A large part includes the size reduction of the handheld devices. Mobile gaming in a wireless environment and the availability to play games at any place is receiving major importance. Thus more and more games are released in this section (including a huge number of different mobile phone games). Thus, the mobile market offers a wide variety of devices, such as the new handhelds like Nintendo DS and Sony PSP. With the increase in opportunities one must first look at the user behavior to understand how to improve current problems. This paper gives an introduction into the differences of current mobile gaming platforms and their capabilities. Furthermore it features a user survey about individual preferences and social coefficients with unexpected results. The current survey system features a database to handle the huge amount of answers (the predecessor used a polling system). Concluding the results of the previous inquiry, this paper contains a lobby tool based on J2ME and C# to increase the matching mechanisms in a local environment.

**Keywords:** Mobile Phone Games, Mobile Games, User Case Study, Handhelds, Lobby Tool.

## 1 Introduction

With a still increasing importance the game market has already become a major part of the entertainment sector over the last decade. Especially interactive multimedia applications like mobile phone games show a rapid evolution. In order to understand the underlying facts one must first look at the technological progress in the handheld devices.

Gaming itself has mutated within the last years; so did its social acceptance. The society obviously has a huge impact on the local gaming scene; South-Korea for instance had the first professional e-sports league meanwhile other countries do not even feature a reliable Internet support [3]. But not only technological factors show great influence; it is also a matter of ethnological factors and motivation towards innovations [10]. Thus for various reasons gaming has become more that just pure entertainment; it has become communication, competition, business and social interaction.

Along with the demand for mobile communication and entertainment the distribution of phones has also significantly increased. Depending on the country up

R. Harper, M. Rauterberg, M. Combetto (Eds.): ICEC 2006, LNCS 4161, pp. 292–297, 2006.

to 90% of a peer group (age correlating group) own at least one mobile phone. The market saturation of the mobile phone therefore offers a great platform for gaming. But how do the new phones (including J2ME) compete against handheld devices? The technical background and market situation is described in section 2.

The rest of the paper is structured as following: Section 2 contains background information about the mobile phone market; Section 3 features our research approach (this includes the online survey based on already gathered data from [1]); Section 4 describes our analysis and the mobile gaming lobby approach; Section 5 refers to related work.

## 2  Background

Mobile multimedia applications are supported by different devices; mobile phones are just one category. Beside them there are PDAs (personal digital assistant) and next generation handheld devices (Nintendo DS and Sony PSP). In order to understand the current situation one must look at the technical data as well as the market segmentation (in the last 5 years). Forrester research points out that 90% of all teenagers (peer group) in Europe and northern America have at least one mobile phone. Other country score lower as a result of the missing technological background. Nevertheless the penetration of mobile phones (due to their size and high innovation) among the older people is significantly lower. None of the other devices shows such a massive dissemination, the need for communication made the mobile phone a common tool. Anyhow one should keep in mind that not every mobile phone is used as a gaming platform; although all of the current products feature one or two games within its retail version.

The technical data is evaluated from a gaming oriented view; thus additional non-gaming relevant features are left aside. From a pure viewpoint of technical data sheets a mobile phone contains the least functionality due to various facts. Its limited displays of the current generation (176x220 pixels – 3.2cm x 4.0cm) cannot compete with the display of a PDA (320x240 / 480x320 pixels touch-screen or even 640x480) and next generation handhelds (256x192 pixels with two touch-screen displays at the DS and 480x272 pixels at the PSP). Another aspect is the lack of memory on the extractable RAM of the mobile phones (max 64MB). The PSP offers a DVD device. The PDAs offer hard disks between two and four GB. The category input devices most conspicuously indicates the major lack of the mobile phones. The cellular input structure (12 buttons + special buttons based on the mobile phone type) do not support rapid movement. Next generation handhelds have the most economic design, supporting touch screens and joy-pads. Even the PDA features a better input through its larger display and the touch screen.

## 3  Research Approach

Our mobile phone research approach is mainly divided into two parts. Figure 1 gives an overview about the complete approach including its relations. For a complete statistic user survey analysis and the input limitation testbed we refer to [1].After completing the first part of the survey there were a lot of unanswered questions.

Basically since game-reviews have become more and more popular the amount of low-quality gaming software reduced. The biggest game-review page is Gamespot.com[14]; it shows that with over 2000 mobile phone games there are less than 5% with a rating of "good" or better. The relative low develop-ment cost leads to a huge amount of games, mostly clones or remakes from successful PC and console games.

Such situation notwithstanding there is a major difference in the mobile phone game expectation between countries. Not only the game genre like in PC versions seems to be an important reason; also the acceptance of mobile phones as a gaming platform itself

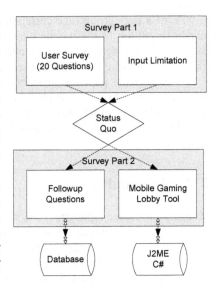

matters. In order to understand how the preferences are divided between the countries we build up a follow-up survey, which includes the results of its predecessor.

**Fig. 1.** An overview about the complete survey, including database & J2ME relation

The set of questions was reduced as much as possible to have a high number of answers (and thus reliability in results). Therefore the database system was designed to offer the survey in four different languages (German, English, French and Spanish).

With this set of questions we ran a small follow-up survey and statistically analyzed it afterwards. Together with the follow-up survey there was also a practical approach. In fact mobility (with 31%) was voted to be the most important advantages of mobile phone games [1]. Although one cannot improve the input devices of all different mobile phone types there is still a software solution for more flexible gaming. The up-to-date mechanism for game finding in the mobile phone sector includes that each of the games features its own connection utility. Especially location aware games suffer a big disadvantage because potential players do not run the game client all the time and thus even if two players would be at the same location (like subway train-station or in the bus) the probability of having both with a running game client is pretty low.

To raise the chance of finding other potential player one should have a general place to look out for ongoing games. At this point the gaming lobby becomes interesting. The idea is a text based lobby chatting application to support a mobile forum. It must be game independent and able to handle even larger number of incoming players without previous network detection (ad-hoc network).

## 4 Analysis

In the prior part of the survey the results were statistically analyzed. We started out with four mayor hypotheses that turned out to be correct. However, there is a surprising outcome because we could not show any kind of correlation between average game-time spend on mobile games and other gaming platforms, which we lead to the minor interest of mobile phone games for hardcore and serious audience. Basically a missing correlation does not necessarily mean that there is none at all. Therefore, the follow-up questions will focus on other handheld devices and the acceptance of mobile phones as a gaming platform. Concluding the analysis of the prior survey [1] we found that the user group is characterized as young and gender indifferent. The mobile phone games seem to have a very short average usage time; although the advantages appear to be equally distributed: the biggest disadvantage by far seems to be the graphic.

Combined with the survey the input limitation testbed shown some interesting results. We assumed that players with cellular input devices and low pixel displays will take at least 20% longer to complete given tasks. However, this did not hold completely true. Arcade games like "Bluetooth Bigplanes" showed nearly no to less than 20% difference; meanwhile fast action paced games (FPS and RTS) greatly decreased in performance due to the very limited input structure. The consequence was more than 100% (sometimes 190%) difference in playing speed between the emulation and mobile phone users.

The second part of the survey started with a follow-up set of questions. The amount of answers through the new ASP / database survey extended the polling system by far. Overall 1123 people participated, 1080 participants within answered all ten questions. We included a small deterministic part (location, sex, age) to statistically analyse correlations with those values. The results underline important aspects of the current mobile phone gaming situation:

The data shows that a majority of over 90% would like to play mobile phone games with their friends; whereas only 42% (36% women, 45% men) would consider playing the same games with random people (see figure 2). We found a minor correlation (0.51) between gender and preference to play mobile phone games with friends. Women tend to prefer not playing those games with strangers even more than men. Hence the game design should seriously take into account that random matching obviously does not fit in the preference of the users.

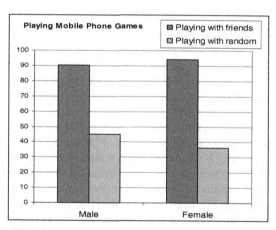

**Fig. 2.** Male and Female opinion on playing mobile phone games with friends / random people

Game preference results have been somewhat surprising. The probe shows a strong correlation between location and favourites in mobile phone games. Most participants in all country favour arcade games (31.5% in Sweden up to 64% in the UK). Overall the other game types (RTS, FPS, action and puzzle) are head-to-head with around 15% each. However there is a huge variance regarding the countries. We assume that the popularity of arcade games is based on their very simple game control mechanism. Nevertheless, only 10% would pay to play mobile phone games (like other MMOGs). On pair with that the average MOS of taking those games serious is 2.1 (1=definitely not serious, 5=very serious) [3]. Both facts together show that location, sex and age independent following holds true: players are not willing to pay or take the current mobile phone games serious. The main goal seems to be quick play with friends.

The game speed setup was rated with a mean opinion score from 1(very unimportant) to 5(very important). With an overall score of 4.43 the majority sets a strong focus on fast game setup. However the preferences varied between countries, ranging from 3.89 in Italy to 4.90 in Germany. This noticeable result leads us to the software solution of a mobile gaming lobby in order to decrease the search and setup time.

Both, PDA and mobile phones have the opportunity to run custom software (3rd party applications). Thus, the gaming lobby was designed in .NET with a support for both C# (for PDAs) and J2ME (Java for mobile phones). Each player only has to pick a nickname and will be automatically connected into the lobby. No further configuration is needed; the underlying ad-hoc network manages the IP addresses on its own. Furthermore, the lobby contains interfaces for different games (generic extendable). Thus, a player must configure the personal profile only once and with that the lobby would be able to start the owned multiplayer games accordingly. The great advantage of game interfaces is that the participants are capable of meeting up with others without having a certain game. The game details are discussed / configured within the chat and its interfaces.

## 5    Related Work

Together with the still growing importance of multimedia gaming applications application, portable devices (and especially mobile phones) offer a wide range of related research approaches. There are three main categories with a close relation to our research work:

There is plenty research material about other mobile devices that are capable of running up-to-date games (like PDAs or handhelds). This includes an overall research approach [2] of next generation handhelds with a focus on performance, protocols and problems that gaming applications on those devices suffer. Another approach is the categorization of requirements for such games [6] and software options for mobile platforms [4]. Both aim to understand the requirements of next generation multimedia applications in a mobile content. Thus, the attempts focus on existing technologies to understand which part can be further upgraded. The ambition is a realization of even more complex applications like distributed databases, ad-hoc network sessions or large scoped applications (such as a massive multiplayer game for mobile phones).

Another approach is the new and rapidly growing technique of J2ME [3], [5]; the java module that helps to build secure applications on a common standard. Techniques such as WAP2 or J2ME significantly changed the function set of current mobile phones. Although there is plenty material for J2ME, especially on the controversial discussion referring to its security, the multimedia real time application approach is not that well analyzed yet. Reason therefore is the rarity of java based multiplayer games and other real time applications (like video streaming). The current camera design of most mobile phones does not support video conferencing. On pair with that the bandwidth is also an issue. However, due to the high amount of work in this section there will be probably more papers in the near future. Another important fact is the constantly increasing amount of bandwidth due to UTMS, HSDPA and WiMAX.

The mobile scenario model features a larger scope. The idea behind this approach is to find a fitting model in order to render user behavior. With an accurate prediction one could test applications on given network structures such as Client/ Server to P2P [8]. Model analysis furthermore helps to provide testbed scenarios [7] and scalability tests that map even huge numbers of clients. With a well designed model one can simulate problematic network situations (like a train with half of the players from a local ad-hoc network suddenly leaves the train station).

# References

1. Fritsch, T., Ritter, H., Schiller, J.:  User Case Study and Network Evolution in the Mobile Phone Sector, ACE 2006, Hollywood, USA, June 2006
2. Claypool, M.: On the 802.11 Turbulence of Nintendo DS and Sony PSP Hand-held Network Games, Netgames 2005 Hawthrone (10th-11th October 2005)
3. Fritsch T., Voigt B.: How Hardcore are you, Netgames 2006 in Singapore  October 2006)
4. Costikyan, G.: Toward the True Mobile Game, Netgames 2005 Hawthrone (10th-11th October 2005)
5. Sierra, A.J., Albéndiz, A.: Comparative Study of Methods of Serialization at J2ME", Applied Simulation and Modeling Netgames 2005 Hawthrone (10th-11th October 2005)
6. Wisniewski, D., Morton, D., Robbins, B., Welch, J.: 2005 Mobile Games White Paper, GDC 2005 San Francisco (7th – 11th March 2005)
7. Petrak, L., Landsiedel, O., Wehrle, K.: Framework for Evaluation of Networked Mobile Games, Netgames 2005 Hawthrone (10th-11th October 2005)
8. Kaneda, Y., Takahashi, H., Saito, M., Aida, H., Tokuda, H.: A Challenge for Reusing Multiplayer Online Games without Modifying Binaries, Netgames 2005 Hawthrone (10th-11th October 2005)

# Designing a Story Database for Use in Automatic Story Generation

Katri Oinonen[1], Mariët Theune[1], Anton Nijholt[1], and Jasper Uijlings[2]

[1] University of Twente PO Box 217
7500 AE Enschede
The Netherlands
{k.m.oinonen, m.theune, a.nijholt}@ewi.utwente.nl
[2] University of Amsterdam
PO Box 19268
1000 GG Amsterdam
The Netherlands
jrruijli@science.uva.nl

**Abstract.** In this paper we propose a model for the representation of stories in a story database. The use of such a database will enable computational story generation systems to learn from previous stories and associated user feedback, in order to create believable stories with dramatic plots that invoke an emotional response from users. Some of the distinguishing characteristics of our proposal are the inclusion of what we call 'narratological concepts' and user feedback in the story database.

**Keywords:** Story database, story representation, automatic story generation.

## 1 Introduction

In this paper we present our ideas about designing a story database which should enable a computational story generation system to learn from annotated representations of existing stories (either human-authored or automatically generated). The story structures represented in the story database can be used by reasoning algorithms for story generation, transforming them for use in new stories. We propose to use a much more expressive knowledge representation model for stories than the representation used in the MINSTREL system of [1] and the KIIDS system of [2]. In MINSTREL a database of story schemas including character goals, actions, and the states of objects, together with knowledge about dramatic writer goals, is used for case-based creative problem solving to generate stories. KIIDS is based on a similar case-based reasoning process as MINSTREL, and uses a case-base of stories built upon a story knowledge ontology related to three basic 'storytelling specific' domains: interactive goal-directed experiences, narrations, and simple simulations. We argue that the story representation model should not only include detailed information about story content linked to the temporal representation of the whole story, but also meta knowledge about which ingredients make up a good story, which we call narratological concepts. We also propose to annotate the stories in the database with user feedback about their emotional impact, so that an interactive

R. Harper, M. Rauterberg, M. Combetto (Eds.): ICEC 2006, LNCS 4161, pp. 298–301, 2006.

automated story generation system can learn from these annotations to construct captivating stories during interaction with a user.

## 2  General Requirements for Story Representation

In our model for story representation we distinguish five related levels, representing different story aspects. In the first two levels the basic story elements, such as the characters, objects, and environment involved in the story are described with their properties and relationships. The semantics of the stories is captured by linking the story elements to the actions, events, and background processes in the evolving story plot represented in the third level. In addition, in the last two levels our model should include meta-knowledge about story structure, which we call narratological concepts, and user feedback about emotional impact.

**Level 1: Semantic networks for story world knowledge.** As a basis for story representation we need a basic general ontology: a semantic network describing the knowledge about the concepts and the possible relations between them in the story domain (see e.g., [3]). A story world description, or world state, is a specific instantiation of (some of) the concepts from the general ontology at a certain point in time, together with the current values of their properties and relationships.

**Level 2: Character representations.** A complex and extensive representation of intelligent characters acting a role in the story is needed. The emotional reaction of the user to what happens to the characters in the story will depend greatly on the emotional-relational properties of these characters. At least information about the characters' physical state, perceptions, beliefs, personality, emotions, social emotional relationships, desires and motivations, action potential, coping strategy, goals, and action plans should be represented in the character model. Gratch and Marsella [4] use similar concepts to simulate the generality of human emotional capabilities, such as appraisal and coping strategies: how characters assess what they perceive, and how they react to this assessment.

**Level 3: Plot structures as a causal and temporal network.** We propose to represent the stories and story fragments in the database as causal network or graph models of actions and events, linked to the representations of the characters and objects that play a role in them [5]. Actions are intentionally performed by the characters in the story, whereas we define events as changes in the world that are not the direct and planned result of any character action. The causal network should also be annotated with time, allowing us to track how the properties of characters and objects change in subsequent world states as a consequence of the actions and events occurring in the story world, as well as background processes that simulate the life, physics, biology, and chemistry in the story world environment.

**Level 4: Representation of narratological concepts.** To enable a computational system to reason about which ingredients make up a dramatic plot, the story representation model also needs to include narratological concepts: meta-knowledge about story structures and their narrative properties. Relevant narratological concepts include *coherence*, *relevance*, and *conflict*. These concepts can be represented as n-ary relationships linking elements from the network representation of the plot (Level 2). Knowledge of these relationships can be used by pattern matching algorithms for detecting dramatic emotional story structures, and for creating new stories by manipulating the structures found in previous stories. We propose to measure the degree of *coherence* of a story by the number of related objects and events covered in a consistent representation of the whole plot. This is similar to the quantitative measure thickness of narrative plot structures proposed by [6], and corresponds to the complexity / richness of the whole story. In our model, the *relevance* of an action, event or background process in a story can be measured from the perspective of a character agent, a community in the story world, or a user. The degree of relevance depends on (1) the strength and importance of its effect on the story world, (2) the number, strength, and importance of the causally or semantically related elements involved with it, (3) the current goals and motivations of the involved characters. This information can be combined with user feedback annotations (Level 5) to determine relevance. In a *conflict*, at least two subjects share a contradicting desire about the state of the same object or about their relationship with the object.

**Level 5: Representation of the cognitive emotional interactor.** The story represent-ation model should also include information about the story or story fragments' potential effects (e.g., suspense) on the user, based on empirically collected user feedback. Then, by automated detection of patterns of narratological concepts that caused certain effects on the user [7] in past stories, the system will be able to predict the audience response to new stories. Later, the potential effects can be derived from how, during interactive story generation, users influence the course of the story from an outsider or a character perspective.

## 3  General Requirements for Story Representation

The Virtual Storyteller[1] is our multi-agent framework for automatic story generation. In this system, plots are generated by autonomous Character Agents that are capable of goal-oriented action planning, and a Plot Agent that steers the emerging plot by (among other things) influencing the Characters' perceptions and manipulating the story world. The resulting plot is represented as a structure of causally linked events, and converted to natural language. The Plot Agent has not been fully implemented yet; an implementation of the Character Agents is described in [8].

Although the Virtual Storyteller does not include a story database yet, much of the information required to develop such a database is already available in the system. Corresponding to Level 1 the Virtual Storyteller makes use of ontologies for plot creation: 1) a basic general ontology defining a classification of objects, and 2) an Action Ontology defining a set of actions that the Character Agents can undertake in the story world, both represented in the W3C standard Web Ontology Language (OWL). See [10] for more details. In addition, the World Agent maintains a story world description (world state): an instantiation of the objects which currently *are* present in the environment, their properties and the relationships between them. In [8]

---

[1] http://wwwhome.cs.utwente.nl/~theune/VS/index.html

we describe an initial implementation of the Character Agents used in the Virtual Storyteller that includes the main concepts from Level 2 of our story representation model: beliefs, goals, actions plans, personality and emotions. Our emotion model incorporates appraisal and coping, specifying how, depending on personality, the Character Agents' emotions are influenced by what happens in the story world, and how their actions are influenced by these emotions. Corresponding to Level 3, the Virtual Storyteller uses a causal plot representation which is an adapted version of the representation proposed by [5]. It includes actions, events, perceptions, goals, goal outcomes, and character 'internal elements' such as emotions and beliefs, linked by motivation, enablement, mental and physical cause relations and annotated with temporal information. See [9] for more details. Levels 4 and 5, the narratological concepts and user feedback annotation, are not yet included in our system but are the subject of future work.

**Acknowledgments.** The authors are involved in the EU Network of Excellence HUMAINE (Human-Machine Interaction Network on Emotion).

# References

1. Turner, S.: The Creative Process: A Computer Model of Storytelling. Lawrence Erlbaum Associates, Hillsdale, NJ (1994)
2. Peinado, F., Gervás, P.: Creativity Issues in Plot Generation. Working Notes of the IJCAI-05 Workshop on Computational Creativity (2005) 45-52
3. Reithinger, N., Pecourt, E., Nikolova, M.: Meta-Data for Interactive Storytelling. Proceedings International Conference on Virtual Storytelling (2005) 172-175
4. Gratch, J., Marsella, S.: A Domain-Independent Framework for Modeling Emotion. Journal of Cognitive Systems Research 5-4 (2004) 269-306
5. Trabasso, T., van den Broek, P., Suh, S.: Logical Necessity and Transitivity of Causal Relations in Stories. Discourse Processes 12 (1989) 1-25
6. Alterman, R., Bookman, L.A.: Some Computational Experiments in Summarization. Discourse Processes 13 (1994) 143-174
7. Szilas, N.: IDTension: A Narrative Engine for Interactive Drama. Proceedings of the Technologies for Interactive Digital Storytelling and Entertainment (TIDSE) Conference (2003) 187-203
8. Theune, M., Rensen, S., op den Akker, R., Heylen, D., Nijholt, A.: Emotional characters for automatic plot creation. Proceedings of the Technologies for Interactive Digital Storytelling and Entertainment (TIDSE) Conference, Lecture Notes in Computer Science Vol. 3105 (2004) 95-100
9. Swartjes, I.: The Plot Thickens: Bringing Structure and Meaning into Automated Story Generation. MSc thesis, University of Twente, Enschede, The Netherlands (2006)
10. Uijlings, J.: Designing a Virtual Environment for Story Generation. MSc thesis, University of Amsterdam, Amsterdam, The Netherlands (2006).

# An Efficient Algorithm for Rendering Large Bodies of Water

Ho-Min Lee, Christian Anthony L. Go, and Won-Hyung Lee

Chung-Ang University,
Department of Image Engineering,
Graduate School of Advanced Imaging Science and Multimedia and Film,
221 Hukseok-Dong, Dongjak-Gu, Seoul, Korea
grancia@gmail.com, chipgo@gmail.com, whlee@cau.ac.kr

**Abstract.** Water rendering is one of the most computationally demanding task in computer graphics. Because of its computational complexity, real-time water rendering requires high-end hardwares. In this paper, we present a new algorithm for real-time rendering of large bodies of water such as open seas and oceans which results in an improved efficiency. Using interactive frustum, water surface can be fluidly calculated as a function of height given and interaction with another player in games. This results in an efficient yet realistic method for rendering large bodies of water without requiring as much computational power.

## 1 Introduction

Realistic water simulation technology has matured with the advent of advanced graphic hardwares. There are many limitations in using the CPU alone. With the advent of GPU's however, developers are now afforded added flexibility to render water in real time. In rendering realistic images of large bodies of water in games, there are four components that need to be addressed: atmospheric conditions, wave generation, light transport, and water surface size[1].

In games, there are many objects like players, NPC(Non Player Character), obstacles, buildings and so on, each of which interacts with one another. Generally, we need high computing power for handling the interaction between objects, and in this light, we should consider efficient computing powers. Real-time rendering also demands high computing power, making it more challenging to implement. In this paper, we describe an efficient approach for realistic large-scale water rendering for games.

## 2 Previous Work

### 2.1 Perlin Noise

The two most common algorithms employed for water simulation are the Navier-Stokes equation and Perlin Noise. The Navier-Stokes Equation is the cornerstone

R. Harper, M. Rauterberg, M. Combetto (Eds.): ICEC 2006, LNCS 4161, pp. 302–305, 2006.

in the field of fluid mechanics and it can show realistic and complex phenomenon of fluid areas. However it is not appropriate because of high computational requirements. In this paper, we use Perlin Noise function for large water surfaces because it requires low computing power. Two functions are necessary to create the Perlin Noise, a noise function, and an interpolation function[3]. The Perlin Noise utilizes a random number generator and represents volume by interpolating random numbers.

## 2.2   Light Transport

To generate realistic simulation of natural water, one must consider in detail the interaction of light with the water body[4]. When light strikes the surface of a water, reflection and refraction phenomena occur on and under the surface. The most common method for the phenomena uses the Snell's law. Equation 1 demonstrates Snell's law.

$$sin\theta_1 \cdot n_1 = sin\theta_2 \cdot n_2 \tag{1}$$

where $\theta_1$ is an incidence angle on water surface, $\theta_2$ is a refraction angle under water surface, $n_1$ means air and $n_2$ means water. In this paper, we use shader programming to get efficient computing power by dividing the load between the CPU and GPU for light transport.

# 3   Water Surface Rendering

## 3.1   Represents Water Surface with Interactive Frustums

Many developers have tried to apply real-time water rendering to games. However, we still have a problem applying it to games because real-time water rendering requires high computing power. In this paper, we propose an efficient algorithm for rendering large bodies of water. This algorithm is based on the projected grid algorithm by Johanson[5]. He proposed a water simulation algorithm which is sufficient for water surface from a low viewpoint, however, the water surface cannot render smoothly when the viewpoint becomes higher. We improved on this algorithm specifically for ocean rendering in games. Fig. 1 shows how we define water surface sizes and interact with other characters. As you can see Fig. 1, when one player's frustum cross with another, height values of the surface frustums for water rendering are balanced automatically. As a result, players get the impression of being on the same water surface.

## 3.2   Water Rendering Range

We utilize two interactive frustums. One is for viewpoint, and another one is for definition of water surface sizes. In Fig. 1, as a height value of viewers, position of the frustum for water surface is defined. Equation 2 describes how the water surface is defined as a function of height.

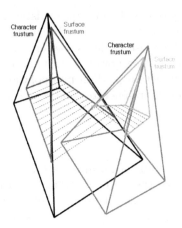

**Fig. 1.** Water rendering with interactive frustums

$$W_{size} = V_{HF} \cdot sin\theta \cdot W_{range} \qquad (\theta < 90) \qquad (2)$$

where $W_{size}$ is the water surface size, $V_{HF}$ is the orthogonal height value from the water surface, $W_{range}$ is the maximum range toward horizon and $\theta$ represents the angle between the surface and the user viewpoint. Thus, as a height value of characters, the water surface size is redefined within $W_{range}$. The traditional projected grid algorithm uses a grid for height value, and conversely, our improved algorithm calculates the grid size as an average of grid coordinates, resulting in improved speed.

## 4    Experimental Results

We experimented using Geforce 6600 GPU, Pentium 4 processor running at 3.0 GHz. Fig. 2 shows the experimental results in terms of different height values: 80, 1000 and 2000 pixels from top-down. In the Fig. 2, the projected grid algorithm shows that cuts the water surface and displays a part of the earth's surface at approximately 2000 pixel-height. However, although when the player's height value is increased, our proposed algorithm still renders realistic water surface efficiently. Moreover, we added objects in space, and it showed increased computing efficiency by about 30%.

## 5    Conclusion

We have presented a method for an efficient rendering of large bodies of water. The method uses an interactive and flexible frustums, Fig. 1 shows how the water surface is defined in terms of height value and interaction with another player. Experimental results have shown our algorithm to render realistic large bodies

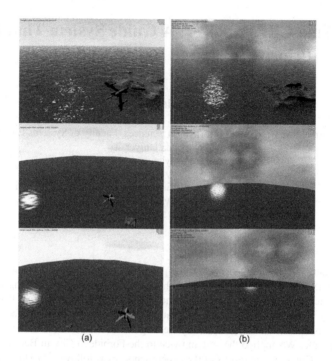

**Fig. 2.** (a) The proposed algorithm    (b) Projected grid algorithm

of water while being flexible when interacting with other players. Moreover, we achieved a 30% increased efficiency in terms of computational costs.

## Acknowledgment

This research was supported by the Korea Culture and Contents Agency, and the Research Grant of Chung-Ang University, Seoul, Korea.

## References

1. Simon Premoze, Michael Ashikhmin.: Rendering Natural Waters. IEEE Computer Society. (2000) 23
2. Jim X. Chen , Niels da Vitoria Lobo.: Toward interactive-rate simulation of fluids with moving obstacles using Navier-Stokes equations. Graphical Models and Image Processing. **57** (1995) 107–116
3. David S. Ebert, F. Kenton Musgrave, Darwyn Peachey, Ken Perlin, Steven Worley.: Texturing & Modeling - A Procedural Approach Second Edition. AP Professional. (1998)
4. Alain Fournier, William T. Reeves.: A Simple Model of Ocean Waves. ACM Press. **20** (1986) 75–84
5. Claes Johanson.: Real-time water rendering. Lund University. (2004)

# Forbidden City Explorer: A Guide System That Gives Priority to Shared Images and Chats

Jun Munemori[1], Thai Minh Tri[2], and Junko Itou[1]

[1] Department of Design and Information Sciences, Faculty of Systems Engineering,
Wakayama University
930 Sakaedani, Wakayama 640-8510, Japan
{munemori, itou}@sys.wakayama-u.ac.jp
[2] Graduate School of Systems Engineering, Wakayama University
930 Sakaedani, Wakayama 640-8510, Japan
s051066@sys.wakayama-u.ac.jp

**Abstract.** We have developed a prototype guide system, which was named The Forbidden City Explorer. This system has real-time information sharing functions including image data, chatting, and mutual location information. It gives priority to shared images and chats, supporting a friendly user interface and simple operation methods, especially creating shared images to be used by general people. We applied the system twice to the Forbidden City in Beijing. Users were Chinese. The results of the experiments are as follows: (1) The evaluation of the image data sharing function was timely. (2) With a simple operation, many shared images and chat messages were created.

**Keywords:** GPS PDA, guide system, Wireless LAN, Forbidden City, shared image, chat.

## 1 Introduction

After years of research, many location aware systems using positioning information have been proposed [1]. GPS receivers have begun to appear in cell phones.

Up to now, we had developed the Beijing Explorer, which is a system for the guidance of the Palace Museum (Forbidden City) in Beijing, China [2]. It was an interactive location aware system, which exchanged a user's positioning information and situation to other users using a PDA with built-in wireless LAN, a Bluetooth communication card and a Bluetooth GPS receiver in real time. Its experiments at the end of 2004 showed that the service using positioning data and shared images, especially photos, are valuable and interesting. However, it is necessary that the system have a friendly user interface and simple operation methods to be used by general people. Furthermore, there are important problems: how to create shared images easily, coordinate chats and images in some way, and find images that are the topics of chats. Therefore, we have developed the Forbidden City Explorer (the Beijing Explorer version II), which gives priority to shared images and chats. This paper shows the development and application of the Forbidden City Explorer.

R. Harper, M. Rauterberg, M. Combetto (Eds.): ICEC 2006, LNCS 4161, pp. 306–309, 2006.

## 2 The Forbidden City Explorer

The Forbidden City Explorer is an interactive location aware guidance system using PDAs. Users of the system can get and present positioning data of other users real-timely. Each participant brings his (her) own system. The GPS receiver of the system shows their positions. So, they don't need to act as a group. They can go sightseeing individually. They can understand the positions of other users and chat with each other. When approaching any historical site, they can take pictures and share them. So, they can understand the contents of the historical site deeply.

The whole system of The Forbidden City Explorer consists of a base station of a wireless LAN and many PDAs (SONY CLIE PEG-NX80V) as clients. The client system uses a wireless LAN for communication with the server. The transmission method is IEEE 802.11b wireless LAN with a speed of 11Mbps (using TCP/IP). Figure 1 shows a screen of the client system. It shows an area of 640m x 800m. Each dot corresponds to 1m on the map [3].

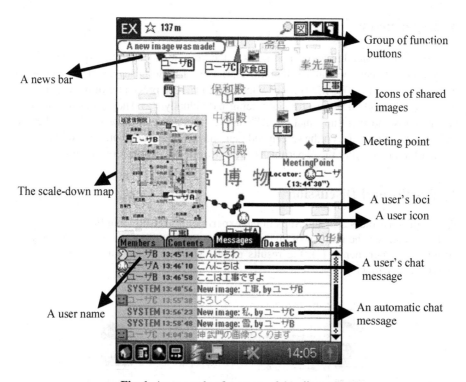

Group of function buttons

A news bar

Icons of shared images

Meeting point

The scale-down map

A user's loci

A user icon

A user's chat message

A user name

An automatic chat message

**Fig. 1.** An example of a screen of the client system

If the user is in the wireless LAN area (about 200 meters in diameter), the system enables the following functions: The client system shows the positions of the user and others. Each position is shown as a face icon in Fig.1. The user can share images and data. By touching any place on the screen, he/she can create them and draw on the image data freely. Hereafter, we shall call it SIO (Shared Image Object). The system will inform the user by sound, news bar and automatic chat messages when shared images arrive (Fig.1). The user can view shared images by tapping on chat messages that contain keywords of those images or using the search function. When the user comes within 15 meters of a building, the image of the building will be displayed. The users can do chats in English, Chinese or Japanese. Chat messages are shown at the bottom part of the screen in Fig. 1. The user can share the waiting point between participants (meeting point-sharing function). The waiting point is shown as the red star icon in Fig. 1. The system shows the loci of the users. The loci are shown as fine lines in Fig. 1. The system has a self-assignment function if they can't get GPS data. Photos taken by PDA can be viewed on the web later.

The state, chat messages, sharing information, and location information of clients can be managed at the server end. The server controls users' position information, shared images, chat messages or any shared information. It operates receiving data, expansion of data, saving, creating and reading log files, and transferring data to other users.

## 3  Experiments

Six participants joined in two experiments at the Forbidden City. The experiments were carried out between the Hall of Supreme Harmony (Tai He Dian) and The Gate of Supreme Harmony (Tai He Men) in the winter of 2005. The procedure of the experiments was as follows: (1) They go for sightseeing individually. (2) They do chats. (3) They take pictures and input informal data. Then, they share it with each other. (4) They decide on a meeting point on the screen and then they meet at the point. Each of them took about 40 minutes. After the experiments, we performed questionnaire surveys.

## 4  Results and Discussion

Part of the chat messages and SIOs in the experiments are shown in Fig. 2.

Table 1 shows the number of chat messages, used  set phrases used and SIOs taken during the experiments. ( ): the results of last year's experiments (the Beijing Explorer's experiments).

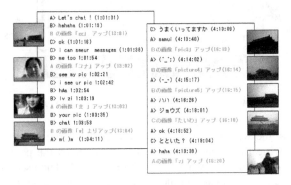

**Fig. 2.** Part of the chat messages and SIOS

**Table 1.** Number of chat messages, set phrases used  and SIOs

|  | No. of chat messages | No. of set phrases used | No. of SIOs |
|---|---|---|---|
| Chinese experiment | 29(17) | 5(0) | 14(6) |
| Japanese experiment | 36(35) | 9(0) | 23(9) |

The time of experiment and users are almost the same as last year but SIOs increased twice (changed from 7.5 to 18.5 images per experiment). The reason may be that the operation was improved to become easier so that the users were able to create more. The total number of chat messages rather increased (changed from 26 to 32.5 messages per experiment) since numerous set phrases were used (changed from 0 to 7 sentences per experiment). The large amount of SIOs means that the users were enthusiastic about creating an SIO.

## 5   Conclusion

We have developed "The Forbidden City Explorer", a prototype system that provides sharing images, chat messages posted by users and performed practical experiments in the Forbidden City, Beijing, China. The experiments were interesting. The numbers of SIOs and messages were increased comparing with the Beijing Explore.

## Acknowledgement

We would like to express our appreciation to everybody in the Institute for Digitization of the Palace Museum for their assistance and Mr. Daisuke Kamisaka, who developed the original Beijing Explorer.

## References

1. Malaka, R. and Zipf, A.: DEEP MAP - Challenging IT research in the framework of a tourist information system. In: Fesenmaier, D. Klein, S. and Buhalis, D. (Eds.): Information and Communication Technologies in Tourism 2000. Proceedings of ENTER 2000, Barcelona. Spain. Springer Computer Science, Wien, New York. (2000) 15-27
2. Munemori, J., Kamisaka, D., Yoshino, T., and Chiba, M.: The Beijing Explorer: Two way Location Aware Guidance System, Proc. of KES 2004 (2004) 905-911
3. Sinomaps :http://www.sinomaps.com

# Reinforcement Learning of Intelligent Characters in Fighting Action Games

Byeong Heon Cho[1], Sung Hoon Jung[2], Kwang-Hyun Shim[1],
Yeong Rak Seong[3], and Ha Ryoung Oh[3]

[1] Digital Content Research Division, ETRI, Daejeon, 305-700 Korea
[2] Dept. of Information and Comm. Eng., Hansung Univ., Seoul 136-792 Korea
[3] School of Electrical Engineering, Kookmin Univ., Seoul 136-702 Korea

**Abstract.** In this paper, we investigate reinforcement learning (RL) of intelligent characters, based on neural network technology, for fighting action games. RL can be either on-policy or off-policy. We apply both schemes to *tabula rasa* learning and adaptation. The experimental results show that (1) in *tabula rasa* leaning, off-policy RL outperforms on-policy RL, but (2) in adaptation, on-policy RL outperforms off-policy RL.

## 1 Overview

Reinforcement Learning (RL) is one of the learning algorithms for Neural Networks(NNs) [1]. The RL NN learns how to achieve the goal by repeating trial-and-error interactions with the environment. Generally, in RL, a NN can be either on-policy or off-policy [2]. With on-policy RL, the NN's decision is reflected to output. Off-policy RL produces no output but observe the decision produced by another static algorithm.

In this paper, we present the RL of NN-based intelligent characters (IC) for fighting action games. We categorize IC's learning into two classes. In *tabula rasa* learning, the IC has no initial knowledge about the game. Thus, it must learn everything. On the other hand, in adaptation, the IC has previously learned about its environment, including game rules and the opponent's action pattern. However, since the environment is abruptly changed now, the IC must re-learn it. For each case, both on-policy and off-policy RL methods are applied, and their performance is compared.

## 2 *Tabular Rasa* Learning

In this section, we address *tabula rasa* learning of an IC. That is, the NN is initially unaware of its environment, e.g. game rules and OC's action pattern, and must learn everything. Both on-policy and off-policy RL methods are applied. Fig. 1 illustrates them.

In Fig. 1(a), the NN senses the state of the environment and produces actions. Then, the IC associated with the NN executes the actions, which affect the environment. The IC and its opponent score according to the fitness of the actions.

R. Harper, M. Rauterberg, M. Combetto (Eds.): ICEC 2006, LNCS 4161, pp. 310–313, 2006.
© IFIP International Federation for Information Processing 2006

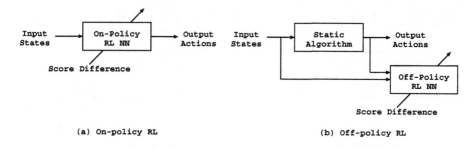

**Fig. 1.** On- and off-policy reinforcement *tabula rasa* learning

Finally, the NN receives a scalar reward value based on the score difference between the two characters. On the other hand, in Fig. 1(b), the IC executes the action produced by a static algorithm, not by the NN. The action is also used to teach the NN. That is, the intermediate learning results do not affect the environment until the learning finishes. In this paper, the static algorithm takes random actions so that the NN explores its environment in an unbiased manner.

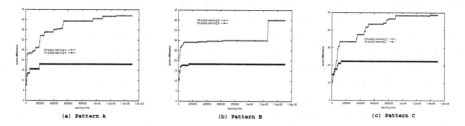

**Fig. 2.** Result of *tabula rasa* learning

We apply the above two methods to the IC of [3], and compare their performance. We use three action patterns. For each case, we use 10 random initial seeds and measure the average of the score ratio between two characters. Fig. 2 shows the results. For all patterns, off-policy RL outperforms on-policy RL. While the score difference quickly converges in on-policy RL, the final score difference in off-policy RL is 2-2.5 times larger than that in on-policy RL. This is because since the NN should learn everything, it would be better to practice as large a variety cases as possible. In off-policy RL, the static algorithm randomly produces output actions. However, in on-policy RL, although the NN is randomly initialized, its output is not sufficiently random.

## 3   Adaptation

With adaptation, an IC can adjust itself to environmental change. Unlike the previous section, the NN has initial knowledge although it is partially unsuitable for the present environment. Fig. 3 illustrates on-policy and off-policy adaptation.

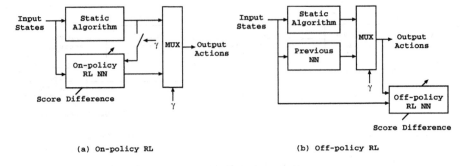

(a) On-policy RL                    (b) Off-policy RL

**Fig. 3.** On- and off-policy adaptation

Fig. 3(a) shows on-policy adaptation. The NN produces output depending on input states. However, as opposed to Fig. 1(a), the output does not always determine which actions the IC will execute in a given input state. The NN controls the IC just at a rate of $\gamma$. At other times, a static algorithm decides output actions. However, in both cases, the NN learns the result of output actions by using generated score difference. Thus, the NN can have new experiences with the aid of the static algorithm. Like *tabula rasa* learning, we use a random generator as the static algorithm. On the contrary, as shown in Fig 5(b), the off-policy RL NN does not produce output. At the beginning of adaptation, it is copied from the previous NN which was trained within the previous environment. Then, it only learns by using the output actions, determined by either a static algorithm or the previous NN relying on $\gamma$, and the resulting score difference until the end of adaptation. However, after finishing adaptation, it produces output to decide the IC's behavior.

These two methods are applied to the adaptation algorithm of [4]. At first, the OC, which is used for this experiment, acts with one of the three action patterns for building IC's initial knowledge. Then, its action pattern is changed to another pattern. Fig. 4 shows the results. In on-policy RL, although the score

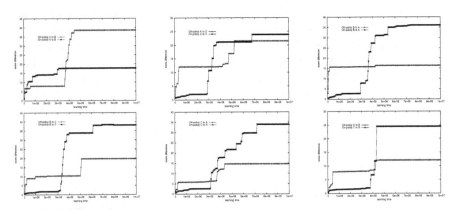

**Fig. 4.** Result of adaptation

ratio is very low during the early stage of adaptation, it strongly increases after all. Thus, as opposed to Section II, on-policy RL outperforms off-policy RL in most cases. This is because the on-policy RL NN immediately learns wrong decisions. That is, when its decision produces bad results, the NN updates the link weights to prevent the same wrong decision. Thus, it has more chances than its rival to try new actions. This allows the exploration of a larger search space. Thus, the on-policy RL NN eventually makes better decision.

## 4 Conclusion

In this paper, on-policy and off-policy RL for an IC in fighting action games based on NN technology are investigated. Both learning schemes are applied to *tabula rasa* learning and adaptation for the IC and their performance is compared. The experimental result tells that (1) when the NN has no initial knowledge (*tabula rasa* leaning), off-policy RL produces better performance, but (2) when the NN has some knowledge, which is partly valid (adaptation), on-policy RL outperforms the rival.

## Acknowledgements

This work was supported in part by research program 2006 of Kookmin University in Korea.

## References

1. R. P. Lippmann. An introduction to computing with neural nets. IEEE ASSP Magazine, vol. 4, no. 2, pp.4–22, 1987.
2. K. R. Dixon, R. J. Malak, and P. K. Khosla. Incorporating prior knowledge and previously learned information into reinforcement learning agents. Tech. Rep., Institute for Complex Engineered Systems, Carnegie Mellon University, 2000.
3. B. H. Cho, S. H. Jung, Y. R. Seong, and H. R. Oh. Exploiting intelligence in fighting action games using neural networks. To appear in IEICE Trans. on Information and Systems.
4. B. H. Cho, S. H. Jung, K. H. Shim, Y. R. Seong, and H. R. Oh. Adaptation of intelligent characters to changes of game environments. CIS 2005, Part 1, LNAI 3801, pp.1064–1073, 2005.

# Capturing Entertainment Through Heart Rate Dynamics in the Playware Playground

Georgios N. Yannakakis, John Hallam, and Henrik Hautop Lund

Maersk Institute for Production Technology
University of Southern Denmark
{georgios, john, hhl}@mip.sdu.dk

**Abstract.** This paper introduces a statistical approach for capturing entertainment in real-time through physiological signals within interactive
playgrounds inspired by computer games. For this purpose children's heart rate
(HR) signals and judgement on entertainment are obtained from experiments on
the innovative Playware playground. A comprehensive statistical analysis
shows that children's notion of entertainment correlates highly with their
average HR during the game.

## 1  Introduction

Motivated by the lack of quantitative models of entertainment, an endeavor for
capturing player satisfaction in real-time through physiological signals during
gameplay is introduced in the work presented here. In this work, we define
entertainment primarily as the level of satisfaction generated by the real-time player-
game opponent interaction — by 'opponent' we define any controllable interactive
feature on the game. Even though entertainment is a highly complicated mental state
it is correlated with sympathetic arousal which can be captured through specific
physiological signals such as heart rate and skin conductivity reported by researchers
in the psychophysiological research field. Herein we investigate the impact of player
satisfaction on heart rate (HR) signals and attempt to capture HR signal features that
correlate with human notion of entertainment. HR signal data and children's
judgement on entertainment are obtained through a gaming experiment devised on the
Playware playground. The 'Playware' [4] intelligent interactive physical playground
combines features and advantages of computer games and traditional playgrounds.
This innovative platform will be described and experiments with children on
developed Playware games will be presented in this paper.

## 2  Capturing Entertainment

There have been several psychological studies to identify what is "fun" in a game and
what engages people playing computer games. Theoretical approaches include
Malone's principles of intrinsic qualitative factors for engaging gameplay [5], namely
challenge (i.e. *'provide a goal whose attainment is uncertain'*), curiosity (i.e. *'what
will happen next in the game?'*) and fantasy (i.e. *'show or evoke images of physical*

R. Harper, M. Rauterberg, M. Combetto (Eds.): ICEC 2006, LNCS 4161, pp. 314–317, 2006.

*objects or social situations not actually present'*) as well as the well-known concepts of the theory of flow (*'flow is the mental state in which players are so involved in the game that nothing else matters'*) [1]. Other qualitative studies include Lazzaro's "fun" clustering — based on Malone's categorization — on four entertainment factors based on facial expressions and data obtained from game surveys on players [3]. Koster's [2] theory of fun, which is primarily inspired by Lazzaro's four factors, defines "fun" as the act of mastering the game mentally.

Following the theoretical principles reported from Malone [5], Lazzarro [3], Koster [2] and Yannakakis and Hallam [7], this paper is primarily focused on the game opponents' behavior contributions — by enabling appropriate learning patterns for the player to be further trained on [2] — to the real-time entertainment value of the game.

## 3  Playware Playground

New emerging playing technologies (e.g. computer games) have contributed to transforming the way children spend their leisure time: from outdoor or street play to play sitting in front of a screen. This sedentary style of play may have health implications [4]. A new generation of playgrounds that adopt technology met in computer games may address this issue. More specifically, intelligent interactive playgrounds with abilities of adapting the game according to each child's personal preferences provide properties that can keep children engaged in entertaining physical activity. On that basis, capturing the child's entertainment and adjusting the game in order to increase it can only have positive effects on the child's physical condition. The Playware playground adopts these primary concepts.

**Fig. 1.** A child playing the Bug-Smasher game

### 3.1  Bug-Smasher Game

The test-bed game used for the experiments presented here is called 'Bug-Smasher'. The game is developed on a 6 x 6 square tile topology (see Fig. 1). During the game, different 'bugs' (colored lights) appear on the game surface and disappear sequentially after a short period of time. A bug's position is picked within a radius of three tiles from the previous bug and according to the predefined level of the bugs' spatial diversity. The child's goal is to smash as many bugs as possible by stepping on the lighted tiles. Different sounds and colors represent different bugs when appearing and when smashed in order to increase the fantasy entertainment factor [5].

## 4  Experimental Data

The Bug-Smasher game has been used to acquire HR physiological data and data of human judgement on entertainment. The game uses two different states ('Low' and 'High') of Malone's [5] three entertainment factors to generate a pool of 8 dissimilar games for children to play. To that end, 28 children whose age covered a range between 8 and 10 years participated in a game experiment. In this experiment, each subject plays two different games (A and B) for 90 seconds each. Each time a pair of games is finished, the child is asked whether the first game was more interesting than the second game i.e. whether $A$ or $B$ generated a more interesting game. The HR of the children is recorded in real-time by the use of a wireless ElectroCardioGram (ECG) device consisting of pulse sensors placed on the chest of the child. Out of the total number of 112 games played in this experiment, in 82 games (41 game pairs) the HR signal was properly recorded.

## 5  Results

Note that, the qualitative features of the HR signals are similar for all children that played the Bug-Smasher game: an initial rapid increase of HR during the first seconds of the game followed by a stable, but noisy, condition of high HR. Given the HR time series over 90 seconds for each game played, the following statistical parameters are computed in order to identify features of the HR dynamics that correlate with entertainment of the child while playing a game: a) The average HR, b) the variance of the HR signal, c) the maximum HR, d) the minimum HR, e) the difference between the maximum and the minimum HR f) the correlation coefficient between HR recordings and the time in which data were recorded, g) the autocorrelation of the signal, which is used to detect the level of non-randomness in the HR data and h) the approximate entropy $ApEn$ [6] of the signal.

In addition, three different regression models were used to fit (least square fitting) the HR signal: linear, quadratic and exponential. The parameters of the regression models under investigation are: a) the slope $s$ of the linear regression ($h_L(t) = st + \alpha$) on the signal b) the parameters $\beta$ and $\gamma$ of the quadratic regression ($h_Q(t) = \beta t^2 + \gamma t + \delta$) on the signal and c) the parameters $A, B, b$ of the exponential regression $h_E(t) = A(1 - e^{-bt}) + B$.

Results obtained show that average HR appears to be the only feature examined that is significantly correlated to entertainment (c = 0.4146, p = 0.0057). The obtained effect of $E\{h\}$ appears to be commonsensical since the Bug-Smasher game belongs to the genre of action physical games where the level of engagement of the user tends to have a significant effect on physical activity. Therefore, if we hypothesize that in such games the level of engagement correlates with average HR, it appears that the higher the average HR during a game the higher the child's perceived satisfaction and the higher his/her physical activity. Moreover, the reported [8] significant correlation between the average response time of children interacting with Playware games and entertainment is consistent with the interplay between engagement, physical activity and entertainment demonstrated here.

## 6 Conclusions

This paper introduced statistical correlations between physiological signals and children's entertainment in physical playgrounds. More specifically the average HR of the child was found to be the only statistic that correlates significantly with the child's perceived satisfaction.

The entertainment modeling approach through HR dynamics presented here demonstrates generality over the majority of action games created with Playware since additional experiments have already shown that the average HR's effect to entertainment generalizes to other dissimilar Playware designed games. Furthermore, preliminary results on a comparative study between HR signals of children playing Playware games and the HR signals of the same children exercising further strengthen the hypothesis that physical activity through entertaining games quantitatively has a dissimilar impact on HR dynamics than that of a non-entertaining form of physical activity. Given these, the proposed approach can be used for adaptation of the game's entertainment features according to the player's individual HR signal dynamics in real-time and as a baseline for validation of any intelligent interactive design applied in Playware.

## References

1. Csikszentmihalyi, M.: Flow: The Psychology of Optimal Experience. New York: Harper & Row (1990).
2. Koster, R.: A Theory of Fun for Game Design. Paraglyph Press (2005).
3. Lazzaro, N.: Why We Play Games: Four Keys to More Emotion Without Story. Technical Report, XEO Design Inc. (2004).
4. Lund, H.H., Klitbo, T., Jessen, C.: Playware technology for physically activating play. Artificial Life and Robotics Journal, no. 4, (2005) 9:165–174.
5. Malone, T.W.: What makes computer games fun? Byte (1981) 6:258–277.
6. Pincus, S.M.: Approximate entropy as a measure of system complexity. Proc. Natl. Acad. Sci. (1991) 88:2297-2301.
7. Yannakakis, G.N., Hallam, J.: A Generic Approach for Obtaining Higher Entertainment in Predator/Prey Computer Games. Journal of Game Development (2005) 1:23–50.
8. Yannakakis, G.N., Lund, H.H., Hallam, H.: Modeling Children's Entertainment in the Playware Playground. In Proceedings of the IEEE Symposium on Computational Intelligence and Games. IEEE (2006) to appear.

# Design Implications of Social Interaction in Online Games*

Kuan-Ta Chen[1,2] and Chin-Laung Lei[1]

[1] Department of Electrical Engineering, National Taiwan University
[2] Institute of Information Science, Academia Sinica
jethro@fractal.ee.ntu.edu.tw, lei@cc.ee.ntu.edu.tw

**Abstract.** While psychologists analyze network game-playing behavior in terms of players' social interaction and experience, understanding user behavior is equally important to network researchers, because how players act determines how well systems, such as MMORPGs, perform. To gain a better understanding of patterns of player interaction and their implications for game design, we analyze a $1,356$-million-packet trace of *ShenZhou Online*, a mid-sized commercial MMORPG. To the best of our knowledge, this work is the first to put forward architectural design recommendations for online games based on analysis of player interaction.

We find that the dispersion of players in a virtual world is heavy-tailed, which implies that static and fixed-size partitioning of game worlds is inadequate. Neighbors and teammates tend to be closer to each other in network topology. This property is an advantage, because message delivery between the hosts of interacting players can be faster than between those of unrelated players. In addition, the property can make game playing fairer, since interacting players tend to have similar latencies to their servers. We also find that participants who have a higher degree of social interaction tend to play much longer, and players who are closer in network topology tend to team up for longer periods. This suggests that game designers could increase the "stickiness" of games by supporting, or even forcing, team playing.

**Keywords:** Design Recommendations, Human Factors, Internet Measurement, MMORPG, Social Interaction.

## 1 Introduction

With an exponentially growing population and the increasing diversity of network gamers, the virtual worlds constructed by MMORPGs (Massive Multiplayer Online Role Playing Games) are gradually becoming a field for the study of social behavior [1, 2]. While psychologists analyze network game-playing behavior in terms of players' social interaction and experience, understanding user

* This work is supported in part by the National Science Council under the Grant No. NSC 95-3114-P-001-001-Y02, and by the Taiwan Information Security Center (TWISC), National Science Council under the Grants No. NSC 94-3114-P-001-001Y and NSC 94-3114-P-011-001.

R. Harper, M. Rauterberg, M. Combetto (Eds.): ICEC 2006, LNCS 4161, pp. 318–321, 2006.
© IFIP International Federation for Information Processing 2006

behavior is equally important to network researchers, because how players act determines how well systems, such as MMORPGs, perform. For example, the dispersion of players across a virtual world affects how well an algorithm performs in distributing the workload to a number of servers in terms of bandwidth usage, load balancing, and users' perceived quality of games.

To gain a better understanding of the patterns of player interaction and their implications for game design, we analyze *how players interact* from packet traces. Analyzing user behavior based on network traces is particularly useful for our purpose, since it naturally connects to network-level factors, such as IP addresses and transmission latency between participating parties. Also, it is easier for commercial game operators to adopt this strategy, because collecting network traces does not increase the load of, or require modification to, game servers. To the best of our knowledge, this work is the first to put forward architectural design recommendations for online games based on empirical analysis of player interaction.

We develop an algorithm that derives patterns of player interaction from a 1,356-million-packet trace of *ShenZhou Online* [3], a commercial MMORPG. The inferred grouping structure is then analyzed from the following aspects: the dispersion of players in a virtual world, the correspondence of network locality and in-game locality, and the "stickiness" of game-playing in terms of social interaction. The main objective is to understand the implications of player interaction for the design of online games, especially architectural design issues.

Our major findings are as follows:

- The dispersion of players in a virtual world can be well modeled by Zipf-like distributions, where 30% of players gather in the top 1% of popular places. This implies that static and fixed-size partitioning of game worlds is inadequate for both server-cluster and peer-to-peer infrastructures [4,5], and dynamic partitioning algorithms should therefore be used [6,7,8,9].
- Players who are neighbors or teammates tend to be closer to each other in network topology. This property is advantageous to both client-server and peer-to-peer architectures, because message delivery between the hosts of interacting players can be faster. In addition, the property improves the fairness of game playing, as interacting players tend to have similar latencies to their servers.
- Players who have a higher degree of social interaction tend to participate much longer. This suggests that game companies could increase the "stickiness" of games by encouraging, or even forcing, team playing. Furthermore, the duration of group play correlates with a group's size and the network distance between players. This implies that real-life relationships carry over into the virtual world, and/or real-life interaction plays a key role during games. The latter also suggests that enriching in-game communication would encourage players to be more involved in team play.
- Larger groups generally lead to longer collaboration due to the enjoyment derived from interaction and social bonds. This suggests that a game could be made stickier by encouraging the formation of large groups.

## 2 Conclusion

In order to understand the implications of player interaction for the design of network games, we analyzed the grouping structure inferred from a packet trace of *ShenZhou Online*, a mid-sized commercial MMORPG. The analysis reveals that the dispersion of players in a virtual world is heavy-tailed, which implies that static and fixed-size partitioning of game worlds is inadequate. We have shown that neighbors and teammates tend to be closer to each other in terms of network topology, a property that is beneficial to both client-server and peer-to-peer infrastructures, because message delivery between the hosts of interacting players is faster. In addition, this property makes games fairer, as interacting players tend to have similar latencies to their servers.

We have also found that participants who have a higher degree of social interaction tend to play much longer than independent or solo players. This suggests that game companies could increase the "stickiness" of games by supporting, or even forcing, team playing. Furthermore, the duration of group play correlates with the size of the group and the network distance between the players. Specifically, players who are closer in network topology tend to team up for longer periods. Larger groups generally lead to longer collaboration due to the enjoyment derived from interaction and social bonds, which suggests that games could also be made stickier by encouraging the formation of such groups.

## References

1. Ducheneaut, N., Moore, R.J.: The social side of gaming: a study of interaction patterns in a massively multiplayer online game. In: CSCW '04: Proceedings of the 2004 ACM conference on Computer supported cooperative work, ACM Press (2004) 360–369
2. Yee, N.: The demographics of groups and group leadership. (The Daedalus Project) http://www.nickyee.com/daedalus/archives/000553.php.
3. UserJoy Technology Co., Ltd.: (ShenZhou Online) http://www.ewsoft.com.tw/.
4. Knutsson, B., Lu, H., Xu, W., Hopkins, B.: Peer-to-peer support for massively multiplayer games. In: Proceedings of IEEE INFOCOM'04, Hong Kong, China (2004)
5. Yu, A.P., Vuong, S.T.: MOPAR: a mobile peer-to-peer overlay architecture for interest management of massively multiplayer online games. In: NOSSDAV'05: Proceedings of the International Workshop on Network and Operating Systems Support for Digital Audio and Video, ACM Press (2005) 99–104
6. Vleeschauwer, B.D., Bossche, B.V.D., Verdickt, T., Turck, F.D., Dhoedt, B., Demeester, P.: Dynamic microcell assignment for massively multiplayer online gaming. In: NetGames '05: Proceedings of the 4th Workshop on Network and System Support for Games. (2005)
7. Chen, J., Wu, B., Delap, M., Knutsson, B., Lu, H., Amza, C.: Locality aware dynamic load management for massively multiplayer games. In: ACM SIGPLAN Symposium on Principles and Practice of Parallel Programming (PPoPP), ACM Press (2005)

8. Hu, S.Y., Liao, G.M.: Scalable peer-to-peer networked virtual environment. In: Proceedings of ACM SIGCOMM 2004 workshops on NetGames '04, ACM Press (2004) 129–133

9. Lui, J.C.S., Chan, M.F.: An efficient partitioning algorithm for distributed virtual environment systems. IEEE Trans. Parallel Distrib. Syst. **13** (2002) 193–211

# TEMPEST: A Text Input System for Musical Performers

Yoshinari Takegawa, Tsutomu Terada, and Shojiro Nishio

Grad. Sch. of Information Sci. and Tech. Osaka Univ. Osaka, Japan
{takegawa, tsutomu, nishio}@ist.osaka-u.ac.jp

**Abstract.** Recently, due to the widespread use of computers, text-based communication methods, such as e-mail and chat, have attracted a great deal of attention. If pianists can apply their musical expressions to the text input, they can input texts with their own emotion richly. Therefore, the goal of our study is to construct TEMPEST (TExt input and Musical PErforming SysTem) that is a text input system to input texts with various musical expressions using a clavier. Since this system provides text input methods considering musical artistry, a performer can input texts like playing music.

## 1 Introduction

Recently, due to the widespread use of computers, text-based communication methods, such as e-mail, blog, and chat, have attracted a great deal of attention. Moreover, various communication media, such as pictures and movies, are used for expressing own emotion, and various new interfaces for such purposes are investigated and developed[1].

Here, the best device for pianists to express their emotion is obviously the piano. A pianist creates a marvelous sense of his emotion using a piano. If pianists can apply their musical expressions to the text input, they can input texts with their own emotion richly. Therefore, the goal of our study is to construct TEMPEST (TExt input and Musical PErforming SysTem) that is a text input system to input texts with various musical expressions by using a MIDI keyboard. Since this system provides several text input methods considering musical artistry, a performer can input texts like playing music.

## 2 Design of TEMPEST

All keys in a keyboard are divided into two types in our method; Text-input keys and Execution keys. The former is used for inputting characters with sounds, and the latter is used for only playing sound.

### 2.1 Text Input Methods

We propose two types of text input method for Text-input keys; Monophony method, and Polyphony method.

R. Harper, M. Rauterberg, M. Combetto (Eds.): ICEC 2006, LNCS 4161, pp. 322–325, 2006.

**Table 1.** The character code chart in two text input methods

| (a) Monophony method | | | | | | (b) Polyphony method | | | | | |
|---|---|---|---|---|---|---|---|---|---|---|---|

| Alphameric | | | | | | | Alphameric | C# | D# | F# | G# | A# |
|---|---|---|---|---|---|---|---|---|---|---|---|---|
| First \ Second | C | C# | D | D# | E | F | C | a | b | c | d | e |
| C | a | b | c | d | e | Enter | C, D | f | g | h | i | j |
| C# | f | g | h | i | j | Space | D | k | l | m | n | o |
| D | k | l | m | n | o | Back | D, E | p | q | r | s | t |
| D# | p | q | r | s | t | MS | E | u | v | w | x | y |
| E | u | v | w | x | y | IC | E, F | z | ! | ? | . | , |
| F | z | ! | ? | . | , | | F | 1 | 2 | 3 | 4 | 5 |
| F# | 1 | 2 | 3 | 4 | 5 | | F, G | 6 | 7 | 8 | 9 | 0 |
| G | 6 | 7 | 8 | 9 | 0 | | G | + | − | * | / | = |
| G# | + | − | * | / | = | | G, A | ( | ) | { | } | ^ |
| A | ( | ) | { | } | ^ | | A | Enter | Space | Back | MS | IC |

## Monophony method

In Monophony method, a user presses two keys successively to specify an input character. Table 1 (a) shows the character-code chart in this method. It uses 10 keys from C note to A note. To generate "h", the user presses C# key followed by D key.

If a user wants to input other characters such as Function keys and Arrow keys, he/she inputs "MS (Mode Shift)" to change the character mode. When the user selects "IC (Input Conversion)", the last entered character is changed to lower-case/upper-case character alternately.

## Polyphony method

Instead of pressing keys in sequence to specify the input character, multiple keys are pressed simultaneously in Polyphony method. Table 1 (b) shows the character-code chart in Polyphony method. This method uses 11 keys from C note to A# note chords that have two notes and three notes. To generate "h", the user presses C, D, F# keys simultaneously. Since this method and Monophony method are independent, they can be used at the same time.

### 2.2   Musical Artistry

To dissolve the lack of artistry in output sounds for Monophony method and Polyphony method, our system translates the output sounds of Text-input keys according to output sounds in Execution areas. Concretely, the system extracts note-numbers that are harmonious with note-numbers played in Execution area, and it replaces note-numbers of Text-input keys by the extracted note-numbers according to the following algorithms.

### Replacement methods of note names

1. **Random method**

   When a Text-input key is pressed, the system randomly picks out and uses one note name played in Execution areas. For example, when C3, E3, G3 and B3 in Execution area are played, the system randomly allocates one of them for Text-input keys.

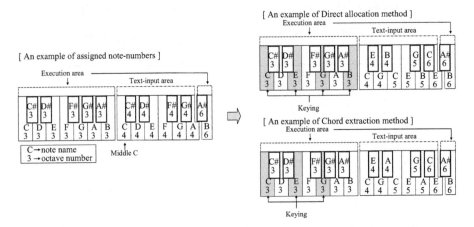

**Fig. 1.** The example of the note replacement algorithm

## 2. Direct allocation method

The system extracts note names played in Execution areas. Then, it allocates the extracted note names in order for Text-input keys. For example, in the situation as shown in the left of Figure 1, when C3, E3, G3 and B3 in Execution area are played, the system allocates C, E, G, B in order for Text-input keys as shown in the upper right of Figure 1.

## 3. Chord extraction method

The system extracts possible chords that include note names played in Execution areas and then it selects one of them randomly. Next, it replaces the note names of Text-input keys by constituents of the extracted chord in order of the key. For example, in the situation as shown in the left of Figure 1, when C3, E3, and G3 in Execution area are played, the possible chords extracted by the system are C (C major triad), CMaj7 (C major seventh), C7 (C dominant seventh), C6 (C major sixth), and the system randomly selects one of them. The lower right of Figure 1 show the case that C6 is selected.

In Random method, since the system replaces the note name of the key whenever a Text-input key is played, the user enjoys unpredictable sounds. On the other hand, he cannot control output sounds. In Direct allocation method, if the note names played in Execution area is same, all keys in Text-input area are assigned the same note names. Therefore, users can control output sounds, at the same time, performances tend to be monotonous. Moreover, in Random and Direct allocation method, in the case that the number of keys pressed in Execution areas is one or two, the system reluctantly allocates the same note name for each Text-input key. On the other hand, Chord extraction method extracts possible chords to resolve this problem. This method has the most unpredictable layout in the proposed three methods, because the system may replace the note names of Text-input keys by the note names not played in Execution areas. Since each method has advantages and disadvantages, users can select a method flexibly.

**Table 2.** Aggregate statistics of the questionnaire

| Question | Not Applying | Applying |
|---|---|---|
| 1. This performance has musical artistry. | 2.12 | 4.35 |
| 2. I am impressed by input characters with musical artistry. | 1.56 | 3.83 |

### Replacement methods of octave numbers

In general keyboards, the righter key has the higher pitch. According to this rule, the system allocates the octave number as shown in the right of Figure 1.

In concrete terms, the system allocates the octave numbers that the left-most/rightmost key in the Text-input area is higher/lower than the rightmost/left-most key in the left/right side Execution area. For example, when the right-most key in the left side Execution area is "B3", and the leftmost key in the right side Execution area is "A#6", the keys in a Text-input area are as shown in the right of Figure 1.

## 3   Evaluation

We have evaluated the effectiveness of the proposed algorithms by the subjective evaluation. In this evaluation, the first author of this paper entered "Osaka University" in applying the note replacement algorithm and not applying it. 48 examinees evaluated the system by ranking (1: worst, 5: best) the questions, and the average of scores are shown in Table 2. From the result, we prove the effectiveness of proposed algorithm for the improvement of the artistry.

## 4   Conclusions

In this study, we have constructed TEMPEST that a user can input texts with musical artistry. We propose the several text input methods to improve the artistry of the text input.

In future, we have a plan to evaluate our system from the point of player's view. Moreover, we will construct text input interfaces using other instruments such as the guitar, the violin, and the maraca. Additionally, we will construct a musical performance chat system as an application.

## Reference

1. Y. Itoh, A. Miyajima, and T. Wanatabe:. 'tsunagari' communication: fostering a feeling of connection betweenfamily members. CHI 2002, pp. 810–811, April 2002.

# Design Strategies for Enhancing Experience-Based Activities

Lena Pareto and Ulrika Lundh Snis

University West, Laboratory for Interaction Technology, SE-461 86 Trollhättan, Sweden
{lena.pareto, ulrika.snis}@hv.se

**Abstract.** Enjoyment and experience-based activities are important in today's society. The purpose of this paper is to explore and better understand how experiences can be enhanced using IS in such experience-based enterprises. The research is based on a case study conducted in collaboration with a Swedish regional museum, where a location-aware auditory museum application for experience enhancement is being designed. The results include design approach recommendations, enhancement strategies and a model for estimating the potential benefits related to enhancements features of the system design.

**Keywords:** design strategies, experiences, enhancements, experience-based activities, value-added, estimation model.

## 1 Introduction

There is an on-going change in our economy: from service-based to more experience-based economies [8]. This change implies an increased focus on enjoyment and experience-based activities and events. Several experience-oriented business sectors, in particular entertainment, education and culture, are growing rapidly with this change. Information systems (IS) have great potential in supporting such sectors, e.g., interactive media can engage or enjoy its users optimally [7], and there are several current attempts of Edutainment IS products. Hence there is a need for in-depth studies of the role of IS in these settings, addressing the following questions: How can IS enhance and support experience-based activities? Are there any differences in the design approaches? How can we understand enhancements and estimate the value added by proposed IS solutions? The purpose of this paper is to explore and better understand how experiences can be enhanced using IS in experience-based enterprises.

## 2 Experience-Based Activities

User experience has for long been of interest in IS design, in particular within the field of human computer interaction. To consider user experience as an effect of using IS products is always of importance when designing IS tools and systems. According to [1] experience means "all the aspects of how people use an interactive product", and user experiences thus refer to how well the IS provides users with successful and satisfying experiences. With this perspective, the experience is due to the IS usage. In

R. Harper, M. Rauterberg, M. Combetto (Eds.): ICEC 2006, LNCS 4161, pp. 326–331, 2006.

contrast, we will in this paper concentrate on experiences "as such". By experiences, we refer to the sensations that results from an activity of experiencing "something", as a means to enjoy or engage in a certain series of activities, an event. This event needs not necessarily be experienced through a product or a system. We focus on activities with the main purpose of generating an experience, IS-based or not, as defined by [4]. Essentially, an experience is a kind of totality, engaging oneself (or together with others) in relationship with an object, or in a situation. The technology part, the IS system, is there to support such an experience-based activity, with the aim to enhance the already occurring experience.

## 3  Research Approach

Our research approach is to focus on *strategies for achieving enhancements of experiences*. We consider the enhancement as the point of departure when exploring design issues for experiences. Enhancements are understood as different ways of adding value to, or increase the attractiveness of an object or a situation. Values such as knowledge, feelings, and sensations are examples of what experience-based activities might generate. However, experiences occur within individuals, and highly depend on, for instance, the individual's interests, preferences and needs. To explore potential enhancements we have analysed activities in relation to user groups, in order to understand different ways of achieving enhancements.

Our findings are based on a case study: an ongoing, collaborative project together with a regional museum. The museum provides exhibits reflecting the local culture, local handicraft and artworks, and is an experience-based, non-profit service. The museum's goals in this project are to attract *new* visitors, to attract visitors to come *more often* and to provide *enhanced experiences* for all visitors, by IS support. The project is exploratory in nature, has proceeded for several years, and has engaged museum staff, researchers, one IT company, and one class of media students. Various user-groups have been in focus; mock-up and prototype systems have been designed, developed and user-tested. Evaluation has been based on attractiveness and enhancement of the experiences using the system in the museum context. From this, a model for estimating the enhancements and its value-adding potential has been developed to judge the different design attempts. Thus, the project is suitable for exploring how an IS application can be used for value-adding purposes, in an experience-based enterprise.

## 4  The Case: An Auditory, Location-Aware Museum Application for Experience Enhancements

The museum of our case is in many respects traditional: it is open to the public; the building is spacious and exhibitions are spread; visitors wander around; most exhibitions are organized around visual objects and visual displays of text information; guided tours can be arranged. The starting point of our research was to design an auditory, location-aware IS system to enhance the museum experience. The choice of an auditory-based system is motivated by the visual nature of exhibitions, as well as the aim to increase accessibility for visitors with visual or language disabilities, non-native speakers, tourists, youngsters and children. A location-aware system, which is a system that "knows where it is" and can act accordingly, can provide context-dependent information without any involvement of the visitor. This allows for a great freedom for the visitor to move around and experiencing objects and exhibitions of their own choice. Thus, an auditory, location-aware system can be used for several purposes: e.g., providing context-dependent information in different languages, additional information, predefined guided tours, complementary sound effects or background music, which can augment the visual experience in the museum. Our responsibility is to propose a design of such a system; i.e., the principal technical solution, the interaction with the device and test applications of auditory content for various user-groups and use situations to ensure a flexible, usable solution. The goal is to design an affordable system, which is beneficial and can enhance the museum visit for as many visitors as possible.

Our proposed system consists of a generic infrastructure of location-aware technology, together with use- and user-adapted auditory content. The visitor carries a portable device and headsets for the auditory information, in an environment equipped with identification tags which tells the device where it is. The appropriate auditory information is loaded into the device, and transmitted to the user when at the location of an information-equipped object or when entering a room.

Five different test applications have been developed so far. The first two were primarily designed as assistive support for users with reduced vision and language comprehension disabilities, but nevertheless we strived for a mainstream application with universal usability [9] in accordance with the findings of [5 and 6]. Extensive user studies, requirement analysis, a mockup wizard-of-oz prototype was developed and user-tested, resulting in a InfraRed-based hardware prototype constructed by the partner IT company. The other three test applications are auditory games based on the exhibitions in the museum: a treasure hunt for children and families, an enigma for Swedish-learning immigrants, and a guess-who puzzle for teenagers developed by digital media students. The games run on a PDA-based prototype, and we have conducted user-tests with representative users and teachers of the corresponding groups.

## 5   Design Strategies for Enhancements of Experiences

The proposed design strategies are presented in three parts: a design approach discussing methodological aspects, a set of enhancement strategies or classifications of different types of enhancements to guide the design, and a model for estimating the potential benefits related to enhancements features of the system design.

### 5.1   Design Approach

The design approach taken in the case study was two-folded: a user-centered, contextual design approach was combined with an explorative, experimental, more technology-driven approach to design. The former approach was primarily used to guide the design work by identifying requirements and design implications for identified target groups, whereas the latter was used for searching new, potential target groups and for exploring additional uses of proposed design solutions. The two approaches were intertwined during the iterative process of forming a usable design solution.

User-testing with simulated or real prototypes in the proper context is crucial for experience-based design. Since the values of applications are more concerned with sensations and emotions than actual needs, it is difficult to predict user reactions and experiences. Moreover, requirements gathering related to the experience aspect (in contrast to ordinary usability issues) need to be experimental and suggestive, since experience-based sensations are difficult to value in advance. This calls for a design approach which combines contextual, user-centered methods with experimental, explorative design in short iterative, cycles with frequent user tests and evaluations.

## 5.2  Enhancement Strategies

In this section we will describe some of the features we have designed and evaluated, as well as the underlying rationale in terms of enhancement discussions. We conclude by summarizing our experience in three general enhancement strategies.

The museum is primarily based on visual artefacts and visual information, which clearly limits the accessibility for individuals with reduced vision. Several participants in our user studies were older women who used to visit the museum but had ceased to do so due to their reduced vision. Providing a solution where a visitor's lack of vision is *compensated* by auditory information, including descriptions of visual phenomena, can change an inaccessible experience to become accessible, which is clearly an enhancement.

Most information provided in the museum consists of written text. There are live guided tours available, but only at certain times and at cost. For visitors who are incapable or reluctant to acquire information through reading, this information has limited accessibility. Underlying reasons for such limited capability are reading disorders, minor cognitive disabilities, or reduced skills in provided languages (children, new immigrants, tourists, foreigners). For these groups, simplified auditory information *compensates* for their reduced capability of reading, and *complements* the written information. For tourists and foreigners, information provided in a language they are accustomed to *compensate* for their language incomprehension and additional explanations may *compensate* for a lack of cultural understanding. Making experience-related information accessible to those who want it, certainly enhances their experience. *Augmenting* the information with background explanations to increase the understanding of an artefact, potentially enhances the experience of it.

The museum is frequently visited by children and teenagers, as part of school projects or at the spare time accompanied with adults. Youngsters of today are normally not thrilled by facts about local culture, handicraft and artworks, or contemporary art and cultural history, unless presented in a way attractive to them. Today, most of the exhibitions are arranged around visual artefacts and objects that cannot be touched or felt, accompanied with written, often fact-based information, which is far away from the entertainment this group is used to. The auditory edutainment games *augment* the exhibitions to become a physical adventure arena with motivational, playful information which engage these users groups into an informative and entertaining experience.

Our user tests indicate that such games can result in a great enhancement of the museum visits for these groups of visitors.

Any visitor could benefit from listening to information rather than reading it: auditory information *complement* visual objects much better than written information, and does not compete for the same cognitive resources. Moreover, visual displays take up space in the room, they cannot be read at a distance and the aesthetics of exhibitions generally do not improve by informative visual displays. With an auditory, location-aware system a variety of information can be provided (e.g., about the artist, painting techniques or history), as well as information at different levels and depths. Finally, sound illustrations accompanying the artefacts or background music can be provided. These examples are *augmentations* of the physical exhibitions that have the potential of enhancing the museum experience for many visitors.

We have identified the following enhancements strategies as useful tools for exploring potential enhancements features:

- *Compensate:* If you compensate for a lack of something, you do something to make the situation better. This enhancement refer to, for instance, compensating for disabilities and is subjected to people, who lacks some abilities needed to take part of the full experience.
- *Complement:* Things or people that complement each other are different or do something differently in a way that makes them a good combination. This enhancement suggests that an experience could be known in many ways. It allows for other ways the event or situation can be experienced.
- *Augment:* To *augmenting an experience* means to make it stronger, by adding something. By supplying more of actual resources or new resources, the experience is augmented in a way such that it provides a richer context.

The enhancement strategies can also be used for categorisation of enhancements in the value-added estimation model below.

### 5.3  Value-Added Estimation Model Related to Enhancements

Exploration and experimentation is fruitful for generating ideas and seeing possibilities, but there comes a point in the design process where convergence is needed and generated features must be analysed and judged against each other and against their corresponding costs. For this purpose we have developed *a value-added estimation model*, to guide the convergence phase, in order to estimate the relation between potential benefit and cost of the proposed features. In this attempt to estimate the enhancements of experiences, we have focused on the *enhancement,* i.e., ways of improving the value, quality or attractiveness of an experience. The enhancement focus allows us to compare relative values of experiences rather than absolute, and this is easier to judge. A relative judgement involves only ordering two emotional experiences, which most users are able to do, whereas an absolute judgement involves some scale of measurement [2] which is problematic to compare between subjects. For this analysis, we used the enhancements strategies as categories of different ways of achieving enhancements. The model consists of a table with the following entries:

**Table 1.** The value-added estimation model

| Enhancement feature content | Enhancement category of feature | Target group | Estimated Enhancement (EE) | Estimated Value (EV) | Cost |
|---|---|---|---|---|---|
| Which information that needs to be provided | Which type of enhancement the feature refer to | For which target group this is likely to be an enhancement. | An estimation of how much value the enhancement may add. Should be guided by user tests. | EV = Estimated Enhancement EE* estimated % of attracted target group | Estimation of production costs |

To break down a complex concept such as enhancement of experiences, helps in understanding its components and their relations. A more grounded estimation of the enhancements value can be done, and the points of uncertainties become explicit. Thus, it can be used to make strategic decisions *before* the technology is developed.

# 6 Discussion and Future Work

Choosing the *enhancement* of experience to be the main unit of analysis in our study was useful in order to better understand different kinds of enhancements, as well as classifying design attempts. It resulted in the three enhancement strategies: *compensating* for something missing, *complementing* something or *augmenting* something in the experience. The museum management found the strategies "mind-trigging" and promising for valuing its IS initiative. However, the suggested design strategies need to be used in other settings to further verify its usefulness.

# References

1. Alben, L. 1996. Quality of experience: defining the criteria for effective interaction design. *interactions* 3, 3 (May. 1996), 11-15.
2. Desmet, P. Designing Emotions. Doctoral thesis, Delft University of Technology, Netherlands, 2002.
3. Dickinson, A., Eisma, R. and Gregor, P. (2003). Challenging interfaces/redesigning users, In *Proceedings of the 2003 conference on Universal usability*, P 61-68, Vancouver, British Columbia, Canada 2003. ACM Press.
4. Forlizzi, J & Battarbee, K (2004) Understanding Experience in Interactive Systems. *Proc of the 2004 conference on Designing interactive systems: processes, practices, methods, and techniques.* 261-268 ACM Press, NY.
5. Law, C., Jacko, J., Peterson, B., and Tobias, J. (2005): Universal designs versus assistive technologies: research agendas and practical applications. In *Proc of the 7th international ACM SIGACCESS Conference on Computers and Accessibility* (Baltimore, MD, USA, October 2005). Assets '05. ACM Press, NY, 2-3.
6. Liffick, B. W. (2003). Assistive technology as an HCI topic. *J. Comput. Small Coll.* 19, 2 (Dec. 2003), 142-144.
7. McClelland, I. (2005). User Experience Design: A new form of design practice takes shape. *CHI 2005*, April 2-7 2005 Portland, Oregon, USA.
8. McLellan, H. (2000) *Experience Design.* Cyber Psychology & Behaviour. 3.1. 59-69
9. Shneiderman, B. (2000). Universal usability, *Communications ACM*, vol. 43, no 5, 84-91. ACM Press.

# Imitating the Behavior of Human Players in Action Games

Atsushi Nakano, Akihito Tanaka, and Junichi Hoshino

Systems & Information Engineering, University of Tsukuba, Japan
{nakano, jhoshino}@edu.esys.tsukuba.ac.jp

**Abstract.** In action games, the computer's behavior lacks diversity and human players are able to learn how the computer behaves by playing the same game over and over again. As a result, human players eventually grow tired of the game. Therefore, this paper proposes a method of imitating the behavior of human players by creating profiles of players from their play data. By imitating what many different players do, a greater variety of actions can be created.

## 1 Introduction

In many action games, a human player manages different behavior every time he/she faces a different opponent. However, when the player faces a computer as an opponent, its behavior is limited in variety since its behavioral patterns are restricted by a finite-state machine or by scripts programmed in advance [1]. Because of this limitation in behavior, a human player can play the same game repeatedly, learn the behavior of the computer-controlled game character, and win easily. This is one major reason why human players soon grow tired of "fighting with a computer." Thus, many players prefer playing with another human player to playing with a computer. Yet this human-to-human play has a major drawback, as there is no guarantee that a player can find a human opponent when he/she wants to "fight."

Recently, it has become easier to find a human opponent over the Internet or other networks, which has alleviated this problem by connecting two human players across a long distance. Still, it remains difficult to find a human opponent with a similar degree of proficiency and/or a similar preference in style of play. Therefore, game players demand computer-controlled characters with many different behavioral patterns, which they can fight at anytime. However, many researchers in this field are focusing on making the computer's artificial intelligence for fighting human players as "tough" as humans. Furthermore, researchers are striving to develop artificial intelligence that is closer to human intelligence. However, such research is not focusing on imitating the behavior of a player that a human player wants to fight.

This paper proposes a system that imitates a player's actions by creating a profile of the player. The profile incorporates the player's tactics and strategies based on play data for that particular player and controls the computer character's behavior by referring to the profile. By changing the player profile for the computer, a human player can face computer-controlled characters with many different behavioral patterns. The human player can also fight a computer-controlled opponent that matches his/her preference simply by choosing the player profile he/she prefers.

R. Harper, M. Rauterberg, M. Combetto (Eds.): ICEC 2006, LNCS 4161, pp. 332–335, 2006.

As shown in Fig. 1, the proposed system records the moment-to-moment actions that a game player takes and the timing of interactions between game players as the play data. From these play data, the system calculates correlations of situations and tactics to the actions taken by the player in such situations. In addition, the system acquires from the play data the strategies (tactic sequences) of the player, which are represented by a sequence of tactics. The acquired tactics and tactic sequences are stored as the player profile of the particular player to be imitated. Then, the system creates imitated actions of the player based on this player profile. The computer evaluates the distance between the situation in the game and the strategy selection criteria in order to create the imitated behavior of the player by choosing and carrying out and carrying out the strategy in the player profile that the imitated player would most likely take.

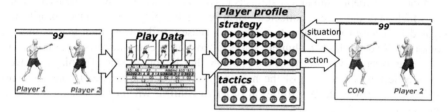

**Fig. 1.** Outline of the proposed system

## 2  Player Profile System

Our proposed system records characteristics of the imitated player in his/her play data as the player's profile and creates actions that imitate the player. This system chooses the actions to take based on the sequence of actions recorded in the profile and reproduces the sequencing of actions. Out of these recorded sequences, a sequence is chosen probabilistically according to the frequency of its appearance. This allows the reproduction of the player's tendency in action as well as the diversity of actions the player could take. In this paper, the correlation between a given situation and the actions taken by the imitated player in that situation, which are observed in the play data, are referred to as tactics. A strategy combining such tactics is called a "tactic sequence", which is a series of tactics. The appearance frequency of each tactic sequence is also obtained from the play data. The player's profile consists of these sequences and their frequencies. The computer character creates the actions of the imitated player by choosing what actions to take based on this player profile.

According to this process, the computer character that is equipped with the player profile of the imitated player makes actions that imitate the player. In addition, by changing the player profile for the computer to use, a human player can "fight" many different opponents with many different behavioral patterns. With our proposed system, a human player can play a game with his/her friend and obtain the friend's play data. Then, the friend's profile can be created. With this profile, the human player can fight with a computer character that imitates the friend's behavioral patterns, even when the friend is not present. The human player can also analyze the behavioral patterns in order to defeat the friend in their next fight. In addition, a player can download other profiles. For instance, the profile of the champion of a game competition can be downloaded and a player can fight the champion.

## 3  Evaluation Experiment

To verify the effectiveness of the system proposed herein, we implemented the system in an experiment. For the experiment, a PC (Intel ® Xeon ™ CPU 2.80GHz, 1.00GB RAM, ELSA Gloria4 900 XGL) and a "joy pad" (Xbox controller) were used. The game used in the experiment was similar to many fighting games. The player who has done more damage to the opponent or brought the opponent's power down to 0 within a certain period of time is the winner.

In the experiment, human test subjects played ten matches between themselves during which play data were collected. Then, using the play data a player profile was created for each of the human test subjects. These profiles were then loaded into the computer. Next, each of the human subjects "fought" a computer character controlled according to the player profile of the opponent he/she fought when the play data were being collected. Then, each of the human players fought a computer character containing his/her own player profile, in order to confirm whether or not the character imitates the player's strategies.

We observed and compared the human players fighting another human player while collecting play data and while the human players were fighting the computer character controlled with the player profile of their respective human opponents. For example, Subject A in red trunks adjusted the timing while fending off the opponent's attacks by dashing backwards(Fig. 2(a)). Then, when the attacking opponent was momentarily vulnerable, Subject A moved closer to the opponent by attacking the opponent with continuous jump kicks. When the opponent fought back, Subject A adjusted the timing again. This was the subject's strategy. When we applied the player profile of Subject A to the computer, we observed that the computer character followed a similar strategy. As shown in Fig. 2(b), the computer character in blue trunks

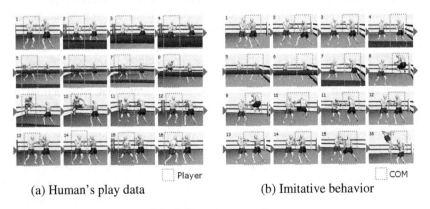

(a) Human's play data                    (b) Imitative behavior

**Fig. 2.** Experiment results

dashed backwards to fend off the opponent's attacks and to adjust the timing (Frames 1 through 6 in Fig. 2(b)), then, when the attacking opponent became vulnerable, just like Subject A, the character got closer to the opponent by attacking the opponent with jump kicks (Frames 7 through 12 in Fig. 2(b)) and continued the attacks (Frames 12 through 16 in Fig. 2(b)).

## 4  Conclusion

This paper proposed a system that enables a computer character to imitate a human player. To do so, the system first acquires tactics and tactic sequences from play data of a player. Then, from the tactic sequences collected it creates tactic graphs that represent the strategic actions of the player. From these graphs, the system selects tactics that suit different situations. We also demonstrated the effectiveness of the system in an evaluation experiment. Furthermore, we created many different behavioral patterns for the computer by changing player profiles, which are the collections of tactic sequences and tactic graphs of the particular players.

Although we tried to obtain a diverse range of behaviors by probabilistically choosing from multiple candidate tactics, such diversity was not actually obtained because of insufficient play data. One solution to this problem could be to create as many player profiles from as much play data as possible, so that more tactics can be acquired. However, the more tactics we have, the more strategies are developed and the more computation is required in order to choose a strategy. Therefore, in order to manage more strategies, it is necessary to employ a more efficient method of choosing strategies, such as clustering strategies depending on the situation.

## Reference

1. Brian Schwab. "AI GAME ENGINE PROGRAMMING", Charles River Media, pp.203-210 (2004)

# Electronic Treasure Hunt: Real-Time Cooperation Type Game That Uses Location Information

Jun Munemori[1], Shunsuke Miyai[2], and Junko Itou[1]

[1] Department of Design and Information Sciences, Faculty of Systems Engineering,
Wakayama University
930 Sakaedani, Wakayama 640-8510, Japan
{munemori, itou}@sys.wakayama-u.ac.jp
[2] Graduate School of Systems Engineering, Wakayama University
930 Sakaedani, Wakayama 640-8510, Japan
s055056@sys.wakayama-u.ac.jp

**Abstract.** The electronic treasure hunt developed this time uses location information and operates avatar. The participant competes for the point looking for the treasure arranged virtually. The feature of this game is that the treasure cannot be obtained if two people do not cooperate. From the experiments the following points became clear that participants evaluated highly the avatar operation system that used GPS location information. The cooperation system by which each player's position became a point allowed location information to be used well.

**Keywords:** GPS, PDA, treasure hunt, cooperation, location information.

## 1 Introduction

Research utilizing location information has grown [1],[2]. There are numerous models of cellular phone equipped with GPS, and present location retrieval services and applications that make the best use of portability are being provided [3] in Japan. The electronic treasure hunt developed this time uses location information and operates avatar. The participant competes for the point looking for the treasure arranged virtually. The feature of this game is that the treasure cannot be obtained if two people do not cooperate. The interest of this system was evaluated from various angles. In this paper, the outline, experiment, and results of the developed electronic treasure hunt are described.

## 2 Electronic Treasure Hunt

The system of this game consists of a movable system and a server. Moreover, the movable system is composed of a PDA (SONY PEG-NZ90), a PHS (NEC, AH-N401C) and a GPS unit (SONY GU-BT1).

This game uses location information and real-time two-way communication acquired from GPS, and is a treasure hunt game for two or more people. The purpose of

R. Harper, M. Rauterberg, M. Combetto (Eds.): ICEC 2006, LNCS 4161, pp. 336 – 339, 2006.

the player is to find the virtual treasure arranged in the university. There are two kinds of treasure, the usual treasure (ten pieces) and special treasure (three pieces). When the special one is acquired, the cooperation of the other players is needed. He looks for the treasure concealed on the map by actually moving in the university, and operating the avatar displayed on the screen through a concrete search method. It is repeated during the time limit. Points are allotted to each treasure. We placed a limit of 5 pieces on the number of treasure to possess. The order is displayed in real time on the main screen while playing the game. When the time limit is up, the person with the most points is the winner.

This game is chiefly composed of eight screens (Initialization screen, main screen, search screen, treasure acquisition screen, treasure list screen, reduction map screen, avatar change screen, result announcement screen). In the game, the main screen (Fig.1) is an important screen. Avatar and various information on each player are displayed in the map of the university that is the stage of the game. Avatar is operated on this screen.

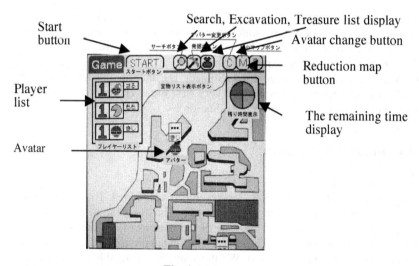

**Fig. 1.** Main screen

The cooperation request is a function to call for one to approach other players when a special treasure is acquired. Cooperation can be requested to a player away by the use of the message transmission function when there is no player that can cooperate nearby. In the emoticon list transmitted by the message, there is a pick mark (Fig. 2). The pick mark transmits to the other party who wants to request this cooperation. On the other hand, the other party replies with a message of "OK (O)" or "NO (X)". These correspond to consent or refusal. At this time, the player comes to think about his strategy from a position with each other party and present order, and to select the other party who complies with the request for cooperation.

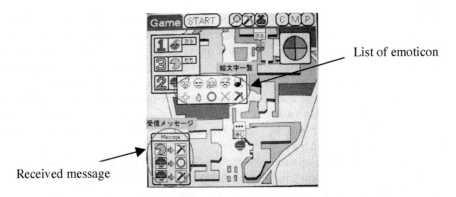

List of emoticon

Received message

**Fig. 2.** Message transmitting function

# 3  Experiment

Experiments were conducted on the Wakayama University premises. Four people participated in one experiment, which were done five times every four days. One experiment was about 30 minutes. The experimental subjects were seven in total. Two subjects participated in five experiments (Subject A and B), one person participated four times (Subject C), one three times (Subject D), and three people participated one time. For the subject of B, this was the very first time. The questionnaire was given with each experiment (The five-stage evaluation).

# 4  Results and Discussion

(1) First experiment
First of all, it is the first evaluation. Seven subjects responded. The evaluations for the operation system of avatar were high (4.3~4.6). The cooperation function seems not to be used easily (3.4) the first time. One of the reasons to add the cooperation func-tion is use of the location information. A high evaluation of the use of the location information was obtained (4.3~4.4). We think that we were able to give the meaning of a position to each other by having added the cooperation function. We think there is no load with the cooperation request using the message transmission function (4.1). However, there is an opinion of not noticing the reception of the message easily, and it seems that it is necessary to improve this. The overall evaluation of enjoyment was 3.9 and it is thought that it was possible to build it in the game well as a new function. The overall evaluations of the game were high (4.4~4.6). Moreover, when interest was evaluated by the rental charge, it was 286 yen on average. It was an evaluation for each verge of the attraction in the game center and the amusement park.
(2) Continuous experiment
Next, we show the results of the continuous experiment that four subjects did (Table 1), followed by a discussion. The cooperation function is considered. The evaluation went up in about the third time in A in Q3 and Q4 in Table 1. Concerning the cooperation frequency, the frequencies tended to increase more beginning in the

middle. It was stated, "The interest of the game was felt again because we cooperated" at the third time from the description type questionnaire of A. It is understood from Q1 and Q2 in Table 1. The evaluation temporarily rises the third time. The cooperation frequency increased from two or three times. Perhaps, it seems that it is because the usage of this function was understood from acquiring this experience. We think that we can slow down getting tired by adding the function (element) for which time is necessary by mastering the game.

**Table 1.** Results of Questionnaire (multiple experiments)

| Question | A | B | C | D | Mean value |
|---|---|---|---|---|---|
| Q1.Was this game enjoyable? | 3→3→4→3→2 | 5→5→5→5→5 | 5→3→4→4 | 5→4→4 | 4.5→3.8→4.3→4.0→3.5 |
| Q2.Do you want to play this game in the future? | 3→2→4→2→2 | 5→5→5→5→4 | 4→3→3→3 | 5→4→4 | 4.5→3.5→4.0→3.3→3.0 |
| Q3.Is it easy to use the cooperation system? | 3→1→4→4→3 | 3→3→5→4→5 | 4→3→4→4 | 5→5→4 | 3.8→3.0→4.3→4.0→4.0 |
| Q4.Was cooperation enjoyable? | 3→2→4→3→4 | 5→5→5→5→5 | 5→4→4→4 | 5→4→5 | 4.5→3.8→4.5→4.0→4.5 |
| Q5.Did the position of each other make you anxious while you were playing the game? | 4→4→4→5→4 | 5→5→5→5→4 | 3→5→4→4 | 5→5→4 | 4.3→4.8→4.3→4.7→4.0 |
| Q6.Was the character operation that used GPS interesting? | 4→3→3→4→3 | 5→5→5→4→5 | 4→3→4→3 | 4→4→4 | 4.3→3.8→4.0→4.0→4.0 |
| Q7.Was there a sense of presence? | 4→3→4→3→2 | 5→5→5→5→5 | 5→4→3→4 | 4→4→5 | 4.5→4.0→4.3→4.0→3.5 |
| Reference: Numbers of collaboreation. | 0→1→5→?→0 | 0→3→6→3→1 | 1→1→3→2 | 1→3→? | |

## 5 Conclusion

We have developed a game that used location information and operated avatar. This game has the feature that participants cooperate in real time. From the experiments the following points became clear.
(1) Participants evaluated highly the avatar operation system that used GPS location information.
(2) The cooperation system by which each player's position became a point allowed location information to be used well. Moreover, it was found that in addition to the fact that it should be used several times until the subject comes to be able to master it, there is the possibility of delaying subjects' getting tired.

## References

1. Fintham, M., Anastasi, R., Benford, S., Hemmings, T., Crabtree, A., Greenhalgh, C., Rodden, T. Tandavanitj, N., Adams, M., and Row-Farr, J: Where On-Line Meets On-The-Streets: Experiences With Mobile Mixed Reality Games, Proc. of CHI 2003 (2003), 569-576
2. Brunnberg, L.:The Road Ranger- Making Use of Traffic Encountera in a Mobile Multiplayer Game, Proc. of MUM 2004 (2004)
3. THINKWARE,INC./IDEANETWORK CO.,Ltd./TAIRA AKITSUURL : http://hakkutu.jp

# Design of Positive Biofeedback Using a Robot's Behaviors as Motion Media

Nagisa Munekata, Naofumi Yoshida, Shigeru Sakurazawa,
Yasuo Tsukahara, and Hitoshi Matsubara

Future University-Hakodate
116-2 Kamedanakano, Hakodate 041-8655, Japan
{g2104042, g2104044, sakura,
yasuo, matsubar}@fun.ac.jp
http://www.fun.ac.jp

**Abstract.** The purpose of this study is to develop a game system that uses biofeedback to provide an attractive entertaining game. In general, negative biofeedback is used for relaxing users; however, in our game system positive biofeedback is used for arousing them. We assumed that the latter biofeedback method could affect the users' emotional states effectively; that is why we call it positive biofeedback. We used skin conductance response (SCR) as a biofeedback signal in our game system because SCR can effectively reflect the mental agitation of users. Therefore, we developed a teddy bear robot to be the motion media for providing feeding back the measured SCR information to users. When the value user SCR increases during interaction with this robot, the robot starts moving its arms and head in relation to the transition of SCR values so that it appears to be agitated. We then conducted two experiments to measure the participants' SCR transitions. From the results of these experiments, we can state that the users' emotional attachment to the robot and the robot's behaviors in reaction to user biological signals are important cues that create positive biofeedback.

## 1 Introduction

Recently, interface systems that can reflect human emotional states by means of biological signals have been focused on, and many researchers have been working on developing this kind of interface. Presenting their own measured human biological signals back to people has been said to help them comprehend their physical and emotional states. Moreover, doing this can provide some entertainment tools for ordinary people. One example is the frequent use of lie detection equipment in various TV programs. This method is called biofeedback, a methodology that helps people perceive their own physical condition and emotion by means of numerical, visualized or audible data in response to their own measured biological signals. Currently, many self-control apparatus using biofeedback are actively being developed, e.g., visual feedback conveyed with light pulses or audible feedback using music or sounds.

In general, biofeedback is used to make patients aware of their involuntary affects or emotions by making it possible for them to perceive these states. In this way,

R. Harper, M. Rauterberg, M. Combetto (Eds.): ICEC 2006, LNCS 4161, pp. 340 – 349, 2006.
© IFIP International Federation for Information Processing 2006

biofeedback is used as an aspect of medical care that helps patients relax. These systems can be said to consist of negative biofeedback that offers people a means of suppressing their involuntary affects or emotions, in other words, help them relax.

This means that this negative biofeedback cannot be applied directly to entertainment because if players fall into relaxed states while playing a video game they will become bored with it and eventually quite the game. Therefore, we have previously proposed positive biofeedback as a way to incite involuntary affects or emotion, in other words, a way to make users excited or agitated. We then developed a video game that exploits such positive biofeedback [1-3].

Concretely, players' measured biological signals used as positive biofeedback dynamically affected the game environment and the behaviors of a game character. For example, when a player became agitated and experienced panic, many enemies started to appear on the computer display. As a result of these studies, we found that this positive biofeedback could stimulate players' affects or emotions, and make them excited and agitated.

The purpose of the study reported here is to propose an enhanced video game by means of positive biofeedback that will make players much more excited and agitated and sustain their agitated mental states as long as possible. Concretely, the measured biological signals are fed back not only into the game environment and the behaviors of a game character, as in our former studies, but in addition, these signals affect the behaviors of a stuffed animal robot (IP ROBOT PHONE developed by IWAYA corporation [4]). This robot looks similar to the game character appearing on the computer display. We then conducted psychological experiments to observe players' mental states during game playing and investigated the effects of presenting positive biofeedback with robot behavior as motion media, and we investigated the players' mental states in response to the information that was fed back.

## 2  Biological Signals

Electrical signals detected from the human body are objective and quantitative data that reflect psychological states and physiological functions. Such signals have been used for diagnosis and treatment in medical care and for the lie detector used in police interrogation [5]. One of the biological signals that a lie detector uses is the skin conductance response (SCR) that occurs when mental states such as agitation, surprise, and excitement induce changes in the conductance on the skin surface [6-10].

We have little awareness of the physiological functioning of our own body because most physiological functions are involuntary, and therefore uncontrollable. The SCR is a typical example. No one is aware of the minute amounts of sweating during mental agitation unless an unusually large amount of mental stress is present. Therefore, observing one's own SCR produces a strange feeling that this is not a feature of one's own body but rather that of another person. People generally believe that inner agitation or excitement during communication in daily life can be concealed. However, the SCR can reveal concealed agitation despite a person's intention to conceal it. The SCR indicator greatly amplifies the amount of involuntary signaling that can take place.

## 3   Materials and Methods

Figure 1 shows the video game system developed in this study. The SCR signal is a reaction to changes in conductance on the surface of the skin due to sweating. Since eccrine glands are most dense on the palm of the hand and sweating is an autonomic response that can be triggered by emotional stimuli, the palm is an ideal site from

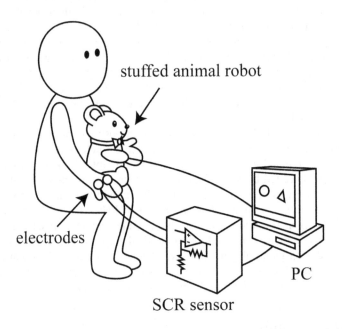

**Fig. 1.** Developed video game system with stuffed animal robot

**Fig. 2.** (a) Game character, yellow bear, on computer display (Normal condition), (b) Stuffed animal robot that is put on the participants' laps

which to obtain measurements of psychophysical activity by using the SCR. The player provides the SCR via two electrodes. The signal was amplified by a SCR sensor, transmitted to a PC through an A/D converter, and it could be displayed at the upper-right corner of the game monitor (see the Figs. 2 (a) and 3 (a). In particular, Fig. 3 (a) displays the transition values of accumulated SCR. (In this paper, we specifically mean accumulated SCR values whenever we mention SCR values). Information from the players' psychological excitement or agitation is thus fed back to them, and this tends to cause them to become more agitated. A positive biofeedback loop of this agitation often arises within this system, and to succeed in the game players must overcome the effects of their own excitement or escalating panic.

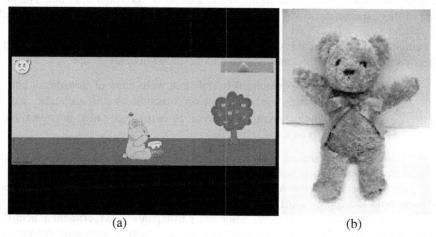

(a)                                        (b)

**Fig. 3.** (a) Game character stung by a wasp, (b) robot bear's corresponding reaction when game character in computer display is stung by wasp. Showing that the character and robot expressed similar behaviors.

The specific game story is as follows. The game character is a yellow bear. This bear is continuously walking from left to right on a plane to take a honey pot into her home. The player's task is to watch this bear calmly. When the player's SCR values are lower than a certain value for specific durations, the bear can reach her house and the player successfully completes the game. On the other hand, if the game player is agitated (e.g., their SCR values increase more than the specified value), the bear also becomes agitated and drops the honey pot. Immediately after the honey pot is dropped, a wasp appears, notices that the bear has the honey pot, and stings the bear. When the wasp stings the bear three times the game session ends without success. The number of wasp stings is displayed at the upper-left corner of the game monitor as a bear face icon; a green face means the bear was stung zero times (Fig. 2 (a)), yellow means one time (Fig. 3 (a)), and red means two times. The duration of this game is designed to be one minute.

While playing this game, players hold a stuffed animal robot on their laps (see Fig. 2 (b)) that is similar in appearance to the game character, the yellow bear, that appears on the game monitor; this robot moves in the same way as the game character (Fig. 3 (b)). For example, when the players' SCR values are increasing, the robot opens its arms and its body trembles as if it feels the pain from a wasp sting. Thus, this game system gives the players feedback in the form of the game character's behavior as visual feedback and the robot's behaviors as tactile feedback.

# 4  Experiments

We conducted the two psychological experiments. The purposes of the first experiment (Experiment 1) were to investigate the effects of the robot's behaviors on participant excitement or agitation and to achieve positive biofeedback. We set up two experimental sessions; one is Session A in which the robot moves in relation to the participants' SCR values, while in the other, Session B, the robot does not. The purpose of this experiment was to compare the SCR values observed in Session A with those from Session B.

Participants were 14 university students (6 men and 8 women: 19 – 25 years old). These participants were randomly assigned to the following two groups:

> • **Group A:** who experienced 6 trials that were pairs of Sessions A and B for three turns in the same order, Session A then Session B; each time, and
> • **Group B:** who experienced the sessions in reversed order, Session B then Session A; for three turns

The purposes of the second experiment (Experiment 2) were to investigate the effects of participants' emotional attachment to the robot on their excitement or agitation and to achieve positive biofeedback. In this experiment, the participants were asked to hold the robot as if holding some waste or an object they disliked and to avoid feeling emotional attachment, while the participants in Experiment 1 held the robot on their laps. The participants in Experiment 2 were 7 university students (3 men and 4 women; 19-25 years old); no members of this group participated in Experiment 1, and they were designated as **Group C**. The participants in Group C experienced the same session order as Group A in Experiment 1, 6 trials that were pairs of Sessions A and B for three turns in the same order, Session A then Session B; each time. Concretely, we compared the measured SCR values of the participants in Group C with those of participants in Group A in Experiment 1.

# 5  Results

## 5.1  Experiment 1

Figs. 4 and 5 show the typical transitions of SCR values in each trial of one participant in Group A and one participant in Group B, respectively. These figures show that the SCR values were higher when the participants played this game in conditions of Session A, while these values were lower when they played in Session B. However, the SCR values in the 6th trial in both groups showed rather higher values than those for the other trials. A possible reason for this phenomenon is that some participants reported, "I got excited about winning this game because it was the final trial in this experiment." Thus, the attitudes of these participants toward the experiment affected the SCR values in the 6th sessions.

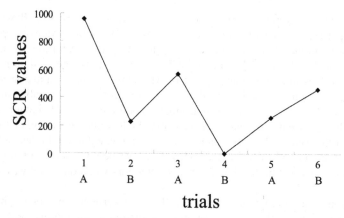

**Fig. 4.** Typical transition of SCR values in each trial of one participant in Group A

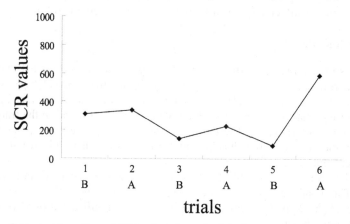

**Fig. 5.** Typical transition of SCR values in each trial of one participant in Group B

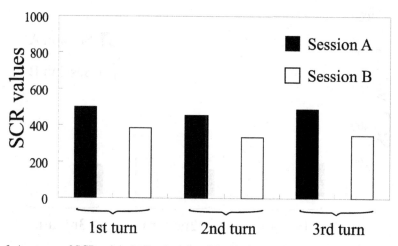

**Fig. 6.** Averages of SCR values in Session A and Session B within each turn of Experiment 1

Fig.6 shows the average of SCR values in Session A and Session B within each turn for Experiment 1. This figure reveals that SCR values of participants playing in Session A were higher than those in Session B for every turn. Additionally, this figure shows a gradually downward trend of SCR values; that is, the first turn revealed higher SCR values in both Session A and B, while the last turn resulted in lower values. This phenomenon is evidence that the participants became habituated to the game, or lost interest in the game environment and/or the robot behavior. Actually, even though individual differences in measured SCR values were found for participants, out of the total of 14 participants, 11 participants exhibited higher SCR values in Session A compared to Session B. Therefore, we believe most participants were affected by the positive biofeedback of robot behaviors when the robot was placed on their laps.

In addition, some participants reported, "I had a warm feeling for the bear robot because it was dynamically affected by my excitement and agitation." or "I hated for the wasp to sting the pretty bear." Thus, we can say that the positive biofeedback from SCR values greatly affected those participants' feelings about the robot.

### 5.2  Experiment 2

Fig.7 shows the average of participant SCR values in Sessions A and B during each turn in Experiment 2. From this figure, one can see that the SCR values of Session A and Session B revealed practically no difference in every turn. Moreover, a gradually decreasing trend that we observed in Experiment 1 was not found in the transition of SCR values in Experiment 2. Therefore, we can say that these participants were not affected by the positive biofeedback from the robot when it was held without emotional attachment.

Fig.8 shows the average of SCR values for all trials of participants in Experiments 1 and 2. This result revealed that the SCR values for participants in Experiment 2 were lower than the participants in Experiment 1; a significant difference ($p < 0.01$) between them is shown.

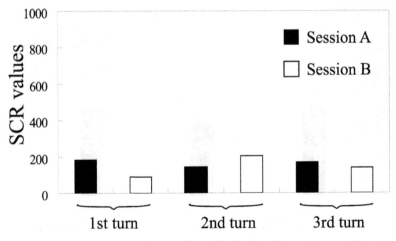

**Fig. 7.** Average of SCR values in Session A and Session B within each turn of Experiment 2

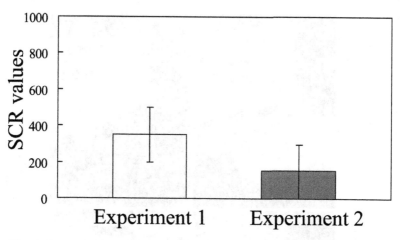

**Fig. 8.** Average of SCR values in all trials of participants in Experiments 1 and 2

## 6 Discussion and Conclusions

From the results of the two experiments described above, we found the following phenomena:

- The SCR values of the participants in Experiment 1 were higher when the participants played this game in the conditions set for Session A;
- The SCR values of the participants in Experiment 2 were lower than those of participants in Experiment 1; and
- The participants in Experiment 2 were not affected by the positive biofeedback derived from the behaviors of the robot because they had no emotional attachment to the robot.

Thus, we can say that the robot's behaviors displayed by means of the positive biofeedback and the act of holding the robot with emotional attachment influenced the excitement or agitation of participants.

In Experiment 1, the participants felt some responsibility to help the game character and the robot avoid the punishments; this was because it seemed to them that drastic transition of their SCR values directly hurt the character and the robot. Furthermore, we can say that the robot's trembling behaviors caused it to look as if is suffered from pain, and this action increased their feeling of responsibility. Therefore, the fact that the participants reacted sensitively to the robot's behaviors was made apparent.

On the other hand, the SCR values of participants in Experiment 2 were lower than those of participants in Experiment 1. Specifically, we can say that the SCR values were not affected by the robot's behaviors. Although the important issue in this game is to avoid punishment of the game character and robot, i.e., their being stung by a wasp, the participants in Experiment 2 seemed not to consider doing this. Therefore, we assumed that these participants did not feel any emotional attachment to the robot.

**Fig. 9.** Participants in Experiment 2 (Group C) holding the robot without emotional attachment

This phenomenon, that some participants did not form an emotional attachment for the robot, could be explained by detailed analysis of the results of Experiment 2. Fig. 9 consists of some snapshots taken when the participants in Experiment 2 were holding the robot without emotional attachment. This figure reveals that these participants accepted the experimenter's instruction, i.e., "holding this robot as if it is waste or a disliked thing." Apparently, they started thinking of the robot as just an appliance that produces a vibration, and did not care about its behaviors. In this case, these participants could not create an appropriate positive biofeedback with the game system; that is, they were unaware of the meanings of the robot's behaviors even though the robot's behaviors reflected the users' biological signals just as in Experiment 1, in which most participants did recognize the meaning of the robot's behaviors.

We found another reason that some participants did not form emotional attachment to the robot, and this reason was not directly related to the experimental conditions of Experiment 2. Some participants reported introspections, such as, "I hate this stuffed animal." and "The robot's behaviors look very eerie." In fact, in the results for these participants, no differences in their SCR values for Session A and B were found, and their average SCR values in all trials were lower than those of other participants in the same group. Thus, if the participants were not interested in the robot itself, they were not affected by the positive biofeedback. Apparently, they did not have any initial emotional attachment with this robot, even though they held it on their laps. We considered that these participants' lack of interest was rooted in their personalities.

In sum, this study described our findings that the emotional attachment of the participants to the robot and the robot's behavior as motion media had significant influences on the participants' excitement or agitation and that we had achieved positive biofeedback in our game environment. Therefore, positive feedback obtained by using the behaviors of robot to which users have emotional attachment would be a key technology to achieve interactive systems that make players excited or agitated. This result should provide some guidance for the design and development of entertainment tools that provide positive biofeedback by using robots as motion media.

# References

1. Sakurazawa. S, Munekata. N, Yoshida. N, Tsukahara. Y, and Matsubara. H.: Entertainment Feature of the Computer Game Using a Skin Conductance Response, In proceedings of ACM SIGCHI International Conference on Advances in Computer Entertainment Technology ACE 2004, pp.181-186, (2004).
2. Sakurazawa. S, Munekata. N, Yoshida. N, Tsukahara. Y, and Matsubara. H.: Entertainment Feature of the Computer Game Using a Biological Signal to Realize a Battle with Oneself, In Proceedings of the 3rd international Conference on Entertainment Computing, pp. 345-350, (2004).
3. Munekata. N, Yoshida. Y, Sakurazawa. S, Tsukahara. Y, and Matsubara. H.: The effect of biofeedback in the game using biological signal (In Japanese), Japan Society for Fuzzy Theory and Intelligent Informatics, Vol. 17, No 2, 243-249, (2005)
4. Sekiguchi. D, Inami. M and Tachi. S.: RobotPHONE:RUI for Interpersonal Communication, In proceedings of CHI2001 Extended Abstracts, pp. 277-278, (2001)
5. Geddes, L. A.: History of the Polygraph, an Instrument for the Detection of Deception. Bio-med. Eng. 8, 154-156, (1973)
6. Dawson, M. E., Schell, A. M., Filion, D. L.: The electrodermal system. In: Cacioppo, J. T., Tassinary, L. G. and Berntson, G. G. (eds.): Handbook of Psychophysiology. 2nd edn. Cam bridge University Press, New York, pp. 200-223, (2000)
7. Ohman, A., and Soares, J. J. F.: Unconscious anxiety, phobic responses to masked stimuli. Jour-nal of Abnormal Psychology, 103, 231-240, (1994)
8. Gross, J. J. and Levenson, R. W.: Emotional suppression, self-report and expressive behavior. Journal of Personality and Social Psychology, 64, 970-986, (1993)
9. Gross, J. J. and Levenson, R. W.: Hiding feeling, the acute effects of inhibiting negative and positive emotion. Journal of Abnormal Psychology, 106, 95-103, (1997)
10. Petrie, K. J., Booth, R. J. and Pennebaker, J. W.: The Immunological Effects of Thought Suppression. Journal of Personality and Social Psychology, 75, 1264-1272, (1998)

# Social Landscapes: Visual Interface to Improve Awareness in Human Relationships on Social Networking Sites

Yuya Nomata[1] and Junichi Hoshino[2]

[1] Systems and Information Engineering, University of Tsukuba,
1-1-1 Tennodai, Tsukuba, Ibaraki, Japan
`nomata@graphic.esys.tsukuba.ac.jp`
[2] Systems and Information Engineering, University of Tsukuba,
1-1-1 Tennodai, Tsukuba, Ibaraki, Japan
`jhoshino@esys.tsukuba.ac.jp`

**Abstract.** This paper proposes Social Landscapes, a visual interface which supports exploring by visually displaying histories of user and interrelations between users in a social networking site. Social Landscapes visualizes the activities of each user through diary postings and the access status to online services, and the number of comments to the diary as landscape scenery. We describe a case study that did not emphasize the analysis of the total social network structure or for user search, but rather emphasized a visualized interface for improving the user's recognition of other users and friends in SNS.

**Keywords:** Information Visualization, Graphical Interface, Social Networking Services (SNS).

## 1 Introduction

Recently, Social Networking Sites (SNS) have been spreading rapidly. SNS are online environments where people create their own profiles for the purpose of connecting with their friends or other users they meet through the site. The main feature of such sites is the expansion of the number of your friends and acquaintances [1]. SNS-registered user cans deepen or build up relationships with existing friends or with friends of friends or unknown users in SNS through varies communications, such as disclosing diaries and giving comments on other users' diaries, and exchanging messages.

This paper proposes Social Landscapes, a visual interface which supports exploring by visually displaying histories of users' activities and interrelations between users in a social networking site. Social Landscapes visualizes the activities of each user through diary postings and the access status to online services, and the number of comments to the diary as landscape scenery.

## 2 Related Works

Heer et al. proposes Vizster [2] as an environment that can discover and analyze the social network of the end user. They produced a graph showing the network of

R. Harper, M. Rauterberg, M. Combetto (Eds.): ICEC 2006, LNCS 4161, pp. 350–353, 2006.

relationships that exists between friends and acquaintances on SNS and reinforced functions such as the search function. Visualization of social networks was performed even before computers were used, and many examples exist [3]. Many of these social networks were visualized as graph networks using nodes and passes and were mainly used to analyze network structures. We did not concentrate on the visualization of the structure and analysis of networks with our design, but rather we focused using the visual design to improve the awareness of the activities of friends centered on the user.

There have been many previous studies done on the visualization history of user activities on online communities. Xiong et al. developed PeopleGarden [4] that depicts the characteristics of each user in the online community using flower metaphors to visualize the records of the articles and the replies submitted by each user. Furthermore, Viégas et al. developed Newsgroup Crowds and AuthorLines [5], a visualizing system that visualizes user activities on a Usenet newsgroup. All of the systems that have been developed were mainly designed to allow analysis to be performed from the outside. Opposed to using visual systems for analysis, Viégas et al. performed user-oriented visualization focused on inner reflections to heighten personal self-realization in PostHistory and Social Network Fragments, which are visualization systems for e-mail [6].

Our objective in Social Landscapes is to convey indications of the SNS activities of our friends and to encourage inner reflection.

## 3   Social Landscapes; Design and Implementation

The purpose for creating a visual design in Social Landscapes [Fig. 1] is not to analyze relationships or the total structure of an SNS but to improve self-realization regarding the user's friends and acquaintances. Therefore, we are not interested in presenting a comprehensive network display of the SNS as a whole.

The visualization utilizes a 3D presentation of the data, using two spatial dimensions for standard graph layouts and the third dimension as a quantitative timeline. Each user is visualized as a pillar called a Pillar Shaped Timeline.

### 3.1   Visualizing Each User Using a Pillar Shaped Timeline

Social Landscapes will display the number of postings in diaries by each friend and their comments using a Pillar Shaped Timeline (hereinafter "PST") object[Fig.2]. A PST object is a method for visualizing an event during a certain period and summarizing quantitative indexes associated with the event [7]. The size of the circle depicted on the base of each area shows the number of friends the user has. In addition, the names of each user will be displayed on the base area like a shadow of the pillar.

The access status of each user is reflected by the color of each PST object based on the time that has elapsed since the last access. There are three levels of color for each user based on the time that has elapsed: 1) A bright color indicates that the last access occurred within the past hour. 2) A normal color indicates that the last access occurred during the past day. 3) A darker color indicates that the last access was over two days ago.

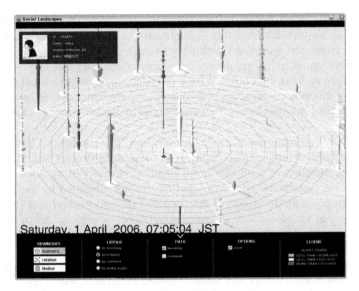

**Fig. 1.** A Screen Shot of Social Landscapes

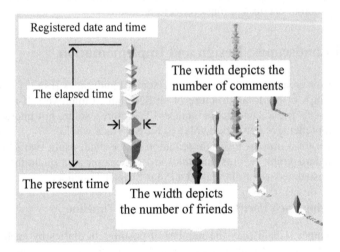

**Fig. 2.** Pillar Shaped Timeline

## 3.2 Implementation

To gain feedback from users on the effects of using Social Landscapes, we implemented a system using Java language and an hsqldb database. We used mixi[8], which is the largest SNS in Japan, as the data source when implementing the system.

By default, the users displayed immediately after start up will only be the actual user, the user's friends who are logged in. The user can select an optional object and display the user's friends and can gradually expand the displayed network if they wish to do so.

# 4  Conclusion

In this paper, we describe a case study that did not emphasize the analysis of the total social network structure or for user search, but rather emphasized a visualized interface for improving the user's recognition of other users and friends in SNS.

In the proposed interface, the users were able to use it passively. As a result, the users were able to gradually connect with a number of users through the system and it was able to the assist in promoting relationships. By displaying the change in access status and diary postings of friends in SNS, this assisted the users to remember the other users, which will hopefully lead to further communication.

# References

1.  1. Donath, J., Boyd, D.: Public displays of connection, In BT Technology Journal Vol. 22, No. 4. (2004) 71-82
2.  Heer, J. and Boyd. D.: Vizster: Visualizing Online Social Networks. IEEE Symposium on Information Visualization(InfoViz), (2005)
3.  Freeman, L.: Visualizing Social Networks, Journal of Social Structure, Vol.1 No.1 (2000)
4.  Xiong, R. and Donath, J. PeopleGarden: Creating Data Portraits for Users, in Proceedings of the 12 th Annual ACM Symposium on User Interface Software and Technology, New York: ACM (1999) 37-44
5.  Viégas, F. B., Smith, M. A. Newsgroup Crowds and Authorlines: Visualizing the activity of individuals in conversational cyberspaces. Proceedings of the 37th Hawai'i International Conference on System Sciences. Los Alamitos: IEEE Press (2004)
6.  Viegas,,F., Boyd, D., Nguyen, D., Potter, J., Donath. J.: Digital Artifacts for Remembering and Storytelling: PostHistory and Social Network Fragments. Proceedings of the Hawai'i International Conference on System Sciences (HICSS-37), Persistent Conversation Track.Big Island, HI: IEEE Computer Society. January 5 - 8, (2002)
7.  Nomata, Y., Hoshino, J.: Graphical Digital Storytelling: visualizing personal histories and relations, ACM SIGGRAPH2005 Sketches and Applications, (2005)
8.  http://mixi.jp/

# Bare Hand Interface for Interaction in the Video See-Through HMD Based Wearable AR Environment*

Taejin Ha and Woontack Woo

GIST U-VR Lab.
Gwangju 500-712, South Korea
{tha, wwoo}@gist.ac.kr

**Abstract.** In this paper, we propose a natural and intuitive bare hand interface for wearable augmented reality environment using the video see-through HMD. The proposed methodology automatically learned color distribution of the hand object through the template matching and tracking the hand objects by using the Meanshift algorithm under the dynamic background and moving camera. Furthermore, even though users are not wearing gloves, extracting of the hand object from arm is enabled by applying distance transform and using radius of palm. The fingertip points are extracted by convex hull processing and assigning constraint to the radius of palm area. Thus, users don't need attaching fiducial markers on fingertips. Moreover, we implemented several applications to demonstrate the usefulness of proposed algorithm. For example, "AR-Memo" can help user to memo in the real environment by using a virtual pen which is augmented on the user's finger, and user can also see the saved memo on his/her palm by augmenting it while moving around anywhere. Finally, we experimented performance and did usability studies.

## 1 Introduction

The vision based hand interface enables more natural and intuitive interaction but it has inherent problems, as follows: First, it is difficult to construct the hand color model when the hand object position is unknown. Thus, it requires the user to be provided additional input events (e.g. mouse button) to learn the hand color model in specific area. In the conventional systems, users wore color gloves to easily extract the hand object from arm where the hand object has similar color distribution as the arm [8]. In this case, user may feel inconvenience. Lastly, the users usually attach the fiducial markers [1] on the fingertips to detect fingertip points as well but it is also unnatural and inconvenient to use.

Therefore, we proposed the following approaches to overcome aforementioned problems. The proposed system composed of three sequential stages, first, detect the hand object from input image (e.g. region of interest) by exploiting the template matching based on invariant features (e.g. Hu moments [2]) and then learn the

---

* This research is supported by the UCN Project, the MIC 21C Frontier R&D Program in Korea and GIST ICRC & CTRC.

R. Harper, M. Rauterberg, M. Combetto (Eds.): ICEC 2006, LNCS 4161, pp. 354–357, 2006.
© IFIP International Federation for Information Processing 2006

detected object's color distribution automatically. It is possible to the extract hand object from arm, even though users are not wearing gloves so they can feel easy. Then, extract the hand object by using the distance transform [3] and radius of palm. Finally, extract the fingertip points by finding convex hull points of the hand object and constraining radius of palm.

We implemented several applications based on the proposed technique. The system "AR-Memo" can help user to memo in the real environment by using a virtual pen, and the user can also see the saved memo on the palm while moving around. In addition, the user can change the color or the thickness of a pen through "AR-Menu" and the user can play "AR-Tetris" game by using two hands. Finally, the proposed system has been evaluated regarding the performance and usability test.

This paper is composed as follows. In section 2, we explain the algorithm and implementation. In section 3, we address application. In section 4, we show the experimentation results and conclusion in last section.

## 2  Algorithms for the Vision Based Hand Interface and Application

Various methodologies have been proposed to learn color distribution of the hand object by using the user's hand on the certain area of a screen and pushing mouse buttons [9]. Most of the conventional methodologies require additional user input so it is uncomfortable. The proposed method automatically learns color distribution of the hand object in consideration of HSV color space. A binary image is obtained based on the intensity of center point of the interest region. After contour processing, the maximum area of object and Hu moment are calculated. If the distance between the detected object and the known hand template object is below threshold, then the hand color distribution is constructed through the three sigma rule.

Next, we try to extract the hand object from the arm, because the hand and arm have the same color. It is very difficult that the size of the hand and its direction change continuously. In this paper, we applied the distance transform to silhouette image of the hand object. The highest intensity value in the silhouette image indicated the center point of a palm area. The size of radius of palm can be obtained by inspecting the intensity value $I_{(x, y)}$ of point is equal to the zero. In order to extract fingertip points, we used "3 coins algorithm"[5]. However, there are too many convex hull points are existed so we consider the constraint that the distance between convex hull points for each point on the fingertips. We set constraint that the points above 1.5 times of palm's radius.

After finding the center point and the radius of a palm, the search window is set to reduce the redundant image processing. The mean shift algorithm [4] can be used to track the hand object but the size of search window expands continuously that contain the similar color object (e.g. face or hands). In the proposed approach, the center point of the search window is set as the center point of palm area and the size of search window is set based on the radius of palm.

We implemented several applications based on the proposed technique.

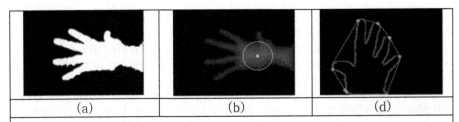

|     (a)     |     (b)     |     (d)     |

**Fig. 1.** (a) Silhouette image of a hand object (b) the center point and radius of palm (b) extracted convex hull points

|     (a)     |     (b)     |     (c)     |     (d)     |

**Fig. 2.** (a) Memo by using a virtual pen (b) a saved image is augmented on the palm. (c) Change color of a pen (d) the user can move blocks using the finger tips in the Tetris game.

## 3  Performance Comparison and Usability Test

The proposed scheme has been coded with OpenCV library [7] and implemented under mobile computer equipped with Intel mobile processor 1.13 GHz and 512 RAM. We used a cheap USB camera; resolution is 320*240(pixels), frame rate 25f/s and HMD, i-visor DH-4400VP [6]. The experiment is executed in the usual indoor environment.

Through the experimental experience, we decided the threshold for template matching based on the distance value. If the distance value is less than 0.01, then we could properly detect the hand object. Fig. 3 (b) represents the mean values and its standard deviations of the detected hand object (e.g. 5-8, figure 3 (a)).

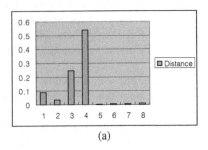
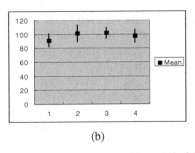

|     (a)     |     (b)     |

**Fig. 3.** (a) The distance between segmented object and the template hand object. 1-4: false detection, 5-8: true detection, (b) Mean and standard deviation value of the hand object.

Next experiment is about detection rate and usability test in two cases. We measured how many times hand object is detected in 5 seconds. When the users wear the gloves, the number of detection per second is 13.56 in an average. In the bare hands case, 11.7 counts per second and 87.5 % of subjects prefer usage of the bare hand more than wearing gloves (6.25 %) and etc are 6.25 %. Also, when fiducial markers are attached on fingertips, the number of detection per second is 14.26 whereas the bare hand case, 10.3 per second. 81.25% of subjects prefer the usage of bare finger more than using fiducial markers (6.25 %) and etc is 12.5 %.

## 4   Conclusion and Future Works

In this paper, we proposed a vision based bare hand interface for interaction in augmented reality environment. The proposed methodology automatically learned color distribution of the hand object and tracking under the moving camera. Also, we extracted the hand object from arm but not using the glove. We also detected the fingertip points but not using the fiducial markers. We implement several applications.

Through experiments, we found the users prefer interaction using the bare hand and the bare finger rather than wearing the glove or attaching marker on user's fingertips, even though performance is little bit dropped. We believed that the vision based bare hand interface will be a natural and intuitive user interface.

As future works, we are now considering to applying estimator for more robust augmentation and designing the hand segmentation model under various lighting condition.

## References

[1] ARToolKit, http://www.hitl.washington.edu/artoolkit/
[2] Hu, M.K., "Visual pattern recognition by moment invariants", IEEE Transactions on Information Theory, IT-8, pp 179-187, 1962
[3] Shapiro, L., and Stockman, G., Computer Vision, 196-197, Prentice Hall, 2001
[4] Gary R. Bradski, Computer Vision Face Tracking For Use in a Perceptual User Interface, Microcomputer Research Lab, Santa Clara, CA, Intel Corporation
[5] Avis, D. and Toussaint. "An optimal algorithm for determining the visibility of a polygon from an edge", IEEE Trans. Comp. C-30 (1981), 910-914
[6] Daeyang i-visor DH-4400VP, http://www.mpcclub.ru/index.php?action=product&id=3340
[7] Open Source Computer Vision Library, www.intel.com/research/mrl/research/opencv
[8] Ross Smith, Wayne Piekarski, and Grant Wigley, "Hand Tracking For Low Powered Mobile AR User Interfaces", In 6th Australasian User Interface Conference, Newcastle, NSW, Jan 2005
[9] Cristina Manresa, et al. "Hand Tracking and Gesture Recognition for Human-Computer Interaction", Electronic Letters on Computer Vision and Image Analysis 5(3): 96-104, 2005

# Studying User Experience with Digital Audio Players

Sascha Mahlke

Centre of Human-Machine Systems
Berlin University of Technology
Jebensstr. 1 – J2-2
10623 Berlin, Germany
sascha.mahlke@zmms.tu-berlin.de

**Abstract.** Several attempts have been made to broaden the traditional focus on the efficient achievement of goals and incorporate a fuller understanding of additional aspects of the user experience. These approaches are especially interesting for the area of entertainment computing, where the efficient completion of tasks is not the main focus. The presented research project investigates the role of non-instrumental aspects as hedonics and aesthetics and their interplay with emotions in shaping the user experience. After introducing an integrative model, a first application of the approach in a study of user experience with digital audio players is described. The findings show that this approach offers a wealth of insights that can be used to improve product design from a user perspective.

## 1 Introduction

Definitions of usability [1] focus on tasks and goals, their efficient achievement, and the cognitive information processing involved. Up to now, these premises have formed the basis for most evaluation methodologies. To go beyond these traditional perspectives and for a better understanding of how people experience technology, various approaches have been suggested that take other aspects of the interaction into account, e. g. non-instrumental quality aspects and the role of emotions [2, 3, 4, 5].

We define the processing of information about the quality of use in relevant experience dimensions as an important component that shapes the user's experience (Figure 1). Furthermore, we differentiate between the perception of instrumental and non-instrumental quality aspects that come into play here. These are differentiated to better understand the importance of each group of quality aspects for the user's experience. On the one hand, qualities of the interactive system that are perceived by the user while interacting with the system influence how the user experiences product use. On the other hand, the way the user processes information about this experience has various consequences for the user's behaviour and judgments [7].

The emotional experience plays another important role as element of the whole user experience, and shows a complex interplay with the perception of quality aspects. We assume that the perceived qualities of the interactive system play a role in the appraisal process of emotional consequences. Overall judgments of products, decision for an alternative or the usage behaviour, are influenced by the perception of quality aspects and the emotional experience.

R. Harper, M. Rauterberg, M. Combetto (Eds.): ICEC 2006, LNCS 4161, pp. 358–361, 2006.
© IFIP International Federation for Information Processing 2006

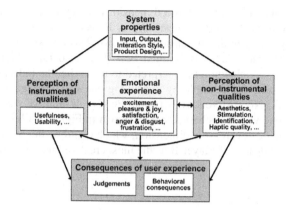

**Fig. 1.** User experience research framework

## 2   User Experience with Digital Audio Players

We conducted a first explorative study using our research framework as the basis for assessing user experiences with interactive systems. We chose four digital audio players for the study because we think this is a typical domain where the user's product experience is of great importance for product choice and usage behaviour. Our main question was whether we could gain more insights into users' assessments of the products by collecting data on many different aspects of the user experience than by simply asking the users for a preference judgment.

Thirty individuals (fifteen women and fifteen men) participated in the study. They were between 20 and 30 years old, most of them students at Berlin University of Technology. Four players were chosen for the study. All were from the same manufacturer, so we did not have to deal with the influence of brand in this case. Nonetheless, players differed in terms of various design aspects.

All participants tested each product in the study. Four short tasks were given to the participants for each product. After accomplishing the tasks, participants filled out a questionnaire that assessed ratings in different experience dimensions. Usefulness and ease of use were operationalized based on Davis [8]. Two dimensions to measure visual aesthetics (classical and expressive visual aesthetics) were taken form Lavie & Tractinsky [3]. Hassenzahl defines the two concepts of stimulation and identification in his approach to hedonic quality that were measured in this study [2]. Additionally, physio-pleasure was surveyed based on the suggestions by Jordan [9]. To measure user's emotional experience we used the self-assessment manikin [10]. After using each of the players, participants made a ranking list of the players.

In the overall ranking, Player C was rated best, followed by Players B and A, while Player D was ranked worst. The data regarding the different quality dimensions and emotional experience give a detailed picture of the users' experiences with the digital audio players. We cannot describe the results in detail but will show a selection concentrating on Players B and D to demonstrate the diversity of insights the approach delivers for improving product design and understanding user experience.

Figure 2 presents the results in those dimensions of experience where we identified significant differences. Regarding ease of use, Player D is rated much better than Player B. But especially in the dimension of physio-pleasure, which relates to sensory aspects of product use, Player B is rated best. It is also rated highest in hedonic quality stimulation, which could be interpreted to mean that the individual striving for personal development, for example by improving one's knowledge and skills, is met best by Player B. No differences between Players B and D were found in the dimension of classic visual aesthetics, but as shown in Figure 3, Player B is rated best in the visual aesthetics expressive dimension, which could be interpreted to mean that users perceived the design of Player B as the most creative and inventive.

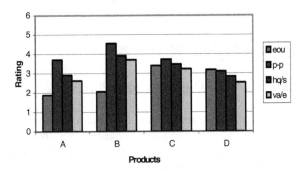

**Fig. 2.** Assessments of ease of use (eou), physio-pleasure (p-p), hedonic quality / stimulation (hq/s) and visual aesthetics / expressive (va/e) for the four digital audio players (higher ratings represent a better assessment)

The emotional state of the users was displayed on two dimensions: valence (pleasure – displeasure) and arousal (arousal – sleepiness). Emotional user reactions were similar for all the players. Descriptively, after use of player C users rated their emotional state as most pleasurable and arousing. Results were less positive for Players B and D, but not significantly.

## 3 Discussion and Future Research

The user experience research framework guided the user-experience-based evaluation process in the study on digital audio players. Following the assumptions of the model, relevant aspects of the user experience were operationalized with questionnaires. After data collection, the user experience process model also helped interpret the data and gave hints for conclusions. The analysis of the user experience data on B and D was able to explain why Player D was ranked worst overall although ease of use was experienced as better. In particular, Player B's significantly better ratings in the dimensions of sensory pleasure, stimulation, and expressive design compensated for its less positive results in perceived ease of use. No significant differences were found with respect to the emotional experience.

Many questions remain open for future research. First, we chose a sample of possibly relevant experience dimensions for the domain investigated. It is unclear whether we have studied all of the dimensions of experience that are relevant [11]. Furthermore, our approach to study emotional aspects of the user experience was a first attempt based on a questionnaire approach. The use of other methods and theories may lead to more useful results [12].

## Acknowledgements

This research is supported by the German Research Foundation (DFG) as part of the Research Training Group 'Prospective engineering of Human-Technology Interaction' (no. 1013). Special thanks to Creative Labs GmbH for supporting the study on digital audio players.

## References

1. ISO: ISO 9241: Ergonomic requirements for office work with visual display terminals. Part 11: Guidance on usability. ISO, Genf (1998)
2. Hassenzahl, M. The effect of perceived hedonic quality on product appealingness. Int. J. of Human-Computer-Interaction, 13 (2001) 481-499.
3. Lavie, T., Tractinsky, N.: Assessing dimensions of perceived visual aesthetics of web sites. Int. J. of Human-Computer Studies 60 (2004) 269-298
4. Mahlke, S.: Factors influencing the experience of website usage. In Ext. Abstracts CHI 2002, ACM, New York (2002) 846-847
5. Norman, D. A.: Emotional Design: why we love (or hate) everyday things. Basic Book, New York (2004)
6. Mahlke, S.: Understanding users' experience of interaction. In: Marmaras, N., Kontogiannis, T., Nathanael, D. (eds.): Proceedings of EACE '05. National Technical University, Athens, Greece (2005) 243-246
7. Davis, F.: Perceived usefulness, perceived ease of use and user acceptance of information technology. MIS Quarterly 13 (1989) 319-340
8. Jordan, P. W.: Designing pleasurable products. Taylor & Francis, London (2000)
9. Morris, J. D.: Observations SAM: The self-assessment manikin. Journal of Advertising Research 6 (1995) 63-68
10. Mahlke, S. Aesthetic and Symbolic Qualities as Antecedents of Overall Judgements of Interactive Products. In: Proceedings of HCI 2006 (2006).
11. Mahlke, S., Minge, M., Thüring, M.: Measuring multiple components of emotions in interactive contexts. In: Ext. Abstracts CHI 2006, ACM, New York (2006) 1061-1066.

# The Development of a Collaborative Virtual Heritage Edutainment System with Tangible Interfaces

Hyung-Sang Cho[1], Binara Lee[2], Sora Lee[2], Youngjae Kim[1], Yongjoo Cho[2], Seung-Mook Kang[3], Soyon Park[3], Kyoung Shin Park[1], and Minsoo Hahn[1]

[1] Digital Media Laboratory, Information and Communications University,
517-10 Dogok-dong, Gangnam-gu, Seoul 135-854, Korea
haemosu@icu.ac.kr
[2] Division of Media Technology, Sangmyung University,
7 Hongji-dong, Jongno-gu, Seoul, 110-743, Korea
[3] Department of Media Art, Jeonju University,
1200 Hyoja-dong, Wansan-gu, Jeonju, 560-759, Korea

**Abstract.** This paper presents an interactive, collaborative virtual heritage system that employs tangible interfaces to make learning experience more interesting and effective. The system is designed for a group of users collaboratively play games to learn a Korean cultural heritage site, the 'Moyang' castle. While most virtual heritage applications focus on the reconstruction of objects or places, it aims to encourage the visitors to get more involved with the activities and increase social interaction to develop collaborative learning experiences. This paper describes an overview of cultural meanings behind the 'Moyang' castle and some details in the system design and implementation for interactive education.

**Keywords:** Virtual Heritage, Game, Tangible Interface, Collaborative Learning.

## 1 Introduction

Nowadays, museums are adapting more interactive techniques for exhibitions and public programs to provide memorable experiences [1]. With the fast growth of the virtual reality technology, it is possible to realize an immersive environment that enables users to experience interactive narratives that promote new patterns of understanding cultural heritages. Recently, interactivity has gotten more attention in the design of virtual heritage applications, such as the use of intelligent tour guide agents, game-style design approaches, and multimodal user interfaces, to increase user's cultural experience and give innovative ways of storytelling behind the scene [3]. The other approaches include the shared virtual heritage environment that allows distributed visitors to navigate the world, examine the architectural details and landscape from different perspectives, and meet with other visitors to develop shared VR experiences [3].

In this paper, we present the development of a virtual heritage system that encourages a small group of co-located users to play collaboratively to learn history and cultural meanings of a Korean traditional castle, 'Moyang-sung', using tangible

R. Harper, M. Rauterberg, M. Combetto (Eds.): ICEC 2006, LNCS 4161, pp. 362–365, 2006.

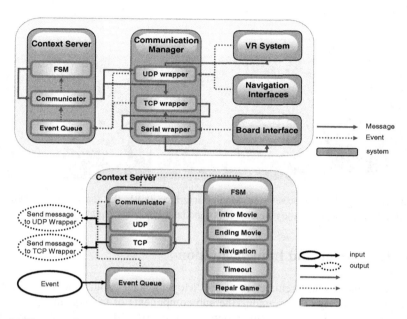

**Fig. 1.** The overall system architecture showing event and message flows among the sub-components (top) and the internal structure of context server (bottom)

interfaces. The castle has a legend called Dapsungnori, which says if anyone goes round on the top of the entire wall three times, he/she can go to the heaven. Our system consists of three main subsystems: the context server, the virtual environment, and the tangible interfaces. Instead of a traditional VR input device like a wand, the tangible interfaces are provided to give a transparency of user interaction with the virtual environment [2]. The tangible interfaces include the 'Matdol (a Korean traditional hand-mill)' interface and the touch-screen interactive navigation map for mimicking 'Dapsungnori', and the building block puzzle game board interface. The board interface allows multiple co-located users to do brickwork by placing tangible blocks on the board to help the group of co-located users engage in the activity together in order to increase social interaction and to develop collaborative learning experiences.

In this game, the users are given a mission to find the destroyed walls and repair the damages as soon as possible. The game task involves the users to walk around the castle walls to find the destroyed parts. Once they find the damage, the same pattern of damage is displayed on the board interface, and the users repair the wall by putting the tangible blocks (i.e., Tetris-pattern blocks made of transparent acryl and magnets) on top of the pattern. The context server maintains the game state from the start to the end as the users interact with the virtual environment and the tangible interfaces. The game ends successfully when the users complete repairing the four damaged walls within 10 minutes, and as a reward of the completion, the users receive an opportunity to experience virtual 'Dapsungnori'. When the game is over with failure, the users will see the whole castle destroyed.

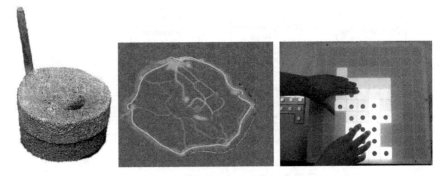

**Fig. 2.** The tangible interfaces - the Matdol interface (left), the touch-screen interactive navigation map (center), and the tangible blocks and board interface (right)

## 2   System Design and Implementation

Fig. 1 shows the overall architecture of the 'Moyang-sung' edutainment system with the event and message flows among the sub-components of the system. The system consists of three main parts: the context server (including the communication manager), the VR system, and the tangible interfaces (i.e., the navigation and the board interface). The context server manages the main game logic and its communication manager controls the event and message handling among the sub-systems. The VR system contains graphics, sound, user interaction, and event processing modules. The tangible interfaces are the navigation devices (one using Korean hand-mill 'Matdol' metaphor and the other, the interactive navigation map) and the building block board. The 'Matdol' interface allows users to rotate its handle to walk through the pre-defined path along with the exterior of the Moyang-sung castle. The touch-screen interactive map shows the layout of the castle and the user positions. The communication manager is connected to the context server via the TCP while the board interface is connected to the communication manager. Communication between the board and the context sever is connected by a transmitter. The transmitter intermediates the RS485 (for the board) and the TCP (for the context sever) protocol. It monitors the board in a half-duplex method.

The context server processes the main logic of the game environment. The context server manages the finite state transition. When users put the tangible blocks on the board interface for damage repair in the virtual environment, an event is generated and the board puts it into the event queue of the context server through a transmitter. The environment is designed for a group of users to sit next to each other and participate in the tangible VR experience together. They can walk through the virtual world using the Matdol or the interactive map interface. The users can move left or right along with the pre-defined path facing the exterior of the virtual Moyang-sung castle by manipulating the 'Matdol' handle.

Fig. 2 shows the 'Matdol' interface, the interactive navigation map, and the tangible board interface used for the 'Moyang-sung' edutainment system. The 'Tetris'-like tangible board interface are provided for users to do brickwork for repairing the damages on the wall. The board consists of 10x10 uniform square cells

(40x40 mm$^2$ for each cell). The users can play the puzzle with five different shapes of blocks (i.e., I, L, T, cross, and square shape) on the board. In the repair mode, the destroyed pattern which is the same pattern shown in the virtual environment is displayed on the board. The block placement or removal on the pattern will be reflected into the virtual wall. Each tangible block has a magnet that can turn on the magnet sensor switch embedded on each cell of the board. The LED lights embedded on the board can light up the multiple-colored pattern to indicate the destroyed part of the wall. This tangible board interface is particularly designed for multiple user applications to play the game together to increase social interaction. However, a single player can also enjoy the system.

## 3 Conclusion / Future Work

In this paper, we presented a collaborative edutainment system using the VR and the tangible navigation and the interaction interfaces for cultural heritage education. The system is designed for a group of co-located users to play games collaboratively in the virtual environment using tangible blocks and enjoy the shared cultural learning experience. Unlike other virtual heritage applications that focus on the reconstruction of cultural objects or places, this system encourages social interaction among users which will help them be more engaged in the learning activities. In the near future, we will also conduct a user study of evaluating the system for collaborative learning as compared to single user learning. We expect that cooperative learning will be more successful in a complex problem solving task because it will help users see the same problem in various perspectives.

## Acknowledgement

This research was supported by the MIC (Ministry of Information and Communication), Korea, under the Digital Media Lab. support program supervised by the IITA (Institute of Information Technology Assessment).

## References

1. Gaitatzes, A., Christopoulos, D., Voulgari, A., Roussou, M. Hellenic Cultural Heritage through Immersive Virtual Archaeology. In Proc. 6th International Conference on Virtual Systems and Multimedia, Ogaki, Japan, October 3-6, 2000, pp.57-64
2. McNerney, T., Tangible programming bricks: An approach to making programming accessible to everyone. Masters Thesis, Media Lab, Massachusetts Institute of Technology, Cambridge, MA. 1999.
3. Park, K., Leigh, J., Johnson, A., How Humanities Students Cope with the Technologies of Virtual Harlem, Works and Days 37/38, 19 (1&2), pp. 79-97, 2001.

# Clustering of Online Game Users Based on Their Trails Using Self-organizing Map

Ruck Thawonmas[1,*], Masayoshi Kurashige[1],
Keita Iizuka[1], and Mehmed Kantardzic[2]

[1] Intelligent Computer Entertainment Laboratory
Department of Human and Computer Intelligence, Ritsumeikan University
Kusatsu, Shiga, 525-8577, Japan
ruck@ci.ritsumei.ac.jp
[2] Data Mining Lab
Computer Engineering and Computer Science Department, University of Louisville
Louisville, KY, 40292, USA
mmkant01@louisville.edu

**Abstract.** To keep an online game interesting to its users, it is important to know them. In this paper, in order to characterize user characteristics, we discuss clustering of online-game users based on their trails using Self Organization Map (SOM). As inputs to SOM, we introduce transition probabilities between landmarks in the targeted game map. An experiment is conducted confirming the effectiveness of the presented technique.

## 1 Introduction

Competitions among online games are becoming very high. Besides acquisition of new players, it is also very important to retain current players. To achieve both of these goals, designers of online games need tools that discover player characteristics so that they can build and provide contents accordingly based on this information.

In our study, we focus on characterizing online game users based on their trails. Having similar trails, or time series of visited locations, indicates that such players have a common interest. This kind of information can thus be used for boosting in-game socializing activities among them, for navigating novice users through showing them moving patterns of certain user groups, and placing game resources such as items at proper locations that match their users, etc. In [1], user trails were also used for examining the distance over time among the members of a social group when users were clustered into social groups in advance. In all of these applications, clustering plays an important role.

---

\* The author was supported in part by Ritsumeikan University's **Kyoto Art and Entertainment Innovation Research**, a project of the 21st Century Center of Excellence Program funded by Ministry of Education, Culture, Sports, Science and Technology, Japan; and by Grant-in-Aid for Scientific Research (C), Number 16500091, the Japan Society for Promotion of Science.

R. Harper, M. Rauterberg, M. Combetto (Eds.): ICEC 2006, LNCS 4161, pp. 366–369, 2006.
© IFIP International Federation for Information Processing 2006

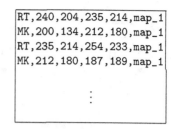

```
RT,240,204,235,214,map_1
MK,200,134,212,180,map_1
RT,235,214,254,233,map_1
MK,212,180,187,189,map_1

          ⋮
```

**Fig. 1.** Landmarks in an online-game map    **Fig. 2.** Typical logs of user moves

In this paper, for clustering users based on their trails, we use a clustering algorithm called self-organizing map (SOM)[2]. As inputs to SOM, we introduce transition probabilities between landmarks (TPL) in a game map. An experiment is conducted for examining whether SOM with TPL can successfully cluster various user types, each having specific moving patterns.

## 2    Transition Probabilities Between Landmarks

Landmarks are recognizable objects in virtual environments. Figure 1 shows six landmarks in a map of an online game currently under development at the first three authors' laboratory. Landmarks are usually used by users for wayfinding. A research group of the fourth author recently developed a route recommendation system [4] that guides the user the most preferred route to his destination. In this recommendation system, a recommended route is the one on which most previous users traveled, among routes from the current-position nearest landmark to the landmark nearest to the user destination.

Figure 2 shows typical logs used in our study. In this figure, each row represents a user move, namely, from left to right, the user name, the xy coordinates at the starting point, the xy coordinates at the destination point, and the name of the map. A sequence of all landmarks passed by, or nearby (within the distance of 30 grids in our experiment), a user is used to represent his trail, e.g., $L_3, L_2, L_6, \ldots$

Let $L$ denote the number of landmarks of interest. The input pattern $\mathbf{x}$, having $n = L \times L$ dimensions, to SOM for user $x$ is the TPL in his trail and is defined as follows:

$$
\mathbf{x} = \begin{bmatrix}
p^x_{1,1} & p^x_{1,2} & \cdots & p^x_{1,L} \\
p^x_{2,1} & p^x_{2,2} & \cdots & p^x_{2,L} \\
\vdots & \ddots & \ddots & \vdots \\
p^x_{L,1} & p^x_{L,2} & \cdots & p^x_{L,L}
\end{bmatrix}
\tag{1}
$$

In the above equation, $p^x_{a,b}$ is the transition probability that user $x$ moves from landmark $a$ to landmark $b$ and is calculated as follows:

$$
p^x_{a,b} = \frac{c^x_{a,b}}{\sum_{i=1}^{L} \sum_{j=1}^{L} c^x_{i,j}},
\tag{2}
$$

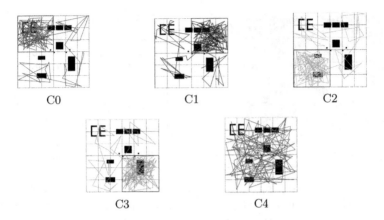

C0     C1     C2

C3     C4

**Fig. 3.** Typical user trails for types C0–C4

where $c_{i,j}^x$ is the number of times that user $x$ moved from landmark $i$ to landmark $j$ in his trail.

## 3   Experiment

In our experiment, user trails were taken from a simulator that generated user trails on a 2D map with the size of 600×600 grids, derived from the online game map shown in Fig. 1. In particular, this simulator generated user trails for the case where there existed in the map five user types C0-C4 whose typical trails are shown as in Fig. 3. Simulated users of types C0-C3 represent, for example, real users who search for particular items in specific areas, while those of type C4 represent real users who roam around the map. There were 50 users for each type, and each user conducted 200 moves.

SOM with the hexagonal topology of size $15 \times 10$ and the Gaussian-kernel neighborhood function was trained in two consecutive phases, each parameterized as follows:

Phase I: $t_{max} = 2000$, $\alpha(0) = 0.05$, and $r(0) = 8$.
Phase II: $t_{max} = 8000$, $\alpha(0) = 0.02$, and $r(0) = 3$.

At the beginning of phase I, weight vectors were initialized with small random values while phase II started with the resulting weight vectors from phase I. Public software package SOM_PAK[5] was used in our experiment.

Figure 4 shows the resulting SOM map, where $\mathbf{X}(\mathbf{Y})$ indicates the location of the winner node for user $\mathbf{X}$ of type $\mathbf{Y}$. It can be readily seen that users were successfully grouped into clusters according to their moving patterns. There are five clusters with the one of C4 at the middle and each of the others at a map corner. The cluster boundary between C0 and C2 and that between C1 and C3 are prominent while boundaries between the cluster of C4 and each of the others are less pronounced.

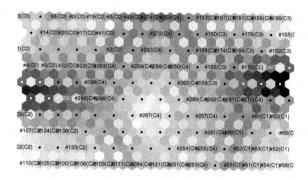

**Fig. 4.** Resulting som map

# 4    Conclusions and Future Work

We have shown in this paper that SOM with the introduced TPL could successfully cluster users based on their trails. Once users in a same cluster are identified, this information can be used in many applications such as those given in the introduction of the paper. Another straight-forward application is that of visualizing user trails in a particular cluster, for example with a tool discussed in [6]

In addition, if one wants to know more about user behavior, besides moving patterns, a visualization technique discussed in [7] can be applied to a user cluster of interest. Our future work related to SOM with TPL is on how to automatically detect landmarks in a large game map and to optimally select them for use in TPL.

# References

1. Börner, K., Penumarthy, S.: Social Diffusion Patterns in Three-Dimensional Virtual Worlds. Information Visualization Journal. **2(3)** (2003) 182–198
2. Kohonen, T.: Self-Organizing Maps. Second Extended Edition, Springer Series in Information Sciences **30** (1997) Springer, New York
3. Oja, M., Kaski, S., Kohonen, T.: Bibliography of Self-Organizing Map (SOM) Papers: 1998-2001 Addendum. Neural Computing Surveys. **3** (2003) 1–156
4. Sadeghian, P., Kantardzic, M., Lozitskiy, O., Sheta, W.: Route Recommendations in Complex Virtual Environments: The Sequence Mining Approach. The International Journal of Human-Computer Studies (to appear)
5. SOM_PAK. http://www.cis.hut.fi/research/som_lvq_pak.shtml (2004)
6. Chittaro, L., Ieronutti, L.: A Visual Tool for Tracing Behaviors of Users in Virtual Environments. Proc. of the 7th Internatioon Advanced Visual Interfaces Conference, ACM Press (2004) 40–47
7. Thawonmas, R., Hata, K.: Aggregation of Action Symbol Subsequences for Discovery of Online-Game Player Characteristics Using KeyGraph. Lecture Notes in Computer Science. Fumio Kishino et al. (eds.) **3711** (Proc. of IFIP 4th International Conference on Entertainment Computing, ICEC 2005) 126–135

# Communication Supports for Building World Wide Internet Game Communities

Jonghun Park, Seung-Kyun Han, Mi Kyoung Won, and Young-Chae Na

Dept. of Industrial Engineering, Seoul National University, Seoul, Korea
{jonghun, jackleg7, mk-}@snu.ac.kr, choyupgi@hanmail.net

**Abstract.** Communities play a vital role in online gaming world for promoting sustainability, and with the increasing popularity of multiplayer online games, they are becoming internationalized. While most online games allow players to communicate and collaborate with virtually any people in the world throughout the game related activities, little has been discussed on the communication support among the players speaking different languages. In this paper, we analyze the communication methods that can be used to facilitate various types of interactions in world wide online game communities, and suggest possible enhancements of them.

## 1 Introduction

Internet has provided an infrastructure with global connectivity on which game companies can develop and deploy online games. In particular, with the popularity of multi-player games, online communities have flourished, and playing online games is becoming a social experience. The feeling of presence and the level of psychological immersion are increased along with the communication among the players, and at the same time they can greatly increase the appeal and longevity of a game. Recognizing that interactions among the players are essential to the success of a game, game developers are increasingly designing games to encourage interactions between game players.

Accordingly, a number of communication supports are currently provided to promote online communities. These can be broadly categorized into in-game, out-of-game, and pre-game supports. In-game communication allows a variety of interaction types, including exchange of advice, social exchanges and small talks, and coordination and scheduling of activities. During the out-of-game communication, players share game tips, relate experiences, discuss strategies, exchange content, and arrange leagues and tournaments. Finally, pre-game communication includes the activities such as matchmaking other players with appropriate level and forming a team on the fly.

Increasingly online games are played by people who speak different languages and communities are becoming internationalized. Despite of this trend, we note that there are few research results that addressed the issues of supporting communication in such world wide game communities where the existing communication methods are limited mainly due to the language barrier. Motivated by this, this paper seeks to analyze various communication methods that can

R. Harper, M. Rauterberg, M. Combetto (Eds.): ICEC 2006, LNCS 4161, pp. 370–373, 2006.
© IFIP International Federation for Information Processing 2006

be employed to better support global game communities, and discuss possible enhancements of them in various forms of interactions carried out in the communities.

## 2    Communication Methods for World Wide Game Communities

### 2.1    Text-Based Communication

Most common form of player-to-player interaction in online games is typed text. Text-based communication include chats, instant messaging, emails, message boards, and blogs. While emails and instant messaging are usually used by players for communicating with fellow players outside the game, most interactions during multiplayer games take place via chats which can be delivered to another player privately or broadcast to a group of players. In many MMORPGs that exhibit a complex social organization, chats are displayed in speech bubbles within the game world. Nevertheless, chats and instant messaging have limited capabilities with respect to personalization, availability of communication cues, and language variety.

Several enhancements can be pursued to address the limitation of text-based communication in global communities. These include (i) automatic sentence translation capabilities (among a few selected languages) as provided by some MMORPGs such as Ultima Online and Everquest, (ii) automatic word by word level translation service, rather than the translation of complete sentence, (iii) binding short keys to certain frequently used pre-defined texts which can be transferred to a recipient in the recipient's language (particularly effective when the players are busy playing games as in many sports games), and finally (iv) recommendation of appropriate expressions in a different language when a popular keyword pertaining to socialization is given.

Furthermore, message boards are frequently used method for out-of-game communication. As in the case of Enjoy Japan (http://enjoyjapan.naver.com), direct translation between the languages with similar roots is a viable method for the message boards defined for international communities. Nevertheless, this approach still requires a lot more work in terms of the automatic language translation research in order to be usable for the languages with different roots (e.g., Korean and English). Therefore, another possibility would be to promote volunteers in a community who interprete different languages, through the introduction of rewarding mechanisms in the community.

### 2.2    Image-Based Communication

For the game players who speak different languages, image-based method can provide an effective way for communication between the players at subconscious, emotional level. Special ASCII symbol combinations, known as emoticons that express emotional tone, would be appropriate as an in-game communication method by which a player expresses his/her current feeling about the other player as well as the current game status. Considering that there are five or six different emotions a player usually uses during a game (e.g., happiness, sadness, anger, fear, surprise, and disgust), it would be worthwhile to provide a service through which a player predefines a certain key for a particular emotion and then uses these different keys to send emoticons whenever necessary.

Another promising approach is to use an iconic language which attempts to represent meanings with icons or flashcons. For instance, the users of GoPets (http://www.gopetslive.com) can send each other messages in icon-based language, called IKU, which substitutes pictures for words, allowing people from different countries to communicate with ease. In GoPets, icons that match a certain keyword can be retrieved. A possible extension of IKU would be to annotate each icon with a text to avoid semantic mismatch, since the same icon may have different meanings to people with different cultures. Furthermore, we note that the usability of an iconic language can be improved if the icon search is empowered by allowing a sentence instead of a keyword to be used as input. This can be accomplished through utilizing the results from the research field of story picturing which automatically generates suitable pictures illustrating a story by extracting semantic keywords from the story text.

### 2.3   Gesture-Based Communication

Many MMORPGs provide a wide library of socials that enable users to make characters in a game gesture through typing commands such as "/smile" and "/bow". For instance, there are 153 socials available in World of Warcraft. These commands can sometimes be assembled into a macro, allowing certain actions to be accomplished entirely automatically.

In addition, avatars can be used to enrich the communication among the players. A player can personalize the avatar through appropriate and meaningful animation of the avatar's body and face, making communications mediated through the avatar more lifelike and natural. Therefore, for some online games in which avatars are displayed throughout the game play, introducing an emotional avatar that makes gestures conveying context of the current game situation appears to be a viable approach.

Avatars can also be employed to improve text-based communication. The affective content of a textual message can be automatically recognized to generate animated avatars that perform emotional coloring of the message using appropriate gestures. Augmented with this kind of capability, avatars can provide an effective means to improve the expressivity of online communication among the users with different language backgrounds.

### 2.4   Multimedia-Based Communication

In-game voice communication has been made possible in recent years, and was incorporated in some games like Tribes 2. However, despite the fact that voice communication enables players to communicate more easily and quickly and amplify emotion in games, it appears that voice communication like one based on VoIP was almost never used in MMP games. Therefore, effectiveness and appropriateness of in-game voice and video communication seem to be depend on the type of game in question.

Out-of-game supports for multimedia-based communication include the sharing of screenshots and video clips of game play and drawing tools based on flash technology that allow users to discuss on some specific subjects such as tactics and strategies necessary for team play. Furthermore, in view of fostering a global community, it appears to be essential to provide means by which users can create and share multimedia files that contain regional characteristics. For example, it would be helpful for two users, say one from USA and the other from Korea, to get acquainted with each other if they can play an online game together while a traditional Korean music selected by the Korean user is played as a background music.

## 3   Conclusion

While it is being recognized that community contributes significantly to the success of on-line games, the community is becoming defined socially, not just spatially. Whether it is MMP or MMORPG, members of a community need to be able to communicate with each other in-game and out-of-game, and the opportunity to play with people rather than AI is one of major motivations for many online gamers.

In this paper, we have discussed various existing communication methods that can be employed to facilitate interactions among game players in global communities, characterized as different languages and cultures, and proposed some possible enhancements of them. While the effectiveness and appropriateness of a specific communication method depend on the type of game in consideration, it appears that the current text-based communication methods can be supplemented and augmented through incorporating various other technologies such as automatic translation, iconic languages, emotional avatars, and cultural multimedia sharing to support more successful, vibrant global game communities.

As a future research work, we envision that considerable attention must be given to the problem of combining research efforts from various disciplines and practices to produce more comprehensive results in the area of communication supports for world wide multi-player online game communities. These results should be able to foster better human relationships and shared experiences through effectively socializing the users from anywhere in the world into the emerging world wide game community.

*Acknowledgments.* This work was supported by the Korea Research Foundation Grant funded by the Korean Government (MOEHRD) (KRF-2005-041-D00917).

# Hardcore Gamers and Casual Gamers Playing Online Together

Anne-Gwenn Bosser and Ryohei Nakatsu

School of Science and Technology, Kwansei Gakuin University
2-1 Gakuen, Sanda 669-1337, Japan

**Abstract.** In this paper, we discuss why Massively Multiplayer Online Games (MMOG) need to attract both *hardcore* and *casual* players and study the evolution of MMOG features for this purpose.

## 1 Hardcore Gamers and Casual Gamers Must Play Together

As opposed to the *casual gamer*, a *hardcore gamer* dedicates most of his leisure time and sometimes even more to his favorite virtual world. Indeed, the average duration of a normal game session can be huge in traditional MMOG like Everquest [4] or Anarchy Online [1]. These games are designed to reward the time devoted to it. Gathering a team of complementary players, traveling through the virtual world to get to the desired location, finding rare items, fighting very powerful Non Player Characters (NPC) are tasks which take time and dedication to complete, but give the final gratification its meaning.

**Why MMOG need to adapt to the casual gamer market:** Economically speaking, the costs currently involved to develop, deploy and maintain such games imply a high number of monthly subscribers for a game to be profitable. To enable the development of more and different MMOG, it seems then necessary to extend their audience. The more obvious way is to reach the *casual gamer* market.

Moreover, MMOG suffer from a bad reputation, often described as addictive desocializing games, equivalent to a drug (*Evercrack* is the nickname of Everquest). Whereas research in this area does not yet explain if MMOG themselves create addiction or attract an audience predisposed to addiction, legislations are discussed all around the world to try and control this issue. This image could be corrected by the design of game-plays more suitable to short playing-sessions.

**Why MMOG need to keep the harcore gamer market:** the success of such a game is highly dependent on the construction of a community. The main feature of a MMOG is to involve each player in a parallel society where they can pursue a second social life. Virtual societies are organized in a number of hierarchic players regroupments. The existence of such organizations is one of the basic features of a MMOG, the very purpose of these games being to interact with other players. These regroupments can sometimes count a very important number of players. Planning a play session for such an organization, managing

R. Harper, M. Rauterberg, M. Combetto (Eds.): ICEC 2006, LNCS 4161, pp. 374–377, 2006.
© IFIP International Federation for Information Processing 2006

common resources, distributing responsibilities, defining and enforcing the common life rules inside the sub-community, and moderating personal conflicts are essential tasks for everyone playing experience. These responsibilities are very time consuming and ask for a strong dedication and good knowledge of the game. *Hardcore gamers* are the people who build the virtual society without which any MMOG would be pointless.

## 2   MMOG Game-Play Features Review

### 2.1   Growing by Interacting with the Virtual World

We will here describe the features involved in the growth of a powerful avatar.

**Competition with the Environment:** by achieving specific tasks, the player can accumulate *experience points* which will be transformed into enhancements of the avatar abilities. This mechanism is commonly called *Player versus Environment* (PvE) and most often consists in killing hostile Non Player Character (NPC). Experience points can sometimes also be obtained through the achievement of *quests* or *missions* assigned by the game.

In a typical MMOG like Everquest, this mechanism is the main feature of the game-design and to ensure the longevity of the game, gaining experience is a slow and sometimes tricky process. If the player actions result in the death of its avatar in the game world, penalties are applied. The avatar can lose experience levels, and has to retrieve its equipment at the location of the unfortunate event. Mistakes thus have very time consuming consequences on the growth of an avatar. Also designed and launched at the beginning of the popularization of the MMOG genre, Anarchy Online provided less frustrating features for the *casual gamer*: the experience loss was limited to the former experience level, and it was possible to retrieve all the equipment of the avatar easily. Still, getting experience was a long process and game-designers have been trying to find alternatives to retain *casual gamers*. In Eve Online [3], avatar learning, once triggered, grows according to time and not to player actions. In World of Warcraft [7], the player gets an experience bonus for being out of the game under some specific but easy to match conditions. These alternatives are risky to deploy: while they allow *casual gamers* to keep the pace with *hardcore gamers* to a certain extent, it is necessary to ensure that the growth of the avatar is not the only reward provided by the game-play (for instance, by making quests entertaining by themselves). Otherwise, it may be perceived as a very unfair mechanism for *hardcore gamers*.

**Items:** avatar abilities can also be enhanced through the possession of specific objects of the virtual world. As these items are only powerful in comparison with other items in the world, they have to be rare and difficult to acquire. In most of the MMOG, including recent ones, finding these objects requires the gathering of a high number of very skilled players with complementary avatars, and a very long and difficult fight against one or several NPC. The expression *camping* thus describes the activity of waiting the spawn of a specific NPC in order to kill it in loop until the drop of a highly desired treasure. In Anarchy Online like in other MMOG, turns between player guilds had to be arranged outside of the game by the guild leaders in order to avoid conflicts for fighting a specific NPC potentially possessing such an item. And usually, the possession of the treasure so much people fought for naturally goes to the most meriting player, that is, to the avatar in need of the object whose player is very involved in the virtual world, that is, to a *hardcore gamer*... This kind of scheme can be retrieved in even the most recent games, like World of Warcraft. However, a game like City of Heroes [2] got completely rid of this feature, the most evident source of conflict between *hardcore* and *casual gamers*. In this game, there is no rare item. The lack of this feature can however be a very bad choice, depriving *hardcore gamers* from in-game recognition of their strong involvement.

## 2.2 Virtual Society

We will here review the features helping to create an in-game virtual society.

**Cooperation between players:** the current main feature implementing player cooperation is the design of complementary classes of avatars. Each class defines strengths and weaknesses, and players thus gain an advantage in collaborating with each other. When Everquest was first released, it was quite difficult to progress in the game alone. This feature forced each player to socialize with other participants very early in the game. However, finding complementary teammates takes time, sometimes more than the team will actually be playing as a whole. Quickly, new regions of the virtual world have been introduced to provide a safe sandbox in which low-level avatars could progress alone. While the progression of an avatar is usually facilitated in a team, current game designs always make possible the progression of an avatar on its own, at least at the beginning. It is however obvious than the less the feature is enforced, the less the creation of each player in-game relationship network will be stimulated and there is a great risk that the MMOG becomes a subscription based solo adventure game.

Player organizations are an essential part of the creation of the virtual society. *Casual gamers* can of course be involved in such organizations, but it is more difficult for them to share resources, especially with other *casual gamers* since they would probably miss each others playing time frame. In Neocron [5], an apartment was available for each player organization, which could be used to store game items in order to facilitate exchanges and collaboration between members. The virtual economy also has a lot of importance in MMOG. In order to ease buy and sell practices for *casual gamers*, games like Everquest (though not from the beginning) and World of Warcraft have implemented in-game markets where players can put items for sale. While enhancing the cooperation between *casual gamers* all these facilities also reduce the chances of building a strong community by limiting contacts between players.

**Competition Between Players:** in most MMOG, players have the possibility to compete with each other by fighting through their avatars. After the lessons learned from Ultima Online [6], in which players could lose everything after a fight and where Player Killers (those players whose favorite entertainment feature is to ruin the other players game experience) were a real plague, MMOG designers have been very careful with this feature. Player versus Player

(PvP) fights are usually strictly regulated, limited to specific zones or servers, sometimes to avatars of the same level or upon explicit mutual agreement. However, while efficiently protecting a pacific *casual gamer* against harassment from an expert Player Killer, these limitations tend to make the PvP feature boring. In order to give a more exciting and controlled background to competition, MMOG designs have included more or less convincing storylines statically separating players in several *realms* competing with each other. The main benefit in this approach is that it enhances the community feeling inside each *realm*.

In Neocron, the PvP feature was less regulated than in most MMOG, and used a system of penalties to try and dissuade Player Killers. Harassment by repetitive killings in an unsafe zone of the world caused the killer to be threatened by powerful law enforcement NPC in the trading areas of the MMOG. The death of the penalized player would also drop a lot of his equipment for other players to take. While this system could still be abused, it had the advantage of being less artificial and kept the PvP immersive thrill by not totally discarding danger.

## 3   Conclusion and Perspectives

In order to retain *hardcore gamers*, time and dedication should still be recompensated, but it should not be the main reward criteria in order to lessen frustration for *casual gamers*. Solutions can be found for instance in making avatar's evolution features rewarding in themselves, providing entertainment and content by using the best of interactive storytelling and AI techniques in a *games-in-the-game* fashion. Indeed, recent games like World of Warcraft and City of Heroes have already demonstrated improvements in these aspects compared to their predecessors. More variety in game-plays is also desirable, including game phases relying more on the player abilities instead of relying only on his avatars' one. For instance, combats or item retrieval relying on instant strategy or reflexes (like in Neocron), whereas currently complex to implement satisfyingly in a MMOG technical context, provide a game-play where skilled *casual gamers* could make a difference whereas not skilled *hardcore gamers* could always use their time for training. Technical research enabling game-design progress in these directions should help providing more variety in commercial MMOG to a larger audience.

## References

1. Anarchy Online. Funcom, 2001. http://www.anarchy-online.com.
2. City of Heroes. Cryptic Studios, NCsoft, 2004. http://www.cityofheroes.com.
3. Eve Online. CCP Games, 2003. http://www.eve-online.com/.
4. Everquest. Verant Interactive, Sony Online Entertainment, 1999.
   http://everquest.station.sony.com.
5. Neocron. Reakktor, CDV Software, 2002. http://www.neocron.com.
6. Ultima Online. Origin Systems, Electronic Arts, 1997. http://www.uo.com.
7. World of Warcraft. Blizzard Entertainment, Vivendi Universal Games, 2004.
   http://www.worldofwarcraft.com.

# High-Precision Hand Interface

Yongwan Kim[1], Yongseok Jang[1], Wookho Son[1], and Kyeonghwan Kim[2]

[1] VR Research Team, Electronics and Telecommunications Research Institute, 161
Gajeong-dong, Yuseong-gu, Daejeon, 305-700, Korea
{ywkim, canfuler, whson}@etri.re.kr
[2] NT Research Inc., 776-2, Daerim-dong, Yeongdeungpo-gu, Seoul, 150-816, Korea
kimk@ntresearch.net

**Abstract.** Virtual reality techniques have been introduced to propose the intuitive interface in virtual entertainment environments. We introduce the intuitive and natural interaction interface supporting the high-precision hand operations. In this paper, we describe the novel sensing mechanism of finger tracking with fast refresh rate and high resolution.

## 1 Introduction

One of the recent key issues for virtual reality technologies is the natural interaction between the humans and a virtual environment. An interface based on hand input to virtual environments would be the most natural method to interact with the world [6].

Since Zimmerman, et. al. (1987) introduced optical fiber sensor-based glove devices, Immersion, Inc. markets the CyberGlove, an instrumented glove primarily designed for manipulation of 3D object in commercial CAD [1,5]. However, these glove devices have a weak point to utilize the hand interface for entertainment environment (temperature/size of user's hand/time consuming calibration) [2].

In this paper, therefore, we suggest the high-precision hand interface with higher resolution, faster refresh rate and robustness compared to the existing sensors such as resistive strip or optical fiber.

## 2 High-Precision Hand Interface

As shown in Figure 1, we present high-precision hand interface which consists of comfortable and precise finger tracking hardware device, hand API, realistic hand model and calibration tool for precise operation.

**Fig. 1.** Glove-type hand interface

R. Harper, M. Rauterberg, M. Combetto (Eds.): ICEC 2006, LNCS 4161, pp. 378 – 381, 2006.

## 2.1   Robust Sensing Mechanism for Finger Tracking

Our glove-type hand interface mounts LEVEX's LVDT(Linear Variable Differential Transducer)-type linear position sensors for measuring the precise micro displacement[7].

As shown in Figure 2, this sensor consists of a primary coil and two secondary coils wound on a coil form. A ferromagnetic core links the electromagnetic field of the primary coil to the secondary coils. Differencing the output of these coils will result in a voltage proportional to the relative movement of the core versus the coils. Compared to the other techniques, LVDT-type linear position sensor with high accuracy operates linearly with an extremely low temperature coefficient. Furthermore, LVDT-type linear position sensor has robust sensing features for finger tracking regardless of size of user's hand. This advantage gives users less calibration time.

**Fig. 2.** Concept of LVDT-type linear position sensor & actual sensor

## 2.2   Direct Measurement for Finger Tracking

As shown in Figure 3, current joint angle of the each finger can be calculated from the measured voltage of sensor because the movement displacement of finger joint(length of arc) is proportional to the central angle($\theta = r\,l$).

Therefore, user's current joint angle can be solved to the following as;

$$At_{(i)} = \frac{Vt_{(i)} - V\min_{(i)}}{V\max_{(i)} - V\min_{(i)}} \times A\max_{(i)} \qquad (1)$$

where, $At_{(i)}$ is user's current $i^{th}$ joint angle and $V\max_{(i)}$ is the maximum voltage value of the $i^{th}$ joint maximally spreaded out. The $V\min_{(i)}$ is the minimum voltage value of the $i^{th}$ joint maximally clenched and $A\max_{(i)}$ is the maximum range of $i^{th}$ joint.

**Fig. 3.** Direct measurement of finger joint angle       **Fig. 4.** Layout of sensor arrangement

As shown in Figure 4, our glove mounts the only 2 sensors for each finger on the assumption that the angle of third joint can be predicted from the angle of second joint because the third joint movement of each finger depends on the $2^{nd}$ joint movement of finger from an anatomical point of view.

## 2.3  Hand Interface API

Hand interface API performs the device initialization, connection, I/O data streaming and supports the easy integration environment to any virtual reality application.

We have migrated OpenSG scenegraph to our Hand interface API. OpenSG is an open source real-time rendering system based on a scenegraph metaphor on top of OpenGL [4]. Hand high-level API performs the collision detection from the scenegraph traversal for various grasp geometrices. We predefine a hierarchical representation of the models using tight fitting oriented bounding box trees. Through the scenegraph traversal, hand high-level API receives current transformation    information about pre-defined objects, and then computes collision status. Hand high-level API support AABB, OBB and polygonal-level API for real-time collision detection.

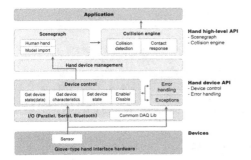 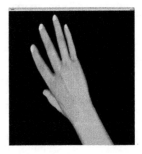

**Fig. 5.** Architecture of hand interface API          **Fig. 6.** Virtual hand model

As shown in Figure 6, to give users natural visual satisfaction, we have implemented a natural deformation of joint movement by using deformable skin mesh control technique. Thus, it is possible to precisely adjust the hand interface hardware comparing the virtual hand model [3].

## 2.4  Calibration Tool

Calibration tool has an important role to store the measured minimum /maximum voltage values, maximum angle range of each finger. As shown in Figure 7, the calibration process is simply done by the two hand gestures.

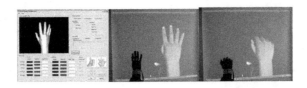

**Fig. 7.** Calibration tool and two hand motion for calibration process

## 3   Experimental Result and Application

We made an experiment on the linearity of LVDT-type linear position sensor. As shown in Finger 8, this sensor is available in strokes from 0.01 to 15mm. Maximum non-linearity is specified as ±0.4% of full scale. This sensor shows the 4kHz update rate, 12bit high resolution and good repeatability.

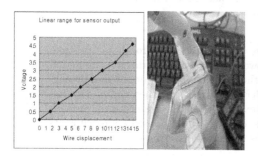

**Fig. 8.** Linearity of sensor output         **Fig. 9.** Interaction using hand interface

As shown in Figure 9, we have developed a car interior review system which is based on a curved display of hemi-spherical. Usability test are operated in this platform such as evaluation of interior of car or information appliance by developed natural and intuitive hand interface.

## 4   Conclusion and Future Work

We introduce the intuitive and natural interaction interface for virtual reality applications. Currently, we are trying to develop the haptic feedback actuators to give users realistic force/tactile sensation and the haptic API including haptic modeling, fast haptic cycle.

## References

1. Sturman, D.J., Zeltzer, D.: A Survey of Glove-Based Input. IEEE Computer Graphics and Applications. (1994) 30-39
2. G. Drew Kessler, Larry F. Hodgers, Neff Walker: Evaluation of the CyberGlove as a Whole-Hand Input Device. ACM Trans. Comput.-Hum. Interact. (1995) 263-283
3. Lander, Jeff: Skin them Bones: Game Programming for the Web Generation. Game developer Magazine. (1998) 11-16
4. OpenSG, http://www.opensg.org
5. Immersion Corp., CyberGlove http://www.immersion.com/3d/products/cyber_glove.php
6. Mentzel, M., Hofmann, F., Edinger, T., Jatzol, B., Kinzl, L., Wachter, NJ.,: Reproducibility of measuring the finger joint angle with a sensory glove. Handchirurgie, Mikrochirurgie, Plastische Chirurgie. (2001) 63-64
7. LEVEX, http://www.levex.co.jp

# Real-Time Animation of Large Crowds

In-Gu Kang and JungHyun Han[*]

Game Research Center, College of Information and Communications,
Korea University, Seoul, Korea
kangin9@paran.com, jhan@korea.ac.kr

**Abstract.** This paper proposes a GPU-based approach to real-time
skinning animation of large crowds, where each character is animated
independently of the others. In the first pass of the proposed approach,
skinning is done by a pixel shader and the transformed vertex data are
written into the render target texture. With the transformed vertices,
the second pass renders the large crowds. The proposed approach is attractive for real-time applications such as video games.

**Keywords:** character animation, skinning, large crowds rendering, GPU.

## 1  Introduction

In the real-time application areas such as video games, the most popular technique for character animation is *skinning*[1]. The skinning algorithm works efficiently for a small number of characters. On the other hand, emerging techniques
for rendering large crowds[2, 3] show satisfactory performances, but do not handle skinning meshes. The skinning algorithm can be implemented using a vertex
shader[4]. Due to the limited number of constant registers, however, the vertex
shader-based skinning is not good for rendering large crowds. There has been no
good solution to real-time skinning animation of large crowds, where each character is animated independently of the others. This paper proposes a GPU-based
approach to independent skinning animation of large crowds.

## 2  Pixel Shader-Based Skinning

This paper proposes a two-pass algorithm for rendering large crowds[5, 6]. In the
first pass, skinning is done using a pixel shader and the transformed vertex data
are written into the render target texture. With the transformed vertices, the
second pass renders the large crowds.

The skinning data for a vertex consist of position, normal, bone indices and
weights, and bone matrices. Fig. 1-(a) shows that position, normal, bone indices
and weights are recorded in 1D textures. A vertex is influenced by up to 4 bones.
The bone matrices are computed every frame, and each row of the $3\times4$ matrix
is recorded in a separate texture, as shown in Fig. 1-(b).

---

[*] Corresponding author.

R. Harper, M. Rauterberg, M. Combetto (Eds.): ICEC 2006, LNCS 4161, pp. 382–385, 2006.
© IFIP International Federation for Information Processing 2006

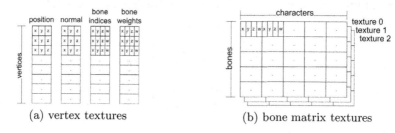

(a) vertex textures                    (b) bone matrix textures

**Fig. 1.** Texture structures for vertex and matrix data

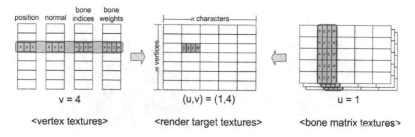

&lt;vertex textures&gt;          &lt;render target textures&gt;          &lt;bone matrix textures&gt;

**Fig. 2.** Skinning and render target texture

Through a single *drawcall*, all vertices of all characters are transformed into the world coordinates, and then written into the *render target texture*. Shown in the middle of Fig. 2 is the render target texture for $n$ characters each with $m$ vertices. For implementing the skinning algorithm in the pixel shader, the vertex shader renders a quad covering the render target. Then, the pixel shader fills each texel of the render target texture, which corresponds to a vertex of a character.

The render target texture in Fig. 2 is filled row by row. All vertices in a row have the identical vertex index. Therefore, the vertex data from the vertex textures are fetched just once, and the cached data are repeatedly hit for processing $n-1$ characters.

When skinning is done, the render target texture is copied to a vertex buffer object (VBO)[7], and then each character is rendered by the vertex shader using a given index buffer. For all of the render target texture, VBO and pixel buffer object (PBO)[8], 32-bit float format is used for each of RGBA/xyzw for the sake of accuracy.

## 3   Implementation and Result

The proposed algorithm has been implemented in C++, OpenGL and Cg on a PC with 3.2 GHz Intel Pentium4 CPU, 2GB memory, and NVIDIA Geforce 7800GTX 256MB. Table 1 compares the frame rates of the vertex shader skinning and the proposed 2-pass skinning. For performance evaluation, view frustum culling is disabled and 'all' characters are processed by GPU. Fig. 3 shows snap-

**Table 1.** FPS comparison of vertex shader (VS) skinning and proposed 2-pass skinning

| # characters | soldier VS | soldier 2-pass | horse VS | horse 2-pass |
|---|---|---|---|---|
| 1 | 2340 | 1545 | 2688 | 1571 |
| 16 | 580 | 1057 | 575 | 1179 |
| 64 | 200 | 565 | 163 | 649 |
| 256 | 56 | 200 | 42 | 219 |
| 1024 | 14 | 55 | 10 | 58 |
| 2048 | 7 | 27 | 5 | 29 |
| 4096 | 3 | 13 | 2 | 14 |

**Fig. 3.** Rendering 1,024 soldiers without LOD and frustum culling

**Fig. 4.** Rendering 10,240 soldiers with LOD and frustum culling

**Fig. 5.** Rendering 5,120 horses with LOD and frustum culling

shots of rendering 1,024 soldiers. The average FPS is 55, as shown in Table 1. In the current implementation, 3 LOD meshes are used: each with 1,084, 544 and 312 polygons, respectively. Fig. 4 shows snapshots of rendering 10,240 soldiers with LOD applied. The average FPS is 60 with view frustum culling enabled.

Finally, Fig. 5 shows snapshots of rendering 5,120 horses with LOD applied. The average FPS is 62 with view frustum culling enabled.

## 4    Conclusion

This paper presented a pixel shader-based approach to real-time skinning animation of large crowds. The experiment results show that the proposed approach is attractive for real-time applications such as games, for example, for rendering huge NPCs (non-player characters) such as thousands of soldiers or animals. With appropriate adjustments, the proposed approach can be used for implementing MMOGs (Massively Multi-player Online Games).

## Acknowledgements

This research was supported by the Ministry of Information and Communication, Korea under the Information Technology Research Center support program supervised by the Institute of Information Technology Assessment, IITA-2005-(C1090-0501-0019).

## References

1. Lewis, J.P., Cordner, M., Fong, N.: Pose Space Deformations: A Unified Approach to Shape Interpoalation and Skeleton-driven Deformation. SIGGRAPH2000 165–172
2. Microsoft: Instancing Sample. DirectX SDK. February 2006
3. Zelsnack, J.: GLSL Pseudo-Instancing. NVIDIA Technical Report. November 2004
4. Gosselin, D. R., Sander, P. V., Mitchell, J. L.: Drawing a Crowd. ShaderX3. CHARLES RIVER MEDIA. (2004) 505–517
5. James, D. L., Twigg, C. D.: Skinning Mesh Animations. SIGGRAPH2005 399–407
6. Dobbyn, S., Hamill, J., O'Conor, K., O'Sullivan, C.: Geopostors : A Real-Time Geometry / Impostor Crowd Rendering System. ACM Transactions on Graphics(2005) 933
7. NVIDIA: Using Vertex Buffer Objects. NVIDIA White Paper. October 2003
8. NVIDIA: Fast Texture Downloads and Readbacks using Pixel Buffer Objects in OpenGL. NVIDIA User Guide. August 2005

# Vision-Based Bare-Hand Gesture Interface for Interactive Augmented Reality Applications

Jong-Hyun Yoon, Jong-Seung Park, and Mee Young Sung

Department of Computer Science & Engineering, University of Incheon,
177 Dohwa-dong, Nam-gu, Incheon, 402-749, Republic of Korea
{jhyoon, jong, mysung}@incheon.ac.kr

**Abstract.** This paper presents a barehanded interaction method for augmented reality games based on human hand gestures. Point features are tracked from input video frames and the motion of moving objects is computed. The moving patterns of the motion trajectories are used to determine whether the motion is an intended gesture. A smooth trajectory toward one of virtual objects or menus is classified as an intended gesture and the corresponding action is invoked. To prove the validity of the proposed method, we implemented two simple augmented reality applications: a gesture-based music player and a virtual basketball game. The experiments for three untrained users indicate that the accuracy of menu activation according to the intended gestures is 94% for normal speed gestures and 84% for fast and abrupt gestures.

## 1 Introduction

For the interactions at immersive 3D gaming environments, it is natural to use means of human-to-human interaction to the human-computer interaction (HCI). The hand gestures are a means of non-verbal interaction. In recent years, many vision-based gestural interfaces have been proposed and most of the previous work has been focused on the recognition of static hand postures. The fusion of the dynamic characteristics of gestures has only recently been taken much interest[1]. *FingerMouse*[2] allows users to perform pointing gestures to control the cursor. *Finger Track*[3] is a vision-based finger tracking system on top of the workspace. Hardenberg and Brard[4] also have developed a finger-finding and hand-posture recognition system. In the system, the finger, moving over a virtual touch screen, is used as a mouse. In a vision-based gesture interface, it is required to discriminate gestures given purposefully as instructions from unintended gestures. Lenman et al.[5] developed a gesture interface using marking menus. A kind of marking menu which is suitable for a pen device, called *FlowMenu*, was also proposed for use with a pen device on wall-mounted large displays[6].

In the gestural interface, hand poses and specific gestures are used as commands. Naturalness of the interface requires that any gesture should be interpretable. But the current vision-based gesture interfaces do not provide a satisfactory solution due to the complexity of the gesture analysis. It is hard to deal with uncontrolled light conditions, complex background of users, and movements of human hands based on articulation and deformation. These reasons increase difficulty both in the hand

R. Harper, M. Rauterberg, M. Combetto (Eds.): ICEC 2006, LNCS 4161, pp. 386–389, 2006.

tracking step and in the gesture recognition step. A compromise would be possible using some sensory devices, using simple shaped markers, using marked gloves, using simple backgrounds, or restricting the poses of hands to frontal directions. Those approaches might not be appropriate for gesture interface since they restrict natural human gestures or environments. Our research is concentrated on the naturalness of gesture interface not imposing strict restrictions on gestures.

Computer vision algorithms for interactive graphics applications need to be robust and fast. They should be reliable, work for different people, and work against unpredictable backgrounds. Fortunately, the problem becomes much easier due to the facts that the application context restricts the possible visual interpretations and the user exploits the immediate visual feedback to adjust their gestures. This paper describes a gesture-based natural interface which is fast and stable without any strict restrictions on human motion or environments.

## 2  Human-Computer Interactions Using Hand Gestures

Our idea of the natural user interface is from the way of a general touch screen system where the system utilizes information both from the user contact point and a touch to the touch sensor to determine the location of a touch to the touch sensor. Touch screens are capable of measuring the touch position for a single touched point. The location of a touch applied by a user is generally determined by measuring signals generated by a touch input and comparing the signals. A touch to the contact point may be an actual physical touch or a proximity touch when a finger is positioned sufficiently close to generate a signal.

For real-time barehanded human computer interaction, we developed a fast hand gesture classification method. We first filter skin color regions and determine the candidate image locations of hands. Then, we detect and track feature points in the skin color regions. The user intension of menu selection is inferred based on the trajectories of feature points near the menu items in a short time interval.

For the proximity touch to a menu item, we locate skin color regions and analyze gestures occurred in the regions. The HSV(hue-saturation-value) model is used to specify skin color properties intuitively. The important property of hue is the invariancy to various lighting environment. For the values $r$, $g$, and $b$ in the RGB color space, each range from 0 to 1, hue $h$ ranges from 0 to 360° and saturation $s$ ranges from 0 to 1. For general digital color images, $r$, $g$, and $b$ have discrete values range from 0 to 255 and the HSV color space also should be quantized to fit into the byte range. The value component $v$ is given by $v=\max(r,g,b)$ and the saturation $s$ is by $s=(v-\min(r,g,b))*255/v$ if $v \neq 0$. If $v=0$, then $s$ is also zero. A fast computation of $h$ is possible by the following rules:

  − If $v=r$ then $h=(g-b)*30/s$.
  − If $v=g$ then $h=90+(b-r)*30/s$.
  − If $v=b$ then $h=120+(r-g)*30/s$.

If the value of $h$ is negative, it is converted to positive by adding 180 to $h$. Since $0 \leq h \leq 255$, $0 \leq s \leq 255$, and $0 \leq v \leq 180$, they fit into a byte array.

Based on the statistics, we filter skin color regions. We only use $h$ and $s$ to eliminate the lighting effects. However, under the very dark illumination, the skin color filtering is unstable. Thus, we exclude the case when intensity is too small. The skin color subspace is bounded by the constraint: ($0 \leq h \leq 22$ or $175 \leq h \leq 180$) and $58 \leq s \leq 173$ and $v \geq 76$. This skin color boundary also works for different human races and different lighting conditions.

Finding fingertip shape requires a fairly clean segmented region of interest. The requirement is hard to be satisfied in a general environment. Instead of finding fingertips, we determine the proximity of hand parts to menu positions and infer the intended user click action using the moving direction of hand parts. We detect enough number of feature points and track them. When a feature point is failed in matching, a new one is detected and added to the feature point set.

The trajectories of all feature points are kept during a fixed interval of time. When one of the skin color regions overlaps one of menu item regions, the trajectories of feature points inside the skin color regions are inspected. If the trajectory shape agrees the user intended menu selection, the corresponding menu item is activated. Unintended gestures include inconsistently moving trajectories containing abrupt change of moving direction, small motion trajectories where the starting positions are near the menu item, and confusing trajectories crossing multiple menu items.

## 3 Experimental Results

We implemented two practical augmented reality applications: a music player and a virtual basketball game. In the music player, several menu icons are displayed on the top of the screen and a user can activate a menu by hand gestures. The music player has four menu items to play, stop, forward, and backward music. Each menu item is shown as an icon located on the top side of the camera view. In the virtual basketball game, a virtual ball is bouncing in a virtual cube space and the real video stream is shown in the background. A user can hit the virtual ball with his hand gestures. The virtual basketball game is shown in Fig. 1. The game player manipulates virtual ball in 3D space by means of hands in the video camera field of view to direct it into the basket.

**Fig. 1.** The virtual basketball game using the bare-hand gesture-based interface

The experiments were performed on a 2.6GHz Pentium 4-based system. The frame size is fixed to 320x240. Color space conversion to HSV space and skin color region filtering requires 15 milliseconds on average per frame. Feature tracking for 500 feature points requires 42 milliseconds on average per frame. The overall processing speed for the interface is about 15 frames per second.

The menu activation accuracy was measured for three untrained users. Each user tried menu selection gestures a hundred times in front of the camera watching the monitor. One of them is requested to do them with fast hand motion. For normal speed gestures of two users, 93 trials and 95 trials were succeeded. For fast gestures of the last user, 84 trials were succeeded.

## 4 Conclusion

We described a barehanded interaction method using human hand gestures applicable to augmented reality applications to help in achieving the ease and naturalness desired for HCI. For the discrimination of intended gestures from accidental hand movements, we utilize a smooth trajectory toward one of virtual objects or menus. We have implemented and tested two simple augmented reality applications: a gesture-based music player and a virtual basketball game. The accuracy of menu activation is about 94% for normal speed gestures. We have still lots of room for improvement in accuracy. Obvious directions for future work for the improvement include applying the unified framework of various user contexts such as velocity of motion, patterns of hand gestures, current human postures, and human body silhouette. Typical applications of our hand gesture interface include remote control of electronic appliances, interaction for a virtual environment, input devices for wearable computers, and user control and response in 3D games.

**Acknowledgments.** This work was supported in part by grant No. RTI05-03-01 from the Regional Technology Innovation Program of the Ministry of Commerce, Industry and Energy(MOCIE) and in part by the Brain Korea 21 Project in 2006.

## References

1. Pavlovic, V., Sharma, R., Huang, T.S.: Visual interpretation of hand gestures for human-computer interaction: A review. IEEE Transactions on PAMI 19 (1997) 677–695
2. Quek, F., Mysliwiec, T., Zhao, M.: FingerMouse: A freehand computer pointing interface. In: Proc. of Int'l Conf. on Automatic Face and Gesture Recognition. (1995) 372–377.
3. O'Hagan, R., Zelinsky, A.: Finger track - a robust and real-time gesture interface. In: Australian Joint Conference on Artificial Intelligence. (1997) 475–484
4. von Hardenberg, C., Brard, F.: Bare-hand human-computer interaction. In: Proceedings of Perceptual User Interfaces. (2001) 113–120
5. Lenman, S., Bretzner, L., Thuresson, B.: Using marking menus to develop command sets for computer vision based hand gesture interfaces. In: NordiCHI '02: Proc. of the second Nordic conference on Human-computer interaction, ACM Press (2002) 239–242
6. Guimbretièere, F., Winograd, T.: Flowmenu: combining command, text, and data entry. In: Proc. of the ACM symposium on User interface software and technology. (2000) 213–216

# PHI: Physics Application Programming Interface

Bing Tang, Zhigeng Pan, ZuoYan Lin, and Le Zheng

State Key Lab of CAD&CG, Zhejiang University,
Hang Zhou, China, 310027
{btang, zgpan, linzouyan, zhengle}@cad.zju.edu.cn

**Abstract.** In this paper, we propose to design an easy to use physics application programming interface (PHI) with support for pluggable physics library. The goal is to create physically realistic 3D graphics environments and integrate real-time physics simulation into games seamlessly with advanced features, such as interactive character simulation and vehicle dynamics. The actual implementation of the simulation was designed to be independent, interchangeable and separated from the user interface of the API. We demonstrate the utility of the middleware by simulating versatile vehicle dynamics and generating quality reactive human motions.

## 1  Introduction

Each year games become more realistic visually. Current generation graphics cards can produce amazing high-quality visual effects. But visual realism is only half the battle. Physical realism is another half [1]. The impressive capabilities of the latest generation of video game hardware have raised our expectations of not only how digital characters look, but also they behavior [2].

As the speed of the video game hardware increases and the algorithms get refined, physics is expected to play a more prominent role in video games. The long-awaited Half-life 2 impressed the players deeply for the amazing Havok physics engine[3]. The incredible physics engine of the game makes the whole game world believable and natural. Items thrown across a room will hit other objects, which will then react in a very convincing way. Even dead bodies that are close to the radius of explosion will be tossed around like rag-doll.

However, there are a number of open issues that still to be addressed especially regarding the integration of physics algorithms with the rest of the graphics system in a game engine. Game developers have to spend lots of time to integrate them into their games. Most physics engines in today's game are pretty weak, especially for articulated character animation. The characters are only dealt with limp and dead rag-doll in physics simulation. Rag-doll simulation appears lifeless because it lacks a control system to generate human behavior[4]. In this paper, we propose an independent physics middleware to incorporate physics into games. We also introduce a new method for simulating reactive motions for data-driven animation. The goal is to generate realistic behaviors under unexpected external forces. A set of techniques are introduced to select a motion capture sequence which follows an impact, and then synthesize a believable transition to this found clip for character interaction.

R. Harper, M. Rauterberg, M. Combetto (Eds.): ICEC 2006, LNCS 4161, pp. 390–393, 2006.
© IFIP International Federation for Information Processing 2006

## 2  Previous Work

In the past ten years, physics has received much attention to improve the realism of virtual environments. Looking through the dynamics literature, a large variety of dynamics formulation can be found, such as Newton-Euler, Gibbs-Appel and Gauss' Least Constraint Principle.

Some software libraries have been developed to perform rigid body simulation. Commercial dynamics libraries such as Havok [3] and PhysX [5] have already been deployed into popular commercial games such as Half Life 2, Max Payne 2, and the future Unreal 3 engine technology. There are also several freely available libraries with comparably robust features. The Open Dynamics Engine (ODE) [6] is a free, industrial quality library for simulating articulated rigid body dynamics. Tokamak [7] is another library freely available, excelling in efficient joint constraints and stacking large number of objects. However, these physics libraries are not designed well to combine with existing applications. It is a challenging work to integrate the physics engines into games.

The most closely related work is Open dynamics framework (ODF)[8]. ODF is an open source project that provides tools to make it easier to get dynamics content into games. These tools are provided as sample code, scripts, and plug-in components that can be integrated directly into an existing tools pipeline or into major digital content creation tools such as 3D Studio Max, Maya, or SoftImage. Unfortunately, ODF is against its primary goal to support various physics engines and becomes a demo application on top of PhysX. Conversely, our goal is to provide an independent physics middleware to incorporate physics into games.

## 3  System Framework

The independent physics middleware was archived by dividing the API in three layers: wrapper, communication, and implementation. The main work was to define an appropriately abstract physical descriptor, then define and implement all sub-descriptors for every concrete application programming interface. First we bound the wrapper layer with low level graphics API of Open GL and DirectX 3D to test the stability. Then we replaced low level graphics libraries with high level game engine (such as OGRE and Irricht) and improved the common interface. PHI was written in C++ and the supported low level physics libraries are at this time ODE and PhysX. PHI encapsulated almost every feature of these physics engines, and added higher level features such as per shape material setting, vehicle dynamics configuration and XML physics script data loading. The physics data allows developer to do quick prototyping, and an exporter that creates rigid bodies with appropriate bounding shapes directly from source artwork.

## 4  Implementation

PHI contains powerful customizable modules for the user to set up various applications. We implemented two set of examples to demonstrate the feasibility of the physics middleware: dynamics vehicle simulation and reactive human motions.

## 4.1 Vehicle Simulation

PHI contains a powerful customizable vehicle module. Users can create cars, trucks or tanks from a set of vehicle specific scripts. Benefit from PHI, vehicle simulation combines physics with graphics well. It is easy to construct a well-looking jeep or armored car running on terrains with full dynamics by PHI (shown as Fig 1). These vehicles are presented as articulated structure of a series of body parts connected by joints, and they driven by motor joints under dynamics. When a large force acts on the vehicles, the joints would break to respond destructive results. We use four groups of spring-damper to simulate the vehicle's suspension and find they work well. Features currently included are the dynamic behaviour of the driving, suspension, steering and firing. The user can create parameterized vehicles which can be driven interactively in a Virtual Environment (VE).

**Fig. 1.** Vehicle Simulation      **Fig. 2.** Reactive human motion generation

## 4.2 Reactive Human Motions Generation

It is very important to create live and vivid animal or biped character in today's game. Simulation human motion with realistic responses to unexpected impacts in a controllable way is challenging work in motion synthesis.

With PHI, we proposed a novel method for incorporating unexpected impacts into a motion capture animation through physical simulation. Fig 2 shows a range of responses when a character falls down for encountering unexpected obstacles. During the fall process, arms of the character are controlled to generate convincing human behaviors: arms are rapidly elevated backward and outward in an attempt to stabilize the forward displaced COM after collision, and then adjusted to track the predicted landing location of the body and generate protective behaviors to avoid injury. The attached video demonstrates our results using real-time screen capture where user interacts with the character.

## 5  Conclusion and Future Work

An easy to use middleware for integrating physics simulation into games has been successfully designed and tested. Both the demo and videos of implementation can be downloaded from the world-wide web at http://www.cad.zju.edu.cn/vrmm/PHI. Using PHI to improve the physical realism of virtual world proved to be effective and robust. In the future work, we will make it possible for PHI with the support of more graphics engines and physics engines. In addition, Collada support will be implemented to aid developers.

## Acknowledgements

This research work is co-founded under Microsoft Research Asia (MSRA) Regional Theme Project 2005, Project 973 (grant NO: 2002CB312100) and NSFC (grant NO: 60533080).

## References

1. Eberly, D.H., Shoemaker, K.,Shoemake, K.: Game Physics. Morgan Kaufmann Pub. (2003) 221-361
2. Kokkevis, E.: Practical Physics for Articulated Characters. Game Developers Conference 2004, (2004)
3. Reynolds, H.,Collins, S.: Havok 2: Game dynamics sdk.(2005).http://www.havok.com
4. Zordan, V.B., et al.: Dynamic response for motion capture animation. ACM SIGGRAPH 2005. ACM Press, (2005) 697-701
5. Morav'anszky, A.: PhysX SDK. NovodeX AG,(2005).http://www.ageia.com/novodex.html
6. Smith, R.: Open dynamics engine. 2005).http://www.ode.org
7. Lam, D.: Tokamak game physics sdk. 2005).http://www.tokamakphysics.com
8. Ratcliff, J.W.: Open dynamics framework. 2005).http://www.physicstools.org

# A Vision-Based Non-contact Interactive Advertisement with a Display Wall

Tetsuo Fukasawa, Kentaro Fukuchi, and Hideki Koike

Graduate School of Information Systems,
The University of Electro-Communications Chofu-shi, Tokyo, Japan 182-8585
{fuka, fukuchi, koike}@vogue.is.uec.ac.jp

**Abstract.** We developed an advertising system that enables users to interact with advertisements on a large display wall without any physical contact. The system recognizes positions of bodies or hands of users in front of the display by stereo cameras. The system recognizes a distance between a user and the display as the user's interests in the advertisement, and changes two display modes according to the distance. One of the modes shows advertisements as many as possible to attract interests of passers-by. The other allows a user to interact with the advertisement on the display by recognizing a gesture of the user.

## 1 Introduction

Nowadays, advertisement is very important to inform consumer about information such as the company and their products. Recently, it becomes popular to display electronic advertisements in large displays such as plasma display panels. However, most of those "electronic posters" on the street provides one-way information. Touch panel display is well known to add interactivity to display walls, but the user has to stand right in front of the display to touch it and this causes difficulty to see the whole screen. To solve this problem, we developed an interactive advertising system that recognizes positions of users in front of the display, and tracks user's hands. When a user stands by the display, it allows the user to interact with it by body or hand gestures.

## 2 Design Principles

We focused on displaying and interaction techniques to show information according to users' interests. Our system has two display modes to show advertisements effectively. It uses the attractive display mode when passers-by are distant from the display, and it shifts to the interactive mode when an interested user approaches the display. In order to recognize the distance between them and his body gesture, it is necessary to track users' positions. We employed stereo vision cameras to get depth data of the image to recognize positions of users. In addition, because we target for public interactive displays on the street, we cannot expect the user to wear any markers or special devices. The system tracks the

R. Harper, M. Rauterberg, M. Combetto (Eds.): ICEC 2006, LNCS 4161, pp. 394–397, 2006.

**Fig. 1.** System overview

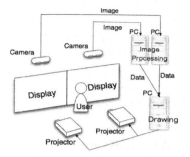

**Fig. 2.** System structure

positions of hands by the stereo cameras simultaneously to recognize a hand gesture. The system detects a hand by applying a simple background subtraction to color images.

## 3  System Implementation

Our advertisement system consists of three PCs, two stereo cameras, two projectors and two screens (see figure 2). The stereo cameras are Point Grey Research's Bumblebee, and they are connected to the PCs via IEEE1394 (FireWire). Bumblebee includes a pair of CCD cameras, and its library calculates a depth image from a pair of color images. It provides a pair of color images and a depth image that they are synchronized. The cameras are set on the ceiling and look downward to recognize users in front of the screens. Each camera covers one screen. Two PCs each are used to track positions of users from images of two cameras. The results are sent to the application PC via Ethernet.

## 4  Recognition Flow

In this section we describe the recognition flow of the system. The process includes two recognition parts: the body tracking part that detects bodies from depth images, and the hand tracking part that detects hands from color images.

### 4.1  Body Tracking Part

In the body tracking part, we use the depth images from the stereo camera for more robust position tracking than color matching or pattern matching. At the beginning of the process, the system obtains a depth image from the stereo camera then scans the pixels whose depth is in the range from 50 to 110 cm from the camera and makes a binary image. Next, the system dilates the binary image to reduce the noise. Finally, it calculates the centroid of each white region.

## 4.2  Hand Recognition Part

Contrary to body tracking part, the hand tracking part uses color images as its input. But it causes difficulty in the recognition because of the same reason in body tracking. Therefore, we employed a very simple recognition technique. The system scans only the upper part of the image so that it detects a hand right in front of the screen. Then the system subtracts background image from it and detects a hand region. Finally the system calculates its centroid.

# 5   Application

We developed an advertisement system based on this recognition system. As described above, this system has two display modes and switches them according to the distance between the user and the display. One of the modes that shows advertisements as many as possible to attract interests of passers-by, is called *Chaos view*, and the other mode, that allows a user to interact with the advertisement, is called *Tower view*.

## 5.1  Display Mode

**Chaos view.** When nobody is detected at the body recognition part, the system considers that no one is interested in current advertisement strongly, and displays the overall of advertisements. (the up of figure 3)

**Tower view.** When the user approaches the screen, the system considers that the user is interested in the advertisements and shifts to this mode that allows the user to manipulate the screen. Tower view mode has two hexagonal columns. Each column has its own theme (e.g. food, music), and its six surfaces are textured with advertisements. (the down of figure 3)

## 5.2  Gestures

In the Tower view mode, a user can manipulate the column by gestures.

**Selecting a column.** When the user stands in front of either of two columns, the column is selected, and displayed larger.

**Rotating a column.** In front of a column, the user can rotate it to see the other surfaces by a peeping gesture. (the upper right of figure 4)

**Carrying advertisements.** When the user touches the column by his hand, he can carry the advertisement on the column. The selected advertisements follow him (the lower left of figure 4)

**Browsing details.** If the user is carrying some advertisements, he can put them on the screen by touching the information area that is placed at the end of the screen. (the lower right of figure 4)

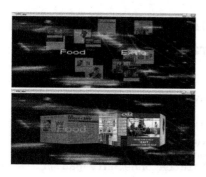

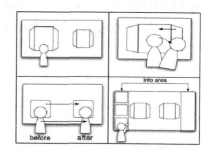

**Fig. 3.** Screenshots of Chaos view (up) and Tower view(down)

**Fig. 4.** Gestures in Tower view mode: selecting a column (upper left), rotating a column (upper right), carrying advertisements (lower left), browsing details (lower right)

## 6  Discussions

Carrying gesture is very attractive, but has some problems on the current implementation. Because there is a gap between the two screens and that area is not covered by two cameras, the system fails to track a user when he walks across the gap. To solve this problem, we should change the angles of the cameras or put the third camera. We found that the peeping gesture is not so intuitive. Some subjects could not find and perform this gesture without our instructions. We could put an instruction board beside the screen, but it is not suitable for public use. We should introduce the other gestures for rotating operation.

## 7  Conclusions

We developed an interactive advertisement system on a display wall. It tracks users and their hands to allow gestural input. The system has two display modes and switches them when a user approaches the screen. At this time only one user can manipulated a column.

## References

1. Daniel Vogel, Ravin Balakrishnan , "Interactive Public Ambient Displays: Transitioning from Implicit to Explicit, Public to Personal, Interaction with Multiple Users" In *Proceedings of UIST'04*. P. 137-146
2. Azam Khan, George Fitzmaurice, Don Almeida, Nicolas Burtnyk, Gordon Kurtenbach , "A Remote Control Interface for Large Displays" In *Proceedings of UIST'04*. P.127-136

# "SplashGame": A Ludo-educative Application Based on Genre and Verbal Interactions Concepts

Marion Latapy, Philippe Lopistéguy, and Pantxika Dagorret

LIUPPA - Laboratoire d'Informatique de l'Université de Pau et Pays de l'Adour
IUT de Bayonne, Château Neuf, Place Paul Bert
64100 Bayonne
{Latapy, Lopisteguy, Dagorret}@iutbayonne.univ-pau.fr

**Abstract.** This paper focuses on interactive applications design. We consider that interactive applications' acceptability can be improved by enhancing their genre dimension, which is inherent in any communication activity. Moreover, we notice that human cognitive predisposition to follow principles of verbal interactions can be helpful to structure the interactions that occur between a user and an interactive application. This paper presents design elements derived from the two former theories and illustrates how these elements are used to describe interactions of a ludo-educative application.

**Keywords:** genre, verbal interactions, design, experimentation.

## 1 Introduction

This paper focuses on the design of interaction systems that are conveyed by interactive applications[1]. We name interaction system a set of interactions that occur between a user and the interactive application he/she is using. We consider that enhancing the genre dimension in interactive applications design aids supporting their acceptability [2]. Indeed, genre can be viewed as a set of rules supported by communication structures, which matches to designers' communication intentions and fulfils users' expectations [5]. Moreover, we aim at basing our purpose on the verbal interaction theory [1], which identifies three dialogical levels of inter-actors communication: interaction, sequence and exchange.

In the second section, we propose concepts derived from these points of view, and organize them within a schema that can be used for the description of interactive applications. In the third section, the named concepts are succinctly illustrated thanks to an experimentative design process.

## 2 Design Elements

The model we propose [3], provides designers with a language for genre interactive applications description. It results, on the one hand, from a mixed survey of three

---

[1] We distinguish leisure oriented interactive applications and production applications which support a human activity in a professional context.

R. Harper, M. Rauterberg, M. Combetto (Eds.): ICEC 2006, LNCS 4161, pp. 398–401, 2006.

levels of the genre study: a theoretical level (genre theory), a specific genres level and a products level, and on the second hand, from concepts derived from verbal interactions principles applied to user / application interactions.

An application treats a domain, which can be either formally (e.g. ontology) or informally described. The genre specificity of an application is defined by a communication intention, which can be considered as expressing the justification of the system usefulness, and associated communication structures which organization is stated in scenarios. The resulting structures, aiming at a specific goal, concern rhetoric. They participate in the implementation of the intention.

On the one hand, among these structures, we stress:

- rhythm (e.g. binary, ternary or enumerated),
- analogy figure (e.g. metaphor, comparison or personification) and
- utterance, made up of an enunciative authority, it defines the author of the statement, and an enunciative mode, it defines the form of the statement expressed by various media (e.g. the narrative one, the explanatory one, the descriptive one, the injunctive one or the argumentative one)

that result from traditional rhetoric and genre theory.

On the other hand, the interaction units are dynamic communication structures that describe interactors' allowed actions. These units, partly derived from the verbal interactions theory, are hierarchically organized in session (the whole interaction), activities (they are genre specific: exercise, research engine, node navigation, buying activity, mission game...) and exchanges (e.g. notification, selection, interrogation, move...) which in turn are composed of interactors interventions.

The interaction scenarios satisfy an intention, they use and organize the communication structures, to be carried out by interactors in order to fulfil this intention.

Depending on the interaction units where they behave, interactors participate to a place system in which they play a precise role. Their interventions are then materialized by the means of capabilities associated to their role.

Despite the fact that genre taxonomy is not stable in time, the former presented model do not depend on any specific genre, it allows designers to use a transversal set of properties to describe interactive applications belonging to any genre.

## 3  Experimentation

The project was initiated as we were requested by an association of lifeguards working in the beaches of Anglet, seaside city located on the Atlantic coast of southwestern France. Each year, this association organizes workshops in Anglet's schools in order to make 8 to 10 years old pupils more aware of the risks to health that can occur when going to the beach during holiday season (May-September).

The association wanted to strengthen its action allowing young pupils to consolidate and evaluate knowledge acquired during the workshops. Our contribution consisted in the design of an interactive application that obeys to ludic and educative principles.

The domain covered by « Splash ! » is organized as follows:

- topological components of the beach (e.g. H-LandingPlatform): label, location, description,
- risks at beach (e.g. ToBeLost): label, rules to be known,
- beach vocabulary (e.g. Current, Flags): label, description,
- beach actors (e.g. BeachGoer, LifeGuard): label, function.

The scenario that organizes session level derives from ludic genre. User plays the role of a lifeguard trainee, which has to keep the beach under surveillance. User can move the trainee over the beach in order to achieve different activities. The goal of the session is reached when the activities are completed successfully.

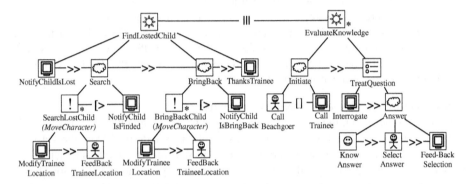

**Fig. 1.** Scenario of the FindLostChild mission[2]

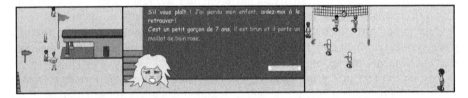

**Fig. 2.** Screen shots of the NotifyChildIsLost intervention

Most of the scenarios that organize activities derive from ludic genre: they organize missions. Each mission is associated to one risk; it ends successfully when the rules associated with the risk are mastered. Mission's success acts like an indicator for user's pedagogical evaluation. Missions consist of intervention exchanges, which occur between user and the application. Interventions are performed in accordance with the interactors roles capabilities, as well as depending on authorized protocols.

The FindLostChild mission, presented in (Fig. 1), is bounded by the NotifyChildIsLost opening intervention and the ThanksTrainee closing intervention, both performed by the application. In the NotifyChildIsLost intervention, the lost child's mother speaks using an injunctive « *Please! I have lost my son,*

---

[2] Presented with an extension of the Concurrent Task Tree notation [4].

**Fig. 3.** Screen shots of the `NotifyChildIsBringBack` and the `ThanksTrainee` interventions

*help me to find out him!* » and then a descriptive mode « *He is a 7 years old boy. He has brown hair and wears a pink swimsuit!* » (Fig. 2).

The sequential (>>) `Search` and `BringBack` sub-missions both consist of an iterative (*) specialized *MoveCharacter* exchange borrowed from the ludic genre. They are respectively interrupted ([>), when the child is found or when the child is brought back to the right place, that is to say the life guards watchtower (Fig. 3).

Simultaneously (|||), while performing the mission, the trainee can be evaluated thanks to the `EvaluateKnowledge` activity borrowed from the educative genre. This activity can be initiated (`Initiate`), either by the user, thanks to the trainee's capabilities (e.g. `CallBeachgoer` or `WhistleBeachgoer`), either ([|) by the application, thanks to a beachgoer's capabilities (e.g. `CallTrainee`). In both cases, the initiating intervention leads to a multiple choice questionnaire like exchange, which questions are asked by the beachgoer. The `Initiate` mechanism is also used in order to notify the trainee of non mastered knowledge.

Material given to « Splash! » design teams to carry out the applications design and coding consisted in the former presented model, guidelines, as well as referential documents about educative, ludic and encyclopedic genres. The authors of this paper observed the use of this material during the design process. Differentiation between the different genres has been clearly appreciated and respected during the whole design process, as well as the focus on interaction's hierarchy. Ludic and pedagogic intentions have been systematically considered in each communication structure. However, the suggested CTT notation for interaction description was considered quite difficult to use. An evaluation of product usage will be done by July 2006.

# References

1. Kerbrat-Orecchioni C. Les interactions verbales - Tome II. Armand Colin (Linguistique), Paris, 1992.
2. Latapy, M., Lopistéguy, P., Dagorret, P. Genre Potentialities For Interactive Applications Design and Acceptation. In Proceedings of ACM Nordic Conference on Computer Human Interaction nordiCHI'04 (October 23-27, 2004, Tampere), ACM Press, New York, 2004, pp. 417-420.
3. Latapy, M., Lopistéguy, P., Dagorret, P., Gaio, M. Usage des interactions verbales pour la conception d'applications interactives centrées Genre, Ergo'IA 2006 (To appear).
4. Paternò, F. ConcurTaskTrees: An Engineered Notation for Task Models, Chapter 24, in Diaper, D., Stanton, N. (Eds.), The Handbook of Task Analysis for Human-Computer Interaction, Lawrence Erlbaum Associates, Mahwah, 2003 pp.483-503.
5. Pemberton, L. Genre as a Structuring Concept for Interaction Design Pattern, position paper for the HCI-SIG Workshop on patterns, London, 2000.

# Shadow Texture Atlas

Kyoung-su Oh and Tae-gyu Ryu

Department of Media, University of Soongsil, Korea
{oks, mordor}@ssu.ac.kr

**Abstract.** In this paper, we present a new method for creating shadow texture atlas with which we can represent the self-shadow. Shadow texture atlas is a texture atlas with shadow information in each texel. Shadow texture is effective to represent high-quality shadow using the graphics hardware because it stores shadow information as color unlike shadow map which stores depth. However, it cannot represent the self-shadow and it takes a long time to create a shadow texture. To overcome these problems we present shadow texture atlas method. Shadow texture atlas can also represent self-shadow information. Moreover, we use shadow map to create shadow texture atlas instead of drawing all shadow casters. Our experimental result shows that our method performs at linear time and its speed is similar to the traditional shadow map method. Furthermore in comparison with shadow map method, our method can use mipmap filtering which is hard to achieve with shadow map method.

## 1 Introduction

Shadow is not common in computer games on account of the expensive costs. Most widely used real-time shadow generation methods are shadow map, shadow texture, etc.

In shadow map method, we render scene from the light's view, and use the depth map to determine which surfaces lies in shadow [1]. However, it can not utilize graphics hardware features such as texture filtering because unlike filtering of color values, filtering of depth values may result in wrong shadow. There were some research to overcome this shortcoming such as percentage closer filtering[2] and variance shadow map[3]. Percentage closer filtering filters the result of the depth comparison. If the shadow map area covered by a pixel is large percentage closer filtering needs many depth comparison. Variance shadow map stores moments of depth distribution function and it uses the Chebyshev's inequality to get upper bound of the probability that the center of each pixel is in shadow. If variance of a pixel is high, light bleeding artifact can occur.

Shadow texture method maps the texture image storing shadow information on rendered objects [4]. Shadow information is represented by texel color, therefore, it can present high-quality shadow effect using hardware accelerated image filtering. However, the projective shadow texture method can not support the self-shadow and it takes a long time to create a shadow texture.

In this paper, we present a shadow texture atlas method. In this method, shadow information is stored in shadow texture atlas that is shadow texture in the form of texture atlas. And we use shadow map when generating shadow texture atlas. Using shadow map, it is possible to generate shadow texture atlas in linear time to the number of

R. Harper, M. Rauterberg, M. Combetto (Eds.): ICEC 2006, LNCS 4161, pp. 402–405, 2006.
© IFIP International Federation for Information Processing 2006

objects in the scene. Advantages of shadow texture atlas method compared with traditional shadow texture methods are support of self-shadow and fast generation time. And advantage over shadow map method is enhancement of image quality using hardware accelerated filtering.

## 2 Shadow Texture Atlas Method

Shadow texture atlas method includes next three steps. First, we create the shadow map. Second, we create atlas of shadow textures for each object with shadow map. And last, we render the scene with the shadow texture atlas.

### 2.1 Shadow Map Creation

To create a shadow map, we perform Z-buffer algorithm with a light source as a view point. As a result, the distance of the closest model to light source is stored in depth buffer. These values are copied to shadow map.

### 2.2 Shadow Texture Atlas Creation for Each Object

With planar projection, we cannot store correct shadow information for concave objects because some positions may be projected to the same texture coordinate. With texture atlas[5], we can map every position on 3D model surface to different texture coordinates. We create shadow texture atlas for each object by rendering.

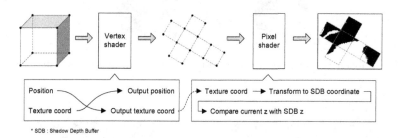

**Fig. 1.** Shadow texture atlas creation

Fig. 1 is a rendering process. The vertex shader outputs shadow texture atlas coordinate as its position. And it also output model space coordinate. Then model space coordinate are interpolated and passed to pixel shader by graphics hardware. Consequently, a pixel shader is transferred a three-dimensional position (value) corresponding to a pixel.

The pixel shader transform model space coordinate into shadow map coordinate. And it compares the z (depth) value of it with a z value obtained from a shadow map. If current pixel's z value is larger than stored value in shadow map then shadow color is assigned. Otherwise illuminated color is output.

### 2.3  Rendering with Shadow Texture Atlas

With stored position and atlas texture coordinate in the each vertex, we can render shadowed objects by mapping shadow texture atlas to each model. By hardware mip-mapping, shadow texture decreases aliasing artifacts. In particular aliasing artifacts which are significant during texture minification are reduced.

## 3  Implementation and Results

We implemented the shadow texture atlas method on a system with Athlon64(3000+), Nvidia 7800GTX. Test model is a geometry image model of the Stanford Bunny.

GU's [6] geometry image generation method minimizes the shape transform of each triangle and incision of 3D model. Because each point on 3D model is mapped to a unique 2D position on the geometry image, we can use geometry image as texture atlas.

We tested with 512x512 size of the shadow map. Test model has 66049 vertices. The size of the shadow texture atlas is 256x256. Fig.2 is comparison of our method with shadow map method. This comparison shows the effect of mipmap filtering.

**Fig. 2.** Rendered output and : (a) shadow texture atlas (left) (b) shadow map (right)

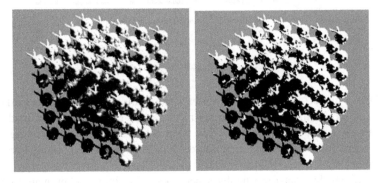

**Fig. 3.** Rendered output. (a) atlas shadow texture (left) (b) shadow map (right).

A 3D model used in Fig. 3 is a low resolution geometry image which has 4096 vertices. Moreover, we use a shadow texture atlas of 64x64 size in for each objects.

**Table 1.** The frame rate

| Scene | Shadow texture atlas | Shadow map |
|-------|---------------------|------------|
| Fig. 6 | 123.46 fps | 126.20 fps |
| Fig. 7 | 16.30 fps | 18.28 fps |

Performances of rendering Fig. 2, 3 are listed in Table 1. Performance of our method is similar to that of shadow map method.

## 4  Conclusions

Shadow texture method has difficulty in representing self-shadows and it takes a pretty long time to create a shadow texture. We presented shadow texture method that uses shadow texture atlas. Our method can create shadow texture representing self shadow in linear time. Advantage compared with shadow map method is image quality when viewer is far from the shadowed models.

## Acknowledgments

This work was supported by the Korea Research Foundation Grant (KRF-2004-005-D00198).

## References

1. Heidmann, T: Real shadows real time, IRIS Universe, 18, 28–31, 1991
2. Reeves, W., Salesin, D., and Cook, R.: Rendering antialiased shadows with depth maps. ACM SIGGRAPH Computer Graphics, v. 21 n4, 283–291, 1987.
3. William Donnelly, Andrew Lauritzen: Variance Shadow Maps. Variance shadow maps, Proc. of symposium on Interactive 3D graphics and games, 161-165, 2006
4. Mark Segal, Carl Korobkin, Rolf van Widenfelt, Jim Foran, Paul Haeberli: Fast shadows and lighting effects using texture mapping, ACM SIGGRAPH Computer Graphics, v.26 n.2, p.249-252, July 1992
5. Bruno Lévy, Sylvain Petitjean, Nicolas Ray, Jérome Maillot: Least squares conformal maps for automatic texture atlas generation, ACM Transactions on Graphics (TOG), v.21 n.3, July 2002
6. Xianfeng Gu, Steven J. Gortler, Hugues Hoppe: Geometry images, Proceedings of the 29th annual conference on Computer graphics and interactive techniques, July 23-26, 2002

# A Chording Glove for Games: Development of a Wearable Game Device

Seongil Lee, Jong Gon Kim, and Byung Geun Kim

Sungkyunkwan University, Department of Systems Management Engineering,
Human Interface Research Laboratory
300 Chunchun-Dong, Suwon, Korea
silee@skku.edu, {gon, billkim}@limeorange.com
http://www.skku.ac.kr/sme/~human

**Abstract.** In this paper, we describe the development of a SKKU glove, a wearable computing device for entertainment and games that can be used in wireless environments. The glove is equipped with chording keyboard mechanism for natural and flexible input and control of games, and a set of accelerator sensors for gathering information from hand gestures. Since the glove can be worn and used only in one hand, it not only provide a natural way to access games, but also helps the gamers with disabilities, particularly those who can use only one hand. The system configuration and the interface for input and control for the glove are presented.

## 1  Introduction

For years, many research efforts have been made in designing various entertainment technologies enjoyable and natural to users. To make access and play games efficiently, users need a convenient access tools and interfaces to give the users primary role to control the games by themselves. This includes how handy their gaming accessories are to carry, and how suitable their computing devices and interfaces are for navigation and control as well as command input.

Like many other emerging technologies, entertainment technologies are characterized by being different from traditional computing devices in the physical appearance and the contexts in which they are used. This paper proposes a glove-based entertainment device that can provide mobile users with accessibility and usability to various gaming environments. The SKKU gloves equipped with a wireless communication module can be a good interactive device to many computers for games since the hands and fingers are the most natural and dominantly used parts of the body in our daily lives. Many simple gestures of the hands reveal so many different contexts which the users deal with. Using hands, humans can naturally develop unique and effortless strategies for interacting with computer games. In other words, hands do not have to hold and manipulate interfacing game devices, but hands can be the interfacing game devices themselves.

R. Harper, M. Rauterberg, M. Combetto (Eds.): ICEC 2006, LNCS 4161, pp. 406–409, 2006.

## 2  Background

Some glove-based input devices, though, have capabilities to make decent control input in addition to their intended functions of gesture recognition and space navigation. Pinch Gloves (Bowman, Wingrave, Campbell, and Ly, 2001; Thomas and Piekarski, 2002) are glove-based input devices designed for use in virtual environments, mainly for 3D navigation, and N-fingers (Lehikoinen, J., Roykkee, 2001) is a finger-based interaction technique for wearable computers also utilizing finger pinching. Pinching is basically the motion of making a contact between the tip of thumb and a fingertip of the same hand. It uses lightweight gloves with conductive cloth on each fingertip that sense when two or more fingers are touching. Pinch gloves were also used in a wearable computer for information presentation with an augmented reality user interface as well as for a text entry mechanism (Rosenberg, 1998).

Most of previous works, however, on glove-based input devices were intended for text input with general computers, not targeted for control devices in entertainment nor game environments. The current works investigate the utilities, functionality, and usability of the chording gloves as a game device.

## 3  System Configurations

### 3.1  System Functions

The design of game gloves began with the arrangement of the functions of the gloves as a game controller. The three functions of the glove system were designed based on the modes that are required in most games: positioning for cursor orientation, controlling for making command inputs, and perceiving for multimodal feedback from the game. The functions were purposed to provide human-friendly nature of fun with the users.

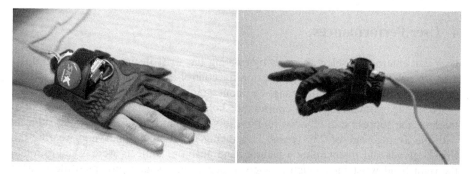

**Fig. 1.** The chording glove for game with the acceleration sensors to detect hand motions in space. The pinching motions generate commands for game. The thumb acts as a ground to conduct electricity to the 4 keys on the fingertips made of silicon.

**Positioning.** Two 2-dimensional **ADXL202** acceleration sensors were used to detect and calculate the amount of the three dimensional hand motions in space. The glove can make directional motions to control the game cursors in 6 DOF motions (Shown in Fig. 1).

**Commanding.** All the commands required by games can be made by the key combination of the gloves, which consist of finger contacts between the fingers with silicon inks. The system uses finger tapping to make input for game control. Chording is possible by making simultaneous tapping with multiple fingertips to the thumb. Two keys are placed on the fingertips of the index and middle fingers on the palm side of leather gloves, and on the thumb for the ground. The keys are made of conductible silicon ink applied to the fingertips with the rectangle of 1.5 cm by 1.3 cm. The keys become "pressed" once the voltage through the silicon ink rises above 3.5 V with contact with the thumb (Shown in Fig. 2). The voltage outputs of chord gloves are connected to an embedded controller that translates chord information into its corresponding control. The corresponding finger force to generate 3.5 V is set to 3.50 N to avoid unwanted activations with light contact between the fingertips and the thumb. The glove weighs approximately 28.5 grams.

### 3.2  System Structure

The 16F874 microprocessor is used for controlling and analyzing the signals from the gloves. The controller also works for functions of converting the signals to control codes and sending them to PC or game stations using a Bluetooth 1.1 (aircode) wireless adapter. The controller works with a 9V battery.

The voltage outputs of chording gloves are sent to an embedded system that translates chord information into its corresponding code, character, or number. The chord glove-based input device can be used in connection with computers or PDAs directly as a portable keyboard/mouse. The controller transmits signals from the gloves to the computing consoles, mobile phones, and other game stations with a Bluetooth module to control them.

## 4   User Performances

User can control the selected target by rotating the wrist in three dimensions. However, an issue was raised in wrist rotation for control activation: setting threshold for activation with limited rotation ranges without degradation in user performance.

To set the optimal ranges for control threshold, we performed a pilot experiment to measure the success rate of wrist rotation in gaming situations for 5 young subjects with the average age of 23.3 years. In a racing game condition, while wearing the SKKU gloves and maintaining a natural hand position, subjects were asked to rotate the right hand wrist far enough to a given degree at a sound prompt while gaming with the gloves to the right (clockwise) and to the left (counterclockwise) directions. Three different degrees were given to the subjects at 45, 90, and 120 degrees in random orders for each direction. A total of 10 trials were measured for each rotation degree. The feedback regarding successful wrist rotation was not given to subjects after each trial at all.

The results showed the best performances in 45 degrees, and the performances drop rapidly as the required rotation degree increases. The wrist rotation for greater than 90 degrees seems not to be desirable since wrist motions with bigger rotating ranges not only lack accuracy but also cause the gaming hand to fatigue easily. Such motions can take the user's fun factor away, which is not desirable for new devices.

## 5   Conclusion

The glove-based game interface in the form of our SKKU chording glove that was developed in our research for controlling game devices showed promises and problems. The glove has distinct advantages over conventional push-button based on-board game control panels in that the glove can be always carried and worn easily. Users can also access games more naturally with the glove-based game device in any position without being restricted by the conventional wire to the game consoles. It is light, and can be carried easily, and takes less space than any other game control device. Since we always use our fingers and hand in a daily life, to make codes in combination by touching the thumb and other fingers together can be easy to remember and natural to perform. The thumb and finger tapping is natural. One other advantage of the SKKU chording glove is that it can be expanded to a universal game device for anybody who may be limited to use only one hand. It can provide access to games for people with physical disabilities.

**Acknowledgement.** The study was supported by the Sungkyun Academic Research Fund from the Sungkyunkwan University granted to the first author.

## References

1. Bowman, D. A., Wingrave, C. A., Campbell, J. M., Ly, V. Q.: Using Pinch Gloves for both Natural and Abstract Interaction Techniques in Virtual Environments. In: Human-Computer Interaction; Proceedings of the HCI International 2001, Lawrence Erlbaum Associates, (2001) 629-633
2. Lehikoinen, J., Roykkee, M.; N-fingers: a finger-based interaction technique for wearable computers. Interacting with Computers, 13 (2001) 601-625
3. Rosenberg, R.: Computing without Mice and Keyboards: Text and Graphic Input Devices for Mobile Computing. Doctoral Dissertation. University College London (1998)
4. Thomas, B. H., Piekarski, W.: Glove Based User Interaction Techniques for Augmented Reality in an Outdoor Environment. Virtual Reality, 6 (2002) 167-180

# VIRSTORY: A Collaborative Virtual Storytelling

Atman Kendira and Laurence Perron

France Telecom R&D Lannion
2 avenue Pierre Marzin
22307 Lannion - France
{atman.kendira, laurence.perron}@orange-ft.com

**Abstract.** From the results of two Human behavior studies in small group interactions we constructed iteratively a Collaborative Virtual Environment named
"VIRSTORY". This system is a digital storytelling with speech and 3D gesture
recognition technologies using like input devices. It includes several modules:
multimodal interaction module, behavior module to animate autonomous expressive characters, etc.

## 1 Introduction

Our aim is to carry out some experiences and use the results to design a multimodal
Collaborative Virtual Environment (CVE) and particularly storytelling environments.
Our recent studies are focused on virtual collaborative games into small groups. In
these particular games, the users are represented by characters in narrative digital
environment and it is primordial to animate the characters in the way that they are
assisted by the Human communication especially non-verbal behavior: gestures, gaze,
life signs, social attitudes, emotion, etc. Voice and gesture are both the basis of
natural dialogue between players and the bimodal interaction support of the digital
storytelling setup. This double function is very interesting for the users but remains a
Human Computer Interaction research field and more specifically multimodal
interfaces [1,2]. In fact, we are focusing on voice and gesture interaction because
these modalities give the user more freedom to create and participate in the story
narration [3]. In the first part of this paper, we investigate through two human
behavior studies a way to permit the "natural" mediated collaboration between users
in creative CVE. In the second part, we present the improvements of CVE called
VIRSTORY that to take into account the results of studies.

## 2 Storytelling Experimentations and CVE Design

At first, we imagine a narrative game for everybody. This game uses cards to illustrate a piece of story e.g.: princess, wolf, etc. Each user must play with her/his pieces
of story and with the other users to elaborate a nice story. This game was the starting
point of VIRSTORY design.

If the primary aim is to conceive VIRSTORY, the secondary aim is to understand
Human behavior especially the non-verbal behavior like gaze, facial expressions, and
gestures of hand to animate a character in CVE [4]. Existing character animation

R. Harper, M. Rauterberg, M. Combetto (Eds.): ICEC 2006, LNCS 4161, pp. 410–413, 2006.
© IFIP International Federation for Information Processing 2006

techniques in CVE prompted us to study sensorial deprivation along two lines of reflection. We wished to establish how subjects interact in a group, and what they do when they are deprived of a form of expression (eyes, hand, and face) as the case with the intrusive device in CVE (cf. Figure 1). The idea was that subjects compensate for the absence of one of these forms of expression either verbally or by means of other non-verbal behaviors not under constraint in the experimental situation. Observations of this experiment showed that characters can already be animated with recurring self-contact gestures and these gestures can be used by example to create animations library. Moreover, these gestures contribute to the feeling of presence that users expect when facing a character without speech analysis.

**Fig. 1.** Four experimental conditions. 1: without deprivation (normal) - 2: with masks to deprive subjects of face expressions - 3: with very dark sunglass to deprive subjects of gaze modality - 4: with their hands under the table to deprive subjects of gesture modality.

In VIRSTORY game (cf. Figure 2) when the user takes a cube, the distant user can see the character with the cube and the colour feedback on the cube. If the character is red then the cube is red, etc. On the bottom of a user's screen is displayed the *"private space"*, consisting of the cubes the user has not yet used in the story (the own cubes of the distant user are not visible). Only cubes already used by either user are visible by both users. These cubes lie on the yellow points that represent the common story-line. The first point is the beginning and the last point corresponds to the end of the story. When a user selects a cube from his private space and moves it to the storyline, this action is seen by both users. As a user moves a cube on the beginning of the storyline and tells "once upon a time", the second user finds a cube to continue the story and so on.

We realized a "Wizard of Oz" experimentation (WOZ) with 20 subjects (9 males and 11 females, 16 adults and 4 children) (cf. Figure 3). This experimentation allows

**Fig. 2.** The VIRSTORY CVE: on the left, the first player – on the right, the second player

understanding the organization of the oral and gesture modalities between themselves, as a function of the habits and competences of the subject (adult/child difference for example). One of the interests of multimodal interfaces is to let a user choose the way to interact as she/he prefers. If pointing with a laser is efficient when this tool is given to a user, the question remains open whether such efficiency is kept without a physical pointing device, for example with computer vision pointing gesture recognition. The experimenter only reproduced gestures performed on objects of the storytelling setup, while other gestures such as wrist or arm rotation to turn a cube were interpreted.

**Fig. 3.** On the left: a child with a laser pointer. On the right: The WOZ experimenter carrying the child's command and the partner in the background playing with the child.

To conclude, such an experiment allows defining a spoken vocabulary, to observe, depending on the context, the importance of a given modality over other modalities. The most important lesson learnt from these experiments is that modality influences the cooperation. The more the subjects pointed and the lesser the story was built in a cooperative manner. When the subjects are centred on the cubes manipulation task, they couldn't manage an efficient narrative communication. The story was build by successive elements without real integration of the distant user.

## 3  VIRSTORY

From previous human studies, we improved VIRSTORY. We included two news modules: one hand, speech and visual gesture recognition and the other hand, a behavior module that is under way in our laboratory (cf. Figure 4). The gesture and speech input modalities are interpreted by MOWGLI (Multimodal Oral With Gesture Large display Interface) module [3] and used like synchronous or not synchronous interface commands in order to interpret and sometimes disambiguate the user's commands. The choice about sequential gesture or speech commands is a result from the WoZ experimentation. In fact, the user points the cube on the screen and after, he uses the oral command (e.g.: "turn") to turn the cube and to see the other faces. The Animation module contains a library of non-verbal behavior like face expressions, postures, animations bodies and some inverse kinematics algorithms.

The first step about Behavior module concerns the relations between the interpreted data (head and arms position, speech detection, speaking time, words recognition, etc.) from MOWGLI module and the running of appropriate behaviors by the Animation module on a 3D articulated character through an agent based system.

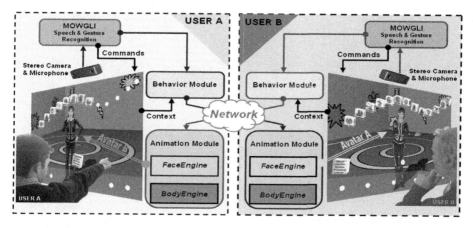

**Fig. 4.** The new VIRSTORY architecture: User A (at left) see user B's character and vice versa

## 4 Conclusion

To conclude, the analysis that we carry out here points out the necessity to work on human studies particularly in situ or in ecological conditions, in order to discriminate transpositions from the real world into the virtual world. Our objectives are also to explore step by step: the multimodal interaction in relation to character animation and strategies of collaboration, the improvement of behavioral module according to the creative task.

## References

1. Buisine, S., Martin, J.C., Bernsen, N.O.: Children's gesture and speech in Conversation with 3D Characters. International Conference of Human Computer Interaction, Las Vegas (2005)
2. Vilhjalmsson, H.: Animating Conversation in Online Games. Entertainment Computing, Lecture Notes in Computer Science, ICEC 2004, (2004) 139-150
3. Carbini, S., Delphin-Poulat, L., Perron, L., Viallet, J.E.: From a wizard of Oz experiment to a real time speech and gesture multimodal interface. Signal Processing (2006)
4. Perron, L.: An avatar with your own gestures. INTERACT'05 Workshop "Appropriate Methodology for Empirical Studies of Privacy", Communicating Naturally through Computers, Rome (2005)

## 4 Conclusion

References

# Author Index

# Lecture Notes in Computer Science

For information about Vols. 1–4106

please contact your bookseller or Springer